Just Sustainabilities: policy, planning and practice

Just Sustainabilities contributes to understanding, theorising and ultimately developing strategies towards the development of more just and sustainable communities in both the global North and South. Through a collection of solutions-orientated books, the series looks at policy and planning themes that improve people's quality of life and well-being, both now and into the future; that are carried out with an intentional focus on just and equitable processes, outputs and outcomes in terms of people's access to environmental, social, political and economic space(s); and that aim to achieve a high quality of life and well-being within environmental limits.

Series editor

Julian Agyeman

Other titles in the series

Julian Agyeman, *Introducing Just Sustainabilities: Policy, Planning, and Practice*

Karen Bickerstaff, Gordon Walker, Harriet Bulkeley, *Energy Justice in a Changing Climate: Social Equity and Low-carbon Energy*

About the editor

Peter Utting is international coordinator of the Center for Social Economy (Centro para la Economía Social or CES), based in Nicaragua, and a senior research associate of the United Nations Research Institute for Social Development (UNRISD). Until August 2014 he was the deputy director of UNRISD, where he coordinated international research projects on social and solidarity economy and corporate social responsibility. He was instrumental in establishing the United Nations Inter-Agency Task Force on Social and Solidarity Economy in 2013. Recent publications include *Business Regulation and Non-State Actors: Whose Standards? Whose Development?* (co-edited with Darryl Reed and Ananya Mukherjee-Reed, 2012), *The Global Crisis and Transformative Social Change* (co-edited with Shahra Razavi and Rebecca Varghese Buchholz, 2012) and *Corporate Social Responsibility and Regulatory Governance* (co-edited with José Carlos Marques, 2010).

About UNRISD

The United Nations Research Institute for Social Development (UNRISD) is an autonomous research institute within the UN system that undertakes multidisciplinary research and policy analysis on the social dimensions of contemporary development issues. Through our work, we aim to ensure that social equity, inclusion and justice are central to development thinking, policy and practice.

SOCIAL AND SOLIDARITY ECONOMY

BEYOND THE FRINGE

edited by Peter Utting

 UNRISD

Zed Books
LONDON

Social and Solidarity Economy: Beyond the fringe was first published in association with the United Nations Research Institute for Social Development in 2015 by Zed Books Ltd, 7 Cynthia Street, London N1 9JF

www.zedbooks.co.uk
www.unrisd.org

Set in Monotype Plantin and FFKievit by Ewan Smith, London NW5
Printed and bound by CPI Group (UK) Ltd, Croydon, CR0 4YY
Index: ed.emery@thefreeuniversity.net
Cover designed by www.roguefour.co.uk
Cover image © Julio Etchart/Panos

A catalogue record for this book is available from the British Library

ISBN 978-1-78360-345-9 hb
ISBN 978-1-78360-344-2 pb
ISBN 978-1-78360-346-6 pdf
ISBN 978-1-78360-347-3 epub
ISBN 978-1-78360-348-0 mobi

Printed in the USA by Edwards Brothers Malloy

CONTENTS

Figures and tables | vii Abbreviations and acronyms | viii
Preface | x

Introduction: The challenge of scaling up social and solidarity
economy. 1
Peter Utting

PART I History, theory and strategy

1 Social and solidarity economy in historical perspective 41
Jean-Louis Laville

2 Prometheus, Trojan horse or Frankenstein? Appraising the social
and solidarity economy 57
John-Justin McMurtry

3 Beyond the business case: a community economies approach
to gender, development and social economy. 72
Suzanne Bergeron and Stephen Healy

4 Can social and solidarity economy organisations complement or
replace publicly traded companies?. 86
Carina Millstone

5 Scaling the social and solidarity economy: opportunities and
limitations of Fairtrade practice 100
Darryl Reed

6 The potential and limits of farmers' marketing groups as catalysts
for rural development. 116
Roldan Muradian

7 Institutionalising the social and solidarity economy in Latin
America 130
José Luis Coraggio

8 Rebuilding solidarity-driven economies after neoliberalism:
the role of cooperatives and local developmental states in Latin
America 150
Milford Bateman

9 Enabling the social and solidarity economy through the co-construction of public policy 166
Marguerite Mendell and Béatrice Alain

PART II Collective action and solidarity in practice

10 Beyond alternative food networks: Italy's solidarity purchase groups and the United States' community economies 185
Cristina Grasseni, Francesca Forno and Silvana Signori

11 Social and solidarity investment in microfinance 202
Paul Nelson

12 Balancing growth and solidarity in community currency systems: the case of the *Trueque* in Argentina 221
Georgina M. Gómez

13 State and SSE partnerships in social policy and welfare regimes: the case of Uruguay. 236
Cecilia Rossel

14 Extending social protection in health through SSE: possibilities and challenges in West Africa 250
Bénédicte Fonteneau

15 Enabling agricultural cooperatives in Uganda: the role of public policy and the state. 266
Justine Nannyonjo

16 Embeddedness and the dynamics of growth: the case of the AMUL cooperative, India 284
Abhijit Ghosh

17 Taking solidarity seriously: analysing Kerala's *Kudumbashree* as a women's SSE experiment 300
Ananya Mukherjee-Reed

18 Demonstrating the power of numbers: gender, solidarity and group dynamics in community forestry institutions. 313
Bina Agarwal

Notes | 330 About the contributors | 339
Bibliography | 341 Index | 372

FIGURES AND TABLES

Figures

1.1 The dimensions of SSE. .56

7.1 The solidarity economy within the mixed economy 143

10.1 GAS registered with www.retegas.org per year. 187

10.2 Motivation for joining a GAS 189

10.3 The main objectives and results of being in a GAS 196

11.1 Pro-social and commercial microfinance funds 206

11.2 Four tiers of MFIs. 218

13.1 Main impacts on SSE when delivering services in partnership
with the state. 239

13.2 Number of beneficiaries of public social services delivered by
SSE actors directly to children and adolescents, 1994–2010 . . . 243

13.3 Impacts of SSE actors' participation in partnership with the state
in service delivery. 245

15.1 New model of agricultural cooperative marketing activities in
Uganda 272

15.2 Old model of agricultural cooperative marketing activities in
Uganda 273

16.1 Capturing the dynamics of embedded reciprocity 294

18.1 Probability of an EC member holding office in mixed-gender CFIs
in Nepal 320

18.2 A schema of lateral and vertical alliances 328

Tables

10.1 Changes in consumption habits. 190

10.2 Changes in lifestyles. 190

10.3 Changes in participation .191

11.1 Kiva.org and Oikocredit 207

12.1 Organisation of the Argentine complementary currency
networks. 231

14.1 Overview of data on MHOs in West Africa 254

17.1 Rural women's workforce participation rate in India, 2009–10 . 306

18.1 EC meetings with women attending in mixed-gender CFIs in
Gujarat and Nepal. 318

ABBREVIATIONS AND ACRONYMS

ACE	area cooperative enterprise
ADS	area development society
BMS	Bombay Milk Scheme
BOT	build–operate–transfer
CDS	community development society
CEC	Community Economics Collective
CFA	Communauté Financière d'Afrique (African Financial Community)
CFI	community forestry institution
CLAC	Coordinadora Latinoamericana y del Caribe de Pequeños Productores de Comercio Justo (Latin American and Caribbean Coordinator of Small Fair Trade Producers)
CORES	Consumi, Reti e Pratiche di Economie Sostenibili (Consumption, Networks and Practices of Sustainable Economies)
CT	*Club de Trueque* (Club of Trueque)
DES	*distretti di economia solidale* (districts of solidarity economy)
EC	executive committee
ECOSOL	Economia Solidária (Solidarity Economy)
FBES	Foro Brasileiro de Economia Solidaria (Brazilian Forum for Social Economy)
FECOFUN	Federation of Community Forest Users of Nepal
FIESS	International Forum on the Social and Solidarity Economy
FLO	Fairtrade International
FT	Fairtrade
GAS	*gruppi di acquisto solidale* (solidarity-based purchasing groups)
GDP	gross domestic product
ICT	information and communication technology
IDS	India Development Services
ILO	International Labour Organization
INAU	Instituto del Niño y Adolescente del Uruguay (Uruguayan Institute for Children and Adolescence)
LDS	local developmental state

LEDA	local economic development agency
MDG	Millennium Development Goal
MFI	microfinance institution
MGNREGS	Mahatma Gandhi National Rural Employment Guarantee Scheme
MHO	mutual health organisation
MIV	microfinance investment vehicle
MTIC	Ministry of Trade, Industry and Cooperatives
MYRADA	Mysore Resettlement and Development Agency
NGO	non-governmental organisation
NHG	neighbourhood group
PACA	Provence-Alpes-Côte d'Azur
PT	Partido dos Trabalhadores (Workers' Party)
RES	Rete Italiana di Economia Solidale (Solidarity Economy Network)
RPO	rural producer organisation
SACCO	savings and credit cooperative
SENAES	Secretaria Nacional de Economia Solidária (National Secretariat of Solidarity Economy)
SHG	self-help group
SSE	social and solidarity economy
SUFFICE	Support for Feasible Financial Institutions and Capacity Building Efforts
UCA	Uganda Cooperative Alliance
UEMOA	Union Economique et Monétaire Ouest Africaine (West African Economic and Monetary Union)
UN	United Nations
UNDP	United Nations Development Programme
UNICEF	United Nations Children's Fund
UNRISD	United Nations Research Institute for Social Development
UTM	Union Technique de la Mutualité (Technical Union of Mutual Health Insurance)
VCS	village cooperative society
WSF	World Social Forum

PREFACE

If there is one question about which most development actors now agree, it's the need for a rethink of development strategies in the context of recurring food and financial crises, jobless growth, persistent poverty, rising inequalities and climate change. The 2012 United Nations conference known as Rio+20 was a unique opportunity to focus global attention on this question. It was also a pivotal event in the genesis of this book. There I had the opportunity to participate in multiple side events at the intergovernmental forum, the 'People's Summit' and gatherings of ecological economists and other scholars. Despite the diversity of world views, explanations of what is going wrong and strategic options to promote sustainable development, considerable attention focused on different ways of organising economic and enterprise activity – ways that better integrate the economic, social and environmental dimensions of development and re-embedded such activity in progressive societal norms.

Of course, much of this reflection involved tweaking 'business as usual' or patterns of production through corporate environmental or social responsibility, eco-efficiency and new regulations associated with private governance and voluntary approaches. Considerable attention was also focused on how the poor might transition to being profitable entrepreneurs. But in various forums the discussion went beyond corporate responsibility and entrepreneurship and empowerment of individual producers. Here, it centred on the practices and potential of collective action and solidarity associated with the production of goods and services by communities, cooperatives, associations and new forms of social enterprise. The umbrella term 'social and solidarity economy' (SSE) was used on occasion as a descriptor for these multiple forms of economic activity that were deemed to be more people-centred and environmentally sensitive.

Despite the bubbling enthusiasm for SSE organisations and enterprises on the fringes of the intergovernmental process, they barely got a mention in the Rio+20 outcome document, *The Future We Want*. Beyond Rio+20, it is noticeable that outside niches within intergovernmental agencies – notably the International Labour Organization (ILO) – and interagency work on cooperatives, SSE as such rarely figures in UN discourse or reports. And among scholars, activists and policy-makers who are pushing the SSE agenda, what is also apparent is the lack of critical inquiry on SSE. 'Small is beautiful', harmonious communities and fairly successful cooperatives and social enterprises seem to be the order of the day. If there is a problem with SSE, it often boils down to the lack of an enabling policy environment and government support.

Upon returning from Rio to my place of work at the United Nations Research Institute for Social Development (UNRISD) in Geneva, colleagues and I set about trying to raise the visibility of SSE within the UN system and to encourage critical inquiry on SSE. At a time when the international development community was actively engaged in crafting the so-called post-2015 development agenda – comprising a set of Sustainable Development Goals to succeed the Millennium Development Goals – it was important to factor the role of SSE into these discussions.

To do so, we launched a global call for research papers on 'The potential and limits of SSE', and we organised, with the ILO and the United Nations Non-Governmental Liaison Service (UN-NGLS), an international conference on the same topic. This book is one of the outcomes of the UNRISD inquiry. Other outputs include a research paper and think piece series (www.unrisd.org/sse). Collaborations among international organisations and associations during the course of the project also led to the formation of the United Nations Inter-Agency Task Force on Social and Solidarity Economy, which was constituted in September 2013 and now comprises over twenty UN and other international intergovernmental and civil society organisations.

The central question addressed in this volume is whether SSE can be scaled up in ways that are consistent with the core values and objectives associated with cooperation, solidarity, the 'triple bottom line', democratic governance and ongoing autonomy from states, profit-maximising business and 'marketisation'.

The critical perspective that infuses the volume is in keeping with the one that frames the Just Sustainabilities series of which it is a part. Such a perspective recognises: 1) the need for deep structural change; 2) the presence of real-world practices or alternatives, and their potential; 3) the constraints, trade-offs, dilemmas and contradictions associated with both internal dynamics and the nature of SSE relations with external actors and institutions; and 4) that the questioning that is a hallmark of critical theory or radical political economy needs to be applied as much to the approaches, models and systems that hold considerable promise as to those that cultivate unsustainable and exclusionary patterns of development.

Numerous people and organisations have facilitated both the work of UNRISD in this field and the framing of this volume. Special thanks are extended to colleagues at UNRISD who provided research, managerial and editorial support, in particular Nadine van Dijk, Cyrus Afshar, Marie-Adélaïde Matheï, Monica Serlavos, Kiah Smith and the UNRISD communications and outreach team. Several colleagues at the UN in Geneva were particularly supportive of the UNRISD inquiry, and for this I would like to thank Anita Amorin, Roberto di Meglio, Simel Esim and Jürgen Schwettmann at the ILO, Hamish Jenkins at UN-NGLS, and Alexis Laffittan and Petra Lantz at the United Nations Development Programme (UNDP). Other colleagues who represent the agencies and networks that are members and observers of the United Nations Task Force on Social and Solidarity Economy are also to be thanked in this regard.

Financial support for different aspects of the UNRISD project was provided by the South–South and Triangular Cooperation Programme of the ILO, Hivos and the Rosa Luxemburg Foundation, as well as UNRISD core funding, which was provided by the Governments of Finland, Sweden and the United Kingdom.

On a more personal note, this book has been finalised just a few weeks prior to my leaving UNRISD after twenty-three years. The fact that the institute launched a global research project on this topic speaks volumes for the unique space it occupies within the UN system – a space that allows for critical inquiry free from government meddling and the taming effects of neoliberal discourse. I must take this opportunity to thank former directors Solon Barraclough,

Enrique Oteiza, Dharam Ghai and Thandika Mkandawire, and the current director Sarah Cook, for having cultivated that space and for having given me a free rein to develop ideas and projects.

The framing of the UNRISD project on SSE, this volume and the analysis presented in the introductory chapter has benefited from the exchange of ideas with numerous people. In this regard I would particularly like to thank Bina Agarwal, Chris Bacon, David Barkin, Jem Bendell, Amalia Chamorro, José Luis Coraggio, Isabelle Hillenkamp, Judith Hitchman, Thierry Jeantet, Jean-Louis Laville, Michael Lewis, Margie Mendell, Ananya Mukherjee-Reed, Orlando Nuñez, Ben Quiñones, Darryl Reed, Paul Singer, Kiah Smith, Daniel Tygel and Ilcheong Yi.

Peter Utting
Geneva, June 2014

INTRODUCTION: THE CHALLENGE OF SCALING UP SOCIAL AND SOLIDARITY ECONOMY

Peter Utting

Introduction

'Things can't go on as they have before' is a sentiment that was mainstreamed at the time of the Global Financial Crisis. Since 2008, it has been further reinforced by the spike in public and political awareness about climate change (IPCC 2013) and inequality.[1] These and other concerns relating to market and state failures have opened up the space for rethinking 'development'. Beyond conventional crisis management responses, alternative pathways, once positioned on the radical fringe or considered not to have systemic or structural significance, are suddenly attracting more attention within mainstream knowledge and policy circles.

Such has been the recent trajectory of 'social and solidarity economy' (SSE). This umbrella term is increasingly used to refer to forms of economic activity that prioritise social and often environmental objectives, and involve producers, workers, consumers and citizens acting collectively and in solidarity. The broadening field of SSE involves not only traditional 'social economy' or 'third sector' organisations and enterprises such as cooperatives, mutual associations, grant-dependent and service-delivery non-governmental organisations (NGOs), and community and other forms of volunteering and giving, but also myriad types of self-help groups organising to produce goods and services, fair trade networks and other forms of solidarity purchasing, consumer groups involved in collective provisioning, associations of 'informal economy' workers, new forms of profit-making social enterprises and social entrepreneurs, and NGOs that are having to shift from a dependence on donations and grants to sustaining themselves via income-generating activities. Various forms of solidarity finance, such as complementary currencies and community-based saving schemes, are also part of SSE, as are some new digital crowdfunding and sharing schemes associated with the 'collaborative economy'. Myriad articulations connect such forms of economic activity to other forms of economy associated with the private sector, the state and the informal economy, as well as to civil society agency in the political realm.[2]

Under the umbrella of 'social and solidarity economy' can be found different world views and understandings of 'development'. Accepting the reality of the capitalist system and its core institutions or 'rules of the game', *social economy* is primarily about expanding the economic space where people-centred organisations and enterprises can operate. It is fundamentally a contemporary variant of 'embedded liberalism' (Ruggie 1982), i.e. it is about re-embedding enterprise activities in progressive societal norms and creating or strengthening institutions that can mitigate or counteract perverse effects of 'business as usual'. *Solidarity economy*, for its part, pushes the envelope of social and systemic transformation. It emphasises issues of redistributive justice, so-called 'deep' sustainability, alternatives to capitalism and the debt-based monetary system, as well as participatory democracy and emancipatory politics driven by active citizenship and social movements activism. This strand of SSE is very much associated with the alter-globalisation agenda popularised by the World Social Forum (Arruda 2005; Santos 2007a). An inchoate movement is forming that connects these two approaches in a counter-hegemonic project[3] that contests the tenets, instruments and outcomes of the neoliberal agenda.

Taken together, SSE is fundamentally about reasserting social control or 'social power' (Wright 2010) over the economy by giving primacy to social and often environmental objectives above profits, emphasising the place of ethics in economic activity and rethinking economic practice in terms of democratic self-management and active citizenship (Gibson-Graham 2006; Dacheux and Goujon 2011; Grasseni et al., Chapter 10). SSE can be conceptualised in terms of a shift towards decommodified economic activities and circuits where, as Vail (2010: 328) points out, 'the social organization and practices of the circuit constitute an alternative logic to prevalent market processes'. Beyond regulating the market, or redistributing the benefits of growth via the state or labour market institutions such as collective bargaining, SSE 'root[s] a bias to greater equality and inclusion' in the organised logic of the economic system and technological innovation (Unger 2006: 21, cited in Vail 2010: 329).

Its potential from both a developmental and emancipatory per-spective relates to the fact that the forms of production, exchange and consumption involved tend to integrate some combination of economic, social, environmental and cultural objectives, as well as the political dimensions of participatory governance and empower-ment (Hillenkamp and Laville 2013; Santos and Rodríguez-Garavito 2013; Utting et al. 2014).

Rightly or wrongly, SSE has long been regarded as a fringe economy within the broader mixed or plural economy that also comprises for-profit enterprise, public sector production and pro-visioning, and the so-called informal economy. But data regarding both the scale and growth of SSE activity suggest that significant scaling up of SSE has not only occurred during different periods of contemporary history but has recently acquired considerable momentum. Furthermore, analysis of the drivers of SSE suggests that this trajectory will likely continue.

Recent data indicate that some 761,221 cooperatives and mutual associations in the world have US$18.8 trillion in assets, US$2.4 trillion in annual revenue and 813.5 million members. Individual cooperative organisations, such as Desjardins in Canada, Mondragon in Spain and AMUL in India, rank among the largest corporations in their sectors in their respective countries. Some 2.2 million self-help groups in India benefit some 30 million people, the vast majority women. SSE makes up a significant part of plural economies in territories such as Quebec (Chapter 9) and Kerala (Chapter 17). The solidaristic certified Fairtrade market (Chapter 5), supplied by an estimated 1.3 million producers and workers in seventy countries, grew from US$1 billion in 2004 to US$6 billion in 2012.[4]

Integrative scaling up? Reflecting the recent diversification and ex-pansion of SSE, there has been a surge of interest within scholarly and advocacy circles to explain what exactly SSE is, to analyse its alternative potential, measure its scale, document good practices, examine its regional manifestations and variations, and identify public policies and legal arrangements that can enable SSE.[5] While this volume touches on all these aspects, it focuses more specifically on the question of whether SSE can be scaled up and sustained while retaining its core values and objectives. For convenient shorthand, we refer to this as 'integrative scaling up'.

As Darryl Reed explains (Chapter 5), the notion of scaling up SSE comprises several dimensions. It may refer to 'horizontal' expansion, i.e. the multiplication of numerous, often small-scale, activities at the grass-roots level or in specific sectors – for example, health service-delivery NGOs in Uruguay (Chapter 13), village-level mutual health organisations in West Africa (Chapter 14) and community forestry groups in Nepal and India (Chapter 18). Scaling up may be 'vertical', as in the case of individual organisations and enterprises that grow significantly in terms of the scale of economic activity and membership, associate in networks or move up value chains – the case, for example, of big cooperative groups such as Mondragon (Chapters 2 and 8) and India's largest food marketing corporation, AMUL (Chapter 16), or what was once the world's largest complementary currency scheme, *El Trueque*, in Argentina (Chapter 12). Furthermore, scaling up may be 'transversal', when SSE expands across sectors and becomes an engine for local economic and social development, and a countervailing power to business and political elites. This has occurred, for example, in the Basque region of Spain (Chapter 8) and in Quebec, Canada (Chapter 9), and appears to be occurring in Kerala, India (Chapter 17). Associated with each of these dimensions are different sets of opportunities and tensions.

Understanding the scope for integrative scaling up requires not only espousing good theory and cataloguing good practices but also undertaking a systematic analysis of the challenges involved. Much writing on SSE is promotional. It runs the risk of romanticising the field and glossing over the tensions and contradictions associated with scaling up. Various disciplinary perspectives yield important insights into what can go wrong but often fixate on particular issues. Neoclassical economic or rational choice theory, for example, has emphasised problems of free riders or shirking; organisational theory points to issues of institutional isomorphism as organisations and managers from different (private, public, collective) fields assume similar characteristics; radical political economy cautions about the capacity of powerful actors not only to repress but also to co-opt 'alternatives'; neo-structuralist analysis critiques so-called neo-populist tendencies within the SSE movement that depict homogeneity and harmony (as opposed to differentiation and conflict) among SSE actors, and ignore the question of how to replace the role of capitalist relations both for developing the forces of production and for the surplus appropriation needed for industrialisation.[6]

Underpinning the focus of this volume, then, is the belief that:

- while SSE has considerable potential in relation to sustainable, inclusive and rights-based development, the scope for realising this potential is heavily constrained by structural contexts, relations with external actors and institutions, trade-offs between different objectives, and internal dynamics within SSE organisations, enterprises and networks;
- under certain conditions some of these constraints and tensions can be mitigated or managed in ways that allow SSE activities to expand while not deviating from core values and objectives; and
- the field of inquiry and advocacy related to SSE needs to be more reflexive, i.e. cognisant of the tensions and compromises involved. It also needs to be more analytically prepared, in terms of both understanding the complexities and contradictions of change and building the evidence base needed to be convincing in its arguments about why policy-makers, activists, scholars and others should be taking SSE seriously. To enhance reflexivity, knowledge and learning, much can be gained by analysis that is informed by multiple disciplines and interdisciplinary and trans-disciplinary methods of inquiry.

What's driving SSE? Various conditions and contexts have emerged in recent decades that are driving the contemporary expansion of SSE. They include heightened risks and shocks related to economic liberalisation and multiple crises, and structural, political, cultural and discursive shifts that have reconfigured power relations, public policy, and people's livelihood strategies and identities. The following are of relevance for the expansion of SSE and the forms it assumes:

- Recurring crises linked to finance, food and energy, as well as awareness of climate change, have fuelled collective and solidaristic forms of coping, producing and provisioning; prompted a repositioning of the role of the state, social protection and regulation in development strategy; and called into question conventional wisdom about growth and industrialisation models (Utting et al. 2010).
- There are new realities and perceptions of vulnerability and

inequality that are linked to processes of deregulation, state retrenchment, financialisation and commodification. These processes have fuelled the growth not only of global corporations, finance capital and the wealth of the '1%' targeted by the Occupy movement, but also of exploitative and hierarchical relations of domination and subordination. Such relations have extended well beyond conventional sites of production to culture, health, consumption and natural resource management (Vail 2010; Jackson 2009).

- New forms of identity politics have reconfigured the subjective preferences of individuals and groups seeking different lifestyles, and the scaling up of struggles for cultural rights, gender and environmental justice are underpinning the formation or expansion of activist and practitioner networks and 'new social movements' (Agyeman 2013; della Porta 2005; Santos 2007a).

- Discursive shifts have elevated notions of equality, rights, empowerment and participation in framings of what ('inclusive', 'sustainable' and 'rights-based') development means (Cornwall and Brock 2005). This can serve to translate perceptions of subordination and insecurity as something 'normal' into awareness of oppression and rights, as well as into concrete forms of resistance (Laclau and Mouffe 1985).

- There has been a social and environmental turn in public policy, manifested in the 2000–15 Millennium Development Goals (MDGs) and the Sustainable Development Goals (SDGs), which are currently being designed via the United Nations, as well as growing attention by governments and international development agencies to social protection programmes, measures to facilitate the economic empowerment of women and small-scale producers, micro-enterprises and entrepreneurs, and alternative pathways to transition from the informal economy (ILO 2013a).

- Ongoing constraints associated with market forces, neoliberal ideology and conditionality have restricted social spending by governments, thereby opening up the space for non-state actors to engage in social service provisioning and 'proximity services' (Borzaga and Defourny 2001; Laville and Nyssens 2000).

- The apparent end of the golden era of NGOs means that such organisations are having to rely less on public grants and more on social enterprise activities that generate income streams through the sale of goods and services.

- Democratic liberalisation has expanded possibilities for active citizenship and claims-making as well as new modes of 'collaborative' governance and consensual forms of hegemonic domination (Sum and Jessop 2013).
- The digital revolution has not only facilitated social organisation, mobilisation and networking, but also enhanced the ability of producers, community organisations and small enterprises to manage economic activities and risk.

The political underpinnings of SSE expansion are particularly important. Commodification, liberalisation (economic and democratic) and crises operationalise certain societal laws. From Foucault (1978: 95) we know that 'where there is power, there is resistance', and the scope for myriad forms of micro-resistance that may (or may not) coalesce into broader networks. From Polanyi (1944) we know that where there is market liberalisation there is a 'double movement' whereby those negatively affected react in various ways to deal with vulnerability and insecurity and to ensure social protection. And we know from Gramsci that elites and intermediary actors located in mainstream knowledge and policy circuits will respond in an attempt to (re-)embed liberalism, (re-)accommodate subaltern interests and (re)stabilise the system (Sum and Jessop 2013). Such developments have major implications in terms of the opportunities, spaces, constraints and dilemmas that relate to the expansion of SSE. The mainstreaming of SSE, then, emanates from interactions among bottom-up contestation and claims-making, technocratic problem-solving and strategising on the part of bureaucracies and policy-makers, and the efforts of political and economic elites to re-accommodate oppositional forces. These dynamics look set to fuel even more the growing interest in SSE as an approach that needs to be enabled through public policy.

SSE and the twenty-first-century development challenge The relevance of SSE in the early twenty-first century needs to be situated in the context of the failure of the twentieth-century solution to the multiple crises of the first half of the century, not least the Great Depression and two World Wars. The model of growth and embedded liberalism that extracted some countries and peoples from chronic vulnerability and insecurity is increasingly being questioned, even within mainstream knowledge and policy circles. The solution was a growth model that, in theory at least, aimed to generate employment under regulated conditions of decent work, an industrialisation model that generated consumer goods for the masses, and a welfare state model that was concerned with social protection and redistribution. This model has failed in numerous respects:

- It is increasingly associated with 'jobless growth'. While competitive strategies and technological developments fuel informalisation, growth is proving incapable of absorbing so-called surplus labour or 'the precariat' (Standing 2011) through conventional formal sector enterprises. The upshot is a situation where the majority of the labour force in Africa, Asia and Latin America make up the International Labour Organization's (ILO's) category of 'vulnerable employment', comprising some 1.5 billion workers (ILO 2013b).
- At the other end of the spectrum is the '1%' exposed by both the Occupy movement and recent literature on inequality (Piketty 2014). The concern that gross inequality not only poses an ethical issue but also impacts on growth and development has re-emerged as a key issue within mainstream circles (UNRISD 2010; UNDESA 2005; World Bank 2005).
- The mid-twentieth-century growth and welfare model assumed a male breadwinner. 'Full employment' meant full male employment and women would be primarily occupied in the private domestic sphere of the home. Eventually women entered the remunerated labour force en masse but often under conditions of 'indecent' work, while having to assume the 'double burden' of paid employment and unpaid care work (UNRISD 2005).
- This model, and the forms of enterprise and patterns of production, industrialisation and consumption associated with it, generated excessive pollution, waste, loss of biodiversity, degradation of habitats and the commons, and global warming (Jackson 2009).
- By concentrating wealth and 'development' in the cities, it generated huge spatial inequalities, siphoning off resources and surplus from sites of local production and surrounding communities, particularly in rural areas, not only to urban centres but also to tax havens, speculative activities and the global North.
- The capacities of welfare states have been undermined by market

forces, neoliberal ideology and fiscal constraints, particularly in contexts of regressive taxation, structural adjustment in developing countries and austerity policies associated with the fallout from financial crises in parts of the global North.

• The model required certain forms of institutional complementarities – for example between finance and production systems, states and markets – as well as social pacts that have been put out of kilter by financialisation and neoliberalism (Boyer 2007), not to mention recurring financial crises linked to deregulation and speculation.

These problems lie at the heart of the twenty-first-century challenge of social development, with its constituent elements of persistent poverty, precarious employment, food and livelihood insecurity, rising vertical and horizontal inequalities, alienation and intergenerational injustice associated, for example, with climate change and debt.

A focus on SSE points to a pathway that not only facilitates coping and needs provisioning and resilience in the above contexts but also interrogates key structural issues. Models of growth and finance, together with social and power relations, need to be addressed head on if the international development community is to do more than tweak 'business as usual' and take seriously the stated goals of sustainable, inclusive and rights-based development (United Nations System Task Team 2013).

Other currents have come together to facilitate this increased space within knowledge and policy circles. The growing interest of governments, development agencies and scholars in SSE goes well beyond its role as a coping strategy in times of crisis or a mechanism for poverty alleviation and employment generation. It also fits analytically with changing understandings of how best to achieve development. Such understandings point to the need to broaden institutional horizons and analytical frames beyond 'states versus markets' and towards public–private partnerships, collaborative or multi-stakeholder governance and 'polycentricity' (Ostrom 2009).[7]

Furthermore, the international context of having to debate and craft a post-2015 development agenda to succeed the MDGs has been conducive to rethinking development. Recognition of the need to address simultaneously issues of poverty reduction, sustainable development and human rights has opened up the terrain for thinking outside the 'business-as-usual' box with its focus on growth, safety nets and market-centred approaches to a green economy. This is reflected in the discursive shifts noted above, where terms that were previously associated with gatherings of social movements and critical scholarship find their way into mainstream circles: for example, 'social and environmental justice', 'food sovereignty', 'empowerment' and 'transformative change'.[8]

Development discourse is playing catch-up with the real-world processes associated with the scaling up of SSE. Governments and international organisations are having to respond after the fact to both developments on the ground and associated forms of contestation and advocacy. In the process, they are realising that SSE can assist them in attaining key objectives associated with poverty reduction, employment generation, local economic development and sustainable development.

Finally, the mainstreaming of SSE also reflects ideological and political shifts that have occurred within the field itself. Different strands appear to be coalescing, despite their often having been at odds about how to relate to 'the rules of the game', structural transformation, the role of the state, collective action and agency. Under the umbrella of social *and* solidarity economy, there are signs that these strands are coming together as part of a broader, more encompassing, movement – or counter-hegemonic project in the Gramscian sense of the term. While some clear differences in approach, ideology and the meaning of development still persist, advocates are now emphasising their commonalities. These relate to the values and objectives of re-embedding markets and enterprise practices in social and environmental norms and reinvigorating the role of communities and citizens in the economy and polity. As Paul Singer, the Brazilian National Secretary for Solidarity Economy, has noted, we seem to be in the midst of the formation of a global SSE movement (UNRISD 2013a).

At a time when SSE is expanding in territories around the world, when civil society networks are positioning SSE as a central plank in advocacy agendas, and when governments and international development agencies are taking greater interest, it is important to examine systematically the tensions and challenges involved in integrative scaling up.

About this book

The eighteen chapters that make up this volume address a range of conceptual and empirical issues associated with scaling up SSE. While several chapters deal with SSE as a global phenomenon and refer to developments in the global North, there is a strong focus on experiences in developing countries, in particular via chapters dealing with countries in South America, South Asia and Africa. The book also examines a diverse range of organisational forms and types of economic activities, including agricultural cooperatives, fair trade, community forestry initiatives, mutual health organisations and NGOs engaged in healthcare provisioning, forms of solidarity finance, and alternative food networks that promote collective provisioning and directly connect producers and consumers. The chapters are organised in two sections.

Part I, 'History, theory and strategy', contains nine chapters dealing with more general historical, philosophical, political economy and strategic questions relating to different forms of SSE or the field as a whole. Part II, 'Collective action and solidarity in practice', comprises another nine chapters that examine the challenges and dynamics of scaling up through the lens of particular SSE organisations or types of initiative. In the remainder of this introductory chapter, we review the main arguments put forward by the different authors and conclude by reflecting on what they tell us about the fundamental challenges of scaling up SSE.

History, theory and strategy The chapters in Part I examine the question of how the meaning, substance and trajectory of SSE have been shaped by the history of institutional change; the configuration of state, market and civil society forces; and philosophical and ideational currents associated with liberalism. They also address the question of how the prospects for integrative scaling up of SSE are shaped by relations with the state and the market. The chapters provide important insights into strategies and institutional arrangements that may address or avoid some of the tensions that often characterise such relations and may foster a more enabling environment.

Learning from history and ideas Historically, the trajectory of SSE has been highly uneven. Periodically, it has expanded; at other times it has contracted or undergone major variations in form or substance. *Jean-Louis Laville* (Chapter 1) surveys a 200-year history of social economy to reveal key institutional and political conditions and contexts that have produced such an uneven trajectory. In so doing, he provides important pointers for the challenge of scaling up SSE. He traces the different stages of SSE: from early nineteenth-century forms of democratic solidarity via associations that emphasised both economic and political empowerment through collective action; through late nineteenth-century 'philanthropic solidarity' that focused on poverty reduction through individual giving; to the resurgence of democratic solidarity in the early and mid-twentieth century, exercised through public authorities tasked with social protection and market regulation. But this latter 'development model ... was based on the synergy between the market and the state, which had the effect of crowding out various forms of associative activity'. Subsequently, non-profit service delivery or 'third sector' organisations expanded to fill some of the social cracks in the system but served a more palliative than transformative function. But combined with elements of the new social movements that had arisen since the 1970s, they paved the way for a resurgence of 'a strong version of solidarity'. And they were precursors to 'another world is possible' – the catchphrase that distilled the essence of both the discourse of the alter-globalisation movement present at gatherings such as the World Social Forum and the practices of myriad SSE organisations engaged in both economic activities and active citizenship. Laville sees SSE as a new theoretical perspective that has developed from 'the tradition of social economy and the resurgence of associative democracy in the late twentieth century'. This broader concept extends the field of interest beyond cooperatives, mutuals and non-profits to grass-roots organisations in non-market spheres of the economy. Furthermore, it recognises the reality of the 'plural economy' and the mix of principles, identified by Polanyi (1944), that govern resource allocation and exchange, including the market principle, redistribution (via the state) and reciprocity (via group solidarity). There is a risk, though, that we are witnessing instead a return to a variant of philanthropic solidarity via microcredit, corporate social responsibility, social business and 'the Big Society'. Drawing on Mauss, Laville argues that in order to avoid the authoritarian pitfalls of history, to correct for market liberalising tendencies that generate human insecurity and crises, to avoid isomorphism and counteract tendencies associated with philanthropic solidarity, what is needed is a robust form of democratic solidarity based on 'a particular relationship between reciprocity and redistribution', as well as a 'reciprocal democratisation of civil society and public authorities'. Key in this regard are questions, discussed in various chapters in the book, of participation and democratic forms of associative activity.

If actors and institutions shape the substance and trajectory of SSE, so too do ideas. *John-Justin McMurtry* (Chapter 2) examines how liberalism has shaped SSE. The apparent unity reflected in the term 'social and solidarity economy' masks divergent normative perspectives concerning the state, collectivities and, indeed, the meaning of development. Drawing on both the normative theory of Rawls, Habermas and Cohen and the economic theory of Sen, Ostrom and Sachs, he examines the implications of the philosophical framing of liberalism for understanding contemporary tensions within SSE. While it is possible to connect different strands within SSE to three distinct historical roots of capitalism (Anglo-American, Continental European and postcolonial development), such roots have been framed by an overarching liberal perspective that has two fundamental drawbacks for theorising and guiding transformative change. It assumes, first, that 'the "rules of the game" are set'; and, second, that the agents of change are individuals and communities whose capacities are severely constrained by those rules or structures. Referring to concrete examples of the cooperative movement, microcredit and alternative energy, McMurtry provides pointers as to how the cleavage between structure and the individual might be overcome. The way forward, he suggests, has two dimensions. One is to ensure that communities rather than states and markets position themselves more effectively as agents of change: 'The purpose here is to articulate both a site of economic and moral activity (the community) and a process (democracy at the community level) that are distinct from the usual drivers of SSE activity'. The other is ideational and procedural, comprising the need for a reflexive process that demystifies the 'rules of the game', clarifies their implications for SSE and 'build[s] towards a more clearly articulated moral position' by ensuring that SSE organisations make their community value clear, measure that value, strategise to enhance impacts, and input community governance. Such processes can, to some extent, address the issue of the (in)capacity of weak agents of change, which is prominent within the liberal tradition.

Neoliberalism and SSE–market relations Turning from liberalism more generally to neoliberalism in particular, *Suzanne Bergeron* and *Stephen Healy* (Chapter 3) pose the intriguing question of whether neoliberalism should always be seen (as is often the case within critical literature) as a tidal wave that swamps any semblance of progressiveness in its path. Drawing on community economics perspectives (Gibson-Graham 2006) and fieldwork, they identify spaces that potentially can cultivate economic and political subjects 'who are guided by motivations of care, ethical concern and collectivity'. Referring to an example from the Philippines, they identify three key elements in the process of forming community economies: 1) the scope for ethical negotiation that exists among different actors, internal and external to the community; 2) the scope for 'bricolage' (Lévi-Strauss 1966), where diverse elements in an economy can be cobbled together in ways that are socially transformative; and 3) the scope for cultivating relations of interdependence and care and practices of mutual assistance. While cautioning that such developments and outcomes are vulnerable to failure and takeover, not pursuing such a path is a sure guarantee that inequality and social and environmental injustice will be reproduced.

Beyond operating within niches at the local level, could SSE ever 'occupy Wall Street' – not in the political sense, but from an institutional perspective? In other words, could SSE assume certain features of big business associated with scale and competitive advantage? And could a more macro-economic or structural shift be envisaged that would be a game changer in terms of the scope for scaling up SSE? These questions are addressed by *Carina Millstone* (Chapter 4). The answer to whether SSE enterprises could compete with publicly traded companies is: with considerable difficulty. This is for two main reasons. First, SSE organisations are not structured to grow in the conventional economic sense; they exist to cater to the preferences and needs of their members: 'SSE organisations have within their aims, membership structure and financing arrangements characteristics that contribute to their success and resilience – but ultimately hinder their growth.' In short, there is often a trade-off between cooperative benefits and identity, on the one hand, and competitive advantage and market share on the other. Second, structural constraints can impede access to credit for SSE enterprises due to their 'less-for-profit' orientation or because they are seen as innately averse to reducing costs through restructuring.

Despite significant hurdles, one possibility for future growth lies within the expanding fields of green economy (renewable energy, more environmentally friendly transport, green buildings), digital enterprise, healthy living, and nutrition and community healthcare provisioning, which may provide important opportunities for value-driven, localised and community-centred enterprises. If consumption patterns were to change in ways conducive to sustainability, SSE organisations could position themselves as 'the natural providers of goods and services to respond to these new considerations of the consumer-citizen'. Millstone also makes the point that even if SSE enterprises could not make any serious dent in the dominance of the corporation, their mere presence in plural economies is a help, given the macro effects of constraining profits that are above the norm, predatory pricing and the creation of oligopolies, as well as facilitating choice, innovations and entrepreneurship.

Beyond the question of whether SSE can compete with big business, there is the even broader question of whether integrative scaling up can occur within the market. Two chapters explore this question by reviewing the performance of agricultural cooperatives and the more recent experience of certified Fairtrade.[9]

Fair trade producers are integrating global value chains dominated by large corporations such as Starbucks and Nestlé. As commercial logic within the Fairtrade system becomes more prominent, and as the balance of interests within governance structures changes, such relations run the risk of diverting fair trade from its original values and objectives associated with small producer and community empowerment, the redistribution of value within value chains and agro-ecology. Indeed, this tension underpinned a major split in the fair trade movement in 2011 when the US labelling organisation Transfair USA split from the umbrella association, Fairtrade International. *Darryl Reed* (Chapter 5) examines systematically the possibilities and tensions associated with the growth of fair trade and its implications for SSE more generally, looking at the three dimensions of scaling up mentioned earlier – horizontal, vertical and transversal – and the trade-offs involved. Closer relations with corporations, for example, may facilitate horizontal expansion of fair trade but compromise vertical and transversal expansion. The outcomes cannot be predetermined: 'it necessarily involves questions of strategy dependent upon experiential-based evaluations of specific conditions, and balancing what might be equally important (social) priorities … versus the promotion of longer-term institutional and structural change'. Drawing parallels with Via Campesina, he identifies as key the need for SSE actors to grow politically in order to effectively engage non-SSE actors on their own terms. This requires autonomous spaces 'so they can mobilise, organise, discuss, learn and strategise' and collaborations between SSE actors 'across different types of spaces and organisations'.

To understand the possibilities and challenges of scaling up SSE, it is instructive to examine the experience of agricultural cooperatives, which have a very long history. This history has been quite chequered, not least due to elite capture at the local level (McGranahan 1975), the contradiction between state or party control of cooperatives in many developing countries, and the principle of autonomy, which is key for ensuring that SSE values and objectives have primacy (Birchall 2003; Wanyama forthcoming). But, as *Roldan Muradian* (Chapter 6) shows in his examination of the experience of farmers' groups, in particular marketing cooperatives, the co-op question is even more complex. Laying out the evidence about the impacts of agricultural cooperatives in rural areas in Africa, he engages with the theory that farmers' collective action highlights the mechanisms through which farmers' groups induce development impacts, and that social dynamics underpin the 'quality' of collective action. Drawing on insights from institutional economics, he shows that the well-known advantages of cooperation (relating to productivity, adding value through processing, strengthening the capacities and capabilities needed to access and mobilise resources, economies of scale, integrating markets on fairer terms and competing economically) tend to accrue to certain types of farmers, in particular those with middle-size holdings who produce perishables or cash crops and have some access to road infrastructure. For small-scale producers, collective action can be costly in terms of time, resources and risks. Furthermore, those producers who face relatively high structural marketing transaction costs, due to factors such as having small landholdings and being a long distance from the road, cannot necessarily expect to be compensated in a significant way through collective action. For larger farmers, the costs of collective action may outweigh the benefits. He therefore puts forward the 'intermediate transaction costs hypothesis': 'collective marketing firms are more likely to emerge and to be effective when farmers face intermediate levels of transaction costs'. Muradian outlines various managerial and organisational challenges facing agricultural cooperatives and other farmers' marketing groups but notes that 'there is not a prescriptive sequence of interventions ... since the three domains of action (marketing, know-how and capabilities) are interdependent'. What is clear, he argues, is that the evidence base needed to support effective interventions is seriously lacking.

SSE–state relations Increasingly, however, states are intervening to support various aspects of SSE. Indeed, since the turn of the millennium, in particular, there has been a sort of 'SSE turn' in public policy in Latin America and Europe, in several African and Asian countries and in certain states and provinces in North America. A growing number of governments have adopted new policies, laws, development programmes and institutions specifically geared towards enabling SSE or some aspects of it[10] (see Coraggio, Chapter 7; Mendell and Alain, Chapter 9; Utting et al. 2014). While advocates of SSE generally see such trends as consistent with their demands for a more enabling policy environment for SSE, they are also hypersensitive to processes of instrumentalisation, bureaucratisation and co-optation – processes that can undermine core SSE principles, not least autonomy. But can SSE practitioners and advocates have their cake and eat it? The remaining three chapters of Part I examine the role of the state in contemporary efforts to enable SSE and ways of addressing the tensions involved.

Referring to developments in several South American countries to institutionalise SSE through legal and political/administrative reforms, *José Luis Coraggio* (Chapter 7) reveals marked differences in approach. Such reforms have occurred in the context of the progressive and popular turn of the past decade and are part and parcel of a shift from policies centred on social assistance to what might be called productive social policy. They are, however, far from similar in content and approach. Examining such reforms in Argentina, Brazil and Ecuador, he highlights the diversity of relations, drivers and approaches involved. Sometimes they are a response to bottom-up forces and new societal practices and politics; sometimes a top-down process to shape economic behaviour. Sometimes they are focused on the excluded; sometimes less so. Referring to Venezuela as well, he observes the dangers of rapidly scaling up SSE through top-down interventions. More generally, the process of institutional reform aimed at enabling SSE is vulnerable to tendencies in the region associated with 'neo-developmentalism', which prioritises an accumulation model centred on resource extractivism, primary exports and industrialisation. It is also vulnerable to electoral competition and the rotation of parties in power, which may put in jeopardy policies ushered in by a particular political party or leader. How might these tensions be addressed? Coraggio insists on the need to look beyond short-term policy and legal reforms to complementarities, articulations and territorial dimensions, i.e. to the 'meso' level. State policy towards SSE cannot be merely social policy; it needs to be enabled through multiple policies (macro-economic, industrial, labour market, etc.). Furthermore, to be sustainable, efforts to enable SSE must be part of a broader project of domestic resource and surplus mobilisation and redistribution. Ensuring that the current trend of institutionalisation empowers SSE rather than reduces it to 'fragmentary forms of self-management' requires not only this type of broader enabling environment but also pressures from below. A powerful grass-roots current of SSE initiatives and projects needs to be articulated with a political discourse and movements, which in turn are aligned with realities on the ground.

Given that SSE organisations and enterprises are grounded in communities, villages, towns, cities and municipalities, a key player in institutionalising and enabling SSE is local government. *Milford Bateman* (Chapter 8) argues that a necessary condition for solidarity economy and cooperatives to expand is 'getting the local institutions right'. He points to numerous failures in this regard: the commercialisation of local service provisioning, microfinance that targets individuals and micro-enterprises as opposed to cooperatives, and models of cooperative enterprise development that position cooperatives at the low end of the value chain while for-profit enterprises appropriate the bulk of surplus. Drawing on historic examples in Europe and contemporary Latin American case studies, Bateman affirms that the mix of cooperatives and enabling local governments has played a decisive role in successful development episodes. In a context where the mainstream development model is in crisis, he insists on the need to learn from history – not only the history of more successful cooperative–local government articulations in Italy, Yugoslavia and Spain, but also that of the 'developmental state'. Such a state supports particular types of formal-sector economic enterprises of varying sizes through a comprehensive set of policies. This combination of insights suggests the importance of the 'local developmental state' as an institutional form that can play a major role in cooperative enterprise development. Referring to examples from Ecuador and Colombia, Bateman shows how local government support policies (credit, training, promotion of farmers' markets, etc.) as well as more direct interventions and investments associated with so-called 'build–operate–transfer' (BOT) models of public investment allow agricultural producers to bypass intermediaries, access export markets and add value through processing. While concerns about capacity and other constraints that often affect cooperatives (see Muradian, Chapter 6) are very real, the 'transfer' dimension of BOT incorporates a time period when both proto- and already existing cooperatives can attempt to build the necessary capacities and competencies needed for sustainability.

But how can we get around the 'can't have your cake and eat it' dilemma? The ways in which SSE actors organise, mobilise and network are crucial in this regard, as is the question of how they participate in policy processes. *Marguerite Mendell* and *Béatrice Alain* (Chapter 9) examine in some depth the 'co-construction' of policy, where SSE organisations organise themselves and are a capable partner in designing and implementing policies. The chapter discusses the main advantages of such an approach and examines the conditions for effective collaborative processes. It also provides examples of good practices and indicates the limits of existing policies that have not been designed or implemented jointly with civil society. Drawing on fourteen case studies from five continents, they show how co-construction is conducive to effective policy-making by reducing information asymmetry and transaction costs, and by improving understanding of the sector's needs, resources and priorities. When a range of SSE actors is involved, these effects are strengthened. Optimal co-construction, however, is dependent on the existence of effective and representative intermediary organisations and networks. Where broad coalitions of SSE actors exist, 'their leverage with government to obtain innovative policy is increased and their capacity to mobilise partners is enhanced'. As examples from Burkina Faso, Ecuador, Poland and South Africa reveal, often these conditions do not persist. The authors note, however, examples where governments have encouraged their creation or have developed initiatives for SSE sectors to join existing networks. Tensions between subsidiarity and conditionality to comply with regulatory frameworks often require hybrid arrangements that give rise to further issues of accountability and modes of service delivery. Effective co-construction also relies on full commitment by the government, which in turn requires sufficient capacity, coordination and resources in all relevant branches of government at both national and local levels. If the main challenge facing governments relates to capacity and coherence, ensuring that SSE networks and intermediaries are 'representative of SSE, strong enough to participate ... and able to remain independent' is the key challenge confronting SSE actors.

Collective action and solidarity in practice To examine in more depth the scope for scaling up SSE in ways that are consistent with its core values and objectives, we turn to the concrete experiences of particular organisations and initiatives. The nine chapters in Part II examine projects in four very different geographical, developmental and institutional settings: the United States of America (USA) and Italy in the global North; South America (Argentina and Uruguay); sub-Saharan Africa (West Africa and Uganda); and South Asia (India and Nepal). The purpose, however, is not to understand regional variations in the trajectories and performance of SSE but to identify significant institutional and political economy conditions and contexts that facilitate or undermine the integrative scaling up of SSE.

Assessing new forms of solidarity in the global North Citizens in the global North are engaged in what some call post-industrial identity politics, which has yielded new varieties of social movements and community action. As commodification extends beyond the conventional workplace into arenas previously associated with the management of common pool resources, community economies, the provisioning of public goods and services, culture and care, so too do relations of subordination and processes of disempowerment (Laclau and Mouffe 1985; Vail 2010). What Polanyi (1944) referred to as the 'double movement'[11] therefore manifests itself in numerous domains. Two such practices involve alternative food networks and solidarity finance.

A prominent feature of SSE in the global North relates to efforts to craft new ways of producing and distributing food that are fairer for producers, healthier – and sometimes cheaper – for consumers, better for the planet and beneficial in terms of social or community cohesion. *Cristina Grasseni, Francesca Forno* and *Silvana Signori* (Chapter 10) examine attempts in northern Italy to create food networks that re-embed economic practice in social relations via forms of collective provisioning and solidarity purchasing that connect consumers and producers via fair trade. Participant observation recorded significant stumbling blocks relating to issues of delegation, leadership and conflict management, as well as a gender imbalance between the largely male steering committees and working groups and a largely female base. But they see SSE as a socio-pedagogic laboratory – a space for creative 'contamination' and cross-cutting innovation, identifying and experimenting with critical issues surrounding delegation and representation, participation and labour division, as well as skill and value construction and 'ethical learning by doing'.

Another field where new forms of solidarity are manifesting themselves in the global North is that of solidarity finance. It is a field, however, that has undergone significant adjustments. The rise of the global microcredit industry in the 1990s was seen by many as evidence that principles of fairness and solidarity stood a chance of restructuring financial systems in ways that were pro-poor. Fast forward two decades and we find a microcredit industry under critical scrutiny for not only having inflated claims about its impacts on poverty but also for having morphed into a commercialised sector that in some contexts has fuelled over-indebtedness (Bateman and Chang 2012). How might microfinance be reconstituted along more ethical and pro-social lines? *Paul Nelson* (Chapter 11) examines this question by looking at the cases of two social investment schemes – Kiva and Oikocredit – that claim to be doing things differently. He identifies five sets of indicators to assess how solidarity finance schemes have fared in terms of building and sustaining institutions associated with SSE. They include the way in which risk is shared and, in particular, whether lending institutions in the global North are prepared to adopt meaningful practices that reduce risk for microfinance institutions. Other variables relate to the level of awareness and the intentions of investors, which in turn relate to the credibility of the claims of the investment vehicle. Also important are 'sustained participation', i.e. of investors prepared to provide 'patient capital' on a regular and long-term basis, and institution-building, particularly to support group or community organisations. In view of the scandals that have rocked the world of microfinance, it is also crucial to assess what these schemes are doing to regulate the industry by setting clear standards for client protection and social impact assessment and to ensure compliance. Nelson notes significant variations in the performance of the two schemes he discusses, but also that both are actively innovating and experimenting with new arrangements aimed at ensuring that pro-social investment can be a component of strategies to build SSE.

Scaling up SSE in Argentina and Uruguay Turning to South America, we examine another problematic experience that relates to alternative finance. Referring to what was once the world's largest complementary currency scheme, known as the *Trueque* in Argentina, *Georgina M. Gómez* (Chapter 12) analyses the tensions that affect SSE initiatives when they grow from small-scale initiatives centred on personal exchange to large-scale, impersonal projects. In the case of the former, exchange is regulated by a variety of mechanisms, including face-to-face interaction that cultivates trust and facilitates monitoring. As impersonal systems emerge, social action needs to be regulated by other institutions. Combining different perspectives from institutional economics, she shows that scaling up was possible only within the limits defined by the interpersonal transfer of trust, the reputation of the leaders to act as a linchpin for the system, and the ability to sustain the process of institutional innovation. In the absence of alternative regulatory mechanisms, such limits eventually caused the system to collapse.

Around the same time that the *Trueque* took off in Argentina, across the border in Uruguay SSE actors, mostly NGOs, started working with the state to provide public social services for the poorer strata of the population. Since then, these partnerships have become more and more frequent, and seem to have become a key catalyst in the welfare system's capacity to integrate population groups excluded from the traditional welfare matrix. As governments and other development actors around the world are rethinking the nature of welfare regimes in contexts of austerity, pro-market ideology and growing interest in public–private partnerships, it is instructive to examine the role of SSE actors in welfare systems and how the intensification of relations with the state affects SSE. *Cecilia Rossel* (Chapter 13) provides a balance sheet that suggests the following. On the plus side, social protection of excluded groups has improved. This sector of SSE has also expanded as a result of increased financial and human resources, and strengthened professional competencies. Furthermore, SSE organisations now have more influence in policy design. On the down side, Rossel notes that increased competition among SSE organisations for state resources has undermined coordination and networks within SSE. Above all, there is a trade-off between dependency and autonomy that can stifle contestation, critical thinking and innovation, and lead to bureaucratisation 'with a strong tendency towards "routine activity and a utilitarian approach"'. This analysis suggests the need to view with caution the growing role of SSE organisations in welfare provision, a trend that is occurring in many countries. It also suggests that if this role is to yield more positive development outcomes, SSE will need to be 'if not strong, then relatively cohesive'.

Experiences from West Africa and Uganda A similar phenomenon, whereby SSE organisations are emerging as significant actors in health systems, is occurring in West Africa. *Bénédicte Fonteneau* (Chapter 14) examines the role and performance of village-level mutual health organisations, which numbered about 500 by the early 2000s, each with between 300 and 1,000 members. Providing a modicum of health insurance and other services, such as health education, governments in the region are now seeing mutual health organisations as crucial future partners in their ambitious plans to extend health cover to large rural and informal economy populations who are currently not covered by private and state systems. The inclusion of such organisations in public policies can be interpreted as recognition of an expanding grass-roots network that is in tune with local needs and can act as 'an interlocutor that represents members' interests vis-à-vis healthcare providers' and in policy dialogues. However, their weak initial conditions pose a major challenge for realising the social turn in public policy. This is apparent in relation to weak governance arrangements and managerial competencies, low levels of contributions and an inability to expand membership, minimalist insurance packages, and mistrust between mutual health organisations and health providers. Furthermore, networking and organising at scales beyond the local level has proved difficult; this is not helped by the fact that mutual health organisations are widely dispersed and disparate, which is partly associated with their very different models of donor support. As in the case of Uruguay, the close articulation of these SSE organisations with public policy has occurred prior to the consolidation of a cohesive organisational structure at local, regional and national levels. In the absence of such organisation and competencies, public policy aimed at supporting mutual health organisations is often top-down. In such contexts, Fonteneau insists that the mutual health organisation 'movement' needs to reflect on how it can scale up and professionalise while staying in tune with members' demands and preferences; and that governments and donors need to reflect on how their support can enable rather than disable representative structures and effective participation.

Public policy in several African countries is also placing great store on the role of a new generation of agricultural cooperatives. *Justine Nannyonjo* (Chapter 15) examines the effectiveness of public policy in Uganda, which, since 2005, has aimed to facilitate the scaling up, conduct and integration of cooperatives in the development process. This has occurred through the incorporation of cooperatives into various poverty eradication and development programmes and plans, legal and administrative reforms, enhanced support services, adding value through processing, and other capacity-building measures that focus on leadership training, business management and entrepreneurship. The chapter also identifies various institutional challenges that hinder the government in fulfilling its policy commitments and that need to be addressed. These include inadequate financial and skilled human resources, and weak links between central and local governments.

South Asia: the cases of AMUL, Kudumbashree *and community forestry groups* To understand the dynamics of scaling, much can be learned from experiences of SSE in South Asia, even if the term itself is rarely used there. The final three chapters of this volume refer to very different experiences in India and Nepal that shed considerable light on what type of institutional and political economy conditions need to be in place to ensure the integrative growth of SSE.

Bringing in a perspective associated with heterodox management studies, which insists on the need to connect micro and macro levels of analysis and to examine how enterprise strategy relates to the broader socio-political context, *Abhijit Ghosh* (Chapter 16) looks at the early conditions that explain the growth of India's largest cooperative organisation, AMUL. Established as an alternative to a private company that exploited milk producers in the Kheda district in Gujarat, the AMUL dairy cooperative expanded to become the country's largest food marketing corporation, with sales of over US$3 billion and 630,000 member producers. Drawing on data from the author's extensive fieldwork, this chapter shows how micro-level strategising and leadership combined synergistically with institutional and technological innovations and an enabling political economy environment, often involving informal political relations and alliances. Key elements of integrative growth included political connections that enabled the cooperative to leverage resources and policy influence; the fit between, on the one hand, enterprise leadership and strategy associated with product diversification and technological innovation and, on the other hand, national circumstances and challenges associated with food insecurity and import substitution; and consistent adherence to the overriding strategic goal of 'serving Kheda's farmers'. Innovations in organisational structure and processes of democratic governance safeguarded the farmers' interests and restricted elite capture.

A vital aspect of upscaling SSE relates to moving beyond its dispersion in disparate locations and intensifying or thickening its presence in sizeable territories, so that SSE constitutes a prominent form within the broader plural economy. Well-known examples can be found in Quebec, Canada, and the Basque region in Europe. A similar situation may be emerging in Kerala, India, which is the focus of the chapter by *Ananya Mukherjee-Reed* (Chapter 17).

She analyses the experience of *Kudumbashree*, a socio-economic programme composed of nearly 4 million women below the poverty line. While Kerala has long had the highest human development indicators in India, it still exhibits significant gender and other forms of inequality. Initiated by the state government in the late 1990s as a poverty eradication programme, *Kudumbashree* has since developed into an extensive network in which marginalised women work collectively to enhance livelihood security and well-being through planning and implementing programmes and projects that address the root causes of poverty. Focusing in particular on how women's groups have become important development actors through their active role in both the implementation of the extensive public employment guarantee scheme and some 44,000 small agricultural collectives, she shows how the creation of strong bonds of solidarity and collective agency has enabled poor women to challenge existing power imbalances and establish innovative organisations. 'The key to *Kudumbashree*'s success,' she argues, 'has been its ability to generate and access [social, economic and political] resources in a comprehensive and systematic fashion through a dynamic relationship between its community and the state.' While this experience has generated significant gains for women, progress is constrained by structural and other conditions. These include low profit margins in the economic sectors in which they operate, the precariousness of demand or orders from private firms in the value chain, the unwillingness of landlords to rent land, and the lack of certainty about the future of government programmes. Mukherjee-Reed considers the feasibility of a number of alternatives, including, for example, greater specialisation and clustering, moving up value chains, forming solidarity value chains and developing their own distribution channels. Other questions remain to be researched, including how the work of organising impacts on women's time and already burdensome workload, the border line between extensive state support and dependency that may stifle autonomy, and the sustainability of the transfers or subsidies involved.

As noted in several of the chapters reviewed above, SSE holds considerable promise from the perspective of women's empowerment and well-being. But women's participation in SSE organisations can be heavily constrained by traditional gender relations and hierarchies.

How can such constraints be overcome? *Bina Agarwal* (Chapter 18) examines this crucial question by looking at the experience of community forestry groups in India and Nepal. She analyses what is an often overlooked area in institutional and political economy analysis, namely the nature of intra-group dynamics, which can have a major effect on the type and quality of cooperation and performance. How does a group's gender composition affect the ability of women to participate effectively in local institutions of environmental governance and the impact of their participation? It is argued here that, in given contexts, the mere inclusion of a larger proportion of women in mixed-gender groups ('women in themselves') can go a long way to improving outcomes, even without a thrust to create a 'women for themselves' social consciousness – although a shift towards the latter can also enhance outcomes. Agarwal's empirical research on community forestry groups in South Asia yields innovative data to demonstrate 'the power of numbers': increasing the proportion of women representatives in the executive committees of these collective institutions can facilitate both the effective participation of women and the functioning and outcomes of the institution concerned. But this analysis also points to the need to organise and mobilise beyond the local level, at multiple scales where governance takes place. And if the power of numbers within community forestry groups is to make a difference in terms of women's empowerment and equality, it is also crucial to build coalitions involving women in other arenas of SSE, such as women's self-help groups.

Strategic pillars of transformative change By way of conclusion, let us return, then, to the central questions and concerns that framed this volume. The first related to the need for a more comprehensive and systematic assessment of the limits, risks, tensions and dilemmas that are associated with the scaling up of SSE. Key elements identified by the authors in this regard include:

- weak initial conditions, assets and competencies, as well as motivational and time-use constraints, that render some SSE organisations not only inherently fragile but also amenable to those populations at the bottom of the ladder in terms of endowments and capabilities (Chapters 3, 6, 8, 10 and 14);
- being locked into commodity and service sectors with low

value-added and limited capacity to mobilise surplus (Chapters 5 and 17);

- disabling environments associated with finance, including restricted or onerous terms of access to credit for SSE organisations, instabilities within financial markets and biases within microcredit associated with individual entrepreneurship rather than group solidarity (Chapters 4 and 11);
- pressures and influences of commercialisation and financialisation that can usher in logics of enterprise activity that swing the efficiency–equity pendulum in favour of efficiency, and can invoke practices associated with the externalisation of social and environmental costs (Chapters 2, 4, 5 and 8);
- related tendencies towards managerialism and institutional isomorphism, where large cooperatives, for example, or 'co-opitalism' (Defourny et al. 1999) may start to assume features typically associated with corporate institutional culture and corporate social responsibility (Chapters 1, 2, 4, 5 and 6);
- elite capture of organisations and the gains of SSE (Chapters 2, 3, 14 and 16);
- trade-offs between scale and social capital, and related difficulties of crafting new regulatory and monitoring mechanisms in transitions from systems of personal to impersonal exchange (Chapters 6 and 12);
- conceptions of social economy that disregard the crucial role of the state in development and change, and fail to recognise the complementarities and synergies between principles of 'reciprocity' and 'redistribution' or democratic solidarity at the level of both groups and the state (Chapter 1);
- limited political will and capacities of state institutions, including local governments, to craft and implement enabling policies, and weak governance arrangements and spaces for the co-construction of policy (Chapters 7, 9, 10, 14 and 15);
- issues of dependency, co-optation, instrumentalisation and top-down interventions related to state policy and programmes (Chapters 7 and 13);
- theories, policies and strategies that ignore structural conditions and contexts that constrain both SSE and the possibilities of designing, implementing and financing enabling policies (Chapters 2 and 7);

- ongoing subordinations of women within governance and leadership structures (Chapters 10 and 18); and
- the challenges of organising beyond the community or local level and engaging in multi-scalar activism and coalition-building (Chapters 9 and 18).

The second concern addressed in this volume relates to the challenge of growing SSE under conditions that support integrative scaling up. Emerging from the chapters are three interrelated sets of explanatory conditions, or what could be called strategic pillars of integrative scaling up: namely, capacity, institutional complementarities and participation.

Capacity The first set of conditions relates to questions of capacity writ large, i.e. the scope for strengthening assets, competencies and managerial and governance processes, be they of SSE organisations themselves or of governmental and other external organisations that seek to support SSE. It also relates to the effectiveness of regulatory instruments and systems.

Capacity-building is partly a question of resources and methods: for example, infrastructure, access to finance and market information, technology up-grading and transfer, and education and training relating to literacy, skills development, cooperative organisation, administration and management. Brazil's National Secretary of Solidarity Economy, Paul Singer, notes that if SSE is not simply to be a response to crisis and the contradictions of capitalism, but is to expand and diversify according to its own dynamic, two aspects of capacity-building are crucial: a system of solidarity finance and a knowledge system for technical and values-oriented training (Singer 1996: 117).

The challenge of capacity-building is particularly pertinent in the context of state institutions that are willing to support SSE but have seen their capacities diminished through decades of neoliberal restructuring. It is also relevant in the context of processes of decentralisation that have transferred responsibilities and administrative authority to local governments but without the commensurate transfer of resources or fiscal authority. Both sets of challenges are particularly apparent in Africa (Fonteneau, Chapter 14) and Latin America (Coraggio, Chapter 7; Bateman, Chapter 8).

As Muradian and Bateman show, capacity-building needs to be factored in early on. As seen in the case of agricultural cooperatives in Africa, various constraints may be particularly acute during the initial phases of cooperative development (Muradian, Chapter 6). Policy responses need to focus on such aspects as marketing, know-how or technology transfer, and enhancing managerial skills. Referring to projects in Colombia and Ecuador, Bateman also highlights the importance of interventions that 'build the required proto-cooperative foundations upon which genuine farmer-owned ... cooperatives can emerge thereafter' (Chapter 8).

Bateman also insists on the key role of local governments – or 'local developmental states' – in capacity-building. Important in this regard are trends associated with decentralisation, noted also by Fonteneau (for Burkina Faso and Senegal), Mukherjee-Reed (Kerala), and Mendell and Alain (Quebec and elsewhere). Under certain conditions, decentralisation can strengthen the capacity of municipal authorities to foster local economic development, promote forms of dialogue and governance that facilitate SSE actors' access to local decision-making, foster equitable partnerships between local authorities and SSE organisations in social service delivery, and serve to connect local- and national-level institutions. Several authors note ongoing challenges, which are well known: the gap between the transfer of responsibilities or authority to local governments and actual resources, as well as the skewed allocation of resources associated with elite capture and clientelism – challenges that ultimately require political action.

The issue of capacity also relates to the question of institutional and social innovation. This requires having the ideas, strategies and ways and means to learn and adapt to complex and changing circumstances, and not least to external pressures and shocks. It also involves the ability to produce new goods, services and processes that meet social needs or create new social relationships and collaborations (Borzaga and Bodini 2012; Murray et al. 2010). Pertinent in this regard are the rapidly expanding fields of proximity services (Laville, Chapter 1; Mendell and Alain, Chapter 9), Fairtrade (Reed, Chapter 5), alternative food networks (Grasseni et al., Chapter 10) and community forestry institutions (Agarwal, Chapter 18). So too are initiatives that insert SSE-related values into the financial sphere. Furthermore, innovation relates to the need to adapt regulatory systems, as in the case of the commercialisation of microfinance (Nelson, Chapter 11) or where SSE initiatives scale up via systems of impersonal exchange (Gómez, Chapter 12). This, in turn, relates to the question of maintaining or cultivating trust or so-called social capital.

'Learning by doing' can be an important source of innovation. Practices of 'ethical learning by doing' were noted by Grasseni et al. (Chapter 10), i.e. when SSE actors expand their preferences beyond material self-interest to encompass other (e.g. environmental or solidaristic) values and objectives. What we might call 'active ethicality' has also been emphasised: McMurtry (Chapter 2) suggests that one of the key means to ensure that SSE stays true to its original values and objectives and 'competes' with for-profit enterprise is by emphasising its ethical value-added.

Institutional complementarities The issue of capacity is intimately connected with a second strategic pillar: institutional complementarities. As Boyer notes, institutional complementarity:

> describes a configuration in which the viability of an institutional form is strongly or entirely conditioned by the existence of several other institutional forms, such that their conjunction offers greater resilience and better performance compared with alternative configurations (Crouch et al. 2005).

As Coraggio suggests (Chapter 7), a focus on institutional complementarity takes us from the micro level of organisations to the meso level of inter-actor and inter-institutional articulations.

Various forms of complementarity have been noted. At the level of the broad principles governing resource allocation and exchange (Polanyi 1944), 'market', 'reciprocity' and 'redistribution' need to coalesce to protect against the excesses of market forces, enable democratic solidarity, and mobilise resources for productive and social ends. This implies the need for complementarities or 'bricolage' among private, civil society and state actors. Whether in theory (Laville, Chapter 1) or in concrete settings (Bergeron and Healy, Chapter 3; Coraggio, Chapter 7; Fonteneau, Chapter 14; Mukherjee-Reed, Chapter 17), we have seen that integrative scaling up of SSE depends crucially on such complementarities. Bateman's notion of the 'local developmental state', closely articulated with cooperative forms of enterprise, emphasises the importance of such complementarities at the local level. This serves as an important corrective to some 'third sector', communitarian or neo-populist approaches that are prone to downplay the role of the state in inclusive and sustainable development.

A focus on complementarity directs attention to the intersections of policy and questions of more effective institutional design. It also relates to the notion of polycentricity referred to earlier. Under certain conditions the different sets of rules that are associated with different actors can mesh in synergistic ways with positive social, environmental and regulatory outcomes (Ostrom 2009). But such an approach runs the risk of ignoring broader structural conditions and constraints – for example, patterns of accumulation and the distribution of land and surpluses – that can stifle or distort SSE and undermine the possibilities of crafting an enabling policy environment (Coraggio, Chapter 7). Therefore, institutional complementarities that relate to the macro level or structural contexts are also key (Boyer 2007).

This structural dimension has implications for what in contemporary development parlance is often called policy coherence. This involves far more than simply better coordination of design and implementation in different policy areas. More fundamentally, it involves reducing the types of trade-offs and contradictions noted by Coraggio (Chapter 7) when governments promote investment, fiscal, trade and labour market policies conducive to the expansion of monocultures, extractive industries, high-input export agriculture and cheap food imports. Such policies can also facilitate patterns of corporate control of value chains that can undermine small-scale agriculture, food security and the environment. Policy coherence requires placing on the policy agenda often neglected redistributive issues that may be vital for providing an enabling policy environment for SSE: for example, progressive taxation, particular forms of subsidy, land reform, policies associated with the care economy, and the restructuring of government transfers and incentives, not least the massive benefits and loopholes associated with 'corporate welfare' (Farnsworth 2012).

Complementarities related to the links between policy at different scales (i.e. at local, sub-national, national and international levels) have also been noted. Referring to Quebec, Mendell and Alain

(Chapter 9) point to the creation of social economy regional poles as a successful example of decentralisation and of designing and instituting mechanisms of information-sharing and coordination between regions and between all regions and the centre.

How financial and production systems connect and interact is another crucial arena of macro-institutional complementarities. Important in this regard is the need for new mechanisms of solidarity finance to facilitate rather than constrain SSE organisations and enterprises (Nelson, Chapter 11; Millstone, Chapter 4; Utting et al. 2014). Traditional gender relations and patriarchy operate in another institutional field that often constrains rather than enables SSE (Hillenkamp et al. 2014). These and other forms of domination, subordination and oppression invoke the need for what Nancy Fraser (2012) refers to as a shift in focus beyond the Polanyian notion of 'social protection' via principles of reciprocity and redistribution to 'emancipation'. Labour market and social (including care) policies that serve to alleviate the double burden of paid work and unpaid care responsibilities, and free up women's time, are of particular significance here (UNRISD 2010; Hillenkamp et al. 2014).

We can also extend the notion of complementarity to the knowledge and policy nexus. The way in which concepts and ideas inform policy and strategy is important. As seen with the history of both communism and contemporary neoliberalism (Laville, Chapter 1; Bergeron and Healy, Chapter 3), when theory and ideology are in the driving seat, the results can be disastrous; they are likely to include major blind spots on the development and policy agenda, distortions in the way in which reality is understood, and policy interventions that have high social and environmental costs (Ocampo 2006: viii). While certain intellectual and political currents associated with SSE run the risk of perpetuating such incoherence, much contemporary theorising of SSE is grounded in real-world practices. With this sequencing, theory can usefully inform understanding, policy and strategy (ibid.). As noted below, 'co-construction' of policy (Mendell and Alain, Chapter 9) is a key mechanism for ensuring that policy is effectively informed by knowledge.

Several chapters suggest that complementarity is also crucial within the field of collective action itself. Both economic and political empowerment go hand in hand (Laville, Chapter 1; Mukherjee-Reed, Chapter 17; Coraggio, Chapter 7; Rossel, Chapter 13). The word 'empowerment' has become one of the contemporary buzzwords in international development discourse (Cornwall and Brock 2005) but its usage is often depoliticised. It is typically associated with economistic interpretations that emphasise the importance of the economic empowerment of women, smallholders and micro-enterprises, and the need to build their capacities as entrepreneurs (Utting 2012). Similarly, much of the literature on cooperatives and other forms of social enterprise or entrepreneurship emphasises this dimension of economic empowerment via, for example, credit, training and legal reforms. Economic and political empowerment are mutually reinforcing: actors who are empowered economically are likely to have greater capacities to enhance competencies, to network and to access markets on fairer terms, while the contestation, advocacy and claims-making associated with political empowerment is crucial for state provisioning, realising rights and holding powerful actors to account.

Participation This brings us to the third strategic pillar – participation – understood in the political sense of the term. As defined by UNRISD in the late 1970s, 'popular' participation refers to the organised efforts of the disadvantaged to gain control over resources and regulatory institutions that affect their lives (UNRISD 2004). Such a definition encompasses various dimensions of the political, including voice, contestation, advocacy, co-construction, negotiation, networking, and building and sustaining coalitions and alliances. In short, it is about 'active citizenship' and reconfiguring power relations (Green 2012; Laville, Chapter 1). This perspective is far broader than that commonly used by mainstream development agencies working within the 'good governance' frame, where selected 'stakeholders' are invited to the table to be consulted. Such a frame often assumes wrongly that confrontation and negotiation between interest groups are passé, and that now we are all 'stakeholders' and 'partners' who can collaborate to solve problems (Mouffe 2005).

But such governance arrangements and logics often ignore two fundamental questions. The first is the need for ongoing contestation both within SSE structures and on the part of SSE actors interacting with external actors and institutions. The second is how to ensure that the SSE actor's 'voice', or their seat at the table, actually translates into them becoming a player who can effectively influence decision-making processes. As seen in the case of fair trade (Reed, Chapter 5), the AMUL cooperative corporation in India (Ghosh, Chapter 16) and community forestry in South Asia (Agarwal, Chapter 18), what matters is the relative balance of social forces or interests within governance structures, as does the presence and institutionalisation of democratic or deliberative spaces within those structures.

In today's networked and globalised world, 'organised efforts' need to play out at multiple scales, well beyond the local level where SSE organisations and enterprises are concentrated. The organisation, mobilisation and advocacy associated with the community forestry groups, associations and federations in Nepal, as addressed by Agarwal (Chapter 18), are a case in point, as are other national movements such the Landless Workers' Movement in Brazil (Santos 2007b). 'Glocal' movements have come to the fore in recent years. These integrate local and national organisations that represent particular types of workers or producers into regional or global organisational and advocacy structures and include, for example, the Global Alliance of Waste Pickers, Via Campesina, Streetnet and Homenet. Moreover, SSE organisations in different countries, regions and sectors are increasingly organising in international networks to exchange knowledge and good practices and to strategise politically. Some, such as the International Co-operative Alliance, have a long pedigree. Others, including the Intercontinental Network for the Promotion of Social and Solidarity Economy and Rencontres du Mont-Blanc, were established fairly recently.

Such alliances point to the possibility of the formation of a counter-hegemonic movement (see endnote 3), which is essential if alternative pathways are to effectively challenge 'business as usual'. The coming together of 'social' and 'solidarity' economy discursively and strategically in recent years is a significant development in this regard. Both liberal and radical currents are accommodated under the SSE umbrella and speak to, rather than past, each other. Put another way, SSE is becoming an arena where two of the most powerful world views that are contesting market liberalism – namely 'embedded liberalism' and 'alter-globalisation' – are finding common ground (Utting 2013c).

As Agarwal suggests, it is crucial to consolidate alliances within the field of SSE itself – in the case she analyses, between community forestry initiatives and self-help groups in South Asia. Consolidating alliances between SSE actors and other groups struggling for social, environmental and distributive justice, such as trade unions, indigenous peoples, farmers, women and so forth, is also key. Referring to tensions within SSE–state relations in Latin America, which relate to dependency, instrumentalisation and top-down interventions, Coraggio (Chapter 7) and Rossel (Chapter 13) emphasise the importance of overcoming fragmentation within the SSE field and building a more cohesive movement.

Within the critical literature on social change, this is often where the story ends, with a scenario in which different struggles against injustice (Santos 2007a), or 'the discontented and the alienated' and 'the deprived and the dispossessed' (Harvey 2010), join forces, or should do so. But there are two other aspects related to the concept of hegemony that need to be factored into strategy. The first concerns the possibilities of cultivating 'common sense' understandings of terms and goals associated with progressive or transformative agendas.[12] Others must come to accept hitherto 'radical' framings as 'normal' normative or cultural guides that pattern identity, preferences, behaviour and action (Laclau and Mouffe 1985; Sum and Jessop 2013). Discursive struggle plays a major role in this regard. Counter-hegemonic contestation and agency require that terms and concepts or particular combinations of 'buzzwords' are linked up (Cornwall and Brock 2005). Such combinations 'evoke a particular set of meanings' (ibid.: 47) that can unsettle conventional wisdom about what is meant by terms such as 'development', 'democracy' and 'sustainability'. Such combinations are also key in efforts to forge alliances between subaltern groups and others who feel 'alienated and discontented' (Harvey 2010).

The umbrella term 'social and solidarity economy' provides ample space for connecting more conventional notions of enterprise, entrepreneurship and social protection with more transformative concepts of rights, equality, active citizenship, ethics, solidarity, emancipation and (social, environmental and distributive) justice. Similarly, under SSE, terms such as 'green economy' are reinterpreted to suggest patterns of economic transition that are not dominated by market logic; instead, they provide spaces for diverse actors and enterprises within the plural economy, restructure production and consumption patterns, and are both green and fair (Cook et al. 2012).

Such articulations are important for the task of building broad-based coalitions for change. Keeping these connections in the spotlight can also guard against hegemonic shifts that dilute transformative agendas, such as 'corporate social responsibility' and philanthropic solidarity (Laville, Chapter 1) and reveal the limits of state interventions that instrumentalise SSE for poverty reduction (Coraggio, Chapter 7).

The second aspect of counter-hegemonic strategy relates to social pacts and compromises, not only with those struggling for transformative justice but with others whose interests and identities intersect with SSE (Bergeron and Healy, Chapter 3; Mendell and Alain, Chapter 9; Millstone, Chapter 4; Nelson, Chapter 11; Reed, Chapter 5; Yunus 2007). These include those associated with for-profit enterprise who may want a stake in the material, reputational or legitimation advantages that derive from links with SSE. Political parties may similarly benefit from closer ties with the SSE movement. Potential allies also include elements of the managerial 'class' or techno-scientific community connected with SSE, as well as those who relate to SSE principles and actors for reasons more closely associated with ethicality and identity, for example so-called ethical consumers and investors.

Alliances and political strategy, must therefore extend beyond progressive social movements and include certain market and state actors, notably those aligned with embedded liberalism. Such SSE–market and SSE–state relations are liable to generate tensions as outlined earlier: for example, those associated with elite capture, co-optation, marketisation and institutional isomorphism. But if and when significant advances can occur with regard to the three strategic pillars of capacity, institutional complementarities and participation, then integrative scaling up might be a real possibility.

PART I

HISTORY, THEORY AND
STRATEGY

1 | SOCIAL AND SOLIDARITY ECONOMY IN HISTORICAL PERSPECTIVE

Jean-Louis Laville

Introduction

To understand the challenges of expanding and consolidating social and solidarity economy (SSE), it is important to examine how such forms of institutions evolved historically. Over two centuries, there have been numerous changes in their character and trajectories, largely accounted for by the relations between state, market and society. This type of analysis is essential if we are to understand both the structural and the institutional determinants of scaling up and the substance of SSE.

As the introduction to this volume explains, the umbrella concept of SSE encompasses very different types of enterprises and associations: cooperatives, mutual associations, social enterprises and non-governmental organisations (NGOs), among others. In this chapter we argue that different historical junctures generate contexts that largely explain the rise and fall of different forms of SSE. Drawing in particular on the experience of Europe and South America, this chapter begins by examining the evolution of democratic solidarity throughout the nineteenth and twentieth centuries, identifying various shifts in orientation. These involved: early forms of associative democracy, the 'welfare state', social economy centred on non-profits and cooperatives; and, more recently, solidarity economy, focused on both economic and political empowerment. It then goes on to specify key differences between these forms and their implications for environmental and social justice.

Market and solidarity in nineteenth-century Europe

The invention of modern solidarity emerged in the early nineteenth century, in the wake of democratic revolutions. The notion of a modern solidarity was defined as an integrating force, not anchored on inherited relations (those of family, kinship and lineage) but created in a deliberate way by humans having acquired clear awareness of the societal bonds that connect them. This recognises the importance of a social link that is neither rooted in religious feeling – as, for example, in the case of charity – nor able to be reduced to a contractual relationship. This also underlines the intentional aspect of this modern solidarity, which acknowledges the interdependency of individuals and groups. Consequently, the move into modernity was not simply a move from community to society; rather, it was characterised by the condition of an open political community that overcomes differences and promotes equality through the recognition of public spaces.

In the first part of the nineteenth century – the era of revolutions, to use Hobsbawm's (1962) expression – modern solidarity was mostly expressed through people organising themselves collectively in associations. Groups that were denied dignity as citizens and suffered exploitation rebelled against their exclusion and poor treatment. The contradiction between alleged equality and the persistence of inequalities placed in sharp relief the incompatibility of political freedom and economic subservience. The solidarity that was being called upon to claim a more open public space was also invoked to organise the economy on an egalitarian basis. In this first stage, a move occurred towards the mushrooming of all types of associations (Dewey 1953). The unfolding of modern solidarity could logically be said to be democratic. It focused on mutual help as much as on protest activities, and had characteristics of collective action through both the self-organisation of workers and producers and contestation via social movements, which implied equal rights among the people involved. On the basis of free access to the public domain for all citizens, it aimed to reinforce political democracy through economic and social democracy. It was thus a moral economy of popular origin (Scott 1976; Thompson 1963) that was undergoing experimentation aimed at maintaining common goods, reinforced by reciprocal obligations and shared conceptions of rights.

In the second part of the nineteenth century, this momentum was cut short. Another definition of solidarity emerged as an alternative to solidarity defined as a principle of democratisation resulting from collective action. The vocabulary of equality was replaced by that of benevolence and paternalism. Philanthropic solidarity corresponded to this second form of modern solidarity, which referred to a vision of an ethical society in which citizens motivated by altruism fulfilled their duties to each other on a voluntary basis. This evolution was inseparable from a pessimistic perspective on liberalism, haunted by pauperism, which recommended both helping the poor and controlling their behaviour. The moral economy of pioneering friendly and mutual societies was therefore replaced by an enterprise of moralisation of the poor, according to Thompson (1963).

Philanthropic solidarity replaced the fight for equality with the fight against poverty, and made solidarity a private affair and an individual responsibility. Supported by advocates of the established order, philanthropic solidarity redrew the associative landscape. By repressing independent associations, by discouraging workers' associations and by simultaneously encouraging charities and patronising associations, this reinterpretation of the nature of associative activity complemented efforts to reinforce the economy by linking power with shareholding. This second stage corresponded to the advent of the ideology of progress, which prioritised the Industrial Revolution and economic growth in order to increase the wealth of nations and to eliminate poverty and social conflict. However, despite the advantages that derived from philanthropic solidarity, the social question remained. Ongoing threats to civil peace made the philanthropic solution untenable; inequalities in the human condition could not be attributed to the responsibility of the individual, and, by the end of the nineteenth century, the fundamental limits of philanthropic solidarity had become apparent.

Bringing in the twentieth-century state

Democratic solidarity regained the upper hand when sociological inquiry opposed economic liberalism and reaffirmed the concern for social cohesion. The holistic vision of society as more than the sum of the individuals of which it was composed critiqued an approach to solidarity confined to the private sphere; it stressed the public dimension of solidarity, centred on rights. However, this form of democratic solidarity differed from earlier versions. Faith in associations was replaced by control of the market by public authorities. The state promoted a specific social mode of organisation, which made it possible to extend the market economy while making it compatible with the citizenship of workers. The divides caused by the market economy had to be corrected through policy and legal interventions – hence the concept of social rights that combined workers' rights within the enterprise with social protection aiming to protect workers against specific risks. The social question led to the separation of the economic (specifically, the market economy) and the social (i.e. a legal mode of protection of society). Such a compromise, based on the partition and complementarity of the market and the social state, was reinforced progressively. After the Second World War, when it proved necessary to support national consensus, this complementarity between the state and the market attained its full significance. The development model that was stabilised in twentieth-century Europe was based on the synergy between the market and the state, which had the effect of crowding out various forms of associative activity. The Keynesian state aimed to enhance economic development through the use of new tools of knowledge and intervention. Public investment in sectors deemed particularly viable, and labour market policy aimed at working conditions and wages, made it possible to find stable ways to accommodate the particular interests of enterprises alongside the general interest of society. But the main shift was in income redistribution, through which the social state became the so-called 'welfare state': the setting up of the latter aimed to fulfil the promise to protect citizens from illness, accidents, old age and unemployment. The generalisation of social protection had to ensure security for a population that had endured the Depression of the 1930s and the sacrifices of two World Wars. The welfare state extended the previous forms of social state with social security and generalised social protection systems. At the same time, the state framed and supported the market as much as it corrected market inequalities; the synergy between the state and the market was expressed, in particular, through new institutional arrangements, including social security and collective bargaining, as well as by gains in productivity.

Crisis, civil society and social innovation

The socio-economic compromise described above underwent a cultural crisis in the 1970s with the rise of experiments in both self-management and new social movements, which unsettled the culture underlying the synergy between the market and the state. Conflicts in enterprises no longer concerned merely collective negotiation, centred on the distribution of the value-added. Contestation also emerged around modes of organisation and the lack of opportunities for salaried workers to express themselves. The trend towards workers' self-management reflected these demands, and resembled earlier forms of associative democracy by distancing itself from the representation granted to workers' movements in industrial society.

More importantly, the nature of contestation could no longer be reduced to the clash between capital and labour; it extended to consumption and ways of life. Although the rallying cries of the new social movements remained disparate, anti-nuclear, environmental and feminist protests articulated and popularised new questions around the social and environmental costs of 'progress' and commodification. Standards and aspirations imposed during the post-war growth period were no longer self-evident. Claims for a better quality of life emerged. What was questioned was the very basis of the development model, which hitherto had enjoyed a broad consensus. The ideology of progress was questioned seriously, as was the future of economic society (i.e. a society shaped by the struggle against scarcity and by productivism) more broadly. These questions led to changes in forms of public intervention. Political activism and social innovation combined to question the status quo and the balance of power, and led to experiments with alternative ways of organising production and exchange.

However, the self-management and alternative trends that had fed upon the social effervescence that followed on from the May 1968 protests in France soon lost their momentum. The capacity of new social movements to attract and unite declined. Their participants began to disperse to other civil society initiatives aimed at building new ways of producing, providing services and living. Some occupied the growing space for NGOs, which, from the neoclassical economics perspective, were a response to market failures in the provision of individual services and to state failures in the provision of collective services. According to this viewpoint, not only were the market, state and non-profit sector separated conceptually, but the latter was promoted as a second- or third-rank option, to be adopted only when the solutions provided by the market and the state were deemed inadequate (Evers and Laville 2004). Some proponents of the non-profit sector also adopted an ideological view that this sector could justify the withdrawal of the state.

In numerous other respects the non-profit model proved problematic from the perspective of democratic solidarity and collective action. The key role of the non-distribution constraint as the basis for legitimacy and trust soon weakened. The reputation of NGOs was often tarnished by elite capture – excessively cosy relationships with states, politicians and business, and the obvious connection of NGO activity with the personal material interests of those who controlled them. Furthermore, market activity through, for example, consultancy and local 'proximity services' (such as educational training or care for the elderly and infirm) penetrated the 'non-profit' field. Other mechanisms for cultivating trust, related to standards and certification, also came to the fore and were adopted by for-profit enterprises that began to compete in the trustworthiness stakes through the discourse and practices of corporate social responsibility.

Under the non-profit model, human decisions often conform to 'rational choice'. In this model, 'society' results from the activity of individuals and their interest-oriented choices, which aim to maximise their advantages (Etzioni 1988). The role of non-profit organisations (NPOs) is restricted to the production of services; other important dimensions, such as social integration and democratic participation, tend to be sidelined.

Beyond the usual NPO and NGO models, some innovations and organisational forms were precursors to 'another world is possible', the scenario popularised by the alter-globalisation movement via the World Social Forum. Various forms of social innovation saw workers and producers re-engaging with economic activities, as though the democratisation of society required the democratisation of the economy. Moreover, these experiences concerned not only production but also consumption and ways of life. Social innovations are observed in local proximity services, fair trade, solidarity tourism, organic agriculture, ethical consumption, short supply chains, renewable energies, recycling and waste valorisation, heritage preservation, microfinance and social currencies, for example. These social innovations involve a redefinition of the social contract on the basis of democratic solidarity. Proponents of this trend are concerned about threats (such as climate change) and irreversible damage to 'natural capital', which no amount of technical capital can replace and which, consequently, should be protected from the logic of the market. They are also concerned with threats to human and social capital, particularly when inequalities grow, and care, education and health are no longer preserved as public or commons goods (Ostrom

1990). This strong version of solidarity puts economy back into its role as a means to achieve goals of social justice and environmental sustainability, whose content results from political deliberation.

Social and solidarity economy: a new twenty-first-century synergy?

In the nineteenth century, solidarity via associations that combined economic, social and political objectives gave way to a social economy comprising a set of organisations with non-capitalist status (cooperatives, associations, mutual societies). But during most of the twentieth century, while such organisations had some economic weight, they had no real political strength. As described above, the social innovations of the last part of the twentieth century were categorised in Europe and South America under the term 'solidarity economy'. This shares commonalities with the social economy but it revives a more political dimension, and it can be defined as a set of activities contributing to democratise the economy through citizens' involvement. According to Lipietz (2001), the solidarity economy adds to the social economy – which focuses on internal functioning – an awareness of the importance of the goals pursued (from environmental to cultural goals) and a necessity to complement formal equality among members with modes of direct participation.

The tradition of social economy and the resurgence of associative democracy in the late twentieth century have generated a new theoretical perspective: the SSE. It critiques the non-profit approach, which tends to dominate international development discourse regarding the role and nature of civil society, and it creates an original framework of analysis by mixing social economy and solidarity economy viewpoints. The core elements of each approach, which are now coming together both conceptually and strategically, include those discussed below.

The social economy The term 'social economy', as understood in Europe, defines a set of organisations that is broader than the non-profit sector (Salamon and Anheier 1997). Indeed, 'non-profit' excludes cooperatives and mutual societies on the grounds that they can distribute part of their profits to their members. This exclusion cannot be justified in many continental contexts for several reasons. Firstly, some cooperatives, such as building cooperatives in Sweden, have never distributed any profits. Secondly, in all cases the distribution of profits is limited, since cooperatives and mutual societies are akin to associations: they are not created with a view to obtaining a return on the capital invested, but rather with the goal of satisfying the general interest or a mutual interest, to contribute to public welfare or to meet social demands expressed by some categories of the population.

Furthermore, social economy organisations are defined legally not by the ban on the distribution on profits, but rather by the fact that the material interest of investors is subject to limits. Consequently, the border is not drawn between for-profit and non-profit organisations but rather between capitalist and social economy organisations, the latter giving priority to the setting up of a collective patrimony over the return on individual investment. In other words, at the organisational level, the social economy framework stresses all of the legal forms that limit the private appropriation of benefits. This limitation on the distribution of profits is what gives social economy organisations their specificity, compared with other productive organisations. Beyond their differences, these organisations share a common tradition – different from the North American tradition – that insists less on the non-distribution constraint, philanthropy and volunteering than on collective actions based on mutual help and the participation of citizens concerned about social problems.

Building on a long history, the social economy perspective imposed itself as a legal approach. This had the advantage of facilitating the statistical identification of the organisations concerned, since it covered three components: cooperatives, mutual societies and non-profit organisations. However, as experts acknowledge, although the adoption of any of these legal forms is 'a significant step towards joining the social economy – this in itself does not guarantee that it will become part of [it]' (Defourny et al. 1999: 30). In certain countries, enterprises are frequently cooperative in name only. Similarly, an associative or mutualist legal form sometimes provides a legal cover for para-public agencies and for-profit economic activities. A normative approach combined with the legal approach has thus gained currency. The resulting definition states that:

> [the] social economy includes all economic activities conducted by enterprises, primarily cooperatives, associations and mutual benefit societies, whose ethics convey the following principles: placing

service to members or the community ahead of profit; autonomous management; a democratic decision-making process; the primacy of people and work over capital in the distribution of revenues (ibid.: 30).

These principles give a more accurate description of the functioning of organisations but also challenge the simplicity of classification offered by the legal approach. This explains much of the ambiguity in the analysis of the social economy, which oscillates between the inclusion of all organisations with the cited legal forms (when the aim is to show their importance in the economy) and the exclusion of some organisations because of the gap between the observable reality and their affirmed principles.

Beyond these legal and normative aspects, social economy is characterised by its system of rules governing the specificities of its organisations. These rules include the voluntary action of a group of persons (Vienney 1994) who are reciprocally linked by a relation of association and economic activity, the equal rights of members, and the fact that the distribution of the operating surplus among the associated persons, when it exists, is proportional to their activities within the enterprise. The cooperative model became the reference point for the whole of the social economy, which led to including in the latter only those associations that are enterprises (Vienney 1980–82). In other words, in the field of social economy, the associative phenomenon is recognised only under the form of entrepreneurial associations. According to this conception, the social economy is composed of non-capitalist enterprises and the indicator of their success is an increase in the volume of their market activities. Questions of internal functioning and the non-market spheres of the economy receive little, if any, attention. Thus, non-profit organisations whose resources largely come from redistribution and volunteering are borderline. They do not fit comfortably within a social economy whose charter, for instance in France, states that its components 'live in the market economy' and develop 'institutions that the traditional market economy does not generate'. This definition evaluates cooperatives, mutual societies and non-profit organisations in terms of the evolution of the relations between their members and in terms of their economic results, examined from the point of view of their degree of integration in the market economy.

The solidarity economy By defining itself as a set of organisations, the social economy leaves open the broader question of its insertion into both the economy and democracy. Questioning these two aspects gave birth to the solidarity economy perspective that has gained prominence during the past two decades, particularly in Europe and Latin America.

From an economic viewpoint, the solidarity economy approach centres on conceptual insights that insist on the plurality of economic principles and propose an expansive definition of the economy based on the following (Polanyi 1944):

- the market principle, which allows the supply of and demand for goods and services to meet – exchange happens on the basis of the setting of prices;
- redistribution, which is the principle according to which production is delegated to a central authority responsible for allocating it; and
- reciprocity, which corresponds to the relationship established among groups or individuals thanks to actions that make sense only insofar as they express a will to demonstrate a social link among the stakeholders.

Today, as in the past, any reflection on the relationship between economy and democracy is enriched by adopting a more realistic, and less ideological, view than the narrowly focused market economy perspective. Another approach is provided by a plural economy perspective in which the market is but one of the components (Hart et al. 2010).

It is true that the relative roles of the three economic principles – market, redistribution and reciprocity – have varied greatly throughout history and were profoundly affected by the rise of modern democracy. Here, not only was the market principle diffused, but the market was made largely autonomous and 'disembedded' from social relations. Despite this, a real democratic and solidarity-based invention also formed, and public redistribution saw its rules enacted through representative democracy. Reciprocity could unfold on the basis of voluntary commitments, in the public space, of free and equal citizens. The recognition of individual rights made possible the development of a solidarity that, in a market context, was defined through the combination of egalitarian reciprocity and public redistribution. The solidarity economy approach thus stresses the mix of these three principles, even though their respective weight and form vary. Combining resources from these three principles is also a way to protect against the phenomena of institutional isomorphism or marginalisation. But such a hybridisation implies linking the economic dimension with the political.

Associations were indeed the first line of defence elaborated by society before being relayed by the state (Evers and Laville 2004: 23–5). One of the benefits of solidarity economy is that it can integrate initiatives of civil society into the public space of modern democratic societies. The relations between these initiatives and public authorities are therefore key. Associations are thus linked to the dual dimensions of politics: non-institutional politics, centred on the potential for active citizenship which supposes that citizens make use of the positive freedom to which they are formally entitled; and institutional politics, centred on the exercise of power. The interactions between public authorities and civil society initiatives translate into mutual effects, the intensity and modalities of which vary greatly over time. On the one hand, the initiatives of various social actors, through their very existence, contribute to the evolution of forms of public regulation. On the other hand, rules enacted by public authorities influence the trajectories of initiatives. Isolating organisations without grasping how they relate to the public sphere amounts to ignoring the institutional dimension.

The challenges of realising democratic solidarity

The history of the twentieth century reveals two difficulties in realising democratic solidarity. The first is represented by the objective of a post-capitalist economy that has been implemented in a dogmatic way through top-down approaches that are disconnected from real-world plural institutions and grass-roots participation. The second consists of a confusion between democratic solidarity and philanthropy, which reduces social action not only to voluntary giving but also to other aspects of state and business practice that relate to 'safety nets' and corporate social responsibility.

The dangers and pitfalls of authoritarian models There was a persistent temptation within radical thought concerned with egalitarianism and social justice to stress the need for a wholesale alternative to capitalism. While this was a failure, it does not mean that there is only one natural economy identified with the market principle. Furthermore, the return of the utopian experiment of a self-regulating market under neoliberal capitalism prompted a societal response that called for a project of democratic transformation. When considering such a project, it is important to remember that the self-regulating market in the 1930s led to authoritarian regimes: it generated so much uncertainty that it created the ground for Nazism and Stalinism. We cannot repeat this terror and we have to be conscious that market ideologists are forging a counter-movement of religious fundamentalisms. To overcome these dangers, it is crucial to mobilise economic principles other than the market (namely reciprocity and redistribution), to institutionally embed the market once more in a perspective of solidarity economy, and to establish non-capitalist enterprises, i.e. recognising the diverse forms of property within the social economy arena.

In order to move in such a direction, democratic solidarity is essential. It starts, as Mauss (1954) insisted, with recognising that this solidarity rests on a particular relationship between reciprocity and redistribution, between the voluntary collective actions of equal citizens and the state's attempts to redress inequalities. The institutional base of SSE includes self-organisation in civil society (unions, cooperatives, mutual insurance and non-profit organisations) and social protection by public rules. It is not a question of replacing reciprocal solidarity with redistributive solidarity, but of combining one with the other to renew the concept of social change.

The twentieth century left us with two extreme cases that we should avoid in the future: on the one hand, there was the subordination of economy to a political will whose egalitarianism was a mask for coercion; on the other, a market society was created whose inequality was justified by an appeal for individual freedom. The contemporary challenge is to find new ways of guaranteeing a plural economy within a framework of democracy.

The public debate over the different meanings of the economy has to be reopened in this light; if not, any discussion about the levers of change or the conditions of transition would be impoverished. If we are to harness our efforts at making the economy compatible with an idea of socio-political transformation, we need to understand and explain the dimensions of economic life that have been obscured by the naturalisation of the economy's current dominant form. Following in the footsteps of Mauss and Polanyi, and taking their contributions separately and together, opens the way to an emancipatory project that is explicitly mindful of a politics that, paradoxically, was banished by revolutionary rhetoric. The plural reality of the economy, including democratic solidarity, can pave the way for a democratisation process in contemporary societies.

The return of philanthropic solidarity The democratisation hypothesis above is contested by another eventuality: the extension of capitalism along philanthropic lines. Contemporary capitalism is less dependent on the mediation of goods to accumulate capital and more sensitive to the capacity for permanent innovation unfolding within itself. The accumulation of capital depends greatly on the accumulation of knowledge. This new regime, which followed the so-called Fordist model of the post-war boom, was said to be patrimonial or shareholder-based, and was linked to numerous innovations in work (just-in-time, re-engineering, total quality management), financial products (derivatives, employee savings plans, pension funds) and trade (the internet, online retailing). For example, Yunus (2007: 48–74), a key proponent of microcredit, argues that capitalism is a half-developed structure that can worthily be complemented by an 'enterprise oriented to a cause rather than to profit'. A 'flood of creativity ... able to change the world' (ibid.: 10) is expected from this innovating entrepreneurship, referred to as 'social business'. The social entrepreneur is then considered a particular type of actor, playing the role of a catalyst for social change – a change agent – putting forward innovative ideas to tackle social and environmental problems. Such philanthropic capitalism is also supported by donor investors concerned about the impacts of their donations; this is 'venture philanthropy', a modernised philanthropy mindful of the evaluation of the social results of its financial contributions. This approach could re-legitimate capitalism if it can cultivate innovation to create economic value and entrepreneurialism, boost growth, and solve the related social and environmental problems. Prahalad (2004) agreed with this when he put forward the 'bottom of the pyramid' approach, whereby the poorest populations – the 4 billion people living on less than US$2 a day – are engaged either as producers and suppliers in value chains or as consumers of products and services. This requires that the enterprise changes its perception of these people's needs in order to meet them. This approach, according to its proponents, is a powerful lever that can be observed in several success stories.

From this point of view, multidimensional innovation helps to reconcile capitalism and society through corporate responsibility: that is, the 'social business' and the 'bottom of the pyramid' make up a system congruent with corporate social responsibility. The new spirit of capitalism combines a humanist societal discourse with renewed competitiveness, with both correlated to a high level of social innovation. At the historic moment when structural adjustment plans implemented in the South are set to spread to the North, the aim is to claim the potential of self-regulation and self-correction contained in the market relationship and in entrepreneurial action.

In democratic solidarity, civil society was taken into account through its public space dimension; however, in the philanthropic solidarity approach, civil society occupies the space of private free initiative according to a liberal tradition. This second version considers the market as an economic expression of civil society and warns of the risks inherent in public interference. This praise of civil society, which is defined as a defence against public intrusion, is shown in the recommendations of international financial organisations about good governance. At the national level, to cite only one example, the English project of 'social impact bonds' finds its place in the 'Big Society' highlighted by a government that advocates proximity solutions provided by civil society as alternatives to state intervention. Born in the 1970s, this school of thought opposes public bureaucracy and the independent private sector, which includes both enterprises and non-profit organisations. Socially oriented private initiatives are expected to work together and cohere, as is proposed by the social business, venture philanthropy and 'bottom of the pyramid' models. However, this resembles the narrow conception of philanthropic solidarity referred to earlier in this chapter, which defined the social question in terms of the fight against poverty and assumed that voluntary social action was key for improving the fate of the poorest. In a nutshell, it prefers individual engagement and ethical awareness over norms emanating from public authorities and political questions.

Conclusion: towards democratic solidarity

The vital challenge for the future is to envisage a reciprocal democratisation of civil society and public authorities (Cohen and Arato 1994). The democratic state will regain legitimacy only if it integrates possibilities for increased participation by salaried workers and users and if it is supported by forms of associative activity influenced by democratic solidarity. The state is responsible for facilitating voluntary commitment, which is an expression of this democratic solidarity. The social state promised an idea of solidarity focused on individual rights and redistribution, but, while it remains necessary, this conception is not sufficient. It also needs to encompass the promotion of common goods and social relations based on respect for the principles of freedom and equality. This cross-fertilisation of public action and civil society by means of a common reference to the democratic society has to be the main conduit for strengthening solidarity.

The dual dimension – political and economic – demanded by the solidarity economy and represented schematically in the diagram overleaf (Figure 1.1) underlines the need for associative, cooperative and mutualist experiments to influence institutional commitments. The focus on the organisational aspect of the social economy has not been able to counter the institutional isomorphism created by the division of, and complementarity between, the market and the welfare state. Furthermore, the focus on the economic success of the enterprises that comprise social economy has sidelined political mediations. Indeed, as a reaction to the perverse effects of that focus on the economic dimension, the solidarity economy experiments of the last decades have reinforced the political dimension of initiatives that aim to be both citizen-oriented and entrepreneurial. These will have no effect if they are unable to promote democracy in both their internal functioning and their external expression.

If we admit that the economic success of isolated experiences is not decisive, we have to reflect on the reasons why such experiences encounter so many obstacles to their diffusion. In this respect, there must be a dominant definition of the economy that discriminates against them. If SSE has no right to full existence, this is due less to inadequacy on the part of its actors and more – and fundamentally – to its relative marginalisation in the configuration of economic and political forces. Through its dual dimension, SSE questions the

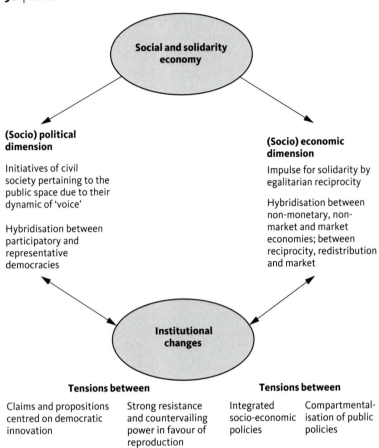

1.1 The dimensions of SSE

categories of the economy at the conceptual and empirical level, refusing to limit economic phenomena to those that are defined as such by economic orthodoxy. It also questions this power of delimitation possessed by neoclassical economic science and fosters a more general interdisciplinary reflection on the definition and institutions of the economy (Granovetter 1985). Such a questioning gives rise to powerful forms of resistance and discrimination from both state and market actors. Understanding the conditions that allow SSE actors to overcome such constraints is key for understanding the scope for scaling up this form of democratic solidarity.

2 | PROMETHEUS, TROJAN HORSE OR FRANKENSTEIN? APPRAISING THE SOCIAL AND SOLIDARITY ECONOMY

John-Justin McMurtry

Introduction

The social and solidarity economy (SSE) is a contested term, and, depending on one's geographic and ideological location, it carries with it various associations. The general understanding of activities in this sector as 'neither public, nor private' gives the appearance of unity, when in reality pressures from both the private and public sphere challenge the very essence of the SSE. Despite these potential challenges, there seems to be general agreement among scholars and practitioners to 'let sleeping dogs lie' and to support the useful fiction that there is a coherent framework uniting the sector (see, for example, Bouchard 2013: 4; Mook et al. 2010: 3–21). The stakes of this silent agreement, however, need to be examined critically, especially for those interested in growing the SSE from the perspective of meaningful community development. Specifically, as the state withdraws from social service provision, the success of this sector is trumpeted as a development panacea and there is an increasing push for 'results' from the SSE by stakeholder groups. That means, for example, control, visible and viable community development, as well as democratic accountability for local communities; measurable, cost-effective (read reduced financial and governance commitment) results for government; and market results (read profitability) from the private sphere. All of these divergent expectations push and pull the SSE in various ways, conceptually and in practice, creating general confusion around its exact meaning among the public and raising key issues for the challenge of scaling up the SSE.

Importantly, these variant expectations also raise the spectre of real and significant failures at a general level, and the potential to destroy or damage the 'movement' in its relative infancy. This possibility is in some ways already a reality, with the definitional ambiguity of the SSE opening up the discursive space for what appears to be less socially oriented policies initiated by opportunistic actors. For example, the retrenchment of central government welfare responsibility in Prime Minister David Cameron's 'Big Society' is couched in the language of the SSE. 'Social enterprise' solutions are being suggested in a broad variety of policy contexts that claim to solve social issues such as poverty, at lower cost, while returning significant returns to investors. While it is too early to say how these new discourses will turn out in practice, there is an obvious need for definitional and practical clarity as we move forward with the SSE.

This chapter engages in this debate with a two-pronged approach. First, using contemporary normative theory (Rawls, Habermas and Cohen) and economic theory (Sen, Ostrom and Sachs), the variant meanings of social, solidarity and the economic are outlined and contrasted at a theoretical level. The purpose here is to locate the 'new' discourse of the SSE in a theoretical context of liberalism generally, and a discourse of 'capacities' specifically. This is not a simple exercise of equating liberal normative thought and the SSE, but rather to trace the debates (mentioned above) within the SSE genealogically back to a philosophical position. This chapter begins such an examination by outlining the historical roots of the SSE – including its three distinct traditions: Anglo-American, continental European and postcolonial development – within capitalism. While these traditions have their own logic, each one articulates a different response to the impositions of capitalism through the lens of liberalism. The chapter concludes by suggesting that we can develop a more robust conception of the SSE by working outside the theoretical framework of liberalism. Three case studies (the cooperative movement, microcredit and alternative energy) are discussed to demonstrate this. They suggest that by developing an ethical value-added framework (McMurtry 2009) we can begin to overcome the limitations of the theoretical roots of the SSE and establish a common understanding of its normative and practical economic goals beyond liberalism and capitalism.

Defining the SSE

The origins of the SSE as a concept are both debated and underexamined. While it is generally accepted that the concept *economie sociale* emerged around 1900, the practices associated with the sector – charities, trusts, cooperatives, non-profits, friendly societies and socially focused enterprises – pre-date this by at least a century formally, and stretch back to the dawn of civilisation in their broadest sense.[1] For the purposes of this chapter, however, this historical and definitional question is reversed. That is, rather than focusing on when we can first identify the conceptualisation of the social economy, I ask what happened around 1900 that created a need to conceptualise activity that had been occurring arguably for millennia. The answer, I believe, lies in the increasingly robust, but uneven, emergence of capitalism as a world system.[2] As this system began to dominate earlier or more mixed economic systems, it became increasingly necessary to be able to define the alternatives to it.[3]

It is also here that the problematic 'neither state nor private' definition of the SSE began to take shape, especially in light of the emergence of communism as a viable economic system in 1917. What are important for our purposes are the ways in which both state-centric communist and, later, social democratic and postcolonial projects, as well as variants of capitalist state projects, have recognised the value of, and potential uses for, the emerging SSE in the face of an increasingly rapacious capitalism. While the uses of SSE in these different contexts varied widely, the motive for identifying and developing it as a policy and practical solution was rooted in the same cause. However, the emergence of the welfare, postcolonial and workers' state largely masked the role that the SSE played within capitalism, and so there was no urgent need for a robust definition for most of the twentieth century. But as the need to articulate alternatives became urgent along with the radical worldwide economic reordering of the 1980s and 1990s, SSE re-emerged as an important concept. Essentially, the three-pronged economic crisis (otherwise known as ascendant capitalism) caused by the collapse of the Soviet Union, globalisation and the undermining of the developmental postcolonial projects – and the resulting decline of the welfare state in the economic West – led to the need for a clearer articulation of alternatives in the form of the SSE at the end of the twentieth century. The problem was (and still is): on what normative grounds is such a claim made?

Theorising the SSE

While the above historical framing of the SSE is not well known or generally accepted, even less developed is an understanding of the philosophical roots of the dominant conceptions of the SSE in versions of liberalism and the capacities argument. Whether conceptualised in the West, in the colonised majority world, or within social democratic and communist countries themselves, all formulations of SSE draw on liberal theory. This has led many on the political left to reject the SSE as a liberal Trojan horse. But this position means that one misses the potential for a radical re-articulation of the SSE (discussed below). Detailing how this liberal understanding of the SSE was imported into more critical political discourses would take more space than is available here, although examining the example of Lenin's New Economic Policy (NEP) is instructive in this regard. The NEP utilised what today would be conceptualised as SSE organisations, namely cooperatives, to facilitate the economic development of the Soviet Union towards communism; this policy option has re-emerged recently in Venezuela and Cuba, but with a different end goal. For Lenin, it was a historical reality, albeit one that he came to rather reluctantly,[4] that liberal vehicles such as cooperatives were needed for this transition.[5] The fact that the SSE has therefore been conceptualised by communists and socialists within essentially liberal terms and as fundamentally liberal institutions has meant that its moral justification, which is rooted in this tradition, has not been considered seriously. It is to the liberal tradition that this chapter now turns.

John Stewart Mill, the most developed of the classical utilitarian thinkers, once famously said that a 'moral revolution in society' would follow the establishment of production cooperatives (Isaac et al. 1998: 198). Further, such organisations would lead to:

> the healing of the standing feud between capital and labor; the transformation of human life from a conflict of classes struggling for opposite interests, to a friendly rivalry in the pursuit of a common good to all; the elevation of the dignity of labor; a new sense of security and independence in the laboring class; and the conversion of each human being's daily occupation into a school of the social sympathies and the practical intelligence (ibid.: 198).

While there is much that can be said about this quote in terms of the SSE,[6] what is central here is the articulation of producer cooperatives, and by extension other elements of the SSE, within the liberal tradition as potential harbingers of a more moral economic order. Specifically (and this is crucial for the argument that follows), the SSE is a site of *moral* development – a 'school of the social sympathies' and the 'elevation of the dignity of labour' – as well as *economic* development for the good of society. Inside classical liberalism, then, and uncritically adopted by Lenin in the NEP, the SSE is seen as a means to a moral and economic end. This articulation of a reunited moral/economic reality is not limited to liberalism but is popular in other non-capitalist moral systems. For example, the desire to articulate a moral economics within religion can be seen in the Catholic church in Leo XIII's encyclical *Rerum Novarum* as well as in the lay Catholic social movement 'distributivism'. A nonreligious example can be found in the British movement for social credit, which emerged as an alternative to capitalism and spread across the British empire after World War II (WWII).

While many instances from other ethnic and religious traditions could be identified as examples of attempts to re-harmonise the moral and the economic, what is important here is that the moral/economic theory of the SSE has two central and fundamentally *liberal* principles: first, an aversion to direct state control of its operation; and second, an aversion to profit as the motive for economic activity. This is, of course, a primary re-articulation of the central definitional problem outlined earlier (and indicates the strength of liberal philosophy within the definitions of the SSE itself).

I now turn to the *positive* liberal normative content of the SSE, as alluded to above by Mill, and to questioning how these principles are articulated in post-WWII liberalism, as well as to the consequences of this position for how the SSE is seen as an alternative to capitalism today. This is important, as how one sees the moral position of the SSE within contemporary capitalism determines the potential role that the SSE can play as an alternative economic activity – liberating Prometheus, capitalist Trojan horse or state-created Frankenstein.

Connecting the dots: liberal philosophy and the SSE

It may seem odd to examine the philosophers John Rawls, Jürgen Habermas and G. A. Cohen as a liberal set, especially as they are contemporaries who explicitly critique each other's work. However, this obvious disagreement belies what is at issue for the SSE – the assumption of a liberal framework in the moral economic activity of the SSE in the post-WWII world. When we turn later to the trio of economists Amartya Sen, Elinor Ostrom and Jeffrey Sachs, the liberal philosophical framework behind the economic understanding of the SSE becomes even more obvious.

Rawls John Rawls is most famous for *A Theory of Justice*, an articulation of robust and moral liberalism framed as a rejection of the classical utilitarian notion of justice (Rawls 1999[1971]: xviii). What is interesting, and not often considered in debates around Rawls, is that he is a strange kind of liberal in that he considers his work to be part of the 'continental' social contract theory of Rousseau and Kant. This bridging work by Rawls is important as we consider below the similarities between his conceptions of economic justice and those of Habermas and Cohen.

> What I have attempted to do [in *A Theory of Justice*] is to generalize and carry to a higher order of abstraction the traditional theory of the social contract as represented by Locke, Rousseau, and Kant ... The theory that results is highly Kantian in nature (ibid.: xviii).

In simple terms, Rawls is attempting to achieve a concept of justice that goes beyond the final moral arbitration of the atomic individual in some form of utilitarian calculus, and to move liberalism towards a notion of justice in a collective, rule-bound and contractual way. Nevertheless, this remains liberalism, through a theoretical sleight of hand in which the regulatory authority, namely the state, guarantees fairness through the structures of society. But actualising the rights, obligations and opportunities resulting from these structures is the responsibility of individuals.

> For us the primary subject of justice is the basic structure of society, or more exactly, the way in which the major social institutions distribute fundamental rights and duties and determine the division of advantages from social cooperation (ibid.: 6).

This resolves the moral/economic problems of capitalism, as there would be a levelling of the playing field on which individuals compete over resources. As Rawls puts it, the problem of capitalism is fundamentally that 'the institutions of society favour certain starting places over others' (ibid.: 7).

This Rawlsian position is a fundamental articulation of a liberal capacities argument that motivates, consciously or not, the policy and practice of the SSE. Justice demands that society provide the conditions for humans to achieve fairness in access to the conditions of life that allow them to realise their individual capacities. However, it is ultimately the obligation of the individual to realise these capacities and opportunities through whatever structures are in place. The SSE conforms morally to this theoretical model because in contemporary capitalism it provides entrepreneurial structures and opportunities to marginalised communities or individuals, the success of which is up to those individuals or communities themselves to realise. Rawls therefore reveals for us the basic liberal moral grounding for the policy option of the SSE: structural opportunity and an individual obligation to realise that opportunity. In fact, this is the fundamental underlying moral principle behind the 'neither state nor market' definition of the SSE.

The problem with this position is, of course, that structural opportunities within a larger unjust system are hard to realise. Simply put, collective economic activity is at an enormous disadvantage within dominant capitalist economy and society. Liberal moral philosophy never addresses this existing collective disadvantage outside changing the 'rules of the game', nor does it address the consequences of resolving inequalities on these larger structures (which is the Promethean possibility). Consequently, by adopting this liberal frame, the SSE can be seen as a means to marketise all aspects of life (a capitalist Trojan horse). Or, if employed as mass state policy, as in Cuba or Venezuela, state policy can further reach into lives and markets (some of which are not capitalist), thereby creating opposite or unforeseen negative consequences (i.e. a Frankenstein).

Habermas Jürgen Habermas, despite his claimed affinity to the Frankfurt School and its more critical stance towards capitalism, repeats this liberal duality of structural opportunity and individual obligation – the capacities argument – in his famous work *The Theory of Communicative Action* (Habermas 1984; 1987). On the surface, Habermas' central concern is with the articulation of a theory that explains and enables a deliberative and communicative populace to resist the excessive impositions of 'systems of money and power' into their 'life-world' (consciously articulated). Thus, he firmly claims that 'the modern life-world asserts itself against the imperatives of a structure of domination that abstracts from all concrete life-relations' (Habermas 1987: 360). What allows the 'life-world' to assert itself against negative social and economic structures is a process of 'communicative action' that is engaged by individuals themselves. According to Habermas (ibid.: 126):

> In communicative action participants pursue their plans cooperatively on the basis of a shared definition of the situation. If a shared definition of the situation has first to be negotiated, or if efforts to come to some agreement within the framework of shared situation definitions fail, the attainment of consensus, which is normally a condition for pursuing goals, can itself become an end.

Habermas provides actors in the SSE an outline of a decentralised structure – communicative action – within which individuals can realise their capacities and values. However, despite this advance over Rawls, the liberal framework is repeated because the structural framework within which these communicative structures are located is not itself engaged. The hard work of recognising, challenging and ultimately rebuilding a society where money and power have become disproportionately and invasively prevalent is left to individuals in communication themselves, without much to guide this process outside the paternalistic demand to 'talk openly about your assumptions'. While the Promethean promise of the structures of communicative action are highlighted by Habermas, the ways in which these communicative communities might overcome these systems is left largely up to them.

Cohen The final thinker to be examined here is the Marxist analytical philosopher G. A. Cohen. While the philosophical and ideological differences between his work and that of Rawls and Habermas are clear and marked, when it comes to conceptualising the framework of possibilities for the SSE, the assumptions are the same. The issue for Cohen in conceptualising justice (which he reads as equality) is the obligation of an individual to develop a moral position in relation to the exclusions of capitalism. His 'critique of Rawls reflects and supports a view that justice in personal choice is necessary for a society to qualify as just' (Cohen 2001: 6). For Cohen, the Marxist faith in the historical necessity of social change and the Rawlsian faith in the state-constructed rules of justice are not sufficient for equality to be achieved (ibid.: 3). Thus, for him, the role of individual moral choice in the creation of justice is of fundamental importance, whereby '*both* just rules *and* just personal choice within the framework set by just rules are necessary for distributive justice' (ibid.: 3, italics in the original). However, the same problem identified by Rawls and Habermas is repeated, despite its acknowledgement; for Cohen, the goal of equality is achievable in a real way only by the atomic decision-making power of the individual, although he recognises the structural limitations imposed on this choice by the very inequality of capitalism. The Promethean possibility of a new moral and economic order is highlighted, but the agent for its recognition is again the atomic, rational individual of liberal philosophical abstraction.

In terms of its moral justification, the SSE is contradictory, as is the liberal framework that has dominated its history. Moral economies are created through a structural framework that creates the *possibility* for justice, the *realisation* of which is the ultimate responsibility of individual social actors. The fundamental circular argument at its core is that individuals must rely on their pre-existing capacities within an oppressive and unjust system in order to realise their capacities. Liberalism, despite its rhetoric from Mill onwards, does not confront the problem of the absence of capacity created by capitalism and social alienation; therefore, it ensures not the Promethean promise of the SSE, but, depending on the dominant ideology behind the structural architecture of its realisation, either the Trojan horse of the capitalist market or the Frankenstein state.

Economics: the playground of liberal assumptions

The liberal assumptions outlined above have embedded themselves within dominant economic thought, perhaps more than anywhere else. What is surprising, however, is how these beliefs have also infiltrated the economic frameworks most closely associated with the economic 'alternative' of the SSE – development, capacities and commons. The most obvious connection between the liberal framework and contemporary alternative economic theory is made by Amartya Sen. For Sen (2009), whose ideas are similar to Cohen's both in content and in their apparent rejection of the liberal framework, a return to the original unification of economics and philosophy is a desirable position. This is especially true if such a position considers both the individual and the institutions that create justice. As Sen argues, 'justice is ultimately connected with the way people's lives go, and not merely with the nature of the institutions surrounding them' (ibid.: x). At issue for Sen is how economics (motivated by theories of justice) can help us understand and articulate individual capacities through the creation of institutions that facilitate such capacities. But again, as with the philosophers discussed above, the key idea is that the goal of justice is the creation of 'lives which people have reason to value' (ibid.: xii), a position that leaves the content of those lives and the creation of their reality radically up to individuals themselves to determine. While the re-harmonisation of ethics and economics is itself a central premise of the SSE, as we shall see below, the practice of the SSE is the site of ethics and yet it is a space that is left fundamentally unaddressed by Sen and others.

The assumption of the liberal frame continues, although in different ways, with the work of Elinor Ostrom. The focus in Ostrom's (1990) work is how collective solutions to crisis situations occur within a 'commons' as opposed to being driven by the rational, self-maximising individual. She calls this the creation of 'common pool resources' – an economic theory that would seem to be tailor-made for the SSE. In fact, what is remarkable about Ostrom's work from the perspective of the SSE is her early anticipation of many of the issues raised by contemporary SSE literature, without seemingly having come into contact with them. For example, she argues that conceptualising common pool economic activity as state or non-state, private or non-private obscures the complex realities of most of these organisations (ibid.: 14). But this question of the state or market is not fundamental for Ostrom. Rather, what is important is how collective economic decisions are made in times of crisis. She argues that:

> an important challenge facing policy scientists is to develop theories of human organization based on realistic assessment of human capabilities and limitations in dealing with a variety of situations that initially share some or all aspects of a tragedy of the commons (ibid.: 23–4).

While she is largely successful in providing a framework for understanding how common pool resources might be articulated within economic discourse, Ostrom leaves the ethical questions of their construction open for debate. The question for her is whether or not common pool resources can be understood economically, rather than how to judge their ethical content in comparison with each other or with dominant economic practice. In short, all common pool resource solutions are normatively equal. While her work can be considered an important corrective to standard liberal development economics, typified by authors such as Jeffrey Sachs (2005), who argue that the economic problems of poorer continents such as Africa are based on their minimal participation in markets, it is clearly an underdeveloped position in terms of articulating a robust and moral theory of the SSE. Thus, Ostrom, like Sen (and, one might argue, Sachs, who has a market development or growth position focused on the least developed countries), continues the liberal cleavage between structure and individual agency, while at the same time arguing for conditions that might improve the capabilities of the least well off.

The SSE in action: thinking beyond the individual

This chapter will now turn from the theoretical problem within liberal thought, which has haunted the SSE, and focus briefly on three practical case studies to demonstrate how this cleavage might be overcome. This could be achieved through a value-based conception of the SSE and a conception of ethical value-added, as exemplified by: 1) the cooperative movement; 2) microcredit; and 3) alternative energy.

Cooperatives The cooperative movement is both within and outside the SSE. It is within the SSE because it conforms to its most basic and developed definitions. It is outside because, as an identifiable and historical movement, it is meaningfully independent in law and in practice and its internal principles exceed any definition of the SSE. It provides two basic experiences from which the SSE can learn, and which go beyond the framework of liberal ethics. First, cooperatives have been able to provide ethical content to the structure of economic cooperation. Seven principles, articulated in individual cooperatives and formalised internationally in 1937, 1966 and 1995, provide a structure upon which communities or individuals can build ethical economic organisations. Furthermore, they develop flexible ethical content that can be applied to a variety of different situations. This is a defining feature of the history of the cooperative movement, its rapid growth, and its adaptability to a variety of different cultural and economic contexts. Key among the seven principles are: democratic member control; the priority of people over capital; and concern for non-members and the community at large. All of these principles form a direct challenge to the precepts of capitalism, and specifically to liberalism's focus on the self-maximising, autonomous individual. Second, and in contrast to the SSE, cooperatives have developed out of the contested context of capitalism and these principles into a *social movement* based on the idea of mutual aid and societal transformation. While there are many examples of individual cooperatives that have stagnated in their ethical and mutual aid activities, as a whole the cooperative movement provides a template for a developing moral economic movement with worldwide reach, hundreds of millions of members, and billions of euros in assets. The SSE would, I believe, do well to look to the cooperative movement as a template for a different moral economic order built on different normative scaffolding.

Microcredit Second, the SSE can look towards the recent movement towards community control of capital through microcredit, most famously in Bangladesh, Africa, and Ireland; this development differs from the older credit unions,[7] which are part of the cooperative movement mentioned above. Within this movement, the promise (and far too often it remains a promise) of controlling capital for goals other than profit remains a key motivating factor. In fact, the idea of microcredit is that the capital contained within a community is sufficient, alongside the labour of individuals within it, to develop that community provided that leakages to capitalist firms are kept to a minimum.[8] By focusing not on the particular business or entrepreneur but on the capital available to a community, the movement towards community credit fundamentally challenges both the normative frame of capitalism – profit – as well as the argument for a central 'distributing' state, and provides a practical mechanism for promoting development at the community level.

Alternative energy Third, the growth of community energy provides another recent example in which a fundamental component of the economy, energy, is at least partially democratised and placed under community control. Here, the potential for the SSE to serve as a Trojan horse for the marketisation of state services is perhaps most pronounced, although its final nature is still a site of struggle in the countries where these policies are most fully developed (such as Scotland, Denmark, Germany, Argentina and Canada, specifically the provinces of Ontario and Nova Scotia). The ambiguous future of these experiments provides us with the most urgent arguments for a more refined understanding of the SSE in order to address the growing criticisms that these policies engender. If, for example, the move to community energy truly creates what the International Labour Organization (ILO 2011) argues should be 'good' as well as 'green' jobs, community control over resources and sustainable local economic development, then this begins to clarify the social elements of alternative energy. If, however, the only requirements of these policies are economic growth and job creation within an alternative energy sector, the promise of community energy does indeed become a Trojan horse for capitalist market penetration of state resources. Like microcredit, what is exciting about the possibility of community-owned energy is the potential for democratising and localising control over vital levers of the economy. However, democratisation and localisation differ from the normative principles of liberalism.

Conclusion: towards an ethical value-added framework

This chapter has focused so far on the liberal normative framework through which the SSE has largely been conceptualised over the last century. While there are many different philosophical, economic, social and political frameworks that have engaged with part or all of the SSE, the fundamental belief remains that individuals and communities must themselves articulate their capacities once the rules of the game are set. In this final section, I wish to turn this premise on its head and argue that what is crucial for the SSE to realise its moral and economic, and thereby Promethean, potential is firstly to build a critical understanding of those rules. Second, the SSE requires a conscious movement to build alternatives that meet the needs of communities that have been excluded and oppressed by the existing structural conditions.

Simply put, the dominant logic in the economic sphere has

increasingly become the logic of capitalism. Governments across the world now essentially accede economic planning in one way or another to the market, as the recent response of 'austerity' to the economic crisis created by private capital demonstrates. Where this is not the response, as in the BRICS block of countries (Brazil, Russia, India, China and South Africa), the state has tended to be an omnipresent player in the economy, creating problems of a different order. Since the SSE by definition is supposed to be neither state nor market in a fundamental way, it requires an articulation that shifts the focus of policy and social movement action to a different actor. For this purpose, I have defined elsewhere the social economy as 'economic activity neither controlled directly by the state nor by the profit logic of the market, activity that prioritizes the social wellbeing of communities and marginalized individuals over partisan political directives or individual gain' (McMurtry 2010: 4). Key here is that the community and its social well-being become the normative site of action rather than state policy or market activity. Economics is engaged with insofar as it serves this need. Further, the social is understood as 'the space of community where the individualism of the market and the alienation of state bureaucracy are replaced with community voice and economic activity responding to community need' (ibid.: 22). In this way, the fundamental site of decision-making for the SSE is the community, and, in whatever way this community considers appropriate, decisions are fundamentally democratic. Such definitions are in direct disagreement with the dominant liberal normative frames of individualism and capitalism, and indeed of representative democracy (or enlightened centralised control) at a state level. The purpose here is to articulate both a site of economic and moral activity (the community) and a process (democracy at the community level) that are distinct from the usual drivers of SSE activity (despite the definitional prohibition mentioned above) – the state and the capitalist market. Liberal philosophy is comfortable with neither the radical decentring of the rules of the game or the economic prioritisation of community decision over individual choice.[9]

The question, however, still remains as to what organisations and individuals might do once they have identified the rules of the game and their unique position in relation to them. After all, even the cooperative movement is, despite its strong articulation as a movement, constantly under scrutiny for its less-than-robust economic performance (for example, the recent failure of the Co-operative Group in Britain to purchase Lloyds Bank despite favourable government support) and its moral dilemmas (for example, the Mondragon worker cooperatives' internationalising process, which has created a significant non-European, non-member workforce with differential wages). How could any SSE organisation even contemplate taking on the rules of the game in a systematic and practical manner?

This chapter suggests a provisional answer in the concept of 'ethical value-added' (McMurtry 2009). Through this concept, SSE organisations would be able to build from where they are – both economically and morally – but they could build towards a more clearly articulated moral position by asking and rigorously tracking the following three questions:

- What social or community value does our economic activity aim to create?
- How can we effectively measure this social or community value in ways that reflect our impacts on community needs?
- How do we plan to increase our impacts on community needs and how can community contribute to our strategic planning?

By asking these questions and formalising them within their operational logic, SSE organisations have the opportunity to start with whatever capacities the organisation has, and build capacity both internally and in relation to the community. They can, in other words, begin to create the rules of their own game, and to demand a place within economic and social policy-making by first opening the doors available to them – those of their community. By so doing, the SSE can avoid the accusation of being a Trojan horse and state Frankenstein, and begin to challenge the liberal normative, economic frame within which it has been put. In fact, this radical reordering of the liberal political and economic (and indeed the state-centric) order is a necessary step for the realisation of the moral and economic claims of the SSE, and indeed its Promethean promise.

3 | BEYOND THE BUSINESS CASE: A COMMUNITY ECONOMIES APPROACH TO GENDER, DEVELOPMENT AND SOCIAL ECONOMY

Suzanne Bergeron and Stephen Healy

Introduction

Over the past decade or so, attention to gender has moved from the margins to the centre of development rhetoric and practice. With this shift, many of the issues once viewed as 'outside' development – such as non-capitalist production and unpaid non-market transactions – are now seen as resources for fostering economic and social progress. So too are attributes once determined as 'non-economic' such as care, cooperation and interdependence. In this sense, the historic gender turn in development can be viewed as a project of potential transformation towards social and solidarity economy (SSE) ends, where space for economic justice, non-market production and social subjectivities of care, cooperation and interdependence is recognised, negotiated and expanded.[1]

While the inclusion of gender and economic difference marks an important shift in thinking, it has not been matched by an attempt to imagine economic development in new ways. This is true of institutional approaches at the World Bank and elsewhere, which largely reduce issues of gender and economic difference – including insights about household labour and women's caring and cooperative motivations – to a 'business case' for investing in women as 'smart economics', aimed at capturing market efficiencies and growth. But it is also true of some left and feminist critics who dismiss this attention to gender and difference as 'business as usual' in which progressive efforts to focus on non-market and care economies are subsumed within a logic of neoliberal capitalism that determines the course of development.

While we are sympathetic to critical feminist concerns, such a framing limits feminist and leftist interventions. It seems to us that critical voices have granted too much power to global capitalism, so that even these emerging possibilities for imagining economy in a different way are viewed as being subsumed within a neoliberal project. Further, we worry that the guiding narratives used to represent the (im)possibility of transformation also shape the performance of that world by portraying alternatives as weak and destined for defeat. This further limits the space available to build on the intentions of progressive frameworks in order to foster economic difference produced within an ethical dynamic of development.

This chapter involves re-reading development by including non-capitalist processes and alternative subjectivities in ways that might open up a space for social transformation relating to both gender equity and SSE. We thereby hope to expand the terrain of development to include unpaid household and community production – as well as values and subjectivities that revolve around justice, care and cooperation. We also hope to contribute to a political project of building upon and transforming gender and development in order to foster ethical dynamics, a goal that we believe is shared by a wide range of feminist and SSE activists and scholars.

Our work draws heavily upon new understandings of economic difference developed by J. K. Gibson-Graham[2] and the Community Economics Collective (CEC) (which Stephen has been a member of for thirteen years) to 'take back' the economy.[3] This work highlights the importance of alternative, non-capitalist economic practices that are otherwise devalued and marginalised in both mainstream and critical discourses, and disrupts the presumptive dominance of capitalism. A further insight of this work is that with a recognition of economic difference comes the possibility of a different political economy of development – one that involves a process of ethical negotiation around shared concerns within the 'community economy'.

Our re-reading of gender and development initiatives for difference and ethical negotiation also connects to the diversity of economic practices and subjectivities brought into being by social movements associated with SSE. Finally, it attempts to engage with some current projects that are rethinking development itself. Here, the history of feminism's encounter with development is instructive for those of us who see the potential in SSE. On the one hand, feminist economics has transformed development in terms of who counts as the subject of development and where development takes place. On the other hand, as critics point out, development has attempted to transform feminism by making women, feminist ethics and household economies fit into a pre-existing discourse of development and the aims of 'business as usual'. One concern is that, as SSE gains attention in the international development community, it too might be domesticated as a poverty reduction strategy (Dinerstein 2013). By highlighting the fragmented and partial nature of capitalism, we create a space in which to acknowledge the contingency of neoliberal projects that emerge from development institutions. This may help us to imagine and bring about forms of SSE that can emerge within development's own polyvalent discourses and practices (Ferguson 2009).

The business case for gender and development: social justice or 'business as usual'?

Of particular note in the contemporary gender-sensitive development discourse is the positioning of activities and motivations that were formerly viewed as being 'outside' the economy but that are now crucial to economic success. In the past, activities associated with social reproduction, such as caring, subsistence production and voluntary and community work, were invisible (Bakker and Gill 2003); now, new projects are addressing this variety of economic practices directly (Bedford 2009). In addition to recognising non-market production, development policy now values motivations and ethics not usually associated with the market, such as care and cooperation. With regard to care, development texts increasingly offer stories about 'rational economic women' (Rankin 2001) whose combination of altruism, cooperation and efficiency make them ideal clients of development projects. Women are targeted for such projects because, in their presumed role as carers, they are more likely to use their income to better their children's and communities' well-being (World Bank 2001; 2012). For example, women migrants are said to send a higher percentage of their remittances home to their families than men because of their caring nature (United Nations 2009). As a result, countries such as the Philippines have specifically targeted women as the ideal migrant workers from the perspective of the home country (Parrenas 2008). Policies that value an ethic of care have even been extended to men to get them to share more care work in their households (Bedford 2009). Women's greater cooperative outlook is now valued as a form of social capital that allows them to engage in collective practices such as micro-credit lending circles – and in what we might even refer to as the 'solidarity economy'. Thus current gender and development policy is not as fixated on capitalist markets or individualistic rationality as in past frameworks.

Ideologically and rhetorically, these recent gender and develop-ment initiatives are tied together by the 'business case' for gender equality (see, for example, World Bank 2006; 2012; ILO 2010; Nike Inc. 2009). This approach sees gender equity as instrumentally valu-able for achieving economic goals or as 'smart economics' (World Bank 2012). The business case now extends to a wide array of conversations about gender equity in development, including those about labour, credit, land and even gender-based violence. For example, the managing director of the World Bank recently stated that the only way to really get the problem of violence against women on the policy map was to show that it causes a loss of gross domestic product (GDP) (Antsey 2013).

This marks a significant shift in thinking from previous decades when the social goals associated with gender equity were viewed as unrelated to, or at odds with, efficiency goals of economic growth and productivity. While the 'smart economics' approach focuses largely on integrating women into waged labour, it also recognises forms of economic difference, including non-market production and an ethic of care. Further, attention has been given to recognising the economic contributions of non-capitalist activities: for example, policies now aim to make households more egalitarian in order to reduce the inequity of women's care burdens, with the belief that these efforts will improve the well-being of family members and also yield economic efficiencies (Bedford 2009). This focus on the household as a locus of gender struggle and a sphere of production marks an extraordinary shift from past practices.

Yet despite the expanded space for tackling gender equity in development, and the acknowledgement that policies must be im-plemented in a broader economic terrain that extends beyond the market, these recent changes have not engendered much optimism on the part of many left and feminist observers, who see the business case for gender equity as 'business as usual': a reformed project of neoliberalism wrapped in a rhetoric of gender equity, care, com-munity and the like that makes it all the more insidious. This shape-shifting neoliberalism is an effort to increase the 'penetration of capital into new spaces and social relations' (Roberts 2008: 535). And the language of gender equity, participation, microcredit and care is an attempt to gain legitimacy with some of its former critics, but what little space this language creates for effecting real change is prone to be co-opted by the mainstream.

When filtered through dominant forms of development discourse, these glimmers of alternative economy become subsumed within capitalist logics. Microcredit fits more closely with the project of expanding global finance rather than with fostering cooperation, by integrating women into circuits of global credit and the marketised production sphere (Karim 2011; Roy 2010). The ethic of care attributed to poor migrant women does not make them more valuable or supported in development, but rather more subject to exploitation in a global care chain that provides remittances to cash-strapped countries when sources of international aid have dried up (Hochschild and Ehrenreich 2003). If attention is paid to caring labour in development policy, unfortunately it is less about acknowledging the contribution this work makes to human well-being and more about removing constraints to women's participation in the capitalist labour force (Razavi 2012). In addition, any consideration of households in development discourse often poses a marketisation solution to women's care burdens, substituting commodity goods and services for those formerly produced in the home through projects of capitalist accumulation (Bakker 2007).

Even the ethic of care is subsumed within reformed neoliberal governance strategies that aim not only to restructure the economy but also to reorient economic subjects in ways that serve politico-economic objectives of neoliberalism. For example, gender and development policies call upon values of care in their attempts at constructing women as altruistic and self-managing economic subjects who do not have to rely on state support (Brodie 2005). These neoliberal projects often reproduce patriarchal and heteronormative structures of power (Bergeron 2011). They maintain traditional gender roles of caring, even as they claim to transform them, in their efforts to harness women's contribution to economic goals such as capitalist efficiency in their presumed identities as wives and mothers (Chant 2006; Molyneux 2006; Roy 2010).

Beyond the business case: reimagining economy and development

Such critiques alert us to the fact that, in certain circumstances, feminist aims can be thwarted when filtered through certain aspects of neoliberal governmentality in development. Furthermore, they provide a useful counter-narrative to the claims made by development institutions that the consolidation of gender policy under the business case constitutes a victory for equity and social justice, when clearly it is not. But we worry that the way in which neoliberal development models are presented in this literature – as a fait accompli – makes it difficult to imagine projects outside such models. The theoretical choice made in representing these innovations in gender and development within a discourse of capitalism as a self-regulating force provides little space for the glimmers of alternative economic and social practices that might emerge from them.

We worry that the ontological commitment to defining everything with reference to capitalism as a determining force takes up political space that might be open for cultivating economic subjects-in-becoming who are guided by motivations of care, ethical concern and collectivity (Graham and Amariglio 2006). In this regard, much of the critical feminist scholarship on the business case is engaged in what has been referred to as the 'politics of denunciation' (Ferguson 2009). Ferguson makes a case for moving beyond this oppositional stance to examine the potential affinities that might exist between neoliberalism and progressive politics. Through a study of the basic income grant programme in South Africa, he shows how a neoliberal social policy aimed at expanding investments in human capital and inculcating rational subjectivities in its clients also achieved progressive, pro-poor outcomes. While Ferguson does not make an explicit link between this politics of denunciation and a discourse of economy organised around a centring order of capitalism, for us that link seems clear.

Many critics view development institutions as handmaidens of neoliberalism. Too much power is ascribed to the capitalist economy as an arbiter of possibility even by those critics – including the feminist scholars we cite above – who acknowledge and value a diversity of economic practices, including non-market household and communal production as well as economic forms characterised by values of care and interdependence (Gibson-Graham 2006). And when development is seen doing the work of global capitalism, it is itself presented as a unified force rather than a site of contradiction and contestation over divergent political projects (Ferguson 2009).

So while we agree that we cannot move forward without acknowledging the ways in which the business case is implicated in the reformed projects of neoliberalism, we also cannot afford to be caught up in a one-sided politics of denunciation that enacts a determining global capitalist order. What if, instead, we could acknowledge these glimmers of caring and interdependence, unpaid and community labour, social policy and concern about equity through an imaginary of development and change in which the possibility for other economies can emerge? How would we begin to decentre projects of neoliberal subjectification by finding space within gender and development where we can foster projects of 'individual self-transformation [which] are the foundation on which alternative economic interventions are built' (Gibson-Graham 2006: xxv)? How might we place care and interdependence at the centre, rather than the margins, of our politics? How could we begin to imagine gender and development in ways that align with SSE aims, placing the diversity of economic activity and thus our ethical commitments to the possible more centrally? These are some of the questions to which we now turn.

Taking back the economy

As feminists, we are encouraged by the circulation of SSE practice, with its focus on cooperation and care, in the wider development project. At the same time, we are concerned that the SSE is being positioned in relation to a constrained, essentialised conception of economic subjectivity as rational and calculating, albeit tempered by an equally essentialist vision of the feminine caring subject. Further, while an ethic of care figures in this discourse, it is valued only as an instrument of economic growth.

This reduction is consistent with broader trends in economic thought. Witness the popularity of Joseph Stiglitz's recent book *The Price of Inequality* (2012), in which he makes the case that economic inequality must be addressed because it leads to less than optimal economic growth. In a similar fashion, in the business case approach, gender equity has been captured by a neoliberal governmental logic of efficacy rather than by ethical first principles. But are efficiency arguments the only ones that can mobilise forces against poverty and gender inequality? Is our vision and political will so limited that, as the World Bank's managing director recently stated, only the 'price tag [of GDP loss] will finally persuade policymakers, communities and societies to take [even] domestic violence seriously' (Antsey 2013)?

Like the inefficiency of inequality, the logic of instrumental gender equity in contemporary development discourse is appealing because it asks so little of us, and the little that is asked is set against the familiar backdrop of a reified economy. Ethical commitment, deliberation and political struggle are not required. What is required is identification of how conditions may be changed so that the economic logic may play itself out. As appealing as this is, we have two objections. First, by privileging a reified economy, it avoids conversations around ethical commitments. Also, only efforts that support narrowly defined goals of human well-being, such as market efficiency and GDP expansion, are given space within these instrumental logics. So while we understand why many feminists working in development have employed efficacy arguments to get a hearing, we worry about the distance this places between them and the normative values that motivate them, and all discussions about the economy, in the first place.

Second, and central to our work here, the positioning of ethical values such as inclusion, care or equity as instruments of economic growth forecloses ways of imagining how those values might be starting points for a different conversation about the economy. The economy we are used to talking about is one where normative commitments are regarded at best as sentimental and at worst as dangerous and misguided. Any discussion of ethics, and an ethic of care in particular, in relation to economics comes with an attendant vulnerability that can be difficult to bear – but this is also what it means to remain faithful to ethical principles.

What if we were to abandon this usual language of economy long enough to explore another that factored in ethics. It is in relation to this question that we would like to consider two central aspects of the work of the CEC, bearing in mind their compatibility with the SSE: the notion of economic difference; and how difference creates the possibility of a different relationship between economics and ethics. From our perspective, economic difference foregrounds the possibility of ethical choice and, in so doing, recasts the process of development as one centred on building an economy through ethical negotiation. Such a reimagining of development and the emergent SSE makes a profound difference in how we understand gender, market and non-market economic activity, and productive and so-called social-reproductive practices.

Economic difference

The pioneering work of Gibson-Graham (2006) and the CEC to imagine a diverse economic landscape begins with challenging an unstated premise of much political economy: the presumed dominance of capitalism and the subordinate position of all other social relationships and spaces – from households to development institutions, non-market production and the state – within capitalist reproduction. While political economy produces masterful representations of naturalised, dominant capitalism, they argue, these representations reinforce the discursive dominance of the very thing they aim to critique, and push to the margins non-capitalist economic spaces, relationships and practices. Instead, what if we were to imagine economy differently, as being made up of heterogeneous forms of production, exchange and distribution? In order to explore this possibility, Gibson-Graham's analysis initially offers a 'thin definition' of the economy as the production, circulation and consumption of goods and services, encompassing market and non-market, goods produced from rational as well as care motivations, and so forth. Gibson-Graham and the CEC also offer a 'thin definition' of capitalism itself: an organisational form that involves waged workers in the production of goods and services where the surplus wealth they produce is appropriated and subsequently distributed by a group of non-producers (a capitalist owner or board of directors). Given these definitions – which do not reduce the economy to capitalism, nor do they reduce capitalism itself to a particular set of practices and values beyond surplus waged labour extraction – it becomes possible to see other forms of economy. By working within the Marxian tradition that identifies class as a process of surplus production, appropriation and distribution, it is possible to recognise different forms of enterprise organisations: for example, an alternative capitalist enterprise could be funded through alternative finance such as crowdfunding. Capitalist firms may or may not own the property or means of production used in their enterprise – choosing instead to rent it. Cooperatives can and do receive finance from mainstream credit institutions. Imagining the economy as a landscape of difference makes these heterogeneous practices visible, which in turn enables us to see the material, cultural and subjective impacts of multiple organisational forms on people's lives (Byrne and Healy 2006; Cornwell 2011; DeMartino 2003).

A number of CEC scholars, drawing upon and extending the important work of feminist economists to make household labour more visible, have examined organisational forms of household economies quite closely; we also find a heterogeneous landscape here. Some households are organised around traditional patriarchal divisions of labour in which women are assumed to take the care role, but there are also independent households (headed by women or men) or households with a more cooperative structure in terms of the division of labour (Cameron 2002). Others have studied how the challenges of informal caregiving for the frail elderly introduce a new division of labour in many households, including community-based mutual aid practices (Healy 2008). Some within the CEC have used mixed methodological research to show how major economic transformation, such as the collapse of the Soviet Union, has impacted on the material economy of households (Pavlovskaya 2004). They have also shown how households, like enterprises, can function internationally in terms of flows of financial support, labour, obligations and acts of mutual aid (Safri and Graham 2010).[4] This understanding of household economies allows us to register such economic activity as both significant and the locus of a potential political struggle. For example, through the lens of the diverse economy, we are able to see the potential relationship between unpaid caregiving labour and supportive institutions in the community or public sphere, or to imagine conditions that could otherwise reduce the significant care burdens that have been put on households as social support has diminished. The diverse economy lens also provides further backing to the crucial feminist policy project of challenging essentialising views of women in households as carers due to domestic gender divisions of labour. Many households – in fact, a sizeable percentage of them – represent alternative forms of economy outside the patriarchal norm, such as individually headed or global households, cooperatives or care among friends, and therefore it is impossible for them to assume the particular division of labour on which this feminised caring subjectivity is based. In its place, we begin to see multiple practices of care and caring subjects, and multiple sites where the ethic of care may motivate economic activity – including capitalist firms themselves – thus challenging the gendered binaries of masculine/feminine, rationality/care, capitalism/household that limit so much contemporary development thinking.

Community economies and subjects-in-becoming

For us, operating within such a landscape of economic difference prefigures the possibility of having intentional, ethically directed conversations about the choices we might make in our individual and collective economic lives. Gibson-Graham (2006) refer to this as a process of forming community economies. From their perspective, we are involved in the process of forming community economies when we move from recognising economic difference to theorising and documenting how economies are structured through relationships between market and non-market spaces, capitalist and non-capitalist entities. Through an ontological reframing of what is commonly viewed as 'given', we move from a politics in which economy acts upon us to something that can be shaped by people and communities (Cameron 2009).

Recasting economic development as a process of ethical negotiation highlights two salient facts. First, while ethics can direct the intentions of those negotiating, they cannot guarantee the outcomes – if there is no human nature guiding our efforts and no economic 'laws' guaranteeing outcomes then there are only the uncertain decisions we make. Second, imagining economic development as an ethical engagement makes us aware that we are not in control of the circumstances in which we build community economies. One implication is that the process may involve us in negotiations with others who have different agendas and motivations, and that engaging in such a process may upset our normative sensibilities (Gibson-Graham et al. 2013).

We offer one example that relates directly to the goals of SSE and to gender and development. Katherine Gibson and the other members of the CEC undertook a participatory action research project in the rural Philippines, funded by the Australian Agency for International Development, in which they worked with a migrant savings group that marshalled remittance income from women domestic workers abroad (CEC and Gibson 2009). This project was part of a programme aimed at decentralising rural development and reducing state involvement. Looking at the stated objectives of reducing government support and encouraging remittances from women already experiencing significant privation, it would be easy to write this off as another project contributing to neoliberal devolution. It is more difficult to see the possibility of producing an economy based on care, guided by solidarity and directed towards justice. Nevertheless, that is precisely what Gibson and the CEC endeavoured to do by making direct use of the diverse economies framework to produce a different development model.

The migrant savings group, called *Unlad Kabayan*, aimed to invest in social enterprises with the ultimate goal of generating employment alternatives to outmigration. So here we already see evidence of difference as migrant workers are putting aside money from what is already too little to live on with the goal of creating social enterprises. Through this process, new economic subjects are coming into being who are motivated by care and solidarity. For example, the group worked with an entrepreneur named Elsa whose social enterprise was a rice-processing centre in her village. As she worked with rice farmers, Elsa found that many of them were effectively locked by debt into a semi-feudal relationship with wholesalers. Her response was to stake everything in order to buy the farmers out of their indebted relationship (ibid.). Elsa also diversified the producer services offered by the mill, introducing ones that might assist farmers, to build a community around her enterprise. As time passed, the rice-processing centre started to offer a number of linked social enterprises that served poor farmers (ibid.). Also, a loan was made to a group of local women who began a social enterprise that produced ginger tea. Many of these women moved from individualised home-based production into this cooperative enterprise, which has fostered networks of support and mutual assistance among its members. The women have been able to save a percentage of their earnings to set up a local revolving credit practice to assist others in the community (ibid.).

We highlight three things in this brief example. First social enterprise development involved ethical negotiations between the entrepreneurs and the community they were hoping to serve. In the first case, the ethical negotiations involved Elsa, the farm families,

Unlad, Katherine and the CEC, development agencies, and the state. Second, while the outcome is perhaps not ideal and is far from certain, it is also an example of how diverse elements in an economy can be strung together in a process of development that results in class transformation from feudal to independent production, from self-employment to cooperatives, among other changes. Third, in the process of building community economies, relations of interdependence and care foster diverse practices of mutual aid (ibid.). This example has implications for how we understand development agencies, practitioners and academics in a process of development recast as ethical negotiation within difference, rather than submission to the dominant logic of capitalism. While risking vulnerability, failure or even being usurped by other agendas is no guarantee of a good outcome, *not* engaging in solidarity practices that can wrest potentially transformative ends from 'neoliberal' initiatives can only mean that things will remain as they are.

Conclusion

It is possible to practise a different approach to economic development that moves out from neoliberalism's conceptual shadow. Drawing on Foucault (2008), Ferguson notes that the answer lies not in the traditional theories of the left; rather it needs to be invented via conceptual and institutional innovation:

> But invention in the domain of governmental technique is rarely something worked up out of whole cloth. More often, it involves a kind of *bricolage* (Lévi-Strauss 1966), a piecing together of something new out of scavenged parts originally intended for some other purpose ... If we can go beyond seeing in 'neoliberalism' an evil essence or an automatic unity, and instead learn to see a field of specific governmental techniques, we may be surprised to find that some of them can be repurposed, and put to work in the service of political projects very different from those usually associated with that word. If so, we may find that the cabinet of governmental arts available to us is a bit less bare than first appeared, and that some rather useful little mechanisms may be nearer to hand than we thought (Ferguson 2009: 318).

Like Ferguson, we also wish to move beyond the mere critique of neoliberalism. We do not mean to minimise here the shortcomings

of the practice of development it inspires or the limits of an economic vision that fetishises the logical efficacy of markets while
essentialising the behaviour of human participants, even while it casts
women in a new position as 'global saviours'. But for us, moving
beyond critique would have to involve developing different ways of
practising development; this includes different ways of valuing market
and non-market, capitalist and non-capitalist economic activity,
but also different ways of understanding and valuing ourselves. It
means recognising that neoliberalism is a discourse linked to the
essentialised subjects it constitutes performatively, and that even
the critique of neoliberalism can serve to increase its effectiveness
by granting it more power than it is due.

Instead, we offer an approach that emphasises the possibility,
through ethical negotiation, to nurture alternative SSE activities
conducive to gender equity and development. By letting go of a
monolithic vision of economy we are able to recognise the diversity
of alternative enterprises (cooperatives, households) and alternative
systems of finance (microcredit) as well as motivations of care,
interdependence, community aid, and so on. And we can see that
these alternatives do not inevitably reproduce neoliberal capitalism;
rather, they are potentially emerging forms of SSE. Likewise, by
rejecting essentialised conceptions of gender, as the feminist critics
rightly insist, we show that communities can still value care, interdependence and attentiveness to others. We also demonstrate that
this can be accomplished without reinforcing essentialist notions of
gender and without risking complicity with a politics that enrols
these qualities in capitalist reproduction, in part by locating care and
interdependence in diverse economic and social locations (Cameron
and Gibson-Graham 2003).

In our view, if economy is divorced from capitalism, if development governance is divorced from neoliberalism, and if care and
cooperation are divorced from their essentialist gender dimensions,
we can begin to imagine a process of development that is directed
towards the totality of interdependent relationships – in households,
firms, communities, commons, and non-market exchange – and this
allows us the chance of a future worth living in. How we acknowledge
these interdependencies is through an ethics and politics of solidarity.

4 | CAN SOCIAL AND SOLIDARITY ECONOMY ORGANISATIONS COMPLEMENT OR REPLACE PUBLICLY TRADED COMPANIES?

Carina Millstone

Introduction

One type of organisation produces the bulk of the world's industrial output: the public limited liability or publicly traded company. The products and services they offer structure our consumption patterns and lifestyles, and have enabled many to lead lives with high levels of material prosperity. However, the model of provision of goods and services they represent has not been cost free. A new product may provide some utility to the consumer, but typically also involves negative environmental and social impacts. This chapter envisages an alternative arrangement for the provision of goods and services, one that simultaneously benefits communities and the environment. Social and solidarity economy (SSE) organisations, if they were able to scale up and compete effectively in the market, could be key actors in such a system.

SSE organisations are diverse, and range from community groups to cooperatives and employee-owned businesses. These organisations all share a common identity based on their values of justice and sustainability; their processes based on cooperation and democracy; and their goals, which are primarily social or environmental. Some organisations are run on a non-profit basis while others are profit-making, although the latter accrue profit for the benefit of workers, members, beneficiaries or communities. As such, an economy in which goods and services are primarily provided through SSE organisations would look very different to our current system and would potentially be more socially equitable and ecologically sustainable.

This chapter explores the potential of for-profit (i.e. not run on a charitable basis) SSE organisations to complement or replace publicly traded companies in the provision of goods and services. The first section provides an overview of the traditional and current landscape of SSE organisations in the United States (US) and the

United Kingdom (UK), the geographic focus here. Next, I assess the inherent characteristics of SSE organisations that may act as drivers or barriers to their growth, and examine how the external economic and environmental climate may present opportunities for such organisations. Finally, this chapter argues that growth is not risk free for SSE organisations, as tensions exist between their purpose and growth through the market.

The SSE landscape and publicly traded companies

SSE organisations have a long tradition on both sides of the Atlantic. They stem from a collective attempt to respond to a market failure: namely the difficulty of individuals to access goods and services through purchase from traditional private businesses due to high cost or lack of offer. In the UK, SSE organisations have their roots in mutual aid groups such as friendly societies, which provided social and financial services to their members and were typically affiliated by trade or religion. In the Victorian period, cooperatives were established to help members access basic foodstuffs. One of the first consumer cooperatives, the Rochdale Society of Equitable Pioneers, was established in Lancashire in the 1840s and provided a blueprint for future cooperative organisations.[1] By the 1900s, mutual organisations dominated the food, retail, mortgage lending and personal insurance sectors (Hutton 2012).

In the US, SSE organisations were also created to respond to the needs of communities or members, pooling their purchasing power. For example, some 400 rural electric consumer cooperatives were developed in the 1930s with the support of the Rural Electrification Administration, as a response to the high expense of infrastructure that made investment unviable for private utilities companies (Deller et al. 2009).[2]

In the late nineteenth century, at the same time as SSE organisations were taking shape, the public company (a limited liability company whose shares are publicly traded on a stock market) was also growing rapidly. This type of company enables large numbers of investors to pool their capital in a single business and receive dividends as a reward for their risk (Hutton 2012). Based on a legal structure designed to ease access to capital and share risk on a scale never seen before, the publicly traded company was able to flourish quickly. Moreover, it also had an in-built *need* to grow to reward its investors, thus forcing it to develop new markets. In practice, this often meant converting poorer people into customers, people who had been SSE organisations' most obvious membership base. The publicly traded company proved an extremely successful way of providing goods and services in the British and American markets. The possibility of widespread individual consumption, brought about by businesses producing large volumes of goods at low cost, made organisational structures designed for individuals to access goods collectively less relevant. SSE organisations began to decline and eventually became marginal. In time, global consumerism also contributed to a loss of local identity, which compounded the erosion of these SSE structures.

The publicly traded company now dominates global industrial output and commerce. The reach of publicly traded companies is global, and their revenue is often larger than the gross domestic product (GDP) of states (Dietz and O'Neill 2013). In 2003, the revenues of the largest 1,000 companies (the overwhelming majority of them publicly traded) represented 80 per cent of global industrial output (Kelly 2012). Cooperatives, on the other hand, represent 3 per cent to 5 per cent of world GDP (Borruso 2012).

The publicly traded company is so dominant that other organisational forms are typically overlooked and poorly understood in the UK and USA.[3] Regulatory, financial, policy and media focus on the performance of publicly traded companies reflects, and results in, a lack of support for organisations with alternative structures (Hutton 2012). For example, in the UK, there is no specific legal act to register a cooperative.[4] In the US, cooperatives contend with a complex regulatory framework, with cooperative incorporation statutes varying from state to state and often applying only to specific sectors. Alternative organisational models are rarely taught in business schools and cooperatives struggle to attract young talent (Borruso 2012).

Despite this, we are seeing a renewed interest in alternatives, especially in light of the current financial and ecological crises. SSE organisations take a number of different forms and are present, albeit unevenly, in most sectors and regions of the UK and the US.

In the US, they include 4,600 community development corporations (which seek local financing to develop residential and commercial property); almost 1,300 community development financial institutions (which offer financial services to low-income individuals or community organisations); and over 240 community land trusts (which buy land in order to secure affordable housing in perpetuity).[5] In addition, there are nearly 30,000 cooperatives (primarily consumer cooperatives), which together have 350 million members and generate approximately US$654 billion in revenue (Deller et al. 2009).

Cooperatives tend to be more common in rural areas; over 85 per cent of cooperative revenue is generated in agriculture, the farm credit system, home loan banks, rural electric services, mutual insurance and credit unions (ibid.). Consumer cooperative models are also becoming popular in education and training, healthcare, energy and transportation. Worker-owned cooperatives, on the other hand, are rare, with only 3,500 people employed in 300 worker cooperatives, clustered in the North East and in the San Francisco Bay Area.[6] Employee stock ownership plans (ESOPs) are a more common way to enable employees to own part or all of the company they work for. Unlike worker-owned cooperatives, ownership does not convey membership, and company governance is not necessarily democratic or run on a 'one member, one vote' principle.[7] There are currently close to 11,000 ESOPs across the US, employing close to 14 million workers (Warren and Dubbs 2010). Some 720 for-profit businesses have also adopted the new 'B-Corporation' or 'B-Corp' status in recent years. While the jury is still out as to whether such corporations should be considered part of SSE, they are purpose-driven businesses established to create public benefit.[8]

In the UK, SSE organisations are commonly referred to as mutual organisations[9] and are established for shared member purposes and owned by their members. In total, there are 18,000 mutual organisations in the UK, the overwhelming majority of which are not-for-profit clubs and societies (Hutton 2012). Organisations run on a for-profit basis include approximately 3,430 cooperatives, 250 employee-owned businesses, 50 building societies, 1,700 housing associations, 60 mutual insurers and 40 credit unions. One in three adults is a member of at least one mutual organisation (ibid.). Additionally, 68,000 small businesses in the UK claim to be 'social enterprises', conducting business primarily for a social or environmental goal.[10]

Despite their large numbers, variety and reach in different sectors and geographies, the overall contribution of such organisations to the British and American economic output is small. In the UK, for example, they contribute approximately 5 per cent of national output (or £110 billion annually) and provide for 3.5 per cent of total employment (ibid.). Even in sectors where SSE organisations are well established – financial services, retail, agriculture – they are eclipsed by their large, publicly traded counterparts. The contribution of SSE organisations to the production of goods and services remains marginal and should not be overstated.

Characteristics of SSE organisations that drive and hinder growth

The membership structure and financing arrangements of cooperatives, mutual organisations and employee-owned businesses can act both as driver and barrier to growth. At the core of their model, for example, consumer cooperatives rely on a loyal base of member-customers, which acts as both a driver of growth and a counterbalancing stabiliser. Their close relationship with member-customers gives cooperatives a good understanding of their market and of customers' needs, driving their success and creating growth opportunities. A study conducted by McKinsey and Company noted that cooperatives and mutual organisations grow at similar rates to publicly traded companies (Borruso 2012) and that their growth tends to come from increased market share, where they outperform their publicly traded counterparts.

However, growth is not the main aim of SSE organisations, and measuring success through growth is misguided. A growth strategy may be pursued but only if it increases member benefits. This is a key difference with the publicly traded company, which is structurally determined to pursue growth as an end in itself. The membership structure can therefore also act as a brake on growth. While members are well placed to identify current need, they may be less adept at identifying future needs and opportunities, stifling innovation and diversification. Moreover, decision-making structures that favour consensus and member participation are likely to be less agile or experimental than more traditional top-down approaches.

A further in-built brake on growth for SSE organisations is their financing arrangements. Employee-owned companies and cooperatives do not have access to equity capital (other than through their members), since they do not have alienable shares – an obvious difference with the publicly traded company, which is structurally designed to attract equity shareholders. This limits the ability of SSE organisations to grow and to compete at scale with publicly traded companies. SSE organisations' imperative to serve existing members may also make them less likely to take on additional debt. This combination of factors means that SEE organisations do not lend themselves well to high-capital sectors: they are largely absent from pharmaceutical, information and new technology areas. This is especially problematic for increasing such organisations' share of overall industrial output, as these sectors are especially high-value and high-growth.

Opportunities for growth for SSE organisations

The interrelated social, economic and environmental crises that we currently face present new opportunities for SSE organisa-tions. Demand from emerging markets, speculation, volatility in commodity prices and climate change require a renewed emphasis on the attributes of SSE organisations associated with community resilience, job stability and the 'greening' of the economy.

The experience of the UK during the financial crisis is suggestive here. Between 2008 and 2011, cooperative businesses significantly outperformed the rest of the British economy, growing by 19.6 per cent, while the UK economy in 2011 was 1.7 per cent smaller than in 2008 (Co-operatives UK 2012). This suggests that cooperatives are more sheltered from economic downturns than their competitors with traditional ownership structures, and that downturns actually present a growth opportunity for them. This resilience may be due in part to the loyalty of their members.

The imperative to grow employment and preserve domestic jobs presents an opportunity for SSE organisations. Worker-owned cooperatives or employee-owned firms tend to have comparable or higher productivity than conventionally owned firms, especially when workers are associated with decision-making relating to process and management (Levin 2006). This is due to high levels of employee or worker engagement, lower staff turnover and higher job satisfaction (Pencavel et al. 2006). As a result, employee-owned businesses tend to generate higher profits than non-employee-owned businesses of the same size. Moreover, these organisations also report greater employment growth (ibid.). In general, employment is more secure (even if the wages may be lower) in employee-owned businesses or cooperatives than in other forms of business. These structures also make company relocations unlikely, and, in times of crisis, reduced employment hours tend to be favoured over redundancies (Levin 2006).

SSE organisations are adept at building resilient communities. Cooperatives exist to serve their members and there are no a priori reasons why member and community benefits should align. However, the principles that underpin the SSE are conducive to developing organisations that serve the needs of their communities. In the UK, half of all cooperatives are found in particularly disadvantaged areas (Co-operatives UK 2012). On both sides of the Atlantic, building community organisation density is seen as necessary both for revitalising depressed areas and for addressing environmental concerns. This presents a growth opportunity for SSE organisations. In the US, for example, the SSE is at the heart of the so-called 'Cleveland model'.[11] This model uses SSE organisations to build community wealth, favouring local economic development by meeting community need rather than by attracting outside investment. Cleveland has a large-scale network of worker-owned and community-benefiting enterprises. Workers are recruited locally, so the organisations build employment in a low-income, minority community. The Cleveland model relies on 'anchor institutions' – local hospitals and universities – as their primary customers. They provide a secure market for the cooperatives while the cooperatives help these institutions 'green' their procurement practices (Alperovitz et al. 2010).

However, there are challenges with replicating this structure. In addition to the difficulties of securing start-up finance, SSE organisations tend to be poorly supported or understood by local authorities. The very nature of SSE organisations requires managing multiple partners, collaborators and interests to make sure that they achieve member or community benefit. This costly and time-consuming organisational effort usually requires dedicated 'local heroes' willing and able to perform this work, as well as third-party support. However, the network-building and collaboration required during the start-up phase ultimately make SSE organisations more resilient, by providing them with exposure and a strong network and supporter base. In the UK, for example,

98 per cent of new cooperative businesses are still in operation after three years, compared with 65 per cent of all new businesses (Co-operatives UK 2012).

Ecological challenges demand both growth in the green economy (sectors such as renewable energy, waste management, green buildings and cleaner transportation) and a greening of the economy (i.e. an improvement of environmental performance in all sectors). As the legal structures of SSE organisations were defined prior to our current ecological predicament, there are no structural reasons why SSE organisations should incorporate environmental concerns more effectively into their practice and products than organisations with more traditional structures. Indeed, some publicly traded companies (such as Puma and Unilever) have taken a lead on tackling ecological sustainability issues.

However, specific features of SSE organisations tend to encourage sound environmental practices. They are typically rooted in their locality, and, as Monique Leroux from Desjardins Group observes: 'as members tend to live in the communities where they do business, they are less likely to engage in massive development projects that could damage the community or drain its natural resources' (Borruso 2012: 64). In the UK, 88 per cent of cooperatives claim to seek to minimise their environmental impacts compared with 44 per cent of comparable small businesses that do not report taking any action (Co-operatives UK 2012). In general, the social goals of SSE organisations are likely to attract members who are also concerned with environmental issues (although this self-selection may inhibit scaling of SSE organisations).

The growth of certain sectors of the green economy – renewable energy, green buildings and others – presents an opportunity for SSE organisations (Warren and Dubbs 2010). The green economy will often require localised initiatives structured around community needs – demands that are aligned with SSE organisations' underpinning values, processes and goals. While some of these activities will require high-capital investments, others will be low-capital and labour-intensive – retrofitting, transportation, food production – and could readily be taken on by SSE organisations with their current membership and financing arrangements. In some instances, cooperatives also have a head start over traditional companies: for example, 11 per cent of the electricity delivered by electric cooperatives in the US is from renewable sources, compared with 8.5 per cent of electricity from investor-owned companies (Deller et al. 2009). Community-owned wind power is also already relatively well established and is a fast-growing sector.

While SSE organisations may capitalise on the business and job creation opportunities of the green economy, they will need to successfully compete with organisations governed by more traditional ownership structures. Given the inherent difficulties in coordinating new community- or member-owned projects, high barriers to entry in these new sectors, and the fact that SSE organisations are not structured for rapid growth, this will not be an easy task. Still, if SSE organisations are successful at capturing the opportunities of the green economy, their success will promote environmental benefits as well as stronger communities and greater wealth equity. These latter social benefits would be lost through corporate ownership of the green economy.

Risks to SSE organisations associated with growth

Growing SSE through the market poses risks for this alternative form of economy, given the tension between market relations and the social character and democratic governance of SSE organisations. If SSE organisations are to effectively complement or displace the publicly traded company in the provision of goods and services, they will need to compete on price. The cooperative model is not in itself a sufficient selling point, and cooperatives need to adopt professional practices to stay in business. For example, successful producer cooperatives in the agricultural sector have become household names – Ocean Spray, Sunkist, Sun-Maid – by pooling their resources and marketing to compete effectively with traditionally owned businesses. But 'acting like a publicly traded company' may have unintended consequences on the social character of the cooperative, due to scale, lack of physical proximity of the growers, and the real temptation for growers to sell out. Some cooperatives, such as the British worker-owned John Lewis Partnership, have arrangements in their founding documents to prohibit the workers from selling the company (Kelly 2012).

Furthermore, the need to compete on price is also inherently problematic for SSE organisations, in that the prices of goods produced by publicly traded companies are often low due to the externalisation of environmental and social costs, such as the inadequate costing of private resource use at point of extraction, or poor environmental and labour standards in producer countries (typically in the global South). The scale of publicly traded companies also means that these externalities are poorly understood. Indeed, most impacts happen in the supply chain and responsibility is diffused at all levels within organisations – numerous investors share risk; ownership and management are separated; and thousands (or more) of employees work in their own silos. SSE organisations would struggle to compete effectively on price and at scale with publicly traded companies without some cost externalisation and practices associated with poor environmental and social performance. This risks the dissolution of their social character, thereby making them less desirable from the perspective of sustainability.

SSE organisations are also at a structural disadvantage when they compete with their publicly traded counterparts. Food cooperatives, for example, introduced organic foods and were leaders in the organic food market until the 1990s. By 2008, sales of organic produce had reached US$23 billion, with the increase in sales coming primarily through publicly traded, mass-market companies (Deller et al. 2009). The challenge for SSE organisations is to achieve replication and scale that could compete with publicly traded companies, so that they can reach a mass customer base while retaining their identity and the benefits derived from their structure.

Some SSE organisations have achieved a scale comparable to their publicly traded counterparts: the Cooperative Group in the UK has 7 million members and an annual turnover of £14 billion (Borruso 2012). However, member participation in governance is low. While this absentee membership does not necessarily undermine the performance of the cooperative, it does undermine some key cooperative principles, namely self-organisation and the democratic participation of members. The distinct identity of the cooperative model and the social and environmental responsibility it tends to foster are threatened by member absenteeism. Responding to this issue, Peter Marks, former Chief Executive Officer of the Co-op Group, experimented with digital participation of its membership in decision-making (for example, crowdsourcing decisions about new store locations) (ibid.). Social media could present opportunities to revitalise member engagement, replacing the physical proximity and locality that have often been at the core of the SSE model with digital community-building.

SSE organisations therefore do not belong naturally to the world of market relations, but occupy another sphere of human exchange, even when they use market mechanisms to bring benefits to their members and communities. Individual consumption of goods and services procured on the market can seem at odds with the collective, civic character of SSE organisations. In fact, consumption has typically been understood as the opposite of citizenship, with citizenship rooted in communal and local identity whereas consumption is associated with individual identity, the global and the faraway (Trentmann 2007). Of course, this does not always hold true, but the consumption of goods and services from large companies does require some abstraction from our civic, social or environmental concerns (due to the externalisation of environmental and social impact, as discussed above).

The emerging 'sharing economy', where products are loaned, usually peer to peer, rather than purchased, is an example of how procuring goods through a traditionally owned company may dilute the social character of procuring the same good through alternative means. Car-pooling, for example, was typically a social and community opportunity, encouraging neighbours to share their cars. Some of these social mechanisms were formalised through the establishment of SSE organisations, and a dozen or so consumer car-pooling cooperatives exist across the US, with the cooperative responsible for maintenance, insurance, car purchase and member vetting. In recent years these cooperatives have been entirely eclipsed by new businesses, such as Zipcar (a short-term car rental company) or Buzzcar (a peer-to-peer car rental agency). These both provide a similar service to members of car-pooling cooperatives, and share clear environmental benefits compared with individual car ownership. However, while car-pooling cooperatives help to build community, a business such as Zipcar does not. The extent to which Buzzcar could help build new digital communities through its use of social media remains to be seen. Moreover, unlike car cooperatives, the profits of these businesses accrue to owners, not to member-users. Thus, while the 'sharing economy' could be seen to promote the values and aims of SSE organisations in the digital age, in its current form it is leading to the further corporate presence in what has traditionally been a space of opportunity for SSE organisations. Social media may simply provide traditional companies with the social knowledge and networks that were previously accessible only to SSE organisations, thus depriving the latter of one of their core competitive advantages. In those circumstances, the sharing economy is likely to become a mechanism for product-sharing dominated by a few corporate actors.

At the same time, SEE organisations present a challenge to publicly traded companies in that they constitute an alternative model with benefits beyond the simple provision of goods and services. The UK's Ownership Commission advocates plurality of ownership structures as a good in its own right, as its absence damages choice, innovation and entrepreneurship (Hutton 2012). In other words, the presence of organisations with alternative forms of ownership, such as cooperatives, can have a positive impact on sectors as a whole. Importantly, a significant presence of cooperatives in a particular sector limits the ability of private firms to extract above-normal profits (Rogers 1994), thereby limiting corporate predatory pricing and the creation of oligopolies, and resulting in a more competitive market. Moreover, SSE organisations may be well placed to deliver public services such as healthcare, as they are close to their members while retaining a financial motive for efficiency.

SSE organisations may also improve sectors by providing products and services whose 'story' may align with the values of an increasing number of consumers. Soper (2007) notes that an understanding of the consumer as an agent seeking to maximise personal satisfaction from spending their disposable income fails to account for the more nuanced consumer patterns that come about from the growing malaise at the social and environmental cost of consumption. This has changed the practice of consumption for a growing number of affluent citizens, thereby presenting an opportunity for SSE organisations to meet this new citizen expectation in their consumption choices. While this has traditionally meant integrating an awareness of the environmental and social impacts of products, it increasingly includes the consideration of their contribution to local economic development, and may in time include questions of the ownership structure, design and processes of producing organisations. SSE organisations would be the natural providers of goods and services that respond to these new considerations of the consumer-citizen.

Conclusion

SSE organisations have a long tradition in both the UK and the US, providing valuable services to their members and benefits to their communities. As organisations that flourish in times of crisis, our current economic and environmental predicament presents growth opportunities for SSE organisations to develop strong communities based on the creation of valuable local employment and to seize the opportunities of the green economy. However, SSE organisations have within their aims, membership structure and financing arrangements characteristics that contribute to their success and resilience – but that ultimately hinder their growth. Moreover, scaling up to compete effectively in the market risks the dissolution of SSE values, processes and goals.

Competing with SSE organisations in the provision of goods and services is the publicly traded company – an organisation structured to grow and to compete on price through the externalisation of its social and environmental impacts. It is unlikely that SSE organisations would be able to replace such a competitor in the provision of goods and services without undermining the attributes that make them socially and environmentally desirable alternatives. However, we can expect them to become less marginal economic actors, which will help create a more plural, resilient economy – an economy that is more appropriate to the needs of our time, and less reliant on one dominant organisational form.

The biggest opportunity for SSE organisations is unlikely to come through competing with the publicly traded company on the latter's terms, but from another challenge: that of the need to reorient our economies for ecological sustainability. While the greening of the economy requires growth in certain green sectors, it also requires both a massive increase in environmental efficiency (or a decrease in environmental impact per unit produced) and an overall reduction in production and consumption in the economies of the global North (Daly 1991).

The publicly traded company exists to grow and does this through the creation of new products and markets, thereby driving production and consumption – when we precisely need to find ways to reduce these patterns. It is structurally ill equipped to contribute to the provision of goods and services outside this growth-based mechanism.

SSE organisations, on the other hand, are not structured to grow. Instead, they have developed and refined processes to effectively provide members and communities with goods and services. They are therefore the kind of organisations that we will need for an economy that does not require growth for a decent standard of living. Advocacy for such an economy may be marginal today, but it will become more pressing as climate change and resource scarcity create volatility and insecurity. This will present an opportunity for the replication and expansion of SSE organisations, as socially and environmentally beneficial, tried-and-tested, non-growth-seeking alternative models for the provision of goods and services.

5 | SCALING THE SOCIAL AND SOLIDARITY ECONOMY: OPPORTUNITIES AND LIMITATIONS OF FAIRTRADE PRACTICE

Darryl Reed

Introduction

While the notion of the social and solidarity economy (SSE) remains controversial with respect to many of its features (especially its core values and what type of actors should be considered a part of the SSE), one thing that all advocates of the SSE agree upon is that it needs to grow in order to better fulfil its mission. But what is the meaning of growing – or scaling – the SSE? Which type of actors are likely to contribute to (or inhibit) such scaling? And what are the challenges and trade-offs involved?

This chapter investigates these issues with regard to the potential contributions and challenges that arise within the specific SSE movement that revolves around the certified Fairtrade (FT) network.[1] Its main aim is to illustrate a conceptual framework that delineates the nature and causes of the basic contributions, tensions and trade-offs associated with efforts within the FT movement to promote the scaling of the SSE. It does this by: identifying potential dimensions of scaling the SSE – the horizontal, the vertical and the transversal; examining how the 'alternative trade' practice within FT contributes to the scaling of the SSE through five activities; investigating how the presence of non-SSE actors within FT complicates the potential of FT to scale the SSE; and, finally, offering some conclusions.

What does scaling the SSE mean?

Any discussion about the meaning of scaling the SSE presupposes some understanding of what the SSE is. As a social practice, the SSE is not a single thing; rather, it is the convergence of a series of overlapping practices and perspectives that have been shaped largely as a response to a neoliberal project of economic globalisation (Coraggio 2012). While this history precludes any uncontested definition of the SSE, there is at least, as the name implies, some common agreement on two points. First, the primary purpose of economic activity should be to benefit people, and not to generate profits. Second, it entails a strong sense of social justice, which is manifested through bonds of solidarity, especially with marginalised groups. In addition, advocates of the SSE tend to agree that it does and should involve a diversity of economic actors, including not only formally incorporated businesses but also social movements, non-governmental organisations (NGOs) and self-help groups, among others. Similarly, a range of formal business types might be included in the SSE (such as cooperatives, mutuals and not-for-profit firms). While diversity is universally acknowledged with regard to the range of actors and firms in the SSE, the limits of diversity are contested. For example, should trade unions be considered part of the SSE, and should public sector enterprises, social entrepreneurs and B-corporations[2] be included?

Such discussions relate to two broader ideological (or normative) questions, as well as to pragmatic concerns (ibid.). The first is whether we want to promote the SSE for inherent reasons (i.e. we have strong preferences for production and exchange based on relationships of solidarity) or for more instrumental purposes (i.e. we believe that it will be more effective than alternatives in poverty eradication efforts, creating employment for marginalised groups, etc.). The second ideological question refers to the role that we want the SSE to play in the larger economy: as supplemental to the capitalist economy (i.e. filling gaps where the corporate economy does not perform well), as a necessary complement to the capitalist economy (i.e. providing competition to ensure competitiveness in markets, including ethical competition) or as a substitute (i.e. as the dominant form of production and exchange in our local economies). These questions raise further normative issues (around priorities, for example) and introduce various strategic considerations (such as those relating to trade-offs in the use of limited resources or risk assessment). These normative questions and pragmatic concerns about promoting SSE activity not only frame the definitional question of who should be part of the SSE, but also help us to understand the potential importance of scaling SSE activity and some of the potential trade-offs involved in such efforts.[3]

There are three main approaches to scaling the SSE: horizontal, vertical and transversal. Some of the costs and benefits involved in pursuing these different strategies are explored below.

Horizontal scaling One of the most immediate concerns of the SSE is how to respond to widespread poverty. To address this issue, a range of efforts have been initiated to promote food security and sustainable livelihoods, including the promotion of production for personal consumption, the formation of individual micro-enterprises and cooperative businesses, and the unionisation of informal work (Santos 2007b). The strategy is generally to supply resources (finance, training, materials, access to land) to marginalised groups to enable them to engage in economic activity. The basic benefit of such programmes is that they help to ensure subsistence for a large number of people, ideally at relatively low costs. Depending on the nature of the programme, they may also have other knock-on effects, such as providing financial independence for women or promoting fairer gender relationships in families.

There are also concerns about such programmes. One of these is how widely they might be extended or replicated, and whether there is sufficient demand for their products. Another is the degree to which these projects may enable members of marginalised groups to move beyond subsistence. Virtually all of these enterprises operate in very competitive market sectors, with very low remuneration. This means that these small 'entrepreneurs' will likely remain trapped in these sectors, as will their children, although prospects may differ depending on whether the enterprises are individual or collective in nature. Collective activity (such as working in cooperatives) may have some advantages insofar as it provides greater opportunity for collective action and may provide support for individual members during times of personal crisis or economic fluctuations.

Vertical scaling In order for (potential) members of SSE enterprises to move beyond subsistence to pursue social, cultural, political and economic development aspirations, they need to focus on the vertical dimension of scale. In the economic literature, scaling up typically refers to productivity advantages that accrue to firms as the average costs of production drop with increased output.[4] The drop in costs and corresponding increase in productivity are usually associated with an increase in the size of the firm, but may also come about as firms associate in networks or in other ways (for example, when primary cooperatives come together to form second-tier cooperatives that provide services). In addition to economies of scale, productivity increases in SSE firms and networks may result from increased learning as growth occurs. Firms may also increase their revenue through efforts to move up the value chain into higher-value processes, such as secondary processing, export, distribution and retail, as well as by developing new product lines that build upon existing capacity and knowledge (Reed et al. 2010).

This strategy of scaling up may be very attractive to SSE enterprises, especially to the degree that they can draw upon bonds of solidarity between units to scale up production and exchange relations. Still, this is easier said than done, as these enterprises exist in competitive markets and scaling up may require significant outlays of capital and knowledge. Additionally, in contexts where SSE enterprises operate within a single sector, such as agriculture, they may be subject to significant market fluctuations. While cooperation helps producers to weather market cycles, if they have invested heavily to scale up then their shared risk can result in shared failure.

Transversal scaling Such vulnerability highlights the potential need to scale the SSE transversally, across different sectors. The goal here is to develop dense, diversified networks of mutually supporting SSE enterprises that can provide a basis not just for the growth of SSE enterprises, but for an entire local economy dominated by SSE production and exchange.[5] Strategically, scaling up on this level requires not only closer links between firms and a supportive policy framework, but also a mobilised consumer base and an engaged citizenry that can drive SSE production and the formation of a business environment that favours SSE enterprises.

While some in the SSE might aspire to such a vision, there is the prospect that pursuing it too directly (or exclusively) might result in lost opportunities to make substantial gains that could benefit small producers and other marginalised groups. On the other hand, it could also be argued that such a scaling project is important not only as a utopian ideal, but more practically in that it can help to keep in check the political and economic power of large corporations, their umbrella associations and the political elites that collaborate with them.

The potential contributions of FT to scaling the SSE

With retail sales of FT now exceeding €4.8 billion in some 125 countries and generating more than €80 million annually in premiums for smallholders, FT is widely viewed as one of the most important SSE success stories and provides important lessons for the scaling of the SSE. In order to understand the contributions of FT to growing the SSE, two fundamental points about FT need to be noted. First, FT is a complex practice that involves a variety of actors and activities. Five primary activities, each involving multiple actors, can be distinguished – production, exchange, regulation, advocacy and mobilisation. Second, FT is a contested practice. Not all actors involved in FT are SSE organisations, and many can be quite hostile to the SSE if it threatens their interests. Moreover, while some actors involved in FT support SSE production and exchange, they may argue that, for pragmatic reasons, it is necessary to work closely with non-SSE actors (especially large corporate retailers and distributors). These pragmatic reasons typically, but not necessarily, involve the horizontal growth of SSE, but there is a concern that they could also undermine long-term vertical and transversal growth. The following section focuses on the SSE actors within the 'alternative trade' side of FT and their potential for growing the SSE, especially in the global South. Later I examine how the presence of non-SSE actors can diminish or undermine efforts by SSE actors within FT to scale SSE production.

FT as SSE production FT involves SSE production, as it is typically undertaken by small producers who join together to market their products or produce. Fairtrade International (FLO) requires small producers to be organised democratically, a requirement that typically is fulfilled through incorporation as a cooperative. Thus, while production may be undertaken individually or in family units, marketing (and sometimes processing) is done jointly through shared membership in a formal organisation.

FT can contribute to the scaling up of the SSE in a variety of ways, most notably at a horizontal level where the FT requirement of democratic organisation can help draw producers into SSE production. Participation in formal cooperative organisations can have many advantages, not least creating relationships with external partners; accessing new resources from outside sources; lowering marketing costs through sharing resources; learning, particularly with regard to production techniques and how markets operate; and encouraging greater sharing of resources in ways that reduce costs and labour for producers, thus increasing their productivity. All of these benefits can happen without FT, but FT may offer an extra inducement for producers to organise (Crowell and Reed 2009; Spear 2000).

The advantages of cooperative organisation noted above may also promote other dimensions of scaling. To the extent that productivity is increasing and learning is occurring, producer cooperatives are building organisational capacity that can potentially be used (along the vertical axis) to produce further economies of scale and to engage in new activities with greater value-added. However, there are frequently major constraints on developing such activities, including knowledge and finance, which FT tries to address in other ways (as discussed below). Similarly, the advantages of cooperation among small producers (such as transport improvements) may spill over to other SSE actors and induce cooperation across sectors (transversal scaling). Again, this will be limited for the same reasons noted above.

FT as SSE exchange The core experience at the heart of FT is that, while small producers typically are not able to engage in fair exchange relations with conventional buyers and distributors, an alternative form of trade based on solidarity is possible with the support of consumers and other SSE enterprises. The solidarity between small producers and other SSE trading partners expresses itself in a number of ways:

- partnership and shared decision-making over the terms of trade, rather than a imposition of terms based on market power;
- transparency and knowledge-sharing, leading to shared autonomy;
- commitment to fairer distribution along the value chain, which includes ensuring that the full costs of production of small producers are covered by the price that they receive;
- trade based on long-term relations, rather than contracts with a one-year horizon;
- commitment to supporting capacity-building and local development, including support for social and physical infrastructure as well as efforts by small producers to capture more value-added by moving up the value chain and developing their own brands

and new product lines – this frequently entails the mobilisation of resources from other actors and support groups;

• long-term relationships with consumers, involving loyalty, more direct trade relations that cut out intermediaries, a commitment to quality products, as well as openness and transparency (Crowell and Reed 2009). This feature of solidarity-based exchange relations – for some, the core component of FT – has tremendous potential for scaling the SSE (especially in the global South).

At the horizontal level, FT exchange relationships are able to pull in more small producers by creating a demand for their products under more favourable conditions – for example, higher prices or long-term contracts. These benefits make it possible for more small producers to work as farmers, or to spend more of their time developing their own land, rather than working as agricultural workers (Bacon 2010). This, in turn, helps to ensure that more land stays in local control and can potentially be used as part of the SSE. On the vertical axis, participation in FT provides producer cooperatives with a variety of new resources that can be used for capacity-building. Knowledge about production techniques (including more sustainable production) can help individual farmers increase quality and in some instances decrease costs. Partners can also bring knowledge about marketing and potential new markets. Technical knowledge about processing and product development can be of tremendous assistance in capturing more value-added, assistance that comes only with trading relationships based on solidarity. Financial and technical support for local infrastructure can help lower costs and increase productivity. Many of the benefits that occur along the vertical scale (knowledge-sharing, increased revenue from increased value-added, new infrastructure) can also be applied to scale up SSE activity in a transversal direction. Specifically, knowledge about production techniques, marketing and finance can be applied to developing new sectors, while new infrastructure (social and physical) can reinforce other fledgling SSE enterprises (VanderHoff Boersma 2009).

FT as SSE advocacy One of the major developments in FT has been the organisation of national and regional producer associations. Their development has followed the growth path of FT itself in that the first national and regional producer organisations arose in Latin America and the Caribbean, emerging out of sectoral organisations (especially for coffee, the first FT product). While regional bodies were subsequently organised in Africa (Fairtrade Africa) and Asia (Network of Asian Producers), the Latin American and Caribbean producer association, CLAC, has remained the strongest and most innovative body. It is also the only one composed entirely of SSE organisations (Coscione 2012).

While producer organisations may provide their members with a range of services, one of their key functions is also advocacy, so as to make the business climate more amenable to the interests of the association's members. Such advocacy work can be directed towards a range of actors and institutions, including legislative bodies, non-state regulatory institutions (including FLO and organic certifying bodies, for example), government agencies, public institutions and NGOs. The purpose of advocacy may be to generate new legislation, to promote new policies, or even to change institutions and their decision-making structures (ibid.; Hutchens 2009).

Advocacy may contribute to scaling in different ways. To the extent that it leads to increased sales, this will enable FT to grow horizontally and incorporate more producers. This can occur through the promotion of FT purchasing policies by public institutions – including the promotion of such practices as FT Towns and FT Universities – as well as through reform to trade laws, including those that facilitate access to markets by removing existing barriers or by providing special status to FT producers (Reed et al. 2010). Advocacy can also promote the adoption of policies that provide FT producers with new resources, such as market knowledge or technical support, from national development agencies, multilateral bodies or large development NGOs. These new resources may facilitate the vertical scaling of FT by promoting economies of scale. In a less direct way, advocacy directed at changing institutional structures (such as producer organisations' efforts to attain membership and decision-making power in FLO) can also contribute to vertical scaling in that it provides producers with increased opportunities for changing policy (Bacon 2010). Advocacy directed towards the development policies of national and regional governments, as has occurred in Ecuador and Brazil, can also facilitate transversal scaling in local economies (Coscione 2012).

FT as SSE regulation Many associate the emergence of FT with the establishment of the first labelling body, Max Havelaar, in the Netherlands in 1988. Over the subsequent decade, as national labelling bodies were established in a variety of northern countries – often with different standards, processes and structures – the need was felt for closer collaboration. This led to the formation of the Fairtrade Labelling Organizations International (FLO), which would later adopt the name Fairtrade International (while retaining the acronym FLO). Initially, only the national labelling bodies (which were composed for the most part of northern NGOs) were members of FLO and had decision-making power. Later, producer organisations were given voting rights and, subsequently, membership status (Hutchens 2009; Reed 2012).

Characterising the nature of FLO in relationship to SSE is not an easy task, given the diversity among the national initiatives and the changes in FLO over time. As a non-state regulatory body, FLO initially had as its primary goal the promotion of SSE activity, but later changed its mission to focus on poverty eradication (Reed 2009). In this sense, it might be considered an SSE regulatory body, especially to the extent that it still promotes the SSE.[6] However, within the organisational structure of FLO have appeared members that some might argue are not SSE organisations.[7]

While characterising FLO unconditionally as an SSE non-state regulatory body is controversial, certain of its policies – especially its requirement for small producers to be organised in democratically controlled bodies – do indeed promote possibilities for scaling SSE activity. Horizontally, certification helps to expand the demand for FT products by assuring consumers of the ethical (SSE) quality of the products.

On the supply side, the benefits derived from FT certification (such as minimum prices) and the requirement for democratic organisation provide small producers with additional incentives to operate within the SSE. Vertically, FT brings in new resources to small producers – through social premiums and the provision of technical support, for example. This delivers a variety of beneficial effects, including cost savings and better quality control. Many of these advantages also spill over to the transversal scale, as social premiums deployed for infrastructure projects benefit the whole community, while other resources increase the capacity of small producers to diversify into other products and services (VanderHoff Boersma 2009).

FT as SSE mobilisation From the beginnings of the alternative trade movement in the 1970s, a variety of organisations have supported what is now called SSE production. Historically, these have included organic and natural food organisations and cooperatives, as well as some social justice and development NGOs. More recently, such supporters have become associated with alter-globalisation movements, which include explicit SSE organisations and networks such as the Intercontinental Network for the Promotion of Social and Solidarity Economy (RIPESS). These organisations engage in educational and promotional campaigns, support advocacy work for trade reform and institutional purchasing policies, and provide direct technical and material support for small producer organisations (Reed 2012).

They have had an impact on the scaling of FT along the horizontal plane by increasing consumer demand through consumer education, promoting public purchasing policies, lobbying and boycotting large retailers. On the vertical scale, such organisations have provided resources and expertise to small producer organisations, as well as advocating for supportive public policy for FT from development agencies and related bodies. On the transversal scale, these organisations have worked with and pressured other SSE organisations (such as cooperative retailers or large northern credit unions) and public agencies to promote more integrated development strategies, which can support and complement FT production and exchange (Hutchens 2009; Reed et al. 2010).

Limits of FT as a vehicle for scaling the SSE

The certified FT movement is not composed entirely of SSE actors. In order to access markets and resources, small producers and northern SSE actors have decided at different times and under different circumstances that it is prudent, if not necessary, not to work exclusively with other SSE actors. Indeed, the transition from alternative trade to FT involved just such a decision. What followed from this decision was a greater role for non-SSE actors, and specifically large corporate bodies, in different features of the new FT network – from production to distribution and retail. This has been characterised as involving the emergence of different types of social economy and corporate value chains within FT (Reed 2009). This section explores how the increasingly dominant role of non-SSE actors in FT affects efforts to scale the SSE.

Heterogeneous production in FT Soon after the first FT labelling bodies were founded, the decision was made by some of them to certify production on estates for certain products, notably tea. When FLO was established in 1997, this decision was reaffirmed, and estate production has since expanded to include all but four products (coffee, cocoa, cotton and honey). While this decision was initially made to address market shortages, over time the extension of estate production has been seen as an important way of increasing FT sales, as it makes participation in FT much more attractive to large retailers, distributors and processors. But this has changed FT from an SSE form of production to a site of competition in which small producers again have to vie with large corporate actors. This restricts the horizontal scaling of SSE production, as small cooperatives confront the irony of having to compete against large corporations within the market that they created in order to overcome the unfair practices of these very actors (Coscione 2012; Reed et al. 2010).

Even in those products where SSE production is still required, there is a strong trade-off involved. In these markets, corporate participation may extend SSE production horizontally by contributing to increased sales, but this may happen at the expense of limited opportunities for vertical scaling. Corporate actors typically do not find it in their interests to share knowledge with small producers, while their perceived mandate to maximise profits leads them to shift as many costs as possible on to those producers. In addition, they do not generally encourage small producers to move up the value chain as this potentially leads to a loss in value-added for them (Renard 2010). These and related dynamics inhibit the prospects for transversal scaling as well.

Heterogeneous exchange in FT From its inception in 1988, FT has not exclusively required SSE exchange relations, as the goal has been largely to gain greater market share by accessing conventional distribution channels while still leaving most of the SSE value chain intact. Over time, however, corporate actors have become much more active in controlling the value chain, thereby altering the potential for scaling SSE activity within FT. There are two distinct cases of how corporate participation influences scaling.

The first involves the four product markets in which FLO still requires production by small producer organisations and where estate production is not certified. In these markets there is potential for horizontal scaling as corporate participation facilitates market growth, as has happened most notably with FT coffee. This scaling is limited only by the demand for FT products, and by the anti-competitive practices of large retailers. There would seem to be few possibilities for vertical scaling in these mixed value chains, however, as corporations have little or no incentive to promote or allow such activities by small producers. Corporations are very selective about sharing knowledge with small producers and promoting capacity-building. They will do this only insofar as it is necessary to increase product quality, reduce costs, improve reliability of delivery, or advance other goals. Typically, they do not want small producers engaged in more value-added processes, such as branding and marketing their own products, as this represents competition for them. Similarly, corporations do not support activities that facilitate transversal scaling (for example, product diversification by small producers) as they prefer producers to focus solely on improving product quality. Thus, when corporate actors are required to work with small producers, there is a trade-off involving scaling. While corporate participation may help to significantly scale production horizontally (bringing in more small producers and allowing small producers to sell more of their crop in the FT market), this may occur at the expense of opportunities for small producers to scale vertically and transversally. This trade-off is exacerbated by the extent to which corporate actors are able to squeeze out northern SSE actors who have typically been supportive of vertical and transversal scaling efforts by small producers (Reed et al. 2010; Renard 2010; Fridell 2007).

The second case involves the majority of FT markets (including bananas and tea) in which corporate actors do not have to work with small producers but have the option of sourcing from large estates. Under these conditions, there are increasingly fewer prospects for FT scaling SSE production, even horizontally. Large estates provide corporate actors with lower-cost structures, and, given that corporations have no extra reason to favour small producers (since produce from small producers and large estates is virtually indistinguishable to most consumers as it all bears the same label), they will favour production by large estates. Small producers are likely to be increasingly restricted to SSE retail and distribution channels unless some other form of intervention is introduced (Coscione 2012; Reed et al. 2010).

Heterogeneous advocacy among FT producers FT producer organisations within the FLO system vary in their composition. CLAC, the oldest of the associations, admits only democratically controlled small producer associations (SSE associations). In Asia, however, a decision was made when the producers' association was formed to also allow estate owners to be members. Similarly, in Africa, estate owners are allowed to be members of the producer association Fairtrade Africa; they are particularly prominent in South Africa in sectors such as wine.

The diversity of membership in producer associations reduces the range of issues on which they are likely to agree to collaborate. CLAC, for example, requires that FT production be undertaken by small producers in sectors where, historically, they have been dominant, and it actively promotes smallholder production in other sectors. It would be difficult to get consensus among the members of other producer associations on this issue, or agreement on measures that would promote such a vision (such as the small producers' label developed by CLAC). In terms of scaling FT, consensus is likely to be achieved among producer organisations only on methods that contribute to horizontal growth, and only if no limitations are placed on estate participation in FT.

Heterogeneous regulation in FT As noted above, while FT as a regulatory body focused exclusively on SSE production in its infancy, over time it has changed its mission to poverty eradication, with SSE production being instrumental to that cause. In this process, two parallel regulatory systems have emerged within FLO: 1) a system of minimum standards according to which corporations are regulated in their dealings with small producers and estates; and 2) a system based on fair trade principles, to which small producers and northern SSE actors aspire. A major problem with this arrangement is that the public is not easily able to differentiate between these two regulatory systems. By not agreeing to the use of different labels to distinguish the two systems, FLO has contributed to unfair competition within the FLO network (Coscione 2012). Small producers operate at a comparative disadvantage vis-à-vis large estates because their costs of production are typically higher for a variety of reasons, while large estates benefit from the image of small producers that is used to market FT. Northern SSE actors (especially those that deal exclusively in FT goods) who seek to support small producers are similarly at a disadvantage. Not only are they not large enough to enjoy the economies of scale of larger retailers, but, more importantly, they have a different business strategy in which they are trying to share value generated along the chain more fairly (Reed et al. 2010).[8]

The implications of these parallel regulatory systems within FLO for scaling the SSE, and the lack of emphasis on trade reform, are stark. On the one hand, estate production in FT limits the prospect of scaling horizontally as corporations will be inclined to source from estates since their costs are lower. This, in turn, undermines the possibility of scaling vertically and horizontally, as small producers are increasingly squeezed out. On the other hand, the cheaper cost structures of multilateral distributors and retailers (combined with greater access to consumer markets) also serve to squeeze out northern SSE actors who import, distribute and retail FR products, thereby limiting their ability to support vertical and transversal scaling by producer organisations.

Heterogeneous social movements in FT As previously mentioned, many organisations actively support FT, including a wide range of religious-based and secular social justice and development NGOs. Some such organisations tend to assume that promoting the FT label is unconditionally a good thing. They may adopt this approach because they do not understand how FT actually functions, because they are unaware of the negative impacts that corporate participation in FT can cause, or because they prioritise poverty reduction over the scaling of the SSE. Such misunderstandings have led to the increased participation of corporations in FT without any significant conditions being placed on them. This failure to impose greater restrictions on corporate participation in FT, it could be argued, has facilitated the degeneration of FT from an SSE movement to a corporate social responsibility practice – a practice that costs corporations relatively little, provides little to small producers, and does not support the scaling of SSE activity, but that offers corporations significant value in terms of public relations while undermining efforts that call for more radical change (Reed and Mukherjee-Reed 2012).

Conclusion

While many academics, policy-makers and practitioners would agree that scaling the SSE is a desirable, if not urgent, task, the nature and practical implications of this task will inevitably be contested. It necessarily involves questions of strategy that depend on experiential-based evaluations of specific conditions, and the balancing of what might be equally important priorities, such as the need to respond to the urgency of abject poverty versus the promotion of longer-term institutional and structural change. These issues of strategy and competing priorities arise in the SSE in relation to different approaches to scaling, and depend on the ways in which SSE actors engage with non-SSE actors to grow the SSE.

While it is not possible to decide such questions of strategy and priority in advance, the case of FT clearly indicates that SSE actors need their own spaces – apart from non-SSE actors – so that they can mobilise, organise, discuss, learn and strategise in arenas where unequal power relations, opposing value commitments and different life-world presuppositions are minimised. It is only out of such spaces that SSE actors can effectively engage with non-SSE actors, whose practices – intentionally or not – often restrict and undermine the growth of the SSE. This is not a new insight, having been incorporated into the practice of organisations such as Via Campesina, including the need to grow concentrically from small to larger SSE circles (Akram-Lodhi 2013). We see similar efforts in FT producer organisations, although these are not always consistent – particular contingencies and power relations constrain the ability to form such spaces in a systematic manner. The FT example illustrates both the need and the potential for SSE actors to collaborate across different types of spaces and organisations to grow the SSE – horizontally, vertically and transversally. While the gains made in FT have not been linear, are far outstripped by the need for further growth, and are under constant attack, they are nonetheless real and point to the forms of collaboration that are necessary to further scale the SSE.

6 | THE POTENTIAL AND LIMITS OF FARMERS' MARKETING GROUPS AS CATALYSTS FOR RURAL DEVELOPMENT

Roldan Muradian

Introduction

Coinciding with the growing interest in social and solidarity economy (SSE), more attention is being paid to agriculture and food within both policy and academic circles, particularly with regard to the fate of small-scale farmers who supply the bulk of food worldwide. This interest has been steered by a variety of factors, including recent spikes in the prices of several food commodities (Timmer 2010) and the realisation of the multiplier economic effects of growth in the agricultural sector, particularly in Africa (Wiggins et al. 2010). There has also been a revival of interest in farmers' collective action and its role in facilitating the market integration of smallholders, enhancing food security and promoting rural economic development. This has been partly in response to growing awareness that the implementation of liberalisation policies (associated with structural adjustment) in developing countries has not led to the expected results in the agricultural sector, and in many cases has even worsened the level of market participation of small-scale producers (Kydd and Dorward 2004). This policy outcome can be explained by the small scale and the unfavourable conditions of production (in terms of location, available infrastructure, etc.) often faced by smallholders, alongside high transaction costs when accessing inputs and technology or when delivering their produce to markets (due to difficulties in meeting standards, having access to efficient transportation or creating appropriate marketing links). In many places, the dismantling of governmental bodies in charge of, or providing support to, smallholders (no matter how inefficient they were) aggravated the incidence of such constraints. At the same time, the size of the average landholding has declined in several developing countries (Hazell et al. 2010).

Major trends in the development of agri-food systems have increased the need for coordination along the value chain, presenting further challenges for small-scale farmers. These include the growing importance of quality and other types of standards, as well as a higher level of market concentration in the downstream parts of value chains; this is particularly the case in the retailing sector, which is increasingly dominated by supermarkets worldwide (Reardon et al. 2009). These trends draw attention to improving coordination mechanisms among agents of the value chain. This is necessary in relation to policies and interventions that aim to enhance both the performance of the agricultural sector in developing countries – in particular through market integration of small-scale farmers (Kydd and Dorward 2004) – and the alignment between different actors or activities and product attributes.

Farmers' groups constitute one of the coordination mechanisms available to small-scale farmers. Farmers' organisations, and in particular marketing groups (either cooperatives or other collective endeavours), can coordinate actions both horizontally (among members) and also vertically (with other value chain agents). These organisations can reduce transaction costs by creating economies of scale for input supply, technological transfer or joint marketing, or by facilitating concerted action between farmers. They can also increase the bargaining power of smallholders vis-à-vis other value chain actors through joint supply systems or indirectly by means of increased local prices. Cooperatives and other types of collective marketing initiatives can thus be considered as transaction cost-reducing institutional settings (Staal et al. 1997).

Such groups have a long and often contested history. In a context of renewed interest in the role of collective action among farmers as a pathway to economic empowerment and rural development, it is instructive to review the lessons of the past. Collective action among farmers may take a variety of forms. This chapter focuses in particular on marketing arrangements, and examines the conditions under which such institutional arrangements can contribute to enhancing the level of market integration of small-scale farmers, and therefore can contribute to rural economic development. Based on a review of the literature, and focusing mainly on African examples, I explore the potential and limitations of farmers' groups in becoming catalysts for economic development in poor, rural areas.

The nature and impacts of agricultural cooperatives

Composed by autonomous members who are also owners, users and social actors, agricultural cooperatives are characterised by a particular set of organisational settings. First of all, from the organisational point of view they are firms; however, from a sociological perspective they are also a community of actors whose interests do not always align perfectly (Nilsson and Hendrikse 2010). Collective decision-making enables cooperatives to coordinate actions among members, which confers advantages on those members, notably in sectors dominated by smallholders. However, such decision-making structures also make them susceptible to a wide range of 'incentive problems' arising from conflicts between collective and individual goals (Borgen 2004). This makes cooperatives particularly complex organisations, whose performance depends on a variety of variables in four main domains: group characteristics (group size, composition, leadership); organisational structure (rules and decision-making); the types of products and markets in which they operate; and the external environment (policies, availability of public goods, etc.) (Makelova et al. 2009).

Understanding the factors that influence the performance of agricultural cooperatives and their capacity to be catalysts for rural economic development requires consideration of not only organisational elements but also of the dynamics of collective action (i.e. factors enabling groups to achieve common goals). The number of factors involved and the complexity of their interactions (in determining the performance of collective endeavours) make cooperatives: 1) prone to fail as business organisations (despite their evident advantages) due to internal conflicts; and 2) a very interesting and challenging subject for research and policy interventions.

In organisational studies, agricultural cooperatives are considered to be examples of hybrid organisations situated between hierarchical and market forms (Menard 2007). They are also reliant on social capital as a resource for the coordination of actions within the group and the creation of links between the group and other players. Social features usually associated with the broad term 'social capital' (trust, commitment, participation, reciprocity, social cohesion, social ties, loyalty) are assumed to be critical factors enabling cooperatives to cope with problems of incentives (Valentinov 2004). The process of building social capital is therefore a key aspect in the analysis of cooperative performance, and in designing interventions that aim to enhance their development impacts.

Several studies have shown that membership in marketing groups has a positive effect on the economic performance of rural households in developing countries. Bernard et al. (2008a) report that cooperative members in Ethiopia obtain better average prices for their products. However, they found that the effects of membership on commercialisation are mixed, depending on land size; in some cases, membership enhances commercialisation only among farmers with relatively larger farms. Francesconi and Heerink (2010) further explain these results by differentiating two main types of cooperatives in Ethiopia according to their orientation; i.e. towards either livelihoods or marketing. While livelihood cooperatives mainly provide inputs and common goods, marketing cooperatives are more market-oriented and are thus more effective in linking farmers to markets. Sizeable effects of membership on commercialisation are most commonly observed among marketing cooperatives. A key conclusion is that farmers' groups are very diverse, and therefore the specific organisational forms should be taken into consideration when conducting impact studies of membership.

Studying the effects of cooperative membership among dairy producers in Ethiopia, Francesconi and Ruben (2012) report that cooperative membership has had a positive effect on milk production and productivity, but a negative effect on fat and protein content. Genet and Anullo (2010) also show evidence of a positive effect of cooperative membership on total income and savings among farmers of the Sidama region in Ethiopia. However, they found no significant effects on household assets. Yang and Liu (2012) report similar results in China, where the presence of farmers' organisations is associated with higher levels of rural income at the local level. Furthermore, Abebaw and Haile (2013) found that cooperative membership in Ethiopia has a positive relationship with the level of use of fertilisers, which might be explained by the fact that Ethiopian cooperatives have a monopoly on the supply of (subsidised) fertilisers.

Wollni and Zeller (2007) have also found cooperative membership to impact positively on prices and participation in speciality markets among coffee growers in Costa Rica. Along the same lines, Mujawamariya et al. (2013) report that prices among cooperative members are higher and more stable among coffee producers in Rwanda. Members, however, still sell part of their production to private traders, due to credit services and the on-the-spot payments they provide. By contrast, cooperatives do not provide credit services, and they pay with some delay.

Although this is difficult to test empirically, cooperatives can also work as a 'competitive yardstick' at the local level. If they were not in place, local prices would likely be lower, suggesting indirect positive economic effects not only among members but also among non-members (Pascucci et al. 2012). Other reported effects of cooperative membership include innovation, the creation of marketing links (Devaux et al. 2009) and the emergence of new international market channels (with strict quality standards) in which small-scale farmers can participate (Roy and Thorat 2008). The benefits of collective marketing groups can also include non-economic development outcomes, such as increasing the level of female education among members' households (Gitter et al. 2012).

In order to assess the effects of farmers' marketing groups on rural development, it is important to first understand who are likely to be members of agricultural cooperatives, as well as considering the mechanisms through which changes in the performance of members are encouraged. Given the wide range of situations surrounding the emergence of cooperatives, it is difficult to generalise about what types of farmers join collective firms. While the empirical evidence on the determinants of cooperative membership is limited, one of the few emerging patterns is what has been coined the 'middle-class effect' (Bernard and Spielman 2009). Referring to Ethiopia and Tanzania, authors such as Bernard and Spielman (ibid.), Franc-esconi and Heerink (2010) and Fischer and Qaim (2012) have found that the likelihood of cooperative membership increases with land size, until a sort of threshold level is reached, after which the relationship between land size and membership is inversed. The consequence is that cooperatives tend not to serve the poorest of the poor (the smallest growers). In a similar vein, Fischer and Qaim (ibid.) and Abebaw and Haile (2013) report a non-linear relation-ship between the distance to the road and cooperative membership among farmers in Tanzania and Ethiopia respectively. As with the relationship between land size and membership, distance to the road is positively related to cooperative membership up to a threshold level, after which a negative relationship between both variables is seen. Therefore, farmers closer to the road are less likely to be members of cooperatives. Interestingly, Ruben and Heras (2012) found that coffee cooperatives located closer to the road showed comparatively lower levels of both performance and social capital in comparison with cooperatives located further away. They attributed these differences to farmers living further away from the road having a greater degree of dependency on coffee for their livelihoods (due to the lack of alternative sources of income, lower incidence of extra-community ties, and so on). Farmers located closer to the road definitively face lower marketing-related transaction costs.

This literature suggests that collective action is more likely to be effective at the intermediate levels of resources, assets or transaction costs. Such patterns might apply equally to farmers' marketing groups, to collective institutions for the management of common pool natural resources, and to collective action in general. For instance, Bardhan (1993) argues that community-based irrigation systems are more effective at the intermediate level of water scarcity. Thus, in the case of collective marketing firms in agriculture, we could formulate an 'intermediate transaction costs' hypothesis: collective marketing firms are more likely to emerge and to be effective when farmers face intermediate levels of transaction costs, such as those related to the type of product, the availability of public goods, and farmers' assets or resources. This hypothesis is based on the notion that collective action is costly, due to the time and resources needed for coordination among members and the risks involved. The benefits of collective action thus tend to offset its costs at intermediate levels of transaction costs. By contrast, when transaction costs are too high (due to small land size or long distances, for example), structural marketing transaction costs are also too high to be reduced significantly by collective action. At the other extreme of the spectrum (i.e. when land size is large and close to the road), the potential benefits of collective action in terms of reduced transaction costs tend not to compensate for the costs of that action, and thus individuals do not have enough incentive to engage in collective action.

From the perspective of transaction costs, the effectiveness of marketing groups is also influenced by the type of agricultural production in which farmers are engaged. The returns of collective action (in terms of reduced transaction costs) are expected to be higher for products that are perishable (fresh fruit and vegetables, dairy products, etc.) or 'high-value' (cash crops). For these products (with relative higher levels of asset specificity), there is more potential for opportunistic behaviour by buyers due to the lack of alternative transactions for suppliers. For instance, a milk processor can gain bargaining power from the fact that milk is perishable, which may imply that it would be difficult for suppliers to find alternative buyers (before the milk gets spoiled) if the milk is rejected. Transaction costs associated with marketing this type of product tend to be higher compared with those for products that can be stored and for which multiple buyers are available. Marketing groups are therefore less likely to deliver great advantages to farmers who specialise in the production of staple agricultural products with well-developed local markets (Levi and Davis 2008).

If marketing cooperatives and other forms of farmers' organisations can become effective catalysts for rural economic development, why are they not more widespread, particularly in poor rural areas of the world? Historically, the cooperative movement has faced many challenges, particularly in developing countries. For example, Holloway et al. (2000: 281), while acknowledging that cooperatives can play an important role in mitigating transaction costs, state that 'African cooperatives have had a generally unhappy history', which they attribute to difficulties around accountability, political interference and financial inefficiencies.

There is little consensus about the determinants of success among agricultural cooperatives in diverse contexts. What is clear, however, is that cooperatives face substantial challenges both in the managerial and the social domains. These can be characterised as structural 'tensions' between different goals or functions of cooperatives, coping with which is a key factor influencing cooperative performance, particularly economic. The following section summarises some of these tensions – understood here as conflicting goals or functions that may jeopardise the cooperative's performance, especially in the long term.

Structural tensions affecting agricultural cooperatives

Social versus business functions Trade-offs between social or developmental and marketing functions are well reported in the literature. Bernard and Taffesse (2012) argue that social programmes (such as the provision of consumption services, literacy training, HIV prevention and the provision of public infrastructure) among Ethiopian cooperatives increase farmers' participation, particularly where farmers have small (but not too small) land sizes. They report that membership among multipurpose cooperatives is nearly twice that of more specialised cooperatives (which, incidentally, also tend to attract members whose average land size is about 25 per cent larger than in other types of cooperatives). However, according to these authors, the implementation of social activities is achieved at the expense of economic performance. A larger and more heterogeneous membership, as well as the multipurpose nature of socially oriented cooperatives, increases internal coordination costs and represents considerable managerial challenges, without bringing further significant gains in reducing other marketing-related trans-action costs. This tension reflects a trade-off between performance and inclusion. Farmers with the smallest land sizes tend to be excluded from agricultural cooperatives since they face difficulties in meeting membership requirements; in addition, the costs of collective action probably offset its benefits among this type of farmer (Bernard and Spielman 2009).

These tensions reflect a key feature of collective firms: they often face trade-offs between equity and efficiency concerns (Bernard et al. 2008b). Equity concerns seem, nonetheless, to remain at the core of cooperatives. For instance, King et al. (2013: 165) argue that the 'cooperative movement is rooted in a social justice framework based on participatory democracy, distributional equity and solidarity'. Such values are fundamental for ensuring members' satisfaction and therefore their commitment to cooperative development. Dealing with the delicate balance between equity and efficiency seems therefore to be the fate of cooperatives.

Membership homogeneity and external links Members' homogeneity is expected to facilitate communication and the alignment of incentives, thus reducing coordination costs. However, homogeneous groups may encounter disadvantages in creating extra-group links, which are usually crucial for properly developing marketing functions. Bardham and Chetemi (2009) report that gender composition affects the performance of farmers' marketing groups. Having males within the group positively influences its marketing functions, which may be explained by the structure of male networks that normally involve more external ties (i.e. outside the group).

Coordination costs and economies of scale The creation of economies of scale is one of the key mechanisms through which farmers' groups can enhance the collective bargaining power of small-scale producers. The scale of operations is a key source of countervailing power in farmers' groups vis-à-vis other agents in the value chain, which is one of the key raisons d'être of cooperatives (Valentinov 2007). From this point of view, increasing the group's size is a reasonable strategy to follow. But the cost of coordinating actions among members also increases with group size. Larger groups require a higher level of delegation of management tasks to the board of directors or the managers, increasing the probability of principal-agent problems (Levi and Davis 2008). There may be misalignment of incentives between managers and members. Such problems occur more often if there is a considerable educational gap between members and managers, as is often the case in cooperatives operating in poor rural areas in developing countries. This explains why, in some circumstances, smaller groups perform better than larger ones despite having lower bargaining power (Chagwiza et al. 2013). The trade-off between economies of scale and coordination costs suggests that there is probably an 'optimal', intermediate level of group size. The actual size would depend on a variety of factors, such as members' heterogeneity, types of product, decision-making structure and the level of social capital among members. Place et al. (2004) have found evidence supporting this hypothesis. They show that medium-sized groups of Kenyan farmers showed a higher level of performance compared with the smallest and largest groups.

External support and autonomy After reviewing collective arrangements for integrating small-scale farmers into agricultural markets in Eastern and Southern Africa, Poole and de Frece (2010: 10) conclude that 'most successful cases of collective enterprise creation have depended on a substantial degree of intervention from Non-Governmental Organisations (NGOs) and international donors'. External agents can facilitate the acquisition of managerial and technological skills, as well as cover the initial high transaction costs involved in the creation of farmers' groups. High set-up costs are a major barrier for the establishment of cooperatives. In addition, the recent boom in agricultural cooperatives in China shows that a favourable policy environment might be very effective in promoting cooperative development (Deng et al. 2010). However, external interference (particularly by the state) has been identified as one of the main reasons why cooperatives fail (Lalvani 2008; Wanyama et al. 2009). The existence of internally crafted rules has been singled out as a key factor determining the success of collective action in general, and agricultural cooperatives in particular (Levi and Davis 2008). The challenge then is to find the right balance between external support and enough autonomy in cooperative development.

Meeting standards and satisfying members As described above, current trends in agri-food value chains make production and product standards important factors in conditioning the market integration of (small-scale) farmers. In sectors dominated by small-holders and where standards play an important role in shaping relations along the value chain, the ability to coordinate horizontally among farmers can confer significant competitive advantages on cooperatives and other collective enterprises (Weatherspoon and Reardon 2003). Several studies have shown positive synergies between certification schemes and collective action (Kersting and Wollni 2012; Pérez-Ramírez et al. 2012; Roy and Thorat 2008) in terms of facilitating market integration and ensuring better prices for small-scale farmers. Nonetheless, meeting strict standards normally entails conflicts with those members who are not able to deliver products according to the specifications. Firstly, vulnerable farmers might exert their rights to influence managerial decisions through a democratic decision-making structure, undermining the standard-setting process. Secondly, exclusion of some members can induce lower levels of trust between members and managers and therefore lower levels of members' commitment and sense of group identification, which would negatively affect the cooperative's performance (Hernandez-Espallardo et al. 2013; Nilsson et al. 2012). In general, members attach strong importance to participation in the cooperative's democratic governance system (Ortiz-Miranda et al. 2010). Higher standards are, however, often achieved through more hierarchical decision-making structures, at the expense of democratic decisions (Bijman et al. 2011). These dilemmas are specific to cooperatives, due to the fact that the owners are also the providers. Hence, meeting quality and other standards in highly coordinated value chains might constitute a significant management challenge for agricultural cooperatives. Indeed, Poulton et al. (2010) argue that the complexity of cooperatives' decision-making structure may be a burden when it comes to responding quickly to changes in buyers' requirements.

Multiple functions Agricultural cooperatives seem to face significant difficulties in maximising the performance of several functions at the same time. Gaps between different functions are probably more likely in marketing groups at early stages of development (for example, in cooperatives that are not yet well consolidated). For instance, Bernard et al. (2008b) point out that market-oriented farmers' organisations in Senegal and Burkina Faso are relatively good at providing information and advice to their members but are relatively weak in facilitating access to financial services, materials and infrastructure investment. Furthermore, Bernard et al. (2008a) and Francesconi and Heerink (2010) show that, overall, cooperatives in Ethiopia can offer better prices, but have a limited capacity to enhance the level of market integration (commercialisation), particularly among the smallest farmers. On the other hand, Fischer and Qaim (2012) report that marketing groups increase the level of commercialisation and income among banana growers in Tanzania, but that the effects on prices are very modest. Mujawamariya et al. (2013) found that coffee cooperatives in Rwanda ensure higher and more stable prices (in comparison with private coffee traders). However, they were not able to pay on the spot or offer credit, which explains why farmers still deliver an important share of their production to traders (who are able to provide these services). These examples indicate the difficulties cooperatives face in maximising the delivery of different services at the same time, which might undermine members' commitment and the performance of cooperatives in the long run.

Coping with tensions in farmers' organisations

The need to deal with the wide variety of tensions outlined above seems to be a particular feature of farmers' marketing groups. These tensions are particularly acute during the early phases of cooperative development, when resources are scarce and managerial capacities are still not well advanced. The incidence of these tensions explains why cooperatives are not widespread, despite their high potential to contribute to the economic development of small-scale farmers who dominate the supply of agricultural products in most parts of the world. The performance of the marketing function of agricultural cooperatives and other collective firms formed by farmers depends to a large extent on how managers, directors and members cope with the tensions described above. Dealing with such tensions constitutes a major managerial and organisational challenge, as their resolution is extremely context-dependent.

The capacity of farmers' marketing groups to address structural tensions can be strengthened through interventions and external support, including a favourable policy environment. Bingen et al. (2003) distinguish three broad types of intervention for increasing small farmers' opportunities to benefit from market participation, depending on their focus: 1) contracting and marketing (creating links with external agents); 2) knowledge transfer (technology mobilisation); and 3) managerial skills and social capital. These three broad areas of action can be summarised as marketing, know-how and capabilities.

A major challenge for cooperatives is that these three domains of action are interdependent and must be addressed together. For instance, the set-up of marketing cooperatives needs considerable investment in social capital (the third type of intervention). However, a key success factor in early stages of collective action is that farmers have clear and significant incentives to cooperate, which normally requires adding value to agricultural products through both technological upgrade (know-how) and alternative marketing channels (external links). Directors and managers therefore need to assess carefully how best to allocate scarce human and financial resources to strengthen these three domains in a complementary way, at the same time. There is not an a priori order or pattern of interventions that managers can follow as a blueprint. The most efficient allocation depends on the collective enterprise's specific combination of factors (endowment) and needs. The evaluation of such endowment and conditions, as well as the design of appropriate responses, constitutes an additional managerial challenge for agricultural cooperatives.

Conclusion

Existing research into the impacts of marketing cooperatives and other collective organisational forms that connect small-scale farmers to markets shows that these organisations have great potential as catalysts for rural economic development. However, as this chapter has indicated, farmers' marketing groups typically face a variety of tensions, particularly during their early stages of development and when operating in poor rural areas. These tensions, which relate to the cooperative organisational form, create significant limitations. Agricultural cooperatives are thus organisations with both the significant potential to foster economic development in poor rural areas of the world and significant limitations to doing so.

Marketing farmers' groups are more effective in facilitating significant developmental effects when farmers engage in agricultural markets with intermediate levels of transaction costs. This is more likely to occur with medium-sized landholdings, perishable and high-value (cash) crops, and intermediate access to public goods (for example infrastructure) by farmers.

There is no prescriptive sequence of interventions to strengthen farmers' marketing groups, particularly at the early stages of their development, since the three main domains of action (marketing, know-how and capabilities) are interdependent. Cooperatives face the major managerial and organisational challenges, which require specific skills, of coping with the wide range of tensions outlined above, assessing the current endowment of the organisation, and designing responses to encourage further development.

In conclusion, collective firms, despite their high potential contribution to rural development within the framework of the SSE, are particularly difficult to manage and to support. This explains why, from a historical perspective, their success is so elusive. Overall, cooperative promotion (through externally funded interventions or state policies) seems to be a particularly daunting task, but one worth undertaking. Furthermore, the evidence available to support the design of such interventions is still very limited. As Obern and

Jones (1981: 345) stated thirty years ago, 'the literature provides little evidence about the factors that are determinants in the success or failure of cooperatives'. Unfortunately, we continue to have limited knowledge about which conditions make collective action among farmers both feasible and effective today. This calls for allocating more resources and research efforts to fill this important knowledge gap.

7 | INSTITUTIONALISING THE SOCIAL AND SOLIDARITY ECONOMY IN LATIN AMERICA[1]

José Luis Coraggio

Introduction

This chapter examines an aspect of the institutionalisation of social and solidarity economy (SSE) in Latin America that relates to the emergence and significance of specific legal and political-administrative forms of SSE. As will become evident, these innovations may be a bottom-up phenomenon involving formal adaptations to new practices and demands generated by society, or a top-down process entailing policy measures instituted by the state as a framework for economic behaviour.

Structural conditions, which reflect a long history of dependence, combined with the neoliberal policies of the last three decades have resulted in massive numbers of poor and indigent people in Latin America (both rural and urban, totalling approximately 180 million), along with the highest level of wealth concentration in the world. In light of this situation, a new SSE must go beyond identifying specific community service needs that are not being addressed by either the market or the state. One cannot expect that there is a critical mass of citizens with sufficient social capital and economic security to assume responsibility for ensuring that their own needs – or the needs of others – are met at the local level. There is a lack of material resources to provide basic necessities and highly unequal access to scientific and technical training. Furthermore, there is a pervasive middle-class stigmatisation of the poor, which hinders the organic development of symmetrical relationships and a sense of solidarity across the social spectrum.

Moreover, paradoxically, current favourable circumstances in the region may weaken the political will to bring about lasting structural changes in the economy. Positive trends in export prices, along with increases in internationally generated state revenues, are providing resources to underwrite massive compensatory social programmes, thus creating a modicum of relief during the present social crisis, the most acute in recent memory. But such a reduction of social suffering can be reversed with further eruptions of the latent crisis in the world economy and/or the political correlation of forces both nationally and globally. In any case, it is not enough to change the economy into a dynamic, self-reproducing social and solidarity system. We need the state (a democratic state with a different relationship to society) and also local and global socio-economic actors to put in place a strong process of profound and sustainable economic transformation in line with SSE values and practices.

The World Social Forum (WSF), inaugurated in Porto Alegre in 2001 as a coalition of social movements opposed to the Davos-centred globalisation scheme, appears to be losing traction due to the difficulties, at both national and international levels, of formulating proposals and forging agreements for concrete political action. Discussion of the solidarity economy was one of the issues that brought together a range of social movements, and these conceptual threads and common concerns retain their relevance and continue to develop, representing a critique of the capitalist economy at the periphery. However, any convergence of these various currents – exemplified in the opposition to the Free Trade Area of the Americas – is a slow process. In addition to the challenges of convergence, proposals for economic change must grapple with the tension between a desire to move beyond the current system and the sectoral demands that arise within that system. As a result, SSE is given different meanings and assigned different priorities by the various movements and individual groups. Therefore, conceptual debate and clarification are needed.

Nevertheless, throughout the past decade, the force of major social movements (in Ecuador and Bolivia), spontaneous collective efforts in response to specific crises (Argentina and Venezuela) and an increased focus by the popular electorate on 'progressive' projects (Brazil, Uruguay and Paraguay) have brought about political changes formalised by broad electoral endorsement. These developments have resulted in a number of changes, as outlined below.

- Governments have adopted more national and popular[2] approaches.
- There has been increased impetus for implementing new public programmes and policies that favour the majority population.

- Nearly all of the countries in question have formally institutionalised SSE by adopting new legal frameworks that recognise SSE principles, establish new state responsibilities and/or modify existing constitutional frameworks.
- A system of specific virtual social networks has been expanded, providing synergy to the processes of socio-economic innovation, particularly with regard to SSE.

Thus, in the course of one decade, significant changes in institutional formats have emerged, though with major differences from one country to another. For example, while legal changes in Argentina and Brazil consist of minor adjustments to already existing frameworks, Brazil has implemented institutional practices to formalise SSE-based policies. In Bolivia and Ecuador, formal changes of major scope have been proposed; although these changes will require lengthy transition periods, they are firmly based on a recognised history of social movements' resistance and the struggle for economic survival. Proposals for significant change are also being advanced in Venezuela; these, however, are idealistic in nature, and will require not only extensive resources but also cultural change.

The following section analyses the nature of institutional and policy changes now occurring in three countries: Argentina, Brazil and Ecuador. It then goes on to identify key variations in approach, using these and other cases as points of reference, and concludes with reflections on the possibilities and challenges of expanding and consolidating SSE in Latin America.

Three countries, three processes

Argentina: a populist social economy policy The Argentine case represents a populist-style approach based on a massive but unstructured mobilisation – from within the state – of people and resources. Its legitimacy is based on its efficacy in solving or alleviating pressing problems in the daily lives of majority populations. Rather than creating a society organised in autonomous, solidarity-based groups capable of creating public spaces for the co-construction of state policy, populism leaves room for a society that, while socially disorganised, can be guided en masse towards specific political goals. This inherent tension can be seen in the relationship between grassroots organisations and the populist party. Ready access to state resources can lead to anomie – and a tendency towards disorganisation – or to passive support for heteronomous political projects.

Policies are conceived from within the governing party or by government officials, in an attempt to: 1) represent and address the immediate desires of the popular sectors; 2) solve problems of governance; and 3) consolidate and maintain an electoral mass that can be manipulated. While there is no co-construction of policy, there is increased participation as a result of the decentralisation of execution, due in part to the bureaucracy's inability to implement programmes on a massive scale. With the new government of 2003, and with a reliance on the self-regulating market showing no sign of ending the employment crisis, social policy has undergone a deliberative change that is designed to incorporate, in a lasting way, so-called 'social economy policy' – an approach that, at its core, consists of promoting mercantile enterprises, albeit enterprises run by workers' associations.[3] A social economy-based sectoral social policy is being institutionalised, focusing on the poor segments of the population and on those facing employment problems, and including efforts to incorporate these workers into the labour market. On a symbolic level, there have been explicit changes in the language being used (for example, referring to 'beneficiaries' as 'rights holders'). At the same time, the Ministry of Labour's progressive labour policies continue to occupy centre stage. These include wage readjustments, restoration of workers' rights (collective bargaining, in particular) and pressure to formalise work, along with family policies involving allocations for children, an expansion of social security and other measures. This approach is seen as the reaffirmation of an orderly model of capitalist development, with a state dedicated to achieving social cohesion. It is not, however, a scheme that provides the means of instituting a new economic perspective, one capable of fostering what could be termed an SSE (for more on this, see Coraggio 2011).

In August 2003, the government shifted the orientation of its social policy, implementing the National Plan for Local Development and Social Economy, 'Manos a la Obra' ('Let's Get to Work'). In addition to its focus on assistance, the plan was designed to promote social inclusion through socio-productive (i.e. inclusive and income-generating) projects involving partnership-based, worker-managed enterprises of five or more individuals. The plan was in part an attempt to deal with pressure from the church and others concerned about the effect of income-transfer policies on the 'work culture'. Given the evident failure of income-transfer and training programmes to promote sustainable income-generating activities, a fund (financed by the World Bank and the Inter-American Development-ment Bank) was created to convert investment resources to non-reimbursable loans for projects with prospects of sustainability.

The plan was expressly aimed at supporting:

- sole proprietor, family, partnership-based and/or community enterprises involving production and/or services;
- the creation of solidarity funds;
- strengthening of cooperatives and mutuals;
- enhancement of spaces for promoting partnerships, consultative boards and civil society organisations;
- training for provincial and municipal technical teams;
- technical assistance and training for beneficiaries to assist them in formulating and executing projects.

The massive scale of the undertaking (with a potential audience of 1.8 million beneficiaries), along with the prospect of a prolonged crisis and the difficulties in rapidly developing the capacities needed for a worker-managed scheme, led to the gradual institutionalisation of an ongoing social economy policy. This policy is officially considered part of economic policy, although in organisational terms it remains under the direction of the Ministry of Social Development.

Numerous policies, laws and institutional reforms have been adopted that aim to formalise the informal economy and provide technical, financial and social assistance to cooperatives, micro-enterprises and population segments associated with SSE. Examples of this process include the following:

- The Secretariat of Social Economy and Local Development (now known as the Secretariat of Social Economy) was created within the Ministry of Social Development), while the National Institute of Cooperatives and Social Economy (Instituto Nacional de Asociativismo y Economía Social or INAES) was incorporated by the Ministry of Social Development. The latter is charged with overseeing legislation and monitoring and promoting the social economy, mainly with regard to cooperatives and mutuals.
- In 2004, the National Registry of 'Agents' of Local Development

and Social Economy was created as a means of registering individual social micro-entrepreneurs. To date, 350,000 individuals have been registered.

- The 2004 administrative decided to reduce the use of monetary (cash or cheque) transfers of subsidies, replacing them with the widespread use of magnetic debit cards. In 2006, law 26.117 ('Promotion of microcredit for development of the social economy') was passed, and the National Commission for Microfinance (CONAMI) was established within the Ministry of Social Development, with an annual budget of US$25 million.
- Coverage by the National Institute of Farm Technology's Pro-Huerta programme and the Ministry of Agriculture's Social Farm Programme was rapidly increased in the wake of the 2001 crisis – a policy that has extended through the 'capillaries' of the national territory and, in 2007, was incorporated in the country's social economy development policy, after extensive deliberation (see Cittadini et al. 2010).
- The Ministry of Labour's Industrial Technology Institute oversees training and counselling programmes for new worker-managed enterprises, including firms rescued from financial failure by their workers. (New 'rescues', however, are not being encouraged.)
- As of 2006, the Ministry of Education has been supporting the creation of technical degree programmes in social economy and local development. Since then, more than a dozen provinces have launched such programmes for training technical workers.
- In 2009, law 26.355/2009 (the 'Collective brand' law), designed to 'improve the market visibility and sales capacity of clusters of economic units', entered into force.
- In June 2011, modifications to the Bankruptcy Act were implemented, giving workers in 'rescued' firms priority in obtaining loans and help in maintaining continuity of production. The law is intended to help some 300 firms affected by the 2001 crisis to formally establish themselves as cooperatives, while also opening up this option for an additional 3,000 firms that employ approximately 200,000 workers and that are currently undergoing bankruptcy proceedings.
- The recently initiated programme Argentina Trabaja is designed to help integrate up to 100,000 unemployed workers in new labour cooperatives, which each employ some fifty to sixty workers. The

target population for this programme consists of indigent – and, generally, unskilled – workers. The programme establishes a fund to cover wages and materials for a limited period of time.

Such programmes view the social economy not as an alternative to firms funded by private capital or public funds, but rather as a supplement – an option to compensate, at least in part, for the ineffectiveness of these firms' policies on investment and job creation.

All of these programmes have encountered problems, due to the state's lack of implementation capacity. They have therefore looked to a range of different stakeholders for assistance – municipal governments, non-governmental organisations (NGOs), universities, and so on – to serve as intermediaries in dealing with policies and funding. Official discourse indicates that territorial integration of these initiatives is a high priority. To this end, various entities have been created to foster local participation, although the results of these efforts have fallen short of enabling true local co-management. A central problem in this endeavour is a lack of will among municipal governments, which are reluctant to open up opportunities for local members of social collectives whose participation has been brought about through national policy. Nevertheless, sub-national governments have positioned themselves, if only for vote-getting purposes, as the discretionary mediators of national resources.

Another important element is the fact that the agenda of one of the two workers' unions – the Confederation of Workers of Argentina (Central de Trabajadores de Argentina or CTA) – now includes a demand for self-managed workers to gain official legal status, an element that is vital in institutionalising the social economy. This goal, however, has yet to be realised.

Finally, it is apparent that a wide range of major experiments in the area of SSE are taking place in Argentina. However, these experiments lack a systematic approach[4] and have not coalesced into an autonomous movement, similar to the one in Brazil. These circumstances militate against such experiments gaining visibility, and – even more importantly – against the possibility of formulating a strategy for constructing an alternative economy.

Brazil: an experiment in the co-construction of public SSE policies[5] While the state discourse in Argentina speaks of a 'social economy', citing the imperative of state-led social protection in times of acute economic crisis, the Brazilian discourse refers to a 'solidarity economy' (Economia Solidária or ECOSOL). This terminology reflects the strong advocacy role that grass-roots organisations have played. It was also used to designate the governmental National Secretariat of Solidarity Economy (SENAES), established in 2003 under the new government of Lula da Silva.

Policy documents of the Brazilian state regard the ECOSOL as a means of addressing unemployment, in preference to the 'structural' option of 'Another Economy' popularised by the World Social Forum. While the ECOSOL approach is broader than the structural option, there is limited scope within this scheme for collective action, which in practice is confined to worker-managed enterprises; the role of public policy is to support, disseminate and provide a framework for these enterprises.

Distinctive to the Brazilian case is the pre-existence of an ECOSOL movement, institutionalised as the Brazilian Forum for Economic Solidarity (FBES). Currently, the FBES consists of three stakeholders: economic solidarity entrepreneurs, civil society promoters and public managers. The FBES originated from the WSF in 2001, and it played a major role in creating SENAES, headed by Paul Singer. FBES activities were dedicated in large part to helping design and monitor implementation of the state's ECOSOL policies. The plan addressed demands for funding worker-managed associations and for the creation of a legal framework for them. The Central Workers' Union (Central Única dos Trabalhadores or CUT), controlled by the Workers' Party (Partido dos Trabalhadores or PT), called on the country's universities to support the ECOSOL enterprises. This led to the formation of Unitrabalho, a network of eighty universities committed to assisting in the creation of ECOSOL enterprises, particularly through the establishment of incubators that provided educational support and training. CUT subsequently supported the formation of productive chains that included ECOSOL as an integral link.

Both SENAES and the FBES have shown a commitment to decentralisation, with an emphasis on creating local and state entities closely linked to national institutions. Institutions within Brazil's states and municipalities, which have closer ties with the target population than do national institutions, have tended to view these programmes as short term and assistance-oriented (Hintze 2011). However, SENAES's stated approach reaches beyond compensatory social policy, proposing that solidarity economy be seen as an alternative means of organising economic processes. In November 2010, shortly before the end of its term and in response to the demands of the second National Conference on the Evaluation of Higher Education (Comissão Nacional de Avaliação da Educação Superior or CONAES), the Lula government created the National System of Fair Trade and Solidarity (Sistema Nacional de Comércio Justo e Solidário).

Public programmes have also shown a commitment to the concept of a horizontal ECOSOL policy, with attempts to link the actions of the different ministries to work together effectively in promoting ECOSOL. Despite these advances, the prospect of a national government initiative to establish ECOSOL as a mainstream policy – and of acceding to the FBES's demand to create a Ministry of Solidarity Economy – remains remote. Obstacles to enacting solidarity economy legislation reflect the state's reluctance to pursue this course as an alternative form of development.

The close relationship between the state and civil society poses a variety of difficult challenges. While there has been a 'bureaucratisation' of the movement – an apparently inevitable development, given the ultimate aim of co-construction – the common origins of ECOSOL organisations and the PT leave such an institutionalisation vulnerable to the possibilities of the PT being supplanted in the government by another party or by an off-shoot movement within the PT. This type of scenario affected the participatory budget process that emerged in the wake of the PT's political success in Porto Alegre. Over the following decade, the party's power declined, eventually resulting in electoral defeat. A similar situation occurred at the national level when the new PT government, under President Dilma Rousseff, sent congress a proposal (on 31 March 2011) in which SENAES and the Solidarity Economy National Council (Conselho Nacional de Economia Solidária or CNES) would be subsumed within the Secretariat of Small and Micro Enterprises – a move that some interpreted as a regressive measure. A concerted mobilisation opposing the plan succeed in scuttling the proposal, which failed to gain broad public support.

As in Argentina, current policy gives little support to the concept of 'Another Economy'. For instance, in Brazil, any SSE proposal at the national level must address a major problem: the inequitable distribution of farmland. Over 100,000 families currently live as squatters awaiting allocations of land. Although 500,000 families have been settled, data from the Landless Workers Movement (Movimento dos Trabalhadores Rurais Sem Terra or MST) indicates that over 4 million Brazilian families are landless. The movement states that there has in fact been an increase in the concentration of landholding under the PT government. The current reality is that there is a lack of political will to bring about an institutional change in the relationship between the unrestricted right to private property and the right to life on the part of the dispossessed.

Ecuador: towards a social and solidarity economy system (Buen Vivir) In the recent past, three of Ecuador's elected presidents have been removed from office by major social movements, which held them to account for failures to fulfil their campaign promises. The year 2006 ushered in the election of the current president, Rafael Correa of the Alianza País party, who convened a constituent assembly to rewrite the country's constitution, in continual consultation with the country's major sectors and social movements.

The new constitution gives formal recognition to various alternative means of organising economic production, establishing as legitimate forms of enterprise public, private, mixed, family, domestic, autonomous, community, associative and cooperative entities. The latter six of these (i.e. excluding public, private and mixed) constitute the popular economy, while the last three are defined as the popular and solidarity economy.

The National Institute of Popular and Solidarity Economy (Instituto Nacional de Economía Popular y Solidaria or IEPS) has been established within the Ministry of Economic and Social Inclusion (Ministerio de Inclusión Económica y Social or MIES), and, after three years of debate, the Popular and Solidarity Economy Act was promulgated in 2011. The National Plan for Living Well (Plan Nacional del Buen Vivir) gives recognition to the IEPS and creates participatory mechanisms for formulating public policies. To date, however, there has been no substantive progress on establishing such mechanisms, due to the resistance of inherited institutions ranging from state bureaucracy to the political culture of social organisations critical of the state.

Article 283 of the constitution of the republic establishes that 'the economic system is social and solidarity-based, and is composed of public, private, mixed, popular and solidarity-based forms of economic organisation, as well as any others that the constitution designates', adding that 'the popular and solidarity economy shall be regulated by legislation and shall include the cooperative, associative, and community sectors'. Given that the Popular and Solidarity Economy Act may be the most highly developed legal institutionalisation of SSE in the region, it will be given a more detailed treatment below.

The law describes the goal of popular-economy organisations as that of:

> meeting needs and generating income on the basis or relationships of solidarity, cooperation and reciprocity, placing a high value on work, while regarding the human being as the subject and end of such activity, seeking, as a goal, living well and in harmony with nature, rather than appropriation, profit and the accumulation of capital.

The law goes on to define the conditions for its legal application to the organisations that it promotes and regulates, stating that they must: 1) seek to achieve the goal of living well and serve the common good; 2) favour labour over capital, and collective over individual interests; 3) encourage fair trade and ethical, responsible consumption; 4) promote gender equity; 5) respect cultural identity; 6) emphasise worker management; 7) manifest social and environmental responsibility, solidarity and accountability; and 8) carry out fair and solidarity-based distribution of profits.

It further establishes that the popular and solidarity economy is composed of associations, cooperatives and communities, as cited earlier, adding that 'popular economic units' (Unidades Económicas Populares or UEPs) – popular-economy organisations that are not necessarily formal or solidarity-based – must be accorded formal legal status, with simplified procedures to facilitate their registration.

More precisely, UEPs are defined as organisations:

> dedicated to the citizen economy: individual, family and domestic

enterprises, retail merchants and artisan shops that engage in economic activities or production, or that market goods and provide
services in a manner that promotes associative partnerships and
solidarity.

Another feature of this law is that, along with UEPs and communities, it includes cooperatives and associations of all sizes –
specifically, the financial cooperative sector, which battled to stay
within the banking sector and thus remain beyond the reach of
the law. The law creates new institutions to ensure the flow of
funds to the solidarity-based financial system, while establishing a
scheme for liquidity funds and deposit insurance, in order to give
these institutions the ability to compete with the banking system in
attracting deposits, while providing, at the same time, regulation to
cover the country's proliferating microcredit initiatives.

The new Ecuadorian constitution encompasses highly significant
changes in the relationship between the economy and nature. It not
only provides for the rational use of 'natural resources' but also
changes the rules for exploiting them (for example, water cannot be
privatised), and, for what appears to be the first time in legislative
history, it incorporates the rights of nature.

It is clear, based on the repercussions emanating from the extensive process of defining these changes, that institutionalising new
forms of the solidarity economy will confront powerful contrary
forces and interests. Success in this regard will require not only
a major social undertaking, but also the strong participation of
politically oriented organisations.

The reality and prospects of SSE: a comparative perspective

In describing SSE, it is important to focus not only on its internal
features, but also on its links with other sectors of the economy.
There are numerous ways of defining the starting point for empirical
economies. One, albeit incomplete, is that of a mixed economy that
encompasses more than the two sectors on which models of the
1960s were based – namely, the state and the market, representing
the public economy and the private sector economy. Reality demands
that the popular economy is finally recognised as a fundamental part
of the region's economies; this, in turn, implies a mixed economy
comprised of three sectors (see Figure 7.1), with a multiplicity of

interacting relationships within them, and between these and the rest of the world.

The three-sector scheme takes different forms in the various countries of the region – a region in which there has been significant progress in expanding the reach of SSE. Considering not only the three cases described above, but also those of Bolivia and Venezuela, a number of distinguishing features stand out. Brazil has a robust business sector, which receives strong institutional support through state resources and co-constructed policies, and also has partially co-constructed policies designed to foster a solidarity economy based on associative microenterprises. In the case of Venezuela, where the country is highly dependent on imports to meet its basic needs, the public economy plays a major role in the extraction of state-owned oil, profits from which are redirected to create an organic popular economy in which the people or workers have greater control over productive activity. In Argentina, where a process of de-industrialisation has taken place since the 1970s, the public economy receives a portion of the profits from agriculture; these earnings are used for monetary transfers and to subsidise poverty reduction programmes. The land erosion resulting from this emphasis on short-term competitive agricultural production had, and will continue to have, serious effects on the country's ecosystems. Bolivia and Ecuador, for their part, are highly dependent on imports. In these countries, the popular economy sector historically has played an important role in rural and indigenous communities, which are now confronted with the dilemma of dealing with national mandates to respect nature.

All of the countries cited above exhibit trends towards a 'return of the state': that is, a growth of the public economy, accompanied by major state efforts to redistribute wealth from the business sector to the popular economy. Bolivia, Ecuador and Venezuela have seen broad mobilisations organised around movements of stakeholders in the popular economy – both men and women – advocating for structural change. The positions adopted by these movements do not call for a variation in the mixed economy structure, but rather a change in the state's regulatory and redistributive role and in the relative weight of the three sectors, with greater priority being given to the popular and solidarity economy. The diagram below attempts to identify where, in this scheme, the solidarity economy resides.

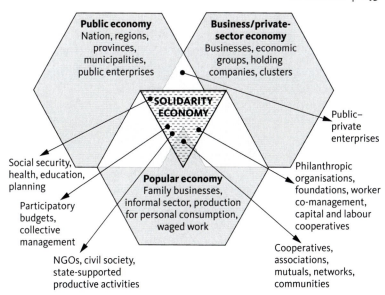

7.1 The solidarity economy within the mixed economy

Here, the scope of the solidarity economy is not limited to associative organisations (i.e. organisations that operate on the basis of *internal* solidarity) within the popular economy, but also includes the state. In this respect, the role of the state consists principally of implementing the principle of redistribution (of income, public goods and means of production), while also serving as a guarantor of social rights and leading the effort to build a sustainable economic system capable of supporting a fully integrated, unified and just society. While the concept that there is a portion of the business sector that has solidarity features is problematic, such businesses can exist; indeed, some are seeking greater solidarity by expanding their philanthropic efforts, either directly or through foundations and NGOs.

The above diagram suggests that, while Argentina and Brazil are working to form associative and worker-managed organisations in the popular economy – particularly in excluded sectors – Venezuela's efforts are aimed at creating cooperative, community, popular, mixed and family enterprises, under the rubric of 'social production enterprises'. Such enterprises are not necessarily created by the poorest segment of the population; some are formed through local community initiatives, others as a result of transforming public or private enterprises to suit the desired scheme, which may include a hybrid form of public/community enterprise. In Ecuador, although the *mixed-economy system as a whole* is to be social and solidarity-based, the constitution stipulates that priority should be given to developing solidarity-based forms from *within* the popular economy, which is not intrinsically based on solidarity. Lastly, Bolivia's stated goal is to establish a plural economy, giving special weight to the community economy, which is part of the popular economy.[6]

Despite the heterogeneity of the various countries and processes, a number of the region's countries are working to redefine what 'an economy' means, leaving room for recognising and publicly promoting an SSE sector, or for restructuring the overall system as an SSE. This trend is in line with shifting political currents that point towards a popular orientation – a trend, however, that is in conflict with neo-developmentalist (or, more broadly, neo-economic) currents of thought.

Although there continues to be a wealth of options available for consideration, certain generalisations can be posited, using the Latin American experience as a basis, regarding the relationship between the dynamic process of developing new economic forms and efforts to institutionalise SSE.

The changes adopted in the social, economic and political realms can be interpreted as part of a Polanyian movement of self-defence by societies confronting the devastating neoliberal programme of the previous three decades. They include the restitution of welfare policies as well as the institution of new forms of state intervention addressing the social economy. Of major importance has been the emergence of ambitious SSE projects involving a structural change in the behaviour of public and private actors, with a corresponding change in a wide range of economic institutions. In some cases, these innovations have failed to obtain all the expected results, given the massive scale on which they are attempted (in Venezuela, for example). In other cases they have become operational after a medium-term process of participation by the state and other concerned stakeholders within the society (Ecuador). In any case, despite decisions reflected in new laws, including those at the constitutional level, the measures are not without a degree of vulnerability, given that they are being implemented in an environment of social conflict, and, being political in nature, are exposed to the vicissitudes of the political scene. There is much to learn from these processes.

One novelty that Latin America brings to the table is an intensity and continuity in spotlighting SSE in public awareness and making it part of the public agenda. In the five countries mentioned here, the most recent decade has seen major political changes, along with a social and political recognition of SSE and the development of new ways of institutionalising it. Numerous SSE networks, disseminating information via the internet, are keeping the issue prominently on the agenda. These networks do not necessarily represent stakeholders in specific territories, although they present paradigms for creating new, sustainable and scale-appropriate economic forms.

As seen in the examples below, there is no single path to institutionalising SSE. In Brazil and Argentina, SSE and its institutions emerge or progress as one additional element in the countries' social and political strategies for 'incorporating or reincorporating excluded sectors in the very economic regime responsible for their exclusion'. In Ecuador, recent constitutional developments incorporate SSE as a central part of an institutional breach, framed as part of a proposal of 'change in the social regime of accumulation'. The same has occurred in Bolivia and Venezuela (Coraggio 2011).

In Bolivia and Ecuador, this is in turn part of the broader goal of 'reversing the incomplete historical process of modernisation' and halting the march towards uniformity in forms of production – an ideal exemplified by the prototypical private or public corporation and by the proletarianisation of workers. Conspiring against this is the neo-developmentalist view cited earlier. The new Bolivian and Ecuadorian constitutions recognise a wide range in current types of economic organisation (such as production for personal consumption, which characterises Ecuador's family economy, and the community production system common to Bolivia and Ecuador). These constitutions aim to institutionalise such diversity as an intrinsic part of a plural economy, according it legal recognition and making it the subject of and the instrument by which policies are promoted and incorporated. In Venezuela, innovation takes place within the framework of a state project whose goal is to foster productivity and achieve a more equitable distribution of wealth – an objective pursued by fostering forms of organisation based on management by worker-owners and/or by local communities. Supplementing this scheme is a system of public enterprises, structured around an 'engineering'-type model or organisation. In all three countries, there is an explicit political will to effect major changes in the economic system and to make it into a system capable of satisfying the needs of all citizens.

In Argentina, as well as in Bolivia, Ecuador and Venezuela, there has been a reaffirmation of the state's role in furthering popular national political projects and providing economic leadership. However, only in the three Andean countries is comprehensive planning at the centre of the development of a new economic regime. Brazil is an example of an internally driven self-centred capitalist economic regime, in which pressures brought to bear by society's stakeholders have gained recognition for SSE as a legitimate, albeit marginal, form of economic activity.

With regard to resources for accumulation and redistribution, the constitutions of Bolivia, Ecuador and Venezuela[7] all call for the nationalisation of profits from hydrocarbons, while Argentine policy relies, for this purpose, on the profits from agriculture and mining obtained as a result of the high international prices for these products. In the case of Brazil, however, changes in policy are designed to promote increased industrialisation while maintaining the role of primary product exports.

In Argentina, Bolivia, Ecuador and Venezuela, one sees a tension: on the one hand, one hears declarations claiming respect for ecological balance, accompanied by a stated desire to move beyond the extractive activities characteristic of the peripheral capitalist economic model; on the other hand, there is an urgent requirement to generate and maintain large surpluses to meet the need for investments to improve the immediate living conditions of the majority of the population, along with a desire to invest in diversifying the economy. Given that these economies are based largely on exporting primary products, the need for a rapid accumulation of large surpluses inevitably entails the continuation of intensive extractionist activities, while ensuring sufficient openness to secure international capital investments to support and expand these activities. The unfolding of the SSE paradigm occurs amidst these competing interests; while it is seen to promote a beneficial interplay between labour insertion and the fulfilment of basic needs, its role is considered subordinate to ensuring conditions for accumulation during the current period of transition. The dynamics of these competing interests mean that a majority of the population is left unable to participate productively in the capitalist extractionist-accumulation system. Hence the need for an SSE approach and the danger of seeing it as a compensatory programme while the employment and income crisis continues.

There is a wide range in the depth of the principles framing the proposed re-institutionalisation – or at least in the depth of intentions behind the actions being taken. While Venezuela, Brazil and Argentina continue focusing on economic growth indicators while pursuing more equitable wealth distribution, the Ecuadorian and Bolivian constitutions' aim is nothing less than a deep change in the value system, replacing modernistic economic values (progress, economic growth, individualism, possessive patterns of consumption) with the world view held by the nations' original peoples – values associated with 'living well' (reciprocity, solidarity, complementarity, community, justice, and balance in their relationship with nature).

In Latin America, the popular economy and its forms of resistance or survival provide the socio-economic and cultural foundation for building a solidarity economy. The rural population and its new forms of organisation – the Movement of Landless Workers in Brazil and Vía Campesina, among others – along with the Piqueteros movement in Argentina, gender-based movements, ethnic movements and strains of liberation theology constitute social forces capable of channelling political will and providing a driving force and meaning for SSE, centred around solidarity-based popular economy practices.

Conclusion

Given the dire social situation that characterises the start of the twenty-first century, new SSE policies can hardly be expected to quickly gain an operational status that is clearly separate from the matrix of 'assistentialist' social policies. In the cases outlined above, there is a clash between: 1) the urgent survival needs of the impoverished and excluded sectors, as well as the targeted public programmes of individuals or small groups related to self-employment designed to deal with this urgent situation; and 2) the longer time frames required to give proper consideration to the possibilities of building a system of SSE and to allow for the cultural changes it entails. Both levels are needed. At the very least it is necessary to intervene at the first level while keeping the second level in mind, in order to shift from a micro to a meso-level perspective (promoting articulation, complementarity, territories and communities).

The Latin American experience indicates that social and other public policies geared towards new forms of production must be seen not as options but rather as necessary complementary parts of SSE policy that involve the redistribution of income and public goods. At the same time, the awareness that the present situation is the product of a profound failure to achieve social integration under peripheral capitalism reopens for the New Left the need to consider deeper and more long-lasting changes to the institutional system. So, providing a dignified life to the entire citizenry will require a significant increase in the surplus, accompanied by the wise investment of resources. At the same time, accomplishing this goal from an SSE perspective involves formulating a strategy to overcome the current extractivist system, which is having devastating effects not only on the ecosystem but also on the future of coming generations. Other sources of social surplus are not easy to obtain – either through expropriation (strong political conflict) or by increasing the overall productivity of the economy (in the medium and long term).

From another angle, the resources emanating from extractive activities make it possible for governments to exploit the international advantages these provide to loosen the grip of foreign debt, while making possible unprecedented levels of autarchy and autonomy. If the new institutions fail, initially, to yield results, there is opportunity – and leeway – for gaining greater understanding and for correcting missteps. However, for reasons of ethics and politics, this leeway is narrowed by the urgency of finding sustainable, long-term solutions to the massive exclusion and impoverishment wrought by neoliberal policies.

Institutional change capable of engendering SSE requires more than legal, policy and administrative reforms. The necessary cultural changes cannot be produced solely by a formal process of centralised decision-making, no matter how well intentioned and democratic such a decision-making process may be. Moreover, re-institutionalisation is occurring amidst global, national and local conflict – a circumstance that SSE policy must take into account.

Hence there is a need to articulate a range of social, political and cultural 'tempos' when re-institutionalising economic processes.

From a substantive economic perspective, there is the central question of what ranking should be assigned to the various principles involved in institutionalising the new economic process: namely, the market principle (which at present enjoys hegemony) and principles such as reciprocity, fair trade, redistribution, non-exploitation of labour, non-extractivism, responsible consumption, and the transformation of ownership structures. Politically, the construction of 'Another Economy' – one that is social and solidarity-based – involves mediated confrontations between power structures inherited from the neoliberal regime, and the dispersion of popular forces with unacknowledged sectoral economic demands.

Moreover, there are valuable, territorially ubiquitous grass-roots initiatives aimed at self-organising their reproductive conditions; these partly rely on – but are not subject to the structures of – public resources. It is possible that, from this mosaic of initiatives and projects, there may emerge a solid SSE component; if this occurs, its viability will depend on aligning its political discourse with effective and broadly encompassing practices. In this regard, institutionalisation is a double-edged approach: it could potentially empower the initiatives by providing the material foundation for people, as subjects, to transform their own circumstances, or it could frame them, politically, as merely fragmentary forms of self-management.

8 | REBUILDING SOLIDARITY-DRIVEN ECONOMIES AFTER NEOLIBERALISM: THE ROLE OF COOPERATIVES AND LOCAL DEVELOPMENTAL STATES IN LATIN AMERICA

Milford Bateman

Introduction

With global neoliberal capitalism coming within a hair's breadth of entirely collapsing in late 2008,[1] the search for a more stable, equitable, dignified, environmentally sustainable and democratic or participative economic model is now more urgent than ever. This chapter explores the construction of an economic model that embodies these aspirations – the social and solidarity economy (SSE) model – and the central role that cooperative enterprises should play in this endeavour. I argue that the key practical task in promoting cooperative enterprises involves 'getting the local institutions right'. I maintain that the optimal, if not only, way to promote the SSE in practice is through the adoption of a local developmental state (LDS) approach, which has achieved enormous success around the globe in relation to both cooperative and investor-driven enterprises. Through a strategic, determined and long-term focus on promoting sustainable cooperative enterprise development, the LDS approach can play a pivotal role in building the solidarity economy from the bottom up.

The discussion that follows proceeds in three parts. First, I identify three historical examples of cooperative development in Europe that yield important lessons regarding the role of local institutions. The analysis moves on to identify another key element in successful development pathways, namely the developmental state that supported certain types of enterprises. While a variety of local institutional models can support this developmental model, it is argued that the contemporary neoliberal approach to decentralisation and market-driven local economic development contradicts key aspects of what worked historically. A final section examines concrete cases in Ecuador and Colombia, where a more effective model, centred on the 'empowered' or 'local' developmental state, is becoming a reality.

Cooperative enterprises as the core of the SSE model

A cooperative enterprise is one that is owned and controlled by its members, who may be basic producers (such as farmers), workers, savers, customers, the local community or other cooperatives. The cooperative movement was born during the rise of industrial capitalism in the early part of the nineteenth century. Cooperatives were seen as a much more democratic, fair, humane and also more efficient enterprise structure in the long term than investor-driven capitalist enterprises, although their establishment and operation in a hostile 'capitalist sea' were not always straightforward. Despite many obstacles, the cooperative sector soon began to register dramatic expansion across the globe, and by the 1900s was a major component of capitalist economies worldwide. In some sectors, such as agriculture and housing finance, agricultural and financial cooperatives actually played a dominant role (Birchall 1994).

From the 1950s onwards, the success of the cooperative enterprise led some to envisage an entirely new economic model – the 'solidarity economy model'. In many ways, this constituted a far better economic model for humanity to aspire to than Western-style free market capitalism or the form of rigid, centrally planned communism then practised in Eastern Europe (except in the former Yugoslavia, as is discussed below). The three examples included in this chapter are of particular importance for policy-makers today, as their experiments have been revisited and re-evaluated very positively by those who now lie behind the modern solidarity economy movement (Santos 2007b).

Italy Starting in the mid- to late 1800s, Italy was a trailblazer for many of the most important advances in the cooperative sector. But it was from the 1950s onwards in the new 'red' communist and socialist regions of northern Italy that a regional version of the solidarity economy model began to emerge. In an attempt to heal the fractures in society caused by the rise of Fascism in the 1930s, the newly elected communist/socialist regional and local governments opted to transform the economy into a more consensus-driven model. Centrally, economic activity was to be more firmly anchored in the cooperative sector. Although the United States (US) government effectively banned any major transfer of Marshall Plan funds to the northern regions on account of their leftist political complexion, numerous locally financed policies and programmes emerged to support the sustainable expansion of industrial and agricultural cooperatives. It helped that new and established co-operative enterprises benefited from a large supply of affordable finance, thanks to networks of financial cooperatives and so-called Special Credit Institutes capably managed by regional governments. Technical support was provided directly by local and regional governments through well-staffed economic development units, and funding also came from various non-state local institutions that could offer business planning advice and business space as well as helping promote technology acquisition and transfer, member training and cooperative education. Creative public procurement policies helped cooperatives get started, to network and cluster productively, and then to begin to access more technically demanding markets (especially abroad) through trusted intermediaries. Eventually, even the initially antagonistic national government in Rome began to pass various banking, taxation and regulatory measures to ensure that the cooperative sector – largely based in the north – was better able to expand sustainably.[2]

By 2003, the 'reddest' region of all – Emilia-Romagna – had the highest number of cooperatives in Italy, the highest proportion of non-agricultural workers employed in cooperatives (nearly 10 per cent in 2001), and the highest proportion of economic activity (more than 40 per cent of its gross domestic product or GDP) generated in the cooperative sector (Bateman 2007). Perhaps most importantly, Emilia-Romagna has regularly topped European 'Quality of Life' surveys due to the very high levels of social capital generated through the cooperative-based economic model. According to Stefano Zamagni of the University of Bologna, 'social capital is highly associated with quality of life everywhere [and] it seems that the co-operatives' emphasis on fairness and respect contribute to the accumulation of social capital here' (Logue 2005: 25).

Spain Moves to build a (regional) solidarity economy have also been very successful in the Basque country of northern Spain. Beginning in the town of Mondragon in the late 1950s, the Mondragon Cooperative Corporation (MCC) was to transform the Basque country from one of the poorest regions in Spain into one the richest. MCC's interlinked network of worker cooperatives now spans the entire Basque region, employing nearly 80,000 member workers in more than 100 cooperatives. As in northern Italy, Mondragon's rapid growth and long-lasting success can be attributed to a dense network of financial and non-financial support institutions, two of which were decisive here: 1) the Caja Laboral Popular (CLP), an institution that mobilised savings within the Basque region and then carefully reinvested these savings back into sustainable cooperative development projects; and 2) an enterprise development unit – *división empresarial* – that provided individual cooperative projects with quality business planning, member training, contact making, product and process development support, access to the latest technologies, and many other forms of support (Bateman et al. 2006). While, like every other company, MCC has been unable to escape the relentless pressure of globalisation and low-cost and low-wage competition from East Asia – in November 2013 its important home appliance unit, FAGOR, was forced into bankruptcy[3] – the fact remains that it has proved a far more robust and socially progressive development model overall than any other comparable capitalist company.

As MCC prospered, the local and regional governments in the Basque country were able to launch their own dedicated cooperative support institutions that could extend the cooperative sector to regions and sectors outside Mondragon and MCC. Soon, even more distant regions of Spain were adopting similar institutional support measures to those in Mondragon, and they too were able to fashion their own economic success. Notably, in the once extremely poor province of Almería, the innovative CLP-like cooperative bank Cajamar proved capable of creating and sustaining a very successful cluster of agricultural cooperatives, an outcome that came to be known as the 'Almeria miracle' (Giagnocavo et al. 2012).

Yugoslavia The former Yugoslavia's pioneering system of 'worker self-management' was the first fully functioning solidarity economy model to emerge at the country level. This solidarity economy model was established in the early 1950s and lasted until the late 1980s. Initially, the state chose to retain some influence over the investment policy of each new worker self-managed unit, fearful that the workers might totally mismanage their enterprise and so undermine the economy. Notwithstanding this situation, the elected managing body within each organisation – the workers' council – was still able and willing to argue successfully on many issues of importance to the enterprise and its employees. In the early 1960s, however, the state opted to end its direct say in enterprise affairs. The result was that the autonomy enjoyed by each worker self-managed enterprise was extended quite considerably, leading to the period of so-called 'market socialism' (Estrin 1983). Although operating imperfectly in many respects, economic performance under worker self-management was initially very sound, and at several times during the 1960s Yugoslavia was officially the fastest growing economy in the world (Horvat 1982). This positive performance occurred despite the need for many adjustments, a massive programme of training for both empowered workers and elected managers, and many other 'learning by doing' requirements during the first years of the new worker self-management system.

The proactivity and innovation of local institutions, mainly operating within and supported by Yugoslavia's historically competent network of local governments (Lampe 1979), proved vital in successfully launching new worker self-managed enterprises and supporting existing ones. It greatly helped that the 1963 Yugoslav constitution assigned the municipal authorities increased power to engage in various local economic development programmes (Seroka and Smiljković 1986). The motive was not only to encourage the creation and preservation of decent employment opportunities while responding to local demands for key products and services, but also to expand the local tax base as much as possible.

The original Yugoslav experiment in the local solidarity economy model was ahead of its time in many ways. The worker self-management system's eventual problems in the late 1970s were mainly a function of renewed political interference and other factors unrelated to the design of the system itself, notably the rise of capitalist-oriented separatist movements in the richer northern Yugoslav republics of Croatia and Slovenia. While unceremoniously phased out in 1988–89 under orders from the International Monetary Fund, Yugoslavia's worker self-management system nevertheless played a pioneering role in demonstrating the feasibility of industrial democracy on a national scale. Indeed, when viewed against the current background of economic collapse, mass unemployment, stratospheric inequality and extreme social dislocation and deprivation, all of which have been the inevitable outcomes of neoliberal capitalism right across southern Europe, with hindsight the many advantages of the worker self-management model are now more apparent than ever before.

Cooperative enterprise development as an aspect of local economic development policy

Despite these historical examples, the question remains as to how best to actually create and maintain genuine cooperative enterprises. Thanks to the emergence of a more accurate depiction of the real economic history of the developed capitalist economies, as well as of the recent East Asian 'miracle' economies, we now understand that the common element in this success was not 'free market forces', as many quite wrongly claim (Friedman and Friedman 1980). Rather, success was largely due to the quality of strategic state support that went into the enterprise development process. This fundamental insight from economic history has given rise to what is known as the 'developmental state' model (Amsden 2001; Chang 2007; 2011; Mazzucato 2013; Wade 1990). The most successful economies are those in which the state (national, regional and local) has most competently and programmatically supported the establishment and growth of the 'right' type of enterprises, broadly defined as small, medium and large enterprises that are:

- formally registered;
- operating at or above the minimum efficient scale;
- operating at the technological frontier;
- innovation and skills-driven rather than low labour cost-driven;
- horizontally (in clusters and networks) and vertically (subcontracting, supply chains and public procurement) interconnected with other organisations;
- able to continually facilitate the creation of new organisational routines and capabilities.

The developmental state model also effectively refused to support what we might describe as the 'wrong' enterprises: those loosely defined as simple, informal or illegal, isolated, low- or no-technology, petty trade-based microenterprises and one-person self-employment ventures (Bateman 2010; 2013; Bateman and Chang 2012; Baumol 1990). The developmental state model contrasts sharply with the contemporary focus on the rapid dismantling of all state capacities and the emphasis on 'market-driven' enterprise development, and especially with regard to the promotion of informal microenterprises – the 'wrong' enterprises – supported by microcredit.

This revised understanding of the role of institutions within enterprise development is not just confirmed by the rapid growth of above minimum efficient scale, innovative and technology-driven enterprises in those countries that adopted the developmental state model; it is also very much confirmed by the bottom-up country and regional cooperative development experience described earlier. Thus, if the SSE is to become a genuine reality through the accelerated promotion of cooperative enterprises, getting local institutional support right is pivotal.

A variety of local institutional models exist to support enterprise development of all kinds. The precise design of these local institutions is important, affecting not only the strategic capability of the institution but also its everyday operational efficiency. In the initial post-World War Two phase of recovery, a variety of public institutions were unapologetically used to drive forward the local economic development process (Weiss 1998). Planning and state intervention had, after all, won the war for the Allied powers and enabled reconstruction. The ascendance of neoliberal ideas in the late 1970s, however, began to discredit all forms of state intervention and planning, including at the local level. But even the most rigid neoliberal accepted that the market was an insufficient force on its own to promote economic development, and so, paradoxically, many institutional interventions were quietly allowed through in order to better promote markets and secure long-term economic success. The principal design constraints for development-focused institutions tolerated under neoliberalism, therefore, were inevitably ideologically driven: first, the imperative that local institutions do not expand pure state capacity; and, second, that there is no cost to the state into the longer term. Accordingly, it was required under neoliberalism that all local enterprise development institutions be (re)configured as for-profit non-state bodies operating with a primary mission to 'earn their keep on the market' in order to achieve 'full cost recovery' (Bateman 2000). Apart from the obvious cost minimisation argument, neoliberals also argued that for-profit institutions would ensure that the services provided were of good quality (so as to win business) and that there was a genuine demand for them (evidenced by the fact that there was a willingness to pay). Supporting a for-profit private institution was preferable to support for state capacity. For most of the last thirty years, this neoliberal approach to local enterprise institutions has dominated in international development policy circles.

However, the rather awkward fact is that the neoliberal commercialisation approach to local institutions does not work in practice. This was the conclusion of the largest ever evaluation of such institutions established in post-communist Eastern Europe, which found that almost none of the local institutions funded by the European Commission could survive by 'earning their keep on the market' while retaining their original mandate to support small businesses and local development (EuropeAid 2000). When it became clear that they could generate far more revenue by working with large companies, governments and international development agencies themselves, most local enterprise development institutions supported by the European Union (EU) abandoned their original mandate. In the absence of any of these lucrative revenue streams, however, the typical response was simply to close down, as indeed almost all such local economic development institutions have done in Eastern Europe since 1990 (Bateman 2005).

Confirmation of the un-workability of the neoliberal commercialisation approach came once again in 2012 in the context of Latin America, thanks to a study commissioned by the United Nations Development Programme (UNDP) (Bateman 2012; for important background to the study and an assessment of its results, see Bateman 2014). This study was tasked to look into the operation of the network of 'market-driven' local economic development agencies (LEDAs) established in Latin America with UNDP technical and financial support. Claimed by UNDP (Canzanelli 2010)[4] to be making a major contribution to the economic development of local communities across Latin America, UNDP's LEDA model was instead found to be in deep crisis everywhere. Amazingly, the very *worst* outcomes were registered in Colombia, which was otherwise portrayed as the *best* performing nation in Latin America (ADEL 2011; Canzanelli 2011). In fact, such was the self-declared success of the LEDA programme in Colombia that both the Colombian government and the EU aid office operating in the country were pushed hard to invest even more resources into what was clearly a dysfunctional structure.[5] The principal problems among LEDAs in Colombia (and which generally apply elsewhere in Latin America and globally) included the following:

- They were clearly financially unsustainable (with one exception).
- They generated almost no added benefits, because they simply competed with other existing local development institutions and universities for the same projects and clients.
- They were unable to meaningfully promote public–private dialogue, because they competed with most key public–private stakeholders for the same contracts.
- Staff in the one and only LEDA in Colombia that proved successful in raising funds by charging user fees and obtaining consulting contracts after competitive tender procedures, operating in the city of Vélez, openly admitted to being on course to be sold off to its current and previous managers for that very reason.

The alternative to the market-driven neoliberal approach to the operation of local development institutions is to be found, I would argue, in a new approach based on an empowered local state. This is the local variation of the 'developmental state' introduced above, which is known as the 'local developmental state' (LDS) model. This specifically holds that local governments and associated local institutions have played a decisive role in many of the most successful episodes of local economic development, and in cooperative enterprise development in particular (Bateman 2000; 2010). Turning now to Latin America, we examine how these roles and development pathways are once again being asserted.

The LDS model and cooperative enterprise development in Latin America

The LDS approach has strategic importance in the context of cooperative enterprise development, and so also in terms of building the SSE. Since 2000, many countries in Latin America have increasingly begun to experiment, not unsuccessfully, with variations on the LDS model in order to support cooperative enterprises, as the following examples demonstrate.

Ecuador With high levels of social inequality and fragility, and with generally much more than half of the population below the poverty line, Ecuador has been one of the countries most active in pioneering a new economic and social model. Recent changes in government policy associated with President Rafael Correa, assisted by significantly increased revenues from the oil and gas industry and rising agricultural exports, have prompted radical plans to promote the SSE model. The intention is to replace the old neoliberal model of economic development in Latin America that was based on de facto rising inequality, unsustainable resource use, and the effective disempowerment of the poor (Green 1997).

It is envisaged that the new economic and social structure in Ecuador will be a mixture of small-scale capitalism, cooperatives and democratically mandated state activism through public ownership. In order to establish this new social economy programme, the Ecuadorian government has also embarked on a major programme of decentralisation. Local or regional state and quasi-state sub-national institutions are now being given more responsibility, encouragement and financial resources than at any other time in Ecuador's history. This very real empowerment of local government has allowed some proactive LDS-type institutions to emerge.

An indication of the potential importance of LDS capacities with specific reference to cooperative enterprises comes from the southern province of Azuay. As part of the national movement to construct a solidarity economy, the provincial economic department has actively sought out potential cooperative enterprise projects. Among the most important to date is one that aims to more effectively include small farmers in the agricultural supply chain.[6] Historically, small dairy farmers in Azuay Province have tended to obtain little benefit from dairy activities, with most of the value going to intermediaries. This is held responsible, at least partly, for both the extent of deep rural poverty in the province and the marked inequality of farmers vis-à-vis the intermediaries with whom they work. Responding to this specific issue, the provincial government's economic development department designed a major new project loosely based on build–operate–transfer (BOT) lines, which went into effect in 2011. The aim was to connect small farmers directly to the market, bypassing traditional intermediaries and thus improving the earnings and security of poor farming communities.[7] The principal intervention was the establishment of Lac Jubones, a dairy processing plant. Lac Jubones was funded by a US$1 million grant from the provincial government. Using public funds, Lac Jubones was initially structured to be 51 per cent owned by the provincial government, with 49 per cent owned by a farmer-owned cooperative – Jiron – composed of the smallest commercial farming operations and some 1,200 individual small farmers. A range of other inputs were provided to the farming community, such as low-cost credit, grants and training in new techniques, in order that they might improve productivity and help manage the activities of Jiron.

In its first year of operation, Lac Jubones became the number two dairy processor on the regional market, second only to a Nestlé subsidiary, with contracts to supply dairy products to several of the most important supermarkets in the province and nationally. Importantly, Lac Jubones not only provides a minimum price for milk, but farmers also obtain security of contract and delivery. Previously, intermediaries would all too often renege on an agreement to purchase milk, leaving farmers with stocks of milk they could not sell. This is a traditional disciplining measure used by intermediaries to 'soften up' their clients (the farmers) and ensure that power within the supply chain was always in the hands of the intermediaries.

With the provincial government now planning for the final part of the BOT deal – the transfer of its shareholding to Jiron – the indication is that a genuine farmers' cooperative will eventually come into being as the majority owner of the state-of-the-art Lac Jubones facility. Based on the success of Lac Jubones to date, the provincial government has now established another proto-cooperative enterprise – Agro Azuay – to essentially do the same thing as Lac Jubones in the fresh fruit and vegetable sector. The ultimate aim of the provincial government is similar to the very successful Danish model (Federation of Danish Cooperatives and Agricultural Council 1993) and will mean that almost the entire agricultural sector in Azuay Province will be organised along farmer-owned cooperative and secondary cooperative lines – and all using the very latest technologies as much as possible.

The creative use of state capacity in the case of Azuay Province contrasts with the traditional stance of many in the global cooperative movement, which is to decry the involvement of the state in most aspects of the cooperative movement out of a fear that the state will eventually 'take over'. The experience outlined here highlights instead that local institutional support is vital not only to all forms of enterprise development, *but particularly to cooperative enterprise development.* Such local institutions can play a much larger strategic development role in Ecuador's overall development ambitions.

Colombia After many years of narco-terrorist and paramilitary violence, Colombia finally began to stabilise in the late 1990s. Part of the approach has been to promote an extensive programme of decentralisation. Sub-national governments in Colombia took advantage of this new freedom and began to develop their own (local) developmental state capacities, policies and programmes that were at odds with the wishes of the central government. In particular, the cities of Bogotá and Medellín have become pioneers in promoting a new local government-driven model of economic development that is building the capacity and flexibility required to address many of the prevailing social and economic problems at the local level (Bateman et al. 2011; Gilbert 2006). This is also providing the local state capacity – the LDS – required to meaningfully promote a regional solidarity economy model.

Agricultural development programmes are key to this goal. Colombia's rural poverty is a result of its vastly unequal landholdings and plantation farming system, and even in sectors where small farmers predominate (such as coffee), benefits have always been appropriated by a wealthy elite involved in processing, packaging, distribution and the final sale (Palacios 1980). But, as the example of Azuay Province in Ecuador shows, having an integrated supply chain structure for agriculture that is driven from the bottom up by farming communities and formally constituted farmer-owned agricultural cooperatives is most beneficial. Similar initiatives are now beginning to emerge in Colombia, as a way to integrate groups of farmers more efficiently into the commercial agricultural system. Two such cooperative projects are explored in more depth below.

Proto-cooperatives and 'local consumption and distribution cycles' in Bogotá One agricultural proto-cooperative project (that is, an initial operating foundation upon which to create a formally registered cooperative) was initiated in the capital city of Bogotá with technical support from the British non-governmental organisation (NGO) Oxfam (Pesquera 2011). The scheme originated in a plan initiated by the office of the mayor of Bogotá in 2004, which aimed to improve Bogotá's supply of fresh food through the 'lowest cost' principle, while also ensuring that consumption in Bogotá would underpin a more economically, socially and environmentally efficient system of food production. Initial investigation by Oxfam confirmed that small farmers in Colombia find it very hard to make a decent living from their activities around big cities, partly because commercially savvy intermediaries control the local market (distribution and retail) and so are able to appropriate most of the value in the agricultural chain. It soon became apparent that the mayor's 'lowest cost' plan was likely to make rural poverty around Bogotá even worse.

Accordingly, a new design was called for – one that saw the 'lowest price' principle replaced by a 'fair price' principle. With financial and other help from the mayor's office, farmers were able to establish their own farmers' market in Bogotá where they could deliver and sell their produce without recourse to the traditional intermediary. As in many global locations (Bijman et al. 2012), cutting out intermediaries often turns out to be far more effective in raising the financial rewards for farmers than simply raising prices (even through the 'fair price' principle). Another innovation was to invite representatives from farming communities to engage in the public–private dialogue process and to argue their case for change and for the new local farming model to be supported more extensively. Following the success of this scheme in central Bogotá, more than thirty municipalities in the area around Bogotá decided to organise their own local markets in a similar way, and soon generated similar outcomes for farmers and the wider community. This 'local production and consumption cycle' model, initially based on communities of farmers but also with the potential to progress gradually towards registered farmer-owned cooperatives, is now being extended to the cities of Medellín and Cali. This project follows a number of others in Latin America, most notably the 'Zero Hunger' programme in Brazil (Da Silva et al. 2011), in that it helps agricultural communities build the required foundations from which genuine farmer-owned agricultural cooperatives can emerge.

Alimentos Nariño Another important example where pro-poor utilisation of local state capacity is under way is in Nariño Province in the south of Colombia. Historically one of the poorest and most deprived provinces in Colombia (further undermined in the 1970s by the presence within its borders of substantial guerrilla and narco violence), the region's economic mainstay is the agricultural sector. However, few farmers in the province have been able to move beyond simple subsistence farming, not least because the traditional landowning elite continues to own and operate the very best land, as well as possessing the best market opportunities for their outputs, either directly or through networks of trusted intermediaries. Poor farmers have generally produced for home consumption and for the local market. Unless decisive action was taken, it was generally thought that this adverse situation was unlikely to change. Influenced by the success of Lac Jubones, the regional governor of Nariño (a former Secretary of Agriculture) began to take just such decisive action. Beginning in Tulcán, a small town on Colombia's border with Ecuador,[8] a project was established that aimed to organise and support the region's small farmers in creating an intermediary enterprise that would help them directly rather than exploit their weak bargaining position. All previous efforts by the farmers to establish some sort of intermediary had been blocked by the region's powerful private agricultural interests, so it was clear that external capacity-building support would be needed.

The project was designed following extensive consultation with farming communities and along the same lines as the BOT project discussed above. It started in 2011 with the construction of a processing company – Alimentos Nariño – designed to process, package and export the output of the several thousand farmers in the locality who had been most eager to participate (because the area was one of the poorest in Nariño). At the same time, a farmer-owned cooperative was established. It owns 80 per cent of Alimentos Nariño, with individual farmers having put up a small sum of money to buy into the venture as farmer members. The cooperative will elect its own officials in due course and will also receive capacity-building support, an important factor given that in the past such ventures have failed because of the weakness of internal cooperative management. Ownership of 10 per cent of Alimentos Nariño currently remains with the regional government, 8 per cent is owned by various sympathetic local businesses and NGOs active with the farmers, and a 2 per cent stake is owned by the LEDA that provided some of the technical support for the project. The regional government plans to recycle any future dividends from its 10 per cent ownership stake into a social venture capital fund that will provide support for new enterprise development.

By 2012, with solid support from marketing professionals hired by the regional government, and even before the processing plant had been fully completed, a major contract was signed with Unifresh, a Miami-based company, which would see it import a range of fresh fruit and vegetables from Alimentos Nariño. Other US-based companies are also interested in linking up with Alimentos Nariño. With a secure market for their outputs, and one that offers better prices than local sale, members of the new cooperative are enthusiastic. They have been taking advantage of training and capacity-building efforts so that their cooperative can achieve long-term success. While still in the early stages of development, this cooperative project represents an important advance in the thinking behind previous so-called 'cooperative' projects; these generally envisaged only the token involvement of the farmers as basic producers organised cooperatively, while entrepreneurs and investors were brought in to own and manage the higher-value parts of the supply chain, which they ran to their own advantage rather than for the benefit of farmers. Instead, local farmers are here being given the chance to cooperatively own and manage their own state-of-the-art processing facility. This will ensure, right from the start, that a very much higher proportion of the value-added generated in the supply chain is returned to them.

Conclusion

The SSE model, and the cooperative enterprises that will inevitably constitute its core, is attracting growing attention worldwide. However, the precise mechanisms and institutions needed to establish and support such enterprises remain vastly under-researched and weakly conceptualised. This chapter has argued that 'getting the local institutions right' is the most important aspect involved in creating the solidarity economy model in practice, and, furthermore, that the LDS approach contains the most fruitful line of enquiry in this regard.

Historical examples from Europe share a common feature with the case studies drawn from Latin America today, in that all were operationalised based on the willingness of local governments to act, change, regulate, promote, finance and otherwise constructively intervene to generate pro-development outcomes. This is certainly not to idealise the LDS-driven process of cooperative development, or to suggest that scaling up such processes will be easy. Nonetheless, given the range of LDS-related policies, programmes and institutional vehicles that have been successfully used to date to support cooperatives, such as in northern Italy and Scandinavia in the past and in Ecuador and Colombia today, it seems reasonable to conclude that such measures can be adapted carefully for local use elsewhere. Indeed, as the manifest failures of global anti-statist neoliberalism have become apparent right around the world, it helps that many, if not most, ideologically driven restrictions on expanding state capacity to promote local economic and social development have come to an end. Accordingly, the opportunity exists as never before to promote the local capacities associated with the LDS model, and thereby rapidly and sustainably expand the role of cooperative enterprises in the local economy. The SSE will thus be closer to becoming a practical reality.

9 | ENABLING THE SOCIAL AND SOLIDARITY ECONOMY THROUGH THE CO-CONSTRUCTION OF PUBLIC POLICY

Marguerite Mendell and Béatrice Alain

Introduction

Existing policy measures embedded within long-established policy settings are increasingly meeting roadblocks, even where there is willingness to introduce policies to promote the development of the social and solidarity economy (SSE). If SSE is to meet its objectives, the experience of numerous countries confirms the urgent need for policy innovation.

'Governing in complexity' (Christiansen and Bunt 2012) requires new approaches to policy formation, more flexible regulatory environments and a shift from a sectoral focus to comprehensive measures. This calls into question the very structure of governing institutions that, for the most part, operate in silos. Their capacity to innovate is restricted to narrowly defined objectives with correspondingly narrow tools. Working across boundaries suggests not only breaking down inter-ministerial or inter-departmental barriers within government or large supra-national and international policy circles, but also collaborating with non-government actors, as those on the ground are best placed to identify policy needs. It means recognising that the state (at all levels) is but one of many knowledgeable actors equipped to solve problems. It also suggests that the best role for the public sector is one of coordination. While transforming the role of government is not easy, some pragmatic and innovative responses by governments are in evidence.

SSE enterprises integrate social, economic and environmental objectives, often generating both profit and social utility. In pursuing these multiple goals, the diverse and evolving organisational forms of the SSE face different constraints and opportunities. All SSE enterprises, whatever their organisational form, require multiple tools – labour market (training), capital (financial instruments), research (partnerships with researchers), commercialisation strategies (access to markets) and enabling public policy. Moreover, because the SSE is rooted locally, it requires both situated and macro policy measures. While individual sectors in the SSE require customised policy, these must be integrated into a systemic approach. Too often, focus on the SSE is reduced to enterprises, organisations or sectors, missing its broader developmental capacity and potential.

Insufficient collaboration between government and civil society is a major barrier for the development of the SSE. This is increasingly recognised in discussions among practitioners, researchers and policy-makers in numerous countries in the global North and South, but it does not always translate into enabling policies that address the multiple constraints and objectives of SSE actors. Top-down policy initiatives, even when well intentioned, often cannot take into account the particular needs of local SSE enterprises and may result in policies that are ineffective and often costly to readjust. Conversely, when demands from SSE practitioners do not take into account the capacity and priorities of government, they have little chance of being addressed. As such, institutional spaces for dialogue between SSE actors and government need to be created for the SSE to reach its potential.

The SSE represents an ongoing process of innovation rooted in communities actively engaged in processes of 'learning by doing'. New approaches to socio-economic development and new forms of partnership between social actors (government, civil society and even the private sector in some cases) are being tested on a continuing basis, calling for corresponding innovations in public policy (Mendell and Neamtan 2010). This raises numerous questions. Are existing forms of governance permeable? Is there room for new forms of governance to emerge and either co-exist with the status quo or replace it? Can governments and/or international policy circles learn to work more collaboratively?

Based on case studies in six countries (Bolivia, Brazil, Canada, Mali, Spain and South Africa) prepared for the International Forum on the Social and Solidarity Economy (FIESS)[1] and other case studies prepared by the Organisation for Economic Co-operation and Development (OECD) and RELIESS,[2] this chapter examines the advantages of multi-stakeholder collaboration in policy processes and the conditions for effective collaboration to formulate and implement public policy for the SSE. The diversity of countries covered by these case studies illustrates how new processes of policy design are emerging under very different conditions. The case studies demonstrate that, where government becomes a strategic enabler, it facilitates the development and growth of the SSE and leads to greater policy effectiveness. However, not all processes of policy formation documented in the case studies are collaborative. The shortcomings of narrow policy measures and traditional modes of policy formation in achieving the broad goals of the SSE are also identified.

Findings: why co-construction?

Through our work over a number of years in Quebec, we have referred to the *co-construction of public policy* to describe a multi-stakeholder process of policy design to enable the development of the SSE. This term is used more frequently today to distinguish it from *co-production* that describes collaborative forms of programme delivery. Current literature describes this as the transmission of 'useful knowledge' to government and suggests that these processes underpin a 'new paradigm of public governance' (Christiansen and Bunt 2012). In our work, we emphasise the circular flow of knowledge and information embedded in this process and involving many actors. Processes of co-construction of public policy are present in many national and local settings and have significant impacts, as identified below.

Co-construction allows the SSE to realise its potential Open dialogue between SSE actors and government leads to more coherent and strategic approaches that transcend a limited and more frequently applied sectoral approach. Because the SSE proposes and develops innovative solutions to complex societal problems, measuring its impact poses challenges for governments generally unable to assess complexity due to the limited lens of ministries, divisions and departments. While this is changing in some areas, governments, by and large, remain constrained by their sectoral mandates. Collaborating with SSE actors to design policy exposes government to the potential of the SSE and to the need to think in broader terms. The cost of not doing so is high for government. Reducing the capacity of the SSE to realise its potential has social, political and economic costs; it increases the risk of policy ineffectiveness or misalignment. The needs of target populations are not met and, in the worst case scenarios, misaligned or narrow policy measures may actually exacerbate the problems they are seeking to solve. Instead, dialogue with government increases the capacity of the SSE to achieve strategic objectives of government, such as employment creation, territorial development and social inclusion. For example, SSE actors questioned in the preparation of the FIESS case study of Spain underlined how their early participation in formal and informal forums helped broaden government's understanding of their capacities and goals. This in turn led to a co-construction process that recognised the multi-sectoral nature and impact of the SSE.

Several countries have adopted framework legislation that enshrines the multi-sectoral impact of the SSE in law. In Ecuador, for example, the constitution calls for more equitable development and includes a National Plan for Wellbeing (2009–13) in which 'establishing a SSE economic system' was identified as a priority. This led to the adoption of the Organic Law of the Popular and Solidarity Economy and the Popular and Solidarity Financial Sector in 2012 and the creation of public institutions to regulate and promote the law.

Although research suggests that the impact of some framework legislation is ambiguous,[3] the adoption of such legislation in October 2013 in Quebec was met with enthusiasm by SSE practitioners and partners, especially because of the contributions of all stakeholders in its formulation. This collaborative process is now embedded in a clause to create a permanent committee of stakeholders to oversee the application of the legislation and/or amendments in the future, and, most importantly, to mobilise knowledge on the SSE as it evolves.

Co-construction reduces information asymmetry and transaction costs By involving all stakeholders, co-construction of policy reduces information asymmetry, thereby reducing transaction costs when implementing or adjusting policy measures. Indeed, it is through discussions that address stakeholders' goals and limitations that 'organisational empathy' develops, which leads to more realistic measures and to objectives that are coherent with stakeholders' priorities and resources. This is the main function of organisations such as the Małopolskie Social Economy Pact in Poland, for example, a multi-stakeholder intermediary organisation that includes government interlocutors and facilitates the exchange of information between participating actors.[4]

This is also the objective of meetings convened by government or civil society to discuss the realities and challenges of the SSE, including the evaluation of existing policy measures and/or new policies required to promote the development of the SSE. Examples of such meetings are the regular national solidarity economy conferences in Brazil, and the National Meeting of the Social Economy and Fair Trade held in Bolivia in 2007.

In 2003, SSE actors in Burkina Faso questioned the government's microfinance strategy. In response, the government convened a national conference to draft a broad outline of a national strategy with stakeholders; this included the adoption of a framework for stakeholder intervention that would better reflect the needs of SSE actors. The government also agreed to convene regular meetings between stakeholders to monitor results. In Ecuador, the Institute for Popular and Solidarity Economics plays a critical role in ensuring that the conditions (delivery time, quality and prices) for procurement from the SSE by various ministries are realistic and beneficial for the SSE. It holds discussions with all parties to understand their needs and capacities, and negotiates with different divisions of government on behalf of SSE actors. Although it may be more costly to elaborate policies through a participatory process, continuous evaluation of policy measures is critical for all stakeholders to better understand the impact of existing policies and to identify needs for new and/or modified measures or programmes.

Organisational innovations within cooperatives and associations require legislation to distinguish their hybrid nature and functions. A paradoxical situation that illustrates the high cost of information asymmetry and policy misalignment arose in Poland at the time of the case study (2009), when not-for-profit social-purpose businesses were not eligible for either European Union (EU) or national funding because of their commercial activities. This exemplified the need for the EU and the national government to recognise these new hybrid enterprises, which were deprived of much-needed public funding because of rigid programme criteria that did not correspond with their reality. That said, while a legal basis is necessary to distinguish such new organisations, it can still limit their capacity if that legislation is not integrated in a broader and more systemic policy framework.

In the case of non-profit organisations, such legislation is also required to raise investment capital in financial markets, as their hybrid status limits their capacity to attract investment. Access to capital is a primary concern of SSE actors in most countries. While many governments provide financing for the SSE, this is insufficient to meet their capital requirements. In Quebec, the Chantier de l'Économie Sociale created new financial instruments that were supported by the provincial and federal governments, precisely because of SSE actors' inability to access financing through existing institutions. The growing social finance and impact investment market is a potential source of capital for the SSE, raising the urgency to address such organisations' legal form where it remains ambiguous.

Initial policy design may not be able to foresee all of the outcomes of a policy or how the environment it applies to will evolve. But by ensuring that all parties are actively involved in an ongoing process of policy evaluation, measures can be adjusted to meet their initial agreed objectives. Within South Korea, for example, it is expected that the newly created Seoul Social Economy Centre, which has commissioned a network of SSE actors to propose and implement SSE policy programmes at the municipal level, will lead to the transformation of the existing SSE policy landscape in Seoul and in Korea as a whole. This experience is interesting and one worth following closely, given the more narrow policy focus on work integration and the top-down approach that have prevailed until now.

Co-construction ensures policy effectiveness By bringing together a greater and more varied number of actors to design and monitor new policy, co-construction leads to more innovative, adapted and effective policy measures and programmes than those designed or implemented unilaterally by government.

The evolution of legislation surrounding work integration enterprises in Quebec is an example of the successful modification of policy measures over the last twenty years as a direct result of continuous dialogue with such enterprises,[5] as well as research carried out to measure their impact on the target population. In contrast, the South Korean government's current requirement for work integration enterprises to create long-term jobs and become self-financing does not benefit vulnerable workers; in fact, it may well penalise the enterprises it seeks to support, as most are unable to survive under such stringent criteria. Moreover, there is a risk that these enterprises might abandon their commitments once the funding period has elapsed. More dialogue between civil society and the state would allow for better understanding of the effects of this policy on SSE enterprises.

Elsewhere, the 2003 Act on Public Benefit and Voluntary Work in Poland (amended in 2010) represents a significant step in institutional innovation for disabled workers in that country. By establishing the need for government to collaborate directly with service providers and by codifying the outsourcing of public tasks – including those related to the labour market, social assistance and disability – the act will address issues of discrimination and the provision of training and support services. It will also address the problem of policy incoherence with regard to social businesses in Poland, as noted earlier.

Processes of inclusion and dialogue are all the more important when governments undertake important structural reforms in regions with deeply rooted or cross-cutting socio-economic challenges. In these cases, desired policy outcomes usually involve changes in the perception and behaviour of citizens, as well as of those who work in, and influence, the public policy system (Sullivan and Skelcher 2002). Examples include municipal programmes for neighbourhood revitalisation in Canada, the United States, Australia and the United Kingdom.

Lastly, it is important for processes of co-construction not only to address the general context in which the SSE is developing but also to produce a specific and detailed development programme with strategic actions and concrete measures for the promotion of the SSE. Such was the case in Spain with the first Andalusian Pact for the SSE signed in 2002.[6] Another example is the network of parent-controlled day-care centres in Quebec, created almost fifteen years ago. This network is now responsible for the majority of childcare services in Quebec and is the third largest employer in the province.

Requirements for effective co-construction

As government and civil society actors are increasingly becoming aware of the advantages of jointly constructed policy solutions, attention is turning to how to facilitate this collaboration. The existence of representative intermediary bodies able to mediate between SSE actors and government is key to this process.

Broad representation within intermediary bodies Intermediaries play an important role in mobilisation and representation, reinforcing the common identity and values of the SSE. When effective, intermediaries educate policy-makers on the specificities and diversity of the SSE and help SSE enterprises navigate the policy environment. They analyse the impact of existing government measures on SSE enterprises and/or individual sectors and offer capacity-building support (training, financing, networking, and so on). Intermediaries can identify best practices and the conditions under which these are replicable, as well as the SSE enterprises and/or sectors at risk. Individual sectors continue to lobby on their own behalf, but have the added benefit of representation by a multi-sectoral body of networks and organisations.

Effective intermediary organisations are well placed to inform policy-makers on the state and needs of the SSE and to suggest modifications to current policy. Many intermediary organisations have developed the capacity to track and evaluate the development of the SSE. Selected examples include:

- the Chambre Régionale de l'Économie Sociale et Solidaire (CRESS) Observatory in France;
- the Observatorio Español de la Economia Social in Spain;
- the Social Policy Observatory of Małopolskie and the Social Economy Development Academy – Phase 1 in Krakow in Poland;
- the Comité Sectoriel de Main-d'œuvre – Économie Sociale Action Communautaire (CSMO-ÉSAC) in Quebec; and
- the Foro Brasileiro de Economia Solidaria (FBES), which, in collaboration with the National Secretariat for the Solidarity Economy, created a National System for Information on the Solidarity Economy.

The Confederación Empresarial Española de la Economía Social – CEPES – in Spain is an example of an intermediary representing a broad coalition of all SSE actors. Two other examples, the Chantier de l'Économie Sociale in Quebec and the FBES in Brazil, are broader still, including SSE enterprises as well as social movements and territorial intermediaries that identify with the SSE. In all three cases, collaborative relationships with government exist. In Brazil, the long-standing relationship between the FBES and the Secretariat for the Solidarity Economy has helped to clarify the complex nature and potential of the Brazilian SSE for all actors. In Spain and Quebec, the existence of such relationships led to the adoption of framework legislation in 2011 and 2013 respectively.

Broad coalitions also allow for new forms of SSE initiatives to be recognised, such as those that operate in the informal economy. Indeed, it is because of the championing of broad coalitions such as the FBES in Brazil that the impact of informal economy initiatives on employment and hunger alleviation has been recognised by public policy. Similarly, the Bamboo Workers' Union in Nepal has been working to highlight the contribution of informal unions and groups to the socio-economic and environmental sustainability of society and to achieve recognition and support for them from other divisions of government beyond the Ministry of Forests and Soil Conservation.

The European Commission's call for a 'coordinated European response' that includes social partners and civil society is an important opening to work with the SSE (EC 2010), as is the recognition that the objectives of this long-term strategy will be best met by developing territorial and social partnerships. It falls upon SSE organisations and networks to create and occupy policy space within these broad commitments. The same holds true for the welcome proposal for partnerships between different levels of government within member countries in Europe.

In addition to intermediary organisations that often represent a diverse constituency of SSE enterprises and organisations, there are also networks that generally represent a type of SSE organisation (for example, cooperatives) or are sectoral organisations, such as the Federation of Community Forest User Groups Nepal. In Mali, at the time of the case study in 2011, the Coordination Nationale des Organisations Paysannes was key in articulating its members' position on the framework law on agriculture. It held regional and national workshops for farmers to present their proposals for the law, and it also provided an overview of the law for its members once it was passed and obtained a mandate from them to monitor its application. In Burkina Faso, the Réseau de Veille sur la

Commercialisation des Céréales brings together agricultural producers, food-processing professionals, transporters, consumers and non-governmental organisations (NGOs), collects and disseminates data, and carries out advocacy and lobbying activities. While these are sectoral networks, in these agricultural countries they perform the role of multi-sectoral intermediaries found in more diversified economies.

Networks that exclusively represent one type of organisation cannot, however, address the impact of other types of SSE organisation. The extent to which different networks are able to work together on issues of common interest influences the development of public policy that enables the SSE. It also determines whether different types of organisations find themselves competing for government recognition and resources, reducing the possibility of collaboration and mutual reinforcement between SSE actors. Governments can accentuate these perverse outcomes when they interfere with the way in which organisations choose to be represented. For example, in Burkina Faso, the arbitrary inclusion by government of different organisations in policy dialogue has exacerbated pre-existing conflicts within the SSE and has weakened the position of the more representative intermediary organisations. A similar example exists in Ecuador, where the Citizen Participation Law institutionalised a process to rank and select representatives of civil society to participate in government discussions, rather than leaving the selection to the organisations themselves. This poses several potential problems, not least of which is the organisations' accountability to the groups on whose behalf they are supposed to advocate.

Towards optimal integration When a network or an ensemble of networks, social movements and organisations are able to form a broad coalition of actors that includes all sectors, types of organisation and regions of the SSE, their leverage with government to obtain innovative policy is increased and their capacity to mobilise partners is enhanced, leading to a more effective process of co-construction. The more open and representative the intermediary, the less it runs the risk of splintering into smaller, competing factions. From the actors' perspective, it requires organisations and movements that are accustomed to working separately to work across boundaries. It also requires spaces for dialogue on general issues of interest to the many organisations and movements involved. This does not imply consensus on all issues but rather commitment to a broad process of deliberative, democratic decision-making.

Governments can facilitate the strengthening of networks and intermediaries by encouraging their creation where they do not exist or by developing incentives for SSE sectors to join existing networks. For example, in the Provence-Alpes-Côte d'Azur (PACA) region in southern France, the regional government supports processes that encourage collaboration between SSE actors within a locality or sector and actively encourages civil society organisations to join or create networks in order to pool resources and coordinate their actions. This is beneficial both for the organisations and for government, which then interacts with fewer interlocutors. If governments can create incentives for civil society to organise, they can also hinder this process, for example through competitive tenders that encourage competition rather than collaboration.

An example from South Africa demonstrates how a lack of coordination in civil society organisations makes it extremely difficult for the particular needs of SSE enterprises to be recognised. Even though the constitution requires government to consult with stakeholders before tabling legislation, the boom in the registration of new cooperatives following the Cooperatives Act of 2005 has not led to any significant developments in legislation for these organisations. The absence of a dedicated agency, ministry or department designed to support cooperatives has meant a lack of resources and insufficient awareness by government of the realities and needs of these organisations. It is one of the factors explaining the extremely low survival rate of cooperatives in the country.

Intermediary organisations must strike a delicate balance between ensuring their survival (including obtaining financing and recognition by government), maintaining a privileged position as interlocutor with government, and not crowding out or suppressing the diversity of actors they represent. Intermediaries that are too centralising may find themselves resented by the organisations and sectors they represent and may lose legitimacy. One successful example of de-centralisation is the social economy regional poles in Quebec; these operate in a similar way to the Chantier de l'Économie Sociale at a regional level and collaborate effectively with the Chantier as well as with local, regional and provincial governments.

Government commitment and capacity Effective co-construction requires full commitment by government to the process. In some instances, there is openness in government to promote the SSE – by enshrining its importance in legislation or by elaborating strategic action plans, for example – but insufficient capacity to act on these intentions. In the best case scenario, the SSE is acknowledged as a key element in the government's overall development strategy, and resources are dedicated to it accordingly. This was the case in Brazil when food security (Fome Zero or Zero Hunger) became a major policy objective of the federal government. One policy instrument stipulated that, as of 2009, 30 per cent of all food purchased for schools by the Programa Nacional de Alimentação Escolar must come from small farms. This has had a very significant impact on the economic viability and stability of small farms and their food production. Another example is the City of Montreal's partnership agreement with SSE actors that recognised the social and economic capacity of the SSE by creating a secretariat for the social economy within the Department of Economic Development. In contrast, while the general principle of social dialogue is reasonably well established in Slovenia, the SSE has not achieved adequate recognition because SSE organisations are not involved in developing enabling public policy.

When governments must operate within extremely tight budgets, effective co-construction can explore cost-effective ways for government to enable the SSE. For example, the participatory budgeting processes implemented at the regional and local level in Ecuador led to a change in government priorities and programmes in favour of social inclusion and the promotion of territorial economic development. In Bolivia, the multi-year strategy for the SSE and fair trade was elaborated with civil society, but budgetary limitations prevented it from achieving its objectives. In Burkina Faso, the consultation process for stakeholders in rural development has never been operational due to insufficient funding. Similarly in Poland, the willingness of local governments to engage with civil society was questioned when local development strategies were designed without any provision to finance their activities.

Differences between intentions and actions may also be the result of poorly trained public officials who lack the expertise to implement policy measures effectively. Decentralising the responsibility for the

SSE is important in order to ensure that programmes are adapted to their territories and can meet their objectives. But this process will face implementation barriers if newly responsible programme officers in local settings are not trained adequately.

In other instances, government interest in collaboration is limited to a particular moment in time or to a specific issue. A more iterative process not only ensures that the initial policy objectives are being met, it also contributes to educating all stakeholders about unforeseen challenges or opportunities that may present themselves along the way. Thus, while the formulation and implementation of the Social Enterprise Promotion Act in Korea was the result of co-construction, the multi-sectoral Social Enterprise Support Committee it created is limited to carrying out the certification of social enterprises, while participating members are appointed by the Ministry of Labour. This clientelist approach to emerging social enterprises and inflexible eligibility criteria severely compromise the potential for innovation within this horizontal space.

Government commitment is also contingent on governing parties. This is why institutional gains, such as general framework legislation, can help avoid dramatic changes in policy. Certainly, some governments have been more favourable to the SSE than others and have created ministries or secretariats for the sector and multi-stakeholder spaces for policy elaboration. For example, programmes promoting the SSE in Canada in 2005 were the result of a process of co-construction at the federal level, but a change of government led to their elimination. In Quebec, however, co-construction is institutionalised and has survived changes in government. Abrupt government changes can also affect the momentum within civil society, as was the case in Brazil; here, the interruption in the dialogue between government and civil society between 2008 and 2010 weakened the SSE's capacity to position itself collectively.

Intergovernmental collaboration In many of the countries surveyed, policies to support the development of the SSE are insufficient or too narrowly focused. The risks of such approaches include: a negative impact on the organisations themselves if contingent funding restricts their activities and limits their capacity to grow; limited impact on poverty reduction and social exclusion if the SSE is narrowly defined; and a high risk of policy failure with its associated costs, both real and political. Designing policy in hybrid and institutional settings that facilitate dialogue and deliberation increases their effectiveness. Where such environments exist, the potential for policy innovation and positive policy outcomes is high.

However, co-construction is necessary but insufficient if the policy instrument is narrow or sectoral. For the SSE, effective co-construction requires a degree of intergovernmental collaboration. Governments that have recognised this have created mechanisms to ensure this type of collaboration. In Brazil, the Inter-Ministerial Team for Systematic Solutions for the SSE and the National Solidarity Economy Council work to ensure that all ministries take the SSE into account. In Quebec, primary responsibility for the SSE was transferred to the Ministry for Municipal Affairs and Land Occupancy, a more horizontal policy space better able to address the inter-sectoral nature of the SSE. In Spain, the general framework law on the SSE includes institutional measures to explicitly include the SSE in different sectoral policies (employment, rural development and social services, for example) and to improve managerial productivity and competitiveness. In contrast, in South Korea, interest in the SSE is mostly confined to its impact on employment, with different ministries focusing on developing specific kinds of organisation. This limited conception of the potential of the SSE and segmentation of government programmes reduce policy effectiveness and obscure the role of the wider SSE, including its role in advocacy for different disadvantaged groups. Also problematic are cases where different government programmes compete with each other, as in Nepal.

The literature on horizontality and collaborative policy identifies the need for a 'lead department' or ministry to coordinate the process (Sullivan and Skelcher 2002). But there is a difference between a convening role and a ministerial mandate that consults only with other departments or ministries. Effective co-construction implies the involvement of all stakeholders, including all affected branches and levels of government, including municipal and regional governments. Such participation was found to be lacking in Slovenia, Poland and Ecuador but well developed in Spain's Andalusian Pacts. In order for municipal and regional governments to play a significant role, they must benefit from enabling national macro policies. Institutional capacity increases as a function of openness to sectoral and jurisdictional realignment, and as a result of linkages between different levels of government (Fung and Wright 2003).

Long-term support to the SSE It is clear that long-term government support for the SSE and its intermediaries is essential to the co-construction process and to allow actors to build on past successes. The Quebec government's multi-year action plan institutionalises the co-construction of public policy.[7] It has significant heuristic value as an example of horizontal coordination within government and collaboration with SSE actors. To achieve this, the government created an inter-ministerial committee and a technical support group that brings together those engaged in the SSE. In Brazil, the Sistema Nacional de Comércio Justo e Solidário, created in 2010, established a series of parameters for government to follow when executing public policies for the promotion of the SSE and fair trade. These policies are designed through an ongoing dialogue with civil society.

Long-term financial support is critical for SSE enterprises and organisations to meet development objectives. Consideration should be given to the diversity of sectors in the SSE and the corresponding variability of financial support they require. In some cases, financial support by government is necessary at the early stages of development and can be reduced as enterprises build scale and market capacity. In other cases, recurrent and long-term financial engagement by government is required by organisations that cannot be expected to be self-financing but that reduce government costs through their public benefit activities. These include organisations providing employment for the disadvantaged (such as disabled and long-term unemployed people) and essential services (day care and home care, for example). These enterprises and organisations internalise social costs that would otherwise be borne by government, and the long-term benefits far exceed the immediate costs to government.

Government must begin to calculate its social returns on investment to capture the large societal benefits from such engagement. The policy universe is complex, including programme funding, fiscal tools, direct financial commitments by government, legislation, procurement provisions, and so on. Most important is the need for a different mindset that understands the overriding benefits to government of actively investing in SSE initiatives. This transforms the logic of subsidy and spending into an expectation of return. This is the rationale that underlies broad supportive measures for the SSE in countries such as Brazil and Ecuador and in regions such as PACA in France and Quebec. It also underpins the support of sectors that have a widespread social and economic impact, such as day care in Quebec and agriculture in Brazil. The social or societal return on investment to government is positive. The greatest challenge, perhaps, is to introduce this logic into policy design.

Conclusion

The SSE is providing solutions to complex societal challenges worldwide. Its capacity to do so is contingent on relations between SSE actors and government and the availability of enabling public policy. The case studies that inform this chapter confirm that, for the SSE to develop its full potential, public policy must take into account the diverse needs and capacities of SSE enterprises, organisations and initiatives. Governments must shift their role from state providers to strategic enablers. The most effective way to achieve this is to create institutional infrastructure for information-sharing and collaborative processes of strategic planning and policy design. The co-construction of public policy considerably reduces information asymmetry, increases ownership of policy and facilitates the implementation of policy measures and their adjustment over time. Co-construction processes generate richer results where independent and capable SSE intermediary organisations exist, where horizontal policy spaces are created – breaking down silos within government – and where actors are able to consider the longer term.

Although co-construction is increasingly understood as a more efficient way of producing enabling policy for the SSE, it is not without its challenges. Governments must navigate between subsidiarity (more autonomy to lower-level authorities) and conditionality (obliging lower-level authorities to comply with a regulatory framework to ensure coherence). When compromises are found, governments must resolve issues of accountability (where does responsibility lie in these hybrid arrangements?) and the delivery of public services (contracts for services and the increased use of quasi-markets, for example).

Both SSE actors and government face the challenge of building and maintaining their credibility to pursue continuous dialogue.

For government, this means ensuring that all government agencies and the levels of government involved are participating fully in the co-construction process. For civil society, it means ensuring that networks and intermediaries are representative of the SSE, that they are strong enough to participate in planning and in executing long-term action plans, and that they are able to remain independent of government or other specific interests.

Research confirms that in the countries where more effective ways of addressing complexity exist, and where this is reflected in policies to enable the SSE, innovation is occurring within government institutions and within civil society organisations – and between them. The challenge is great but the urgency to move in this direction is far greater.

PART II

COLLECTIVE ACTION AND SOLIDARITY IN PRACTICE

10 | BEYOND ALTERNATIVE FOOD NETWORKS: ITALY'S SOLIDARITY PURCHASE GROUPS AND THE UNITED STATES' COMMUNITY ECONOMIES

Cristina Grasseni, Francesca Forno and Silvana Signori

Introduction

This chapter outlines and compares data from four case studies of alternative food networks in Italy and the United States (US) to better understand the factors that have an impact on their capacity to expand. The studies comprised a survey of solidarity purchase groups in Lombardy; ethnographic observation of a network of such groups in one of Lombardy's provinces, Bergamo; a qualitative study of anti-mafia solidarity economy activism in Sicily; and an ethnography of solidarity economy initiatives in Massachusetts (US). The range of methodologies employed[1] have contributed to mapping and measuring previously uncharted aspects of the social and solidarity economy (SSE), as well as assessing limits and strategies in developing novel economic circuits.

The networks we studied engage in collective provisioning of food and some other goods and services as forms of 'solidarity purchase' arranged directly with producers, thus taking into account their costs and difficulties. They encompass different types of civil society and social movement repertoires, as they develop into second-order associative networks. Such networks conform to a 'substantivist' model that re-embeds economic practice into social relations (Gudeman 2012; Polanyi 1968). As Gibson-Graham and Roelvink (2011: 29) argue, 'a different representation of the economy' enables 'new economic subjects who can begin to take ethical action in the economic realm'.

Our thesis is that Italy's solidarity purchase groups or *gruppi di acquisto solidale* (GAS) and districts of solidarity economy or *distretti di economia solidale* (DES) embody such 'performative efficacy' as they organise and inspire novel economic circuits that are directly supported by local actors. From this point of view, GAS are in many ways similar to a collaboratively and collectively organised form of community-supported agriculture (CSA). CSA is a phenomenon born in Massachusetts at the end of the 1980s (White 2013) that is contributing significantly to making alternatives visible in contemporary American foodscapes (Hinrichs and Lyson 2009). However, while CSA usually operates as the initiative of one or more farming entrepreneurs, GAS are organised networks of consumers that trigger an ethical entrepreneurial response.

Understanding the practical challenges and contradictions that emerge as SSE expands and interacts with decision-makers and the media will allow potential donors and developers to accompany and enable SSE organisations as they learn to overcome these hurdles. Our thesis is that the SSE may work as a space of creative cross-fertilisation, or cross-cutting innovation, bridging different networks of activist groups. As such, it can work as a socio-pedagogic laboratory, identifying and experimenting with critical issues about delegation and representation, participation and labour division, as well as skill and value construction.

The emergence of solidarity purchase groups in Italy[2]

A national survey carried out by the farmers' union Coldiretti has claimed that 18 per cent of Italians (about 7 million people) are involved in forms of collective provisioning. These include car-pooling, condominium shopping groups and collective agreements with farmers (Rubino 2012). Of these, about 150,000 people may be involved in solidarity-driven collectives such as GAS.

GAS are grass-roots networks that collectively organise direct provisioning, mostly of food and other everyday items (such as detergents and basic toiletries), but increasingly also of textiles and 'alternative' services such as renewable energy and sustainable tourism. The charter of the GAS national network (www.retegas. org) explains that solidarity means cooperation and sympathy with producers, the environment and other GAS members, or *gasistas* as they call themselves.[3]

Gasistas buy 'in solidarity' with producers in the sense that they take into account the difficulties and costs faced by small and local farming enterprises. For instance, 80 per cent of GAS interviewed in Milan stated that in at least one case they paid for crops in advance of planting. With advance payments, the farmers

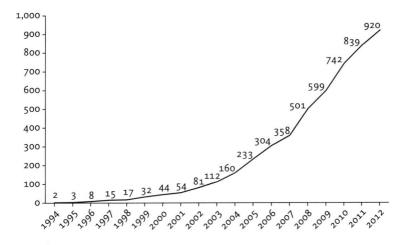

10.1 GAS registered with www.retegas.org per year (*source*: www.retegas.org).

have cash for crop preparation and are guaranteed that, whatever the season, the crop will be sold at the negotiated price. This is a radically different system to those imposed by large distribution channels.

Since the first GAS was established in 1994, about 1,000 GAS have registered with www.retegas.org (Figure 10.1), but this is not the full picture. A pilot project in and around the town of Bergamo mapped approximately double the number of previously known GAS.[4] A parallel initiative in Rome found similar results (Fonte et al. 2011). According to Retegas, it is safe to assume that at least 50 per cent more GAS exist than the 1,000 currently registered.

Our survey of 1,658 *gasista* families in Lombardy further established that 43.1 per cent of the groups engaged between twenty-one and forty families each, while 36.3 per cent involved groups of between four and twenty families. Larger groups do exist but the majority are small- to medium-sized networks of families who get together to establish strategies for collective and solidarity-driven purchases.

The survey shows that total annual household expenditures are approximately €742 per household. Considering that each group enrols an average of twenty-five families of four people, each GAS would cater for the needs of around 100 consumers. Projecting these data on to the number of GAS groups in Lombardy (the 429 identified), the economic weight of these groups would account for about €8 million.

In the next section, we outline our statistical portrait of *gasistas*. Our claim is that participating in a GAS socialises members in alternative socio-economic circuits, which empower consumers seeking direct and collective relationships with providers. In the following two sections, we argue that GAS sociality not only increases families' opportunities for affordable and quality food in times of crisis, but also re-embeds provisioning in a relational fabric. GAS have a political impact on context-specific regional economies, increasing social engagement and active citizenship – vis-à-vis the role of the mafia in Italian economy, for example. In sum, GAS function as de Tocqueville's 'schools of democracy', building social capital beyond mere consumption (Forno et al. 2014). Finally, we highlight some elements of similarity and difference between Italian DES and Massachusetts community economies, illustrating promising parallel developments of the solidarity economy in comparable contexts.

Solidarity purchase groups as family-driven collectives

Who are *gasistas*? The majority (60 per cent) work as clerks, teachers or professors. We should think of them mostly as office workers. On the whole, *gasistas* are unmistakably *families*: only 6.6 per cent are single, while 47.6 per cent are couples with children over five years old and another 24.4 per cent are couples with children under five. Their level of education is also significant: 49.5 per cent of the interviewees have a degree or a higher degree, and another 38.1 per cent have high school diplomas that give access to higher education.

The following chart records types of motivation for joining a GAS. Despite the crisis, the main driver is not to get better quality at a lower cost but to protect one's own health, implying that *gasistas* seek better quality food (in most cases, organic) by directly supporting smallholders (see Figure 10.2).

We asked only the person in each family who does most of the GAS-related work to fill in the questionnaire: 62 per cent of respondents were women, 49.6 per cent were aged between thirty and forty-four, and 42.9 per cent aged between forty-five and sixty. This hardly fits the stereotypical portrait of the political activist.

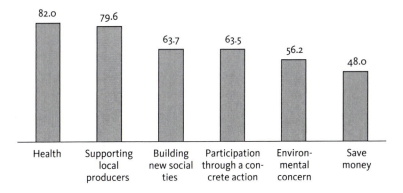

10.2 Motivation for joining a GAS (percentage of respondents who 'agree' or 'agree very much') (*source*: CORES, 'Inside relational capital' project).

Gasistas are *provisioning activists*, in that they are the same people who would typically bear the burden of providing for their families (mostly working middle-aged women). They refashion that burden by socialising it in a solidarity purchase group.

GAS collectively buy bread, pasta, flour, milk, dairy products, oil, fish, meat, detergents, wine, preserves, juices, jams, fruit and vegetables. About half also buy clothes. Most organise this form of collective purchase through monthly meetings, where *gasistas* meet face to face and discuss what to buy, from whom and in what quantities. 'Product coordinators' (*referenti*, namely the people in charge of organising the purchase of a specific product for the entire group) report on their liaisons with each producer involved regarding prices, logistics and product quality.

Gasistas are not rich and they should not be confused with gourmet food lovers. Conviviality may play a part in GAS practice, with farm site visits and occasional dinners or fairs. But GAS are first and foremost solidarity-driven provisioning collectives. In Lombardy, where the cost of living is more expensive than elsewhere in Italy, *gasista* family income ranges between €2,000 and €3,500 (gross per month) in 56 per cent of cases and is less than €2,000 in 22.3 per cent. Thus, any changes in their consumption and provisioning styles are significant, as one assumes that they are not dictated by a 'radical chic' fad or by a question of taste, but by learning new lifestyles through operating within the constraints of fairly tight working family budgets (see Grasseni 2014).

As illustrated below (Tables 10.1, 10.2 and 10.3), the CORES survey shows how consumers' shopping baskets, consumption styles and even civic participation have changed, sometimes dramatically, after joining a GAS.

TABLE 10.1 Changes in consumption habits (percentage of respondents)

	Increased	Decreased	Introduced	No change	n/a
Vegetables	50.4	0.4	0.7	47.4	1.2
Organic	79.4	0.2	7.7	11.6	1.1
Wholemeal	52.9	0.6	10.0	35.2	1.4
Legumes	38.5	0.5	3.7	56.3	1.1
Local	80.6	0.2	5.4	12.6	1.1
Seasonal	68.1	0.1	2.8	27.8	1.2
Cereals	45.1	0.3	12.8	40.5	1.3
Meat	3.1	42.5	0.2	52.0	2.2
Fairtrade	39.6	1.4	5.6	51.8	1.5
Mafia-free	44.6	0.6	14.7	38.5	1.5
Ecological	41.4	0.6	25.0	31.9	1.1

Source: CORES, 'Inside relational capital' project.

TABLE 10.2 Changes in lifestyles (percentage of respondents)

	Yes	No	Already did	n/a
Decreased purchasing of pre-cooked food	24.8	5.1	69.4	0.7
Decreased shopping in supermarkets	41.4	47.9	9.7	0.9
Increased purchases in local shops	27.5	33.0	37.9	1.6
Started producing food at home	38.3	31.9	29.0	0.9
Started growing vegetables	16.2	54.8	27.6	1.4
Started to use the car less	17.6	46.9	34.5	1.0
Increased recycling	32.5	6.7	60.0	0.9
More attention to energy consumption	29.3	22.9	46.3	1.4
More attention to water consumption	28.6	6.1	64.3	1.0

Source: CORES, 'Inside relational capital' project.

Setting up and managing GAS can be difficult. Often highlighted are problems relating to the effective involvement of *all* members in the running of the group (57 per cent), and the difficulty in find-

TABLE 10.3 Changes in participation (percentage of respondents)

	Yes	No	Already did	n/a
More interested in problems concerning my town of residence	26.0	30.3	42.5	1.2
More interested in politics in general	7.9	35.8	55.0	1.3
More able to cooperate with people in general	39.7	16.1	42.9	1.4
Feeling more able to influence public policy	23.9	60.8	13.8	1.6

Source: CORES, 'Inside relational capital' project.

ing volunteers for new tasks (12.7 per cent). Managing a group is time-consuming: most GAS are organised on a system of volunteer task-sharing, to ensure the smooth running of finance, logistics and operations at no additional operational cost. The vast majority of groups are based on a simple mailing list (no Facebook pages!) and meet in person once a month to make consensual decisions about orders, deliveries and all other activities. Many *gasistas* (62.3 per cent) reported that 'we try to rotate roles and tasks, but they tend to remain allocated to the same people'. Logistics plays an important role. The main reason for abandoning a producer is allegedly 'logistics problems that are down to the producer'.

Qualitative and quantitative data highlight that solidarity economies work both as coping strategies for young families with children and as a social, economic and political laboratory. Nevertheless, in the next section we highlight how they develop different dynamics in different regions, drawing on specific territorial political subcultures and socio-economic contexts.

Re-embedding the economy into society

CORES has focused on the repertoires and networking strategies of GAS networks in Lombardy and Sicily, as they expand in two very different economic and social contexts. Lombardy and Sicily are large regions (9,200 and 9,900 square miles respectively, roughly the size of Massachusetts). While Lombardy has approximately 10 million inhabitants, Sicily has about half that figure, although it is still the fourth most populous Italian region. Lombardy's gross domestic product (GDP) is comparable with that of Massachusetts, while Sicily's GDP is about a quarter. GAS have flourished mostly in north and central Italy, which are endowed with a lively and capillary associative fabric; there are only fifty-nine registered GAS in Sicily.

Notoriously, the mafia has solid roots in Sicily, although there is increasing evidence of its economic ramifications at all levels in every region of Italy; for instance, scholars, journalists and administrators have denounced how the Milan (Lombardy) area is rife with money-laundering activities (Varese 2011; Dalla Chiesa and Panzarasa 2012; Portanova et al. 2011). Specifically, the Sicilian mafia historically grew with agricultural monocultures, and mafia 'infiltrations' in lemon cultivation have been documented since 1872 (Rizzo 2011). Mafia rackets control the entire food supply chain, from workers' recruitment to logistics and distribution, including significant sales of fake 'Made in Italy' foodstuffs. They also direct the recruitment of slave-like labour (an estimated 400,000 workers) through *caporalato*, namely the dependency of local bosses who recruit teams of day workers (FLAI 2012).

Because of this, farming cooperatives that work land expropriated from mafia clans struggle to find access to distribution networks (Forno 2011). Gaining direct access to dedicated customers is a condition of survival for these producers. Their active search for this kind of direct transaction is evidenced by the many letters that GAS receive from agricultural cooperatives and family farmers, at both national and local level.

According to Mauro Serventi, the founder of the first GAS in Parma in 1994, 200 GAS were founded in southern Italy in the wake of the 2008 GAS assembly, which took place, significantly, in Sicily. There, GAS meet the specific local need of supporting a 'clean', mafia-free local economy in a context of tragically high unemployment.[5] As financial uncertainty and the environmental crisis increase food and energy prices, networks of organic producers in Sicily are attempting to meet the demand for organic and transparent provision of fruit and vegetables (notably olive oil and citrus fruits) from northern Italian GAS. 'Districts' and networks of solidarity economies aim to facilitate a mutually beneficial encounter between critical consumers and virtuous producers. One significant example is *Sbarchinpiazza* – literally 'dropping the anchor in the square' – an itinerant sale of Sicilian oranges that was organised by the Sicilian agricultural consortium Arcipelago Siqilyah in early 2012.

The 'Archipelago', which is a network of orange growers working in partnership with GAS, hosted orange fairs in about twenty towns in northern and central Italy. The special relationship between GAS and orange producers ensured that only producers already known to local GAS could participate in the fair. The point of holding a public market instead of just unloading trucks of oranges for *gasistas* was to make these transactions visible and to increase their appeal to a larger public. *Sbarchinpiazza* is publicly performed as an act of economic transaction combined with social pedagogy: *gasistas* buy oranges from Sicily in solidarity with southern farmers. Actually meeting the farmers gives the *gasistas* a chance to learn how re-engineering supply chains is a necessary condition to break up complex chains of corruption and organised crime. For instance, some of the oranges sold in this way are produced by cooperatives working on mafia-confiscated land.

This example shows how questions of practice precede, inform and literally unpack wider political and epistemic strategies within the *gasista* experience. Figuring out how to deliver oranges from a farm in Sicily to a Lombard family a thousand miles away is a way in which that particular economic circuit can be liberated from a mafia-ridden distribution chain. In *Sbarchinpiazza*, the economic transaction was obviously key, but the surrounding seminars, speeches and entertainment informed and sensitised both *gasistas* and the general public to the fact that environmentally concerned consumers should also be socially and politically concerned.[6]

Forno and Gunnarson (2010) have studied *pizzo*-free entrepreneurship in Sicily. They maintain that promoting mafia-free shops through 'buy-cotting' innovates the political repertoire of anti-mafia activism through critical consumerism.[7] *Sbarchinpiazza* is a further example of how GAS offer a neutral meeting place for different types of political activism, of economic subjectivities, and of social aspirations that would otherwise not necessarily intersect in fruitful ways. GAS, as circuits of alternative provisioning, work as second-order networks. In our research experience, the key protagonists of the solidarity economy movement have had prior exposure to environmental activism, unions or the global justice movement. Solidarity economy networks offer them a common ground to liaise through novel and collaborative projects, starting from the basic act of food provisioning. However, participant observation with the Bergamo

GAS network in 2009–10 recorded significant stumbling blocks on issues of delegation, leadership and conflict management. This may well relate to the fact that GAS sociality is close-knit and that cross-fertilisation across networks happens through personal acquaintances and participation in the same working groups, as we explain in the following section. Furthermore, ethnographic observation revealed an initial gender imbalance between the largely male steering committees and working groups and the 'base', 70 per cent of which was composed of women. This imbalance, however, was reduced somewhat following more inclusive debates and assemblies in 2011 and 2012.

Solidarity purchase groups as laboratories for sustainable citizenship

GAS originate for the vast majority (39.4 per cent of cases in Lombardy) from existing networks of friends, and in a further 21.2 per cent of cases from pre-existent GAS. *Gasistas* often use metaphors such as 'budding' and 'grafting', but also 'nurturing seedlings' and 'sowing seeds', to describe their own diffusion. Most of their growth trend was concentrated in the austerity years of 2010–13. This resulted in unprecedented media exposure, as GAS were sometimes championed as a DIY solution to the economic crisis, although they were often confused with other forms of bulk-buying or collective purchase (as in the Coldiretti survey mentioned above). This showcasing increased requests from people to join such groups, as well as offers from self-promoting producers to become GAS providers. However, in some cases, this situation created parasitic behaviour in associations that depended on voluntary work. In fact, this is a key difference between GAS and a consumer cooperative, which can delegate assignments to salaried workers but charges running costs to its membership. In other words, GAS practice is also solidarity-driven because it allocates workloads equally among group members. In 75.5 per cent of cases, every member is a 'product coordinator': this means that he or she is responsible for gathering orders for that particular product, liaising with the producer, picking up deliveries and organising distribution to the other members of the group. Only 5.6 per cent of GAS in Lombardy allocate this task to a consumer cooperative or service provider. However, in 18.9 per cent of cases the GAS is run by a tighter group that coordinates, manages and distributes deliveries to all the other members.

Crucially, one of the limitations of GAS is a lack of formal support from local administrations: 73 per cent reply that they have no support while 70.5 per cent state that they collaborate with non-governmental organisations (NGOs) and citizens' associations. This is indicative of the degree of mistrust of political institutions in Lombardy, as in Italy more generally, which is counterbalanced by an equal degree of activism in local associations, NGOs and grass-roots initiatives. Then again, only 23 per cent of Lombard GAS have taken on a formal profile as an association, despite the injunction by law to do so if the GAS wishes to have its activities recognised as tax-exempt by the Italian government (Government of the Italian Republic 2007). Nevertheless, 93.7 per cent of *gasistas* have participated in some form of association in their lifetime. A range between 3 per cent and 30 per cent currently participate in specific associations, from women's rights to pacifist, environmentalist or religious organisations. A further 80 per cent had participated in the mobilisation against the privatisation of water, 64 per cent against the reintroduction of nuclear power plants in Italy, and 52 per cent in defence of public schooling. What is lacking, therefore, is not an associative culture – on the contrary, such a culture pervades society. Rather, the problem is that GAS actively resist efforts to professionalise, organise and normalise their associative activity.

Interestingly, there is a discrepancy between the motivation for joining a GAS (Figure 10.2) and the objectives and results achieved after joining (Figure 10.3). We believe that there is a seamless connection between the practice of solidarity within GAS (namely, the way in which they work as collective micro-organisations) and this result. In the survey, 82 per cent of interviewees maintained that their main motivation for joining a GAS was their own health. Nevertheless, in response to the question 'What are the main objectives and results of being in a GAS?', the most common response was 'to encourage more responsible lifestyles with regard to the environment' (50.1 per cent). Only 11.7 per cent gave the answer 'to protect one's health and that of one's family'. In other words, while individual motivation may well be self-centred, participation results in an awareness of broader goals of social and political relevance, such as responsibility towards the environment. Notably, *gasistas* cite supporting local producers as a specific result in 29.6 per cent of cases, while 20.1 per cent mentioned it as a main objective of a

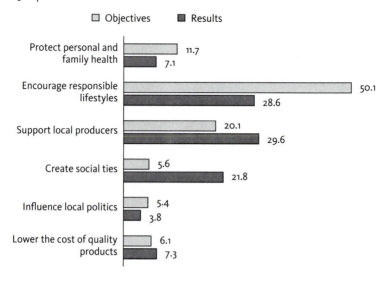

10.3 The main objectives and results of being in a GAS (percentage of respondents) (*source*: CORES, 'Inside relational capital' project).

GAS. As perceived by *gasistas*, then, there are still ample margins for increasing support to local economies.

Our thesis is that, through GAS practice, specific relations of trust are built or extended across networks, thus facilitating virtuous feedback, cooperation between different groups, and the establishment of new economic circuits (Forno 2013; Grasseni 2013). In fact, in Lombardy, which hosts the highest number of GAS in Italy, second-order networks have begun to connect GAS with agricultural cooperatives, ethical banks, time banks and entrepreneurs. These networks have been described as districts of solidarity economy or DES (Tavolo per la Rete Italiana di Economia Solidale 2010).[8] Tavolo RES, the working group for a national network of solidarity economy, indicates that ten out the existing twenty-five DES projects in Italy are located in Lombardy, where GAS density is highest. Ethnographic observation confirms that GAS work as laboratories for 'sustainable citizenship' (Micheletti and Stolle 2012); for example, 'citizenship markets' have been established in the Bergamo area since 2011. These are a solidarity-driven version of farmers' markets, to which farmers are admitted only after being screened by a solidarity economy activist association, Market and Citizenship. Through a self-evaluation questionnaire devised by Market and Citizenship in collaboration with local GAS, each producer wishing to sell at the market is asked to identify their own position vis-à-vis food sovereignty, food democracy, food justice, food responsibility and food quality.[9] Under the name 'Farmers' Market and More' (*Mercato agricolo e non solo*), citizenship markets are held every fortnight in three locations in and outside the town of Bergamo.[10] In brief, these GAS-monitored farmers' markets make the produce of GAS providers available and visible to a wider public, often within the framework of other events, such as book presentations, solidarity economy fairs, or public debates on sustainable agriculture, clean textiles and transparency of price. While featuring local foods, they are not just about food and provisioning, as they aim to reintroduce citizenship in economic transactions.

By purchasing from trusted and selected producers, customers ensure that they are not complicit with the exploitation of indentured or illegal labour (as in the case of the Sicilian oranges). Equally, the markets promote organic farming and shorter food supply chains, supporting the cultivation of crops for consumption instead of mono-cultures, thus increasing local food availability. In doing so, GAS are facilitated by the fact that they often operate in a scenario of geographical, social and temporal proximity with small-scale agriculture.

Nevertheless, GAS activism does *not* always necessarily develop into DES. Ethnographic research in the Bergamo area reveals that even networking among different GAS is laborious and time-consuming. While best practice related to logistics spreads quickly across networks (for instance on how to organise collective orders and deliveries), investing human resources on new projects is more difficult, especially because GAS depend mostly on the voluntary work and time of their own members (Grasseni 2013). Positive contamination of repertoires happens only between networks that have an effective overlap via specific people and practical collaborations. In fact, districts tend to develop where a tight-knit group of activists develop GAS-supported pilot projects and obtain external seed funding. This would happen more easily if GAS routinely supported ethical banking; however, about 56 per cent of interviewed *gasistas* in Lombardy say that they do not practise forms of ethical investing (Signori 2006), and only 7 per cent invest their entire savings in ethical investments.

On the whole, *gasistas* creatively rethink provisioning, making use of both digital communication and face-to-face sociality. Through collective practice and deliberation, *gasistas* re-appropriate their role of both 'co-producers' and critical 'consumers': through their everyday collective choices, they contribute to a more sustainable food provisioning system and participate in a cultural effort to re-socialise consumers to the contexts of production. The most successful districts, such as DES Monza-Brianza, successfully manage short supply chains – for instance, for bread from locally harvested wheat (Maroni and Ponzini 2013) – and collective contracts for green energy.[11]

Nevertheless, network leaders underline the challenges of consolidating and expanding solidarity economy networks, mentioning specifically the constant risk of burn-out of SSE volunteers, who often run complex organisational and relational tasks in their spare time. Moreover, as one leader of DES Monza-Brianza noted, it is difficult to 'convert' producers to the SSE philosophy of mutualism and solidarity when they themselves do not buy and consume within social and solidarity networks: 'I buy from them, but they do their shopping at the supermarket!' According to these insights, the main challenge of implicating SSE in broader processes of transformative change is precisely that of involving larger sectors of society in critically rethinking food and provisioning systems, so that solidarity purchase does not remain a moral exercise in ethical consumerism.

Conclusion: towards an agenda for comparative analysis

The uniqueness of solidarity purchase groups lies in their collective dimension and in their motivation to consider themselves not merely as the end users of a shortened supply chain, but as co-producers of the very conditions of production, in that they enable the farmers to produce outside conventional market constraints. Through a networking dynamic, a variety of social and economic actors coalesce to create novel economic circuits, which respond to community need. This is more typical of the cooperative culture than of what are largely identified as 'alternative food networks' (Goodman et al. 2012). For instance, it was the demand for ethical as well as organic oranges from GAS that encouraged Sicilian smallholders to join forces and propose themselves as an 'Archipelago' of suitable producers for GAS networks.

Similarly, in the US state of Massachusetts a number of environmental and food justice groups, as well as workers' cooperatives, are engaged in economic practices that serve local community needs, such as in urban farming, recycling and weatherisation.[12] Their economic practices are expressed through groups for community-oriented collaborative action and collective self-provisioning, rather than as consumer cooperatives. In the Boston area, for example, these include the collective preparation of preserves and yoghurt from locally harvested fruits in public and private green spaces in a spirit of 'community cooperative enterprise' (Morrow and Dombroski forthcoming). Furthermore, expanding coalitions of worker-owned cooperatives in central and western Massachusetts in sectors such as community-supported agriculture, car mechanics and printing are increasing scholarly understanding of solidarity economies well beyond a dismissive reading of them as 'alternative networks' (Cornwell and Graham 2009).

Italian DES and US community economies both challenge an orthodox distinction between producers and consumers and an orthodox definition of 'economy', as suggested by J. K. Gibson-Graham's diverse economy framework (Gibson-Graham et al. 2013). They sometimes share styles and repertoires of participation with the cooperative movement, and contribute to the diffusion of a context-based and voluntary work-based collaborative culture, devoid of the disenchanting effects of the professionalisation of cooperative entrepreneurship (see Forno 2013).

In the Pioneer Valley of Massachusetts, for instance, several scholars are studying a flourishing of community economies based on cooperative development (Healy and Shear 2011); these share with DES the primacy of volunteer work, a stress on collective self-provisioning and self-help, and a focus on community well-being as a common objective. Italy's DES and these US community economies are comparable and complex processes that re-embed the economy into a social and relational fabric of reciprocity. Although they are rooted in locally specific associative cultures, GAS/DES and community economies share the ambition of creating sustainable and just economies.

They also share the characteristic of involving scholars in co-research to achieve a clear representation of solidarity economies as embedded and diverse (Democrazia Km Zero 2012; Tavolo per la

Rete Italiana di Economia Solidale 2013). In the case of CORES, collaboration with local GAS leaders and with the nationwide Tavolo RES was a vital precondition for obtaining access and widespread support for the online survey, which was endorsed by the founder of the first GAS and achieved an exceptionally high response rate (71 per cent in Bergamo and 48 per cent throughout Lombardy), despite *gasistas'* well-known suspicion of formal investigation of their activities. In central and western Massachusetts, on the other hand, collaborative research with local scholars is helping chart and organise nascent solidarity economies, for example through community mapping initiatives and training in ethnographic interviewing skills. Local projects for neighbourhood empowerment are also active in developing green job opportunities for youth, social and visual media, as well as community events.[13]

While groups such as Worcester Roots are active in decontaminating and reclaiming urban soil for farming, in Lombardy 'participatory guarantee systems' are being developed by three DES to involve both farmers and GAS representatives in local pacts in lieu of institutional certification for organic farming (Contessi 2014). The project was presented publicly by the DES of Como, Monza-Brianza and Varese with a conference on 16 February 2013. This involved identifying consensual protocols for converting conventional farms to organic, or for keeping pesticides at a minimum, in case-by-case negotiations. Participatory guarantee systems aim to find viable and local solutions to usually compromised circumstances, such as nitrogen pollution in the soil and water from excessively fed cattle grazing the land. The potential toxicity of post-industrial ground, the loss of fertility in fields that have been farmed intensively for decades and land-grabbing by large-scale certified organic agribusinesses are all concerns of these actors. Rather than applying an abstract evaluation grid in the name of audit-like accountability, GAS/DES activists prefer to invite transparency from the producers about the actual barriers, so that a protocol and a road map can be agreed upon collaboratively. The spirit of peer review and horizontality in participatory guarantee systems is very much in line with other short supply chain projects that DES have developed in Lombardy, such as the bread short supply chain of DES Brianza (Vergani 2013; Maroni and Ponzini 2013).

Among the many parallels between Italian and American solidarity economies is the grass-roots recognition that actions need to be put in place to fill the gaps of top-down development policies, either in the context of post-industrial decline or in the wake of natural calamity. For example, in Italy, GAS collectively mobilised to buy from Abruzzese farmers struck by an earthquake in 2009 and Parmesan producers affected by another in 2012. Buying at 'solidarity prices' from locations where logistics and produce conservation had become critical due to post-quake circumstances was a way of acting economically but beyond mere profit. In Massachusetts, solidarity economy activists are addressing sustainability by demanding that green jobs are developed in response to community needs and in a spirit of social solidarity[14] and that alternative food provisioning also addresses 'food justice' (Hope and Agyeman 2011).

These many parallels between phenomena that have developed largely without awareness of each other's existence confirm Amin's definition of social economies as an outcome of local circumstances and contexts (Amin 2009), but also CORES's thesis that the main wealth created within solidarity economies is the capacity to rethink economic practice in terms of active citizenship. Many factors remain open to observation and subsequent investigation, such as the diversity of local interpretations of cooperative culture and their capacity to adapt roles and expertise as networks scale up and a certain degree of professional specialisation sets in.

11 | SOCIAL AND SOLIDARITY INVESTMENT IN MICROFINANCE

Paul Nelson

Introduction

Can cooperation, association and solidarity – the features of the social and solidarity economy (SSE) – exist on a large scale in international finance? This chapter reviews efforts to build and expand such financial relations through two mechanisms to mobilise financial capital from individuals and social networks in wealthy societies for microfinance services in low-income and transition societies. The two models are exemplified by Kiva, an internet-based lending scheme, and Oikocredit, an international social investment network based in Christian churches. Both encourage not donations but investments by individuals (and, in the case of Oikocredit, institutions) through funds that use capital investment to lend to microfinance institutions (MFIs), and to cooperatives and small businesses.

Markets, including global financial markets, and the values-driven practice of microfinance intersect in multiple ways. These intersections are likely to become increasingly problematic as microfinance continues to grow and to be seen as profitable under some circumstances. Pro-social investment – investment based on both financial and social performance – has made private, cross-border finance increasingly important for microfinance. Oikocredit was the second largest private source of finance for microfinance in 2009, and its new investments alone in 2012 were US$265 million. Kiva. org reports loans totalling US$370 million over its eight-year history. Loan portfolios in the hundreds of millions of dollars may be small in the context of global financial flows, but they loom large in the flows of capital to low-income borrowers and savers, which totalled an estimated US$25 billion in 2012.

The commercialisation of microfinance services themselves – lending and savings through special for-profit banks – and the use of investment revenues to capitalise non-profit microfinance lenders have sparked debates about profiting from poor borrowers, and have created perverse incentives that led some MFIs to over-lend and compromise the well-being of clients.

In this context, non-profit social investment funds face significant challenges, and play a potentially important role in microfinance, by allowing investment capital to become a source of capital for MFIs without being driven by the need to extract profits. Social investments create a capital stream that is not dependent on donor subsidies. The choice to invest in economic enterprises of the very poor opens the possibility of deepening knowledge, empathy and solidarity among investors and borrowers. Social investment funds may create an enduring institutional framework to mediate these relationships, through religious or secular networks. Finally, they have the potential to be economically viable financial institutions that build into their operation some of the flexibility and capacity for empathy – characteristics of solidarity relationships – that are important in responding to the economic conditions of borrowers.

I take a broad view of social solidarity. Creating solidarity across national lines and across huge differences in wealth is of interest for the concrete economic and social benefits it can deliver to borrowers. But here the investor participates as well, and, at best, pro-social investment schemes could offer the investor the opportunity to enter into respectful and reciprocal relations with microfinance borrowers through investment. Both Kiva.org and Oikocredit explicitly aim to establish relationships of solidarity, and they have substantial records. Kiva has been the object of scathing critiques for creating the appearance that individual lenders could choose and lend directly to particular entrepreneurs. This criticism calls into question whether the relationships that Kiva appears to facilitate are a strong and genuine basis for solidarity. My objective is not to compare Kiva and Oikocredit, which have somewhat different functions in the microfinance investment world, but to use the approaches that they offer collectively to illustrate the potential and the actual dimensions of solidarity in these forms of pro-social lending, as well as the challenges in realising this potential.

The components: microfinance and pro-social investment

Cooperative credit institutions, especially among the poor and particularly among women, exist in almost every culture. Most commonly known as rotating savings and credit associations (ROSCAs), they allow ten or a dozen individuals to save cooperatively by pooling small contributions from each, monthly, and allowing one member each month to receive the collected sum. Credit and consumer cooperatives, buying clubs and informal labour-sharing arrangements are similar expressions of cooperation, and of the SSE. SSE is understood here to include forms of production and exchange that aim to satisfy human needs, build resilience and expand human capabilities through social relations based on cooperation, association and solidarity and is also often associated with values of democratic governance and egalitarianism (UNRISD 2013b).

Non-bank financial services for people not eligible for bank loans have expanded rapidly since the 1970s in the form of microfinance. Microfinance is now an international industry with for-profit, official and non-governmental organisation (NGO) participants, standard-setting agencies, growing sets of norms and entrenched ideological camps and debates. Discussion of the merits of commercial-ising microfinance gained wider notice in 2011, after large-scale for-profit microfinance lenders in Andhra Pradesh, India were the subject of exposés revealing excessive lending, indebtedness and catastrophic economic results for some clients.

Microfinance is recognised as a component of some forms of local SSE. Gutberlet (2009) shows how microfinance contributes to solidarity relationships among recycling cooperatives in São Paulo. She finds that a microfinance fund managed by women recyclers has given the cooperatives access to capital without the additional costs imposed by intermediaries, and that the availability of capital and the presence of inclusive governance structures provide important material benefits.

This chapter begins from the premise that such positive contributions are possible in many local and regional microfinance initiatives, and examines the possibility that investors can also be part of relationships built on informed solidarity and mutual bene-fit. Most microfinance lending is capitalised at least in part by international sources. The mix of official development assistance, charitable sources and savings and investment has shifted over the years. Official aid from bilateral and multilateral donors still provides more than two-thirds of reported cross-border financing for microfinance, with private sources at US$8 billion (33 per cent) in 2011 (Lahaye et al. 2012). For several years, private finance has grown at a somewhat faster rate (19 per cent per year) than public sources (17 per cent per year), and private finance is likely to remain a significant factor.

The forms of private investment have also grown and diversified. Two primary non-profit forms – microfinance investment vehicles or MIVs (investment funds of various kinds) and online intermediaries promoting peer-to-peer investment – are represented by Oikocredit and Kiva.org respectively. A variety of other investment intermediaries practise both forms of investment: Danish MYCR and Indian DhanaX are examples that promote peer-matched lending; Calvert Funds and others also serve as investment intermediaries for MFIs (Davis and Gelpern 2010). These two examples of non-profit finance are examined and compared with commercial microfinance investing, exemplified here by BlueOrchard Microfinance Investment Managers.

Commercial microfinance investment has implications for MFIs (which lend to individual low-income borrowers) and for borrowers themselves. As commercial for-profit investment funds came to see microfinance as a profitable investment, they increasingly targeted the best-established, most profitable MFIs. The preference for these so-called 'tier one' MFIs is not new – aid donors often showed the same tendency – but it was pronounced as investment managers sought to minimise risk and maximise returns. CGAP, the Consultative Group to Assist the Poor, reports that 90 per cent of international investment in microfinance flows to tier one MFIs (Grameen Foundation 2010). This pressure is often thought to affect the mission and orientation of microfinance lenders, and of the borrowers themselves. An investment fund is less likely than an NGO or official donor to be tolerant of returns that fall short of expectations because an MFI made loans to higher-risk borrowers. Indeed, debt offerings such as the US$40 million BlueOrchard fund involve commitments to place investor representatives on the board of directors of the MFI, to monitor lending and financial practices.

The tension between repayment rates and outreach to very poor borrowers is longstanding, and large-scale private investment intensified the tension and in some cases tipped the balance. Rosenberg (2007: 1) worries that balancing commercial and social objectives becomes harder, 'especially when there are choices to be made about whether money goes into shareholders' pockets or clients' pockets'.

These pressures – sometimes labelled mission drift – mean that the role of non-profit, poverty-focused investment organisations is now particularly important.

Pro-social investment

Pro-social investment, as examined here, should be seen in the context of a larger movement for socially responsible investment in which investors avoid certain categories of investment (tobacco, weaponry and fossil fuels, for example) and/or actively invest in industries they support (organic agriculture, renewable energy). Private investment in microfinance takes several forms, and typically combines investors' interests in profitability and security with a concern for social impact or return, in different measures. Dieckmann's (2007) study for Deutsche Bank sharpens the distinctions among types of private MIVs. While all microfinance investors stress the 'double bottom line' of social and financial returns, he distinguishes three categories (Figure 11.1). Large 'commercial microfinance funds' put greater emphasis on financial returns than do 'quasi-commercial funds', promoted as socially responsible investing and marketed with a greater emphasis on social impact. The most strongly oriented towards social returns are non-profit microfinance development

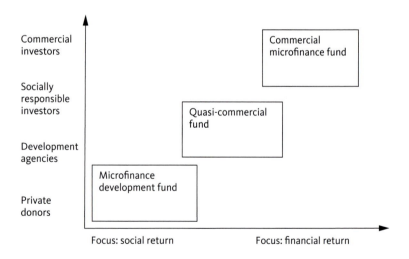

11.1 Pro-social and commercial microfinance funds (*source*: Adapted from Dieckmann 2007).

TABLE 11.1 Kiva.org and Oikocredit

	Size and scale	Social performance	Online presence
Kiva.org	HQ in San Francisco	Kiva loans are managed by the 'field partners' – MFIs that post individual entrepreneurs' profiles on the Kiva website	The foremost online peer lending platform – an online loan is made on its website every 22 seconds on average
	Founded in 2005		
	110,000 loans: total US$89 million		Encourages donations as well as investments
	US$399 average loan		
	Investment: minimum US$25; average US$703		Gifts cover staff costs, so all investments go to borrowers
	Average: 9.39 investments per individual		
	83 full-time staff; 12 in field		
Oikocredit	HQ in Amersfoort, Netherlands	Emphasises its involvement in social performance standards	Online investing possible through MicroPlace
	Founded in 1975		
	45,000 investors; 267 loans*	Project partners sign and adhere to smart campaign standards for client protection	Online recruitment is not a significant factor
	222 full-time staff		Accepts donations but does not encourage them
	36 regional or country offices		
	36 support offices or associations		Pools donations to purchase shares

Note: * Oikocredit loans are to MFIs (and credit unions) not to individual borrowers, and they average €825,000 (US$1.08 million). MFIs in turn lend to hundreds or thousands of individual borrowers, so loan figures are not comparable to Kiva's. See the estimates of the number of individual borrowers supported.

funds, which 'primarily target the development of MFIs by granting capital at favourable financial conditions without necessarily seeking a financial return' (ibid.: 12).

Kiva and Oikocredit both fit squarely in the microfinance development fund category, as do funds sponsored by Accion International, Deutsche Bank itself, and a handful of others: they are non-profit organisations facilitating investments (see Table 11.1). Kiva's online lending format, which the organisation presents as peer-to-peer lending, has attracted journalistic and scholarly attention. Published studies have already examined the effects of group formation among prospective lenders on loan size and frequency (effects are minimal), and have tested laboratory findings about altruistic behaviour by asking whether lenders prefer borrowers who are socially proximate, of the same (or different) gender, or even have the same first name or initial (Galak et al. 2011). Roodman (2009) succeeds in showing that Kiva's claim that investors choose and invest in an individual is not strictly true – Kiva in fact allocates funds to an MFI that supports the proposed entrepreneur, then collects investments that keep the capital flowing – but he also argues that Kiva's actual practice is superior to the peer-to-peer image it promotes.

Kiva Founded in 2005 by Matt and Jessica Flannery, Kiva allows individuals to lend as little as US$25, selecting an individual micro-entrepreneur. Kiva's gallery of individual borrowers are provided by microfinance lenders (Kiva's 'field partners'), who also handle management, oversight and repayment of the loan once funds are available.

Kiva reports that a million lenders have made loans totalling more than US$370 million in sixty-six countries. For MFIs, then, Kiva is an opportunity to bring capital into their operations and make loans to specific borrowers. To more than a million lenders to date, Kiva is an opportunity to lend (at zero interest) rather than donate, and to enjoy at least the perception that they are choosing and then lending to an individual, rather than to an organisation or programme. Kiva affirms this prominently in its mission statement: Kiva exists to 'connect people through lending to alleviate poverty' (Kiva.org 2013).

In 2009, Kiva created a mechanism that allows individual lenders to affiliate in 'lending teams' and to cooperate to make a loan as a group. Hartley (2010) shows that the experience of groups (school groups, church members, friends, family) has been mixed, with little evidence that the psychology of group lending has led to more or larger loans.

Kiva, critics claim, relies on an 'ideology of entrepreneurial charity' by letting its lenders experience the satisfaction of being charitable without actually giving up any money (Bajde 2013). Sinclair (2014) popularised this critique in a widely circulated blog post, arguing that Kiva operates a profitable charity exploiting its individual lenders' desire to help, while charging high interest rates and running up high costs. Kiva's online response shows that the original critique misinterpreted key financial reports (Flannery and Shah 2014), but the broader critique, that 'entrepreneurial charity' has an attraction for Kiva's investors, is surely true. The value of Kiva's particular methodology depends in part on whether it succeeds in informing and mobilising a broader public about poverty and the obstacles and opportunities that confront very poor people who borrow from microfinance lenders.

Oikocredit Oikocredit was established in 1975 and had US$656 million in loans outstanding as of November 2012, most to MFIs, credit unions or cooperatives. Founded as an agency of the World Council of Churches, as the 'Ecumenical Development Cooperative Society', Oikocredit is now an independent agency headquartered in the Netherlands. In 2013, it reported 48,000 investors worldwide, 3,000 of them new investors in 2012 (Oikocredit 2013).

Oikocredit promotes and markets its 'ethical investment alternative' through networks of national offices and national and local volunteer support associations across Europe and North America. It sees investing as more than solely a financial decision, calling itself a 'worldwide movement of investors':

> Oikocredit is about people investing in people. It is a ... worldwide financial cooperative that promotes global justice by empowering disadvantaged people with financial inclusion, and a worldwide network of investors who make it possible (ibid.).

Structured as an international cooperative, the flow of finance and services in Oikocredit began with investments by 48,000 investors, of which 595 were cooperative members in 2012. New investments totalled US$256.5 million in 2012; it has made 2,632 investments in its history, working with 854 partners. National offices and volunteer 'support associations' in Western Europe and North America work to raise investment capital. Lending that capital, monitoring social performance, communication and other functions are led by an international headquarters office in the Netherlands and supported by forty-two national and regional offices.

Oikocredit lends to partner institutions – primarily MFIs but also credit unions and cooperatives. MFIs borrow capital primarily in order to re-lend to individual small borrowers. In 2011, these project partners lent to a total of 26 million borrowers. Oikocredit chooses these project partners to balance financial security with the desire to support new institutions that are reaching more marginalised borrowers. To increase its emphasis on 'mission-driven MFIs', it has a multiyear commitment to prioritising lending in agriculture, lending to small- and medium-sized enterprises, and lending in Africa (Oikocredit 2012).

Who invests in Oikocredit shares? Western European investors are greatest in number and total investments: the top four countries in number of investors and net investment inflow in 2011 were Germany, Austria, the Netherlands and France, with the United States (US) fifth (ibid.). Oikocredit has had greater success winning very large institutional investors in Europe, but US and Canadian affiliates have also recently seen rapid growth in investments. Volunteer support associations are responsible for recruiting significant investments in all the investing countries. Some of this investment, and the development education work that supports it, is done on a face-to-face 'retail' basis through individual presentations in churches and civic organisations. Institutional investors – pension funds of religious orders, hospitals and other institutions, individual houses of worship, and other religious bodies – account for many of the largest investments and are often recruited by staff of national offices.

Commercial microfinance investment: BlueOrchard BlueOrchard Microfinance Investment Managers, based in Switzerland, 'is a leading asset manager in Impact Investing, with specific expertise in debt financing for microfinance institutions worldwide. Since its inception in 2001, BlueOrchard has made in excess of USD 2 billion in loans to microfinance institutions globally.'[1]

Below, Conning and Morduch (2011) describe the workings of a US$40 million BlueOrchard Fund, illustrating risk dynamics that are important for our understanding of the non-profit alternatives. The 2004 debt issue, called BlueOrchard MF Securities I, provides diverse risk and investment options:

> Ninety investors pooled money that supported nine micro-lenders. The deal involved five tranches, with varying returns and risk. In the most subordinated position was an equity tranche. Above that were three subordinated tranches priced at the return on US Treasury plus 2.5 percentage points. These tiers were taken by social investors, foundations, and non-profits, many with a strong international presence. In more privileged positions [i.e. with less risk] were senior notes earning US Treasury plus 1.5 per cent with a 75 per cent guarantee from the Overseas Private Investment Corporation, a US government agency. Here the investors ranged from individuals to pension funds. The deal allowed institutions in Cambodia, Russia, Peru, Bolivia, Nicaragua, Ecuador, and Colombia to reach more under-served – and allowed a large group of socially-minded investors to avoid taking much risk (ibid.: 18).

Microfinance, investment and the elements of SSE

Pro-social investment funds by definition have two sets of purposes: to mobilise capital for positive social objectives, and to permit investment and savings. In this context, how can we assess the contributions of microfinance investment to building institutions of an SSE? I propose five broad indicators, in addition to the widely discussed indicators of social performance – gender impact, debt management and client rights and protections – which are subsumed in the fifth indicator. These are: 1) risk-sharing and responsiveness; 2) knowledge and intention; 3) sustained participation; 4) institution-building; and 5) influencing the industry.

These indicators emphasise the creation of enduring cooperative and solidarity relationships and institutions. Some are economic in nature (risk-sharing and distribution), others social (knowledge and intention, institution-building), and some relate to governance (participation and influence). Collectively, they provide a means of assessing which elements of social solidarity are present in microfinance investment, and of refining or testing our understanding of

SSE at the transnational level. In the following section I use publicly available information from Oikocredit and Kiva.org to begin to answer the questions implicit in these indicators.

Risk-sharing and responsiveness Investors typically seek to balance security with returns on investment, and will often sacrifice higher potential returns in order to gain security. Borrowers, in most transactions, bear most or all of the risk, with lenders protected by physical collateral or other arrangements.[2] Microfinance schemes distribute risk in a variety of ways, including by organising groups of borrowers who provide a kind of social guarantee of repayment, and by choosing borrowers carefully to balance risk against security of revenue flows through repayments. Microfinance repayment rates are famously reported to be higher than those of many conventional bank loans, often above 95 per cent.

In lending for microfinance, solidarity entails accepting risk. Pro-social funds for microfinance and lending to other small- and medium-scale enterprises have in general been very safe, but are uninsured. Investments in Oikocredit and through Kiva.org are not guaranteed or insured. While Oikocredit has consistently paid dividends and repaid principal since 1974, investments of this kind entail some risks, and when individuals or houses of worship invest substantial portions of their savings, endowments or pension funds in such an investment fund, they weigh this risk. Kiva.org also advises prospective investors that investments are not guaranteed, although the organisation emphasises the historical 99.01 per cent repayment rate. (Some have argued that Kiva's high repayment rate indicates that it is treated as a privileged creditor by its MFI partners.) Its 'risk and due diligence' statements specify that, because much of the vetting of individual borrowers is done by field partner MFIs, risk is distributed unevenly across investors. That is, an investor whose chosen borrower defaults bears that individualised risk, rather than the risk and loss being spread across a lending portfolio. Three specific factors are useful to assess risk-sharing, as described below.

Willingness to provide equity investment Equity investment and forms of loan guarantees entail costs and risks for the investor, and their presence is an indicator of a solidarity approach to risk. Most private finance for MFIs comes as loans, but some MFIs express the need for equity financing, in which the investor buys a minority share in the enterprise. Equity lending has several advantages for the MFI: it provides a permanent financial partner and a source of capital that can be used for organisational expenses, and sometimes it makes it possible to secure other loans and investments by making the investor a partial guarantor of loans. Equity investment ties up investment capital, and when an organisation such as Oikocredit agrees to begin expanding equity investments in partner agencies, it is seen as a commitment to the partners' long-term growth and strength. Oikocredit's total equity portfolio is some US$45.7 million, 6.7 per cent of its US$680 million portfolio (Oikocredit 2012). Most of Oikocredit's equity portfolio is in MFIs, but it has also purchased minority shares in fair trade and renewable energy enterprises. Its equity investments are geographically diverse, but most (sixteen) are in Africa. Kiva recruits only debt financing (loans) from its investors; its function is to bring individuals into microfinance investing by setting the threshold very low and giving investors the choice of individual enterprises.

Willingness to provide local currency loans, bearing the risk of currency value fluctuations More than 70 per cent of all international debt financing is in hard currency, a practice that exposes the MFI to risks associated with the changing values of currencies. Loans made in the national currency of the borrowing MFI place this risk on the lender. Local currency lending is an option for Oikocredit but not for Kiva.org, all of whose loans are in US dollars. Oikocredit's shareholder members first authorised such local currency transactions in 2007. The cooperative also maintains a local currency risk fund, of approximately €36,000 in 2011, funded by donations and other sources as a protection against these risks (ibid.: 45).

Willingness to absorb costs associated with natural disasters or extreme market failures Borrowing MFIs occasionally confront situations that make it virtually impossible to repay – in the aftermath of a natural disaster or during wartime, for example (Briceño 2005). After the Haitian earthquake in 2010, Oikocredit and other lenders made donations or refinanced or rescheduled their loans to Haitian MFIs, so that the MFIs could restructure or write off loans to individuals whose lives and businesses were devastated, and be ready to lend in support of recovery and reconstruction. In the Haitian case, the fact that Oikocredit was an equity investor (i.e. a part owner) of the MFI Fonkoze facilitated decision-making in the post-disaster period.

Knowledge and intention Solidarity involves an understanding and awareness of other actors, and social investment that capitalises microfinance and builds solidarity will feature investors who are aware and actively supportive of the uses of their capital. This places a substantial focus on the intentions of investors; some will object (correctly) that this is less important than the economic and social effects of microfinance activities on borrowers.

In examining the possibility of finance that creates solidarity relationships between investors in rich societies and users of microfinance (mostly) in poorer societies, knowledge and intention matter. This premise is subject to debate: who cares what the wealthy investor in Chicago or Stuttgart knows, as long as his or her capital is enabling microfinance lending on terms and with institutional arrangements that are advantageous to the borrowers? The answer in principle is that each individual's awareness is of value and that a genuine effort to be in a relationship with a far-removed neighbour is a step in the development of that person's human capabilities. In this sense, developing social solidarity is a process of developing the awareness and deepening the humanity of rich as well as poor people.

The more pragmatic answer is that investment with awareness is more likely to remain available, over the longer term, when there is a change in conditions that make investing in microfinance funds less advantageous. For most of 2010–13, for example, Oikocredit's available 2 per cent return on investments was competitive, and performed far better than the most secure investments in banks or US Treasury notes. When interest rates for other investments eventually rise again, the investor who was attracted by the mission of microfinance, and developed a deeper understanding of it, is more likely to remain an investor rather than moving for higher returns.

Knowledge and intention might best be assessed by direct interviews with investors. This chapter takes a more preliminary first step by examining how the agencies characterise their investments, and how they educate investors and others. Oikocredit, with a face-to-face outreach strategy and strong commitments from church bodies, particularly in Western Europe, carries out vigorous education and outreach aimed at deepening the knowledge of volunteers and investors, and at educating a broader potential investor public about microfinance. Initiatives in 2011 included a study tour to Guatemala for investors and others, speaking tours in investor countries by staff and field partners, and media outreach including advertising in popular religious periodicals. The Oikocredit Academy provides training in outreach and communication twice a year and sponsors study tours, lecture tours by staff of borrowing partner agencies, and other means of informing the potential investor public.

Kiva presents investors and prospective investors with a wealth of material on its website, including a lengthy essay on microfinance, resources on understanding the social performance of loans and other information. But Kiva investors' knowledge and intention continue to be based on the appearance that they are investing in the business activity of a particular micro-entrepreneur. This marketing scheme has proven highly effective in raising individual investment capital, but is a shaky foundation at best for building relationships of solidarity. Kiva also recruits and supports unpaid Kiva Fellows every year. Fellows are placed with an MFI and provide training and communication services, while gaining personal (and sometimes professional) experience.

Sustained participation An investor who opts to renew a certificate, to make a new investment or loan, or to increase his or her investment demonstrates a high level of commitment. Two concrete measures of sustained participation are available: 1) the duration of the loan (how patient is the capital?); and 2) the presence of repeat investments or decisions to renew existing commitments. One of the signals of economic anxieties during the recession of 2008 was the growing number of 'redemptions' of investments by investors who chose not to renew.

Oikocredit refers to its financial role as providing 'patient capital' loans to MFIs that are relatively long term (four to five years). Kiva's individual investments are generally shorter term, but many of its arrangements with field partners have been enduring. Data about repeat investments are readily available only for Kiva, which reports that the average investor makes 9.39 loans.[3] The presence or absence of sustained commitment and repeated investment is an important indicator of whether social investment in microfinance may be creating links of solidarity. For social investment organisations, and for these two in particular, it raises specific questions: can internet-mediated relationships inspire the kind of loyalty and commitment that face-to-face networks such as Oikocredit have managed across the decades? Can the personal empathy that motivates an individual to invest in support of a single person be sustained and grown on a large scale when institutions intervene and the appearance that one can invest in a single individual or enterprise is lost?

Institution-building The issues of group formation, institution-building and governance arise at both ends of the investment trans-action. Many microfinance schemes rely on group lending, under which peer pressure functions to keep repayment rates famously high. Few microfinance transactions build permanent institutions at the community level, although small-scale lending has encouraged the creation of cooperatives. Many pro-social investors are individuals; others are institutions (pension funds, for example); a few actively encourage the formation of groups, either local or virtual; and (in the case of Oikocredit) some rely on local and national groups and on a global system of governance by members in a cooperative structure.

At the regional and even global level, microfinance has also led to the formation of significant self-governing institutions. For example, Grameen Foundation, created to support and promote the micro-finance work inspired by Bangladesh's Grameen Bank, encourages the adoption of Grameen-style lending methods. Regional federa-tions of MFIs have become standard: the South Asia Microfinance Network, for example, is governed by a board of its seven national MFI members.

As a cooperative, Oikocredit has a distinctive international self-governing structure, which also encourages deepening participation by volunteers. Members of the international cooperative own shares in Oikocredit and vote at annual general meetings on organisational policy questions, to elect board members and to ratify policy de-cisions made by staff. Group formation occurs at another level in Oikocredit, where individuals participate in support associations formed locally to promote investments. Interestingly, Kiva has sparked several studies of online group formation and its effect on investment, but similar research has not yet been conducted on Oikocredit's face-to-face group formation.

Forming identity-based lending teams is not a form of demo-cratic self-governance, but it is potentially a way of building social capital and leveraging that social capital to encourage lending. At Kiva.org, groups allow members to 'connect with each other and rally around shared goals' (Kiva.org n.d.). Some groups are open to new members while some are closed; some are local, family, professional or regional. The two perennial leading groups are 'Kiva Christians' (11,000 members, 197,000 loans) and 'Atheists, Agnos-tics, Freethinkers and Skeptics' (25,000 members, 366,000 loans). Hartley (2010) reports on group-lending dynamics among groups of different size and identity factor, and between open and closed membership groups. He does not report on the question most of interest here: do team members invest differently than non-team individuals?

We can approximate an answer by reporting the average size and number of investments for some leading teams, and for Kiva investors as a whole. 'Christians' and 'Freethinkers' members have averaged 17.8 and 14.5 loans per member respectively, compared with 9.39 for all investors. Is the team dynamic simply encouraging multiple small investments? Possibly. The average individual loan by Kiva investors is just under US$50, the average per 'Christian' is US$35, and the average per 'Freethinker' is US$29. If group members lend more frequently – and Hartley (ibid.) shows that they do – and if teams help to recruit investors, then the lending team construct is a positive one for Kiva.

Influencing the industry: non-profits and the mission of micro-finance Commercial microfinance lenders have come under criti-cism for marketing loans and allowing some clients to go more deeply into debt than is prudent. Commercial private investment in microfinance is sometimes seen as a driver of this kind of lending, and non-profit MIVs face what may be a critical challenge – to invest sustainably while helping set clear standards for client protec-tion and social impact or performance, and pull the microfinance industry towards compliance. Finally, I examine non-profits' role in the standard-setting process and their record as investors in less established, riskier and capital-starved second- and third-tier MFIs.

In recent years, the microfinance community has been rocked by revelations of the impact of large-scale commercial micro-lending

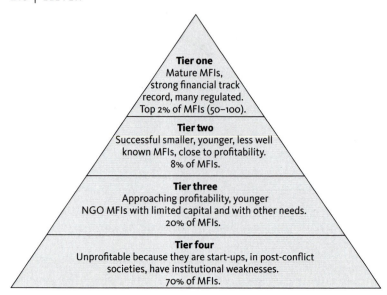

11.2 Four tiers of MFIs (*source*: Adapted from Meehan 2004: 7).

in South Asia and Mexico. Reports of unscrupulous lending practices by for-profit microfinance lenders, and of extreme levels of indebtedness among poor farmers who had been encouraged to borrow repeatedly by agents of the banks, led to widespread scepticism about microfinance. The dramatic growth and profitability of the Mexican MFI Compartamos, which launched the industry's first public stock offering in 2008, further fuelled the debates over social mission, profitability, and the future of privately financed microfinance lending (Malkin 2008).

Here, the role of mission-driven non-profit MIVs such as Oikocredit becomes important. Much of the rapid increase in private investment in microfinance was driven by the rise of a tier of successful, profitable and secure MFIs. These tier one MFIs make up perhaps only 2 per cent of the total number of MFIs, but they attract a great deal of capital: Meehan (2004) estimates 90 per cent. Tier two MFIs are seen as progressing towards mature status, but have less access to investment capital. Tier three and four MFIs have no access to financial capital (see Figure 11.2).

The profitability of these tier one MFIs attracted finance capital into the microfinance industry in the early 2000s and drove the growth of for-profit MIVs (Dieckmann 2007; Ming-yee 2007). The rapid growth of for-profit microfinance and the challenges it poses to the credibility of microfinance as an enterprise mean that upholding and strengthening the social mission of microfinance has been doubly important in retaining the social and economic impact of microfinance and public perceptions. For-profit lenders have provoked serious concerns about the interest rates charged by some MFIs, aggressive marketing of loans to clients who may already be in significant debt, and the need for stronger client protections and standards for MFIs (Schmidt 2013).

MFIs and some non-profit investment vehicles have taken steps to reinforce social performance and public and investor perceptions, and Oikocredit has been actively involved. The most prominent package of client protection standards, launched in 2013 as a vehicle for certifying MFIs, is led by the Smart Campaign, 'a global movement to embed a set of client protection principles deep within the microfinance industry' (Smart Campaign 2013). Complementing these standards, Grameen Foundation and Oikocredit have been among the leaders creating and implementing measures for monitoring and reporting social performance, and for measuring concrete material benefits to borrowers, through the Progress out of Poverty Index.

Conclusion

Microfinance has come in for significant criticism in recent years and faces real challenges in the decade ahead. Developments discussed in this chapter that relate to its expanded investment base and newly reinvigorated self-regulation efforts mean that it could become a key component of strategies to build SSE. Beyond identifying several strategies for research and action, this chapter has pointed to three main conclusions.

First, investment in microfinance can create conditions for solidarity relationships that extend from investors in North America or Europe to borrowers mainly in the global South. There is reason to believe that many investors through Kiva.org and Oikocredit are motivated by a desire distinct from charity, to transform economic possibilities by committing resources of their own. Whether this is true or not in particular cases depends a great deal on how MIVs perform as institutions: how they market, mobilise and educate potential investors, and on the quality of financial regulation within the microfinance industry and in the countries where it operates. These investment funds – and, additionally, non-profit funds like them – make up a significant minority of cross-border private microfinance investments. A next step in assessing investment will be a closer look at commercial investment vehicles.

Second, while knowledge and awareness on the part of investors may be significant, the quality of financial institutions has a major impact on outcomes. The relatively ineffective oversight and regulation of commercial MFIs in Andhra Pradesh allowed market forces to make microfinance an economic trap for some borrowers. On the supply side, the very extensive private investment from Germany is driven by effective and well-known bank-managed investment funds. Deutsche Bank's commercial microfinance investment funds have been joined by the GLS Bank, a 'social and ecological' bank that is further expanding pro-social investment among Germans (Oikocredit 2012).

Third, the issue of scale, and of the possibility of rapid growth to meet the financial needs of more of the 2.5 billion people without adequate financial services, poses enormous challenges. The present modest growth of investment for microfinance (19 per cent in 2012) would have to accelerate dramatically to expand services significantly. But periods of rapid growth have presented regulatory challenges and have been associated with serious abuse, as in Andhra Pradesh. Research that examines other periods of rapid growth in MFI lending could help to clarify the conditions that allow growth without serious problems.

12 | BALANCING GROWTH AND SOLIDARITY IN COMMUNITY CURRENCY SYSTEMS: THE CASE OF THE *TRUEQUE* IN ARGENTINA

Georgina M. Gómez

Introduction

The concern that social and solidarity economy (SSE) initiatives should scale up to increase their economic impact and efficiency needs close scrutiny. On the one hand, the connection between SSE initiatives and the principles of locality, solidarity and small scale are almost automatic; according to some authors, these are essential principles of the SSE (Moulaert and Ailenei 2005; North 2005). On the other hand, capitalist discourse presents local, small and non-profit-maximising economic schemes as essentially inferior in terms of efficiency, rationality, universality and productivity (Gibson-Graham 2008). SSE networks are seen as too small, too local, too ephemeral and too dependent on the limited resources of members (North 2005). SSE alternatives need to scale up to be effective and to have more economic impact. However, the understanding of the processes and implications of scaling up is still modest, especially in relation to losing inclusiveness, local embeddedness and meaning for the SSE members. This chapter seeks to study these processes in the context of complementary or community currency systems.

Community or complementary currency systems are schemes in which groups of individuals exchange goods and services using a self-created and self-regulated currency. The means of payment is accepted voluntarily by the members of the networks, which are normally composed of individuals but sometimes businesses and local government agencies as well. In industrialised Anglophone countries, the best known variants are local exchange trading systems and time banks. Advocates promote them as environmentally friendly initiatives to insulate the local economy from the downturns of the national and global economies, enhance social cohesion within a community and sustain livelihoods during periods of economic distress (Pacione 1999; Seyfang 2001; 2002). They operate in fifty-six countries and the largest have managed to attract a few thousand members. In Argentina, however, they grew massively in scale and scope.

The Argentinian variant, called *Trueque*, was an income-generating scheme created within the SSE as a response to the neoliberal structural reforms of the 1990s. Between 1995 and 2006, Argentina hosted the largest contemporary example of a complementary currency system. The organisers made the conscious choice to scale up the scheme in a sort of 'Keynesianism from below', as Fernando Sampayo, one of the main organisers, called it. Each group or network used its own currency and chose its own organisational arrangements and standards of monetary regulation. The *Trueque* reached its peak in terms of membership during the worst crisis in Argentina's economic history, which slashed gross domestic product by 25 per cent between 1998 and 2002. The number of participants is estimated to have reached 2.5 million in 2002 (Hintze 2003). Subsequently, however, it declined rapidly, given the inability of the organisers to regulate activities on such a scale. Some groups and networks fared better than others and remained active a few years longer (Gómez 2010; North 2007). This trajectory makes the *Trueque* an excellent case study through which to explore the challenges that growth in scale and scope poses for SSE schemes – in this case, those centred on exchange.

This chapter addresses two key questions. What challenges and advantages appeared with the growth in scale, which is understood here as an escalation in the number of members, geographical coverage and diversity of products? How did it affect social cohesion and economic impact? The analysis draws on Douglass North's (1989; 1990) distinction between personal and impersonal exchange. Personal exchange is characteristic of small and local community schemes, which are loaded with values and shared meanings but often remain limited in their social impact and income generation effects. Impersonal exchange addresses larger economic circuits, such as the regular economy of a region or country, in which economic action is guided by institutions. North also describes impersonal exchange as being more efficient, productive, durable and capable of unleashing economic development in the long term, but warns about the increased uncertainties and transaction costs that it entails in comparison with personal exchange. For SSE initiatives, this chapter shows that scaling up is possible within the limits defined by the interpersonal transfer of trust, the reputation of the leaders to act as a linchpin for the system, and keeping the process of institutional innovation active. The analysis in this chapter is informed by twelve months of fieldwork conducted during 2003 and 2006. Extensive interviews were conducted with those who initiated the *Trueque* and with local and regional coordinators. A survey of participating households, which yielded 386 responses, was also carried out.

The next section discusses the literature on scaling up the SSE and the transition from personal into impersonal exchange. This is followed by an analysis of how scaling up took place in the *Trueque* and the challenges that arose until the network broke up. The chapter concludes with some reflections on the implications of scaling up for SSE initiatives and three necessary conditions that could sustain it.

SSE as institutional innovation

Advancing social economy initiatives is about creating new values and institutions, as proposed by Moulaert and others (Moulaert and Ailenei 2005; Moulaert and Nussbaumer 2005). These authors show that when established mechanisms of economic growth and distribution falter, ingenious social forces may develop new social and economic spaces with mechanisms of solidarity, reciprocity and redistribution to satisfy material and immaterial needs. They analyse the social economy as *social innovation* because it generates institutional innovation that addresses new forms of social relations and governance. Shared moralities of solidarity and reciprocity embed economic relations at the local level and can constrain self-interest, allow actors to bypass the limits of pure rationality, and modify the interactions typical of anonymous markets (Granovetter 1985; 1992). For instance, this is the case of economic activity embedded in social relations of family, religion and ethnicity (Beckert 2003).

Most economic activity is embedded in ties of various qualities, and some degree of trust among actors is essential even in atomised market exchange relations to enable the parties to believe that transactions will be realised (Etzioni 1988; Zelizer 1989). Luhman (1996) defines trust as a set of expectations about others' actions that could result in a negative response if not fulfilled. It thus affects decisions to act in a certain manner, reducing exchange risk and uncertainty and diminishing the likelihood of having to enforce contracts. The benefits of trust include the fact that agents exchange fine-grained information, solve problems together and can generally arrange the coordination of their economic actions in a more effective way than on the basis of the information contained in prices (Helper 1990; Larson 1992).

Returning to the conceptualisation of the SSE proposed by Moulaert and Nussbaumer (2005), its first aspect was institutional innovation. Institutions are socially embedded systems of rules, in which those rules are tendencies to behave in certain ways (Hodgson 2006). Agents may refuse to act or act differently by virtue of their agency, but that does not mean that the inclination to act in a certain way does not exist. Institutional innovation in relation to the SSE therefore represents a process by which institutions are changed from the bottom up via collective action, negotiation and contestation at the local level (Gómez 2009). The action taken deviates from what is expected by the reciprocal agreements of a specific community.

The process of institutional change that binds a community is sometimes portrayed as the result of communities of cooperation. Moulaert and Nussbaumer (2005) consider that institutional innovation kindles cultural emancipation, social cohesion, interpersonal and intergroup communication and collaboration and decision-making mechanisms. However, Boyer and Hollingsworth (1997) contend that institutional innovation is as much a political process as it is a social process in which agents pursue divergent interests. They argue that institutions are either points of compromise between actors with divergent interests or frozen points of power asymmetries in which powerful groups are able to cement their strength. SSE initiatives, with their shared morality of solidarity and reciprocity, connect to local institutions and may reproduce the same power struggles and asymmetries present in the community.

Scaling up SSE

SSE initiatives represent new ways of producing and distributing value in the local economy. They rely on trust and solidarity and, in turn, foster trust and solidarity. This description automatically restricts them to a small scale, which also means that resources are limited and their economic impact is necessarily modest. However, this is contested by Gibson-Graham (2008), who see complementary and community currency systems as small economic systems within a diverse economies framework.

As has been known to economists since the time of Adam Smith and his publication of *The Wealth of Nations* (1776), specialisation and the division of labour play key roles in economic development. However, as has been acknowledged rather recently, such processes are not costless and can lead to higher risks and uncertainties, generically known as 'transaction costs' (Williamson 1985). Transaction costs are defined at the micro level as costs other than price incurred in trading goods and services (Swedberg 1990), or, from a more macro view, as the costs of running the economic system (Arrow 1969). Williamson (1981) argues that with an interface in the market that works well, transfers occur smoothly; otherwise, there are frictions between the parties, misunderstandings, delays, breakdowns and other malfunctions or 'market failures' that add to uncertainty and increase the total cost of exchange. Provisions need to be made to mediate the exchange of goods and services in order to allow for the benefits of the division of labour and economic growth.

At the small scale of SSE initiatives, the benefits of specialisation and division of labour are minimal, but transaction costs are a minimal problem as well. Transactions in the SSE are embedded in a social setting of trust and common values that simplifies and reduces these problems. Individuals in small groups can transfer goods between each other with 'simple personal exchanges'; that is, they engage in repeated dealings with each other and have a great deal of personal knowledge about each other's attributes, characteristics and features as well as their products. Norms of behaviour are seldom written down because trust is the crucial element in facilitating transactions. Formal contracting does not exist and formal specific rules are rare and largely unnecessary. However, if they seek to scale up, the risks and uncertainties of opportunism, free-riding and transaction costs start to appear. Douglass North (1989; 1990) refers to scaling up as a transition from personal to impersonal exchange conditions. In a world of impersonal exchange, transaction costs are high between strangers because there are potential gains in cheating, shirking and opportunism. Measuring the attributes of what is being traded and enforcing terms of exchange become problematic and costly. However, production costs in such societies are lower because specialisation and division of labour are not limited to the extent and needs of the small group as agents engaged in personal exchange relationships. Douglass North (ibid.) thus sees development as a consequence of successfully achieving the institutional innovation that supports the transition from personal exchange to impersonal exchange and reduces uncertainty and complexity and allows economies to grow.

In the case of scaling up small networks, such as SSE initiatives, Uzzi (1996) elaborates that third-party referral and previous personal relationships extend trust in newcomers. In a 'word of mouth' system, expectations based on trust are transferred to newly introduced actors, which immediately equips the new economic exchange with resources from pre-existing embedded ties. In this way, transactions are less uncertain – not as a result of what the newcomers have done but because of the social relations existing before they joined the network. Perhaps what is missing is the notion that negative social relations such as hatred, distrust and rivalry may also be transferred, as elaborated by Boyer and Hollingsworth (1997). In subsequent scaling up, trust is allocated to impersonal, long-lasting and impartial institutional structures.

Scaling up in the *Trueque*

The first Argentinian complementary currency system was established in a suburb in Buenos Aires in May 1995, after a period of trial and error with different mechanisms of exchange. Called *Club de Trueque* (CT), it was initiated with thirty members as a spin-off project of an environmental non-governmental organisation (Gómez 2009). Its three leaders saw that the CT had tremendous potential because many people in the country had surplus goods, skills and productive capacity to exchange with others. The scaling-up process of the *Trueque* was initially gradual, but quickly gained momentum. Immediately after the first CT became a working reality, participants started spreading the news about the scheme to relatives, friends and neighbours: that is, the initial growth in the number of members relied entirely on word of mouth and thus was still embedded in personal exchange. As membership grew, people travelled considerable distances to participate in the CT. The organisers decided that distant participants would be better served if they had a club nearer their homes and embedded in their localities. One of the organisers, Carlos de Sanzo, explained:

> It made a lot more sense to motivate people to organise a CT in their locality than to let them travel two hours to come here. All they needed was a group of willing neighbours and a bit of know-how, which we could gladly give.

The replication of the CT in other locations became an ambition of the initiators as soon as they saw that the system was working. According to de Sanzo, the initial success and potential of the scheme to alleviate the economic problems of the disenfranchised middle class made them 'want to spread it everywhere'. In the hope of finding partner groups, the initiators re-established old contacts with socialist and environmentalist activists, offering workshops on the scheme in the city of Buenos Aires. The goal was to 'infect others with our enthusiasm', says Horacio Covas, another initiator. Their discourse went beyond that typically associated with SSE, which emphasises locality and small-scale trust relations (North 2005). The desire to expand and achieve wider economic impact impregnated the *Trueque* and structured agents who worked towards scaling up.

That goal was achieved at the beginning of 1996, when a second group was formed in the city centre and a third in a northern suburb. The three groups decided to stay interconnected in order to allow participants of one jurisdiction to trade in another. But this created new problems. When there was a single CT, exchanges were mediated with a system of cards. The organisers would write the value of the products that participants brought to the market and the value of what they took with them. At the end of the day they would register the transactions and calculate each participant's balance. With three linked CTs, this would take endless hours and set limits on the extent to which they could expand. One of the leaders then proposed printing vouchers for fixed amounts to be used in the CTs. The others liked the idea because of its practicality and because it allowed participants to move across the various CTs. So each local market printed its own currency (vouchers called *créditos*) as a means of payment, although all of them were accepted throughout the network. These currencies were the first step beyond the scale of personal exchange.

Printing vouchers to circulate as fiat currency among the

participants of the various clubs unleashed the potential of the initiative as an income-generation scheme. However, when participants started coming from three different networks and exchanged products with three different currencies, the complexity of their trade also increased and problems typical of scaling up and impersonal exchange began to appear. While all groups shared a common past of political militancy as a source of solidarity or common morality, in reality the trust required to trade with distant participants derived primarily from the reputation of the leaders as initiators of the CT. Several individuals in each group had known and trusted the initiators for several years and their trust was transferred to the other members. Barreiro and Leite (2003) report that the members' trust was mainly in the leaders, and then in the cluster of institutions that made up the *Trueque*.

The mechanism by which trust expanded to the network in three localities corresponds to the process described by Uzzi (1996) of the interpersonal transfer of trust from old to new members. As explained by Horacio Covas, one of the initiators of the scheme: 'It happened almost by inertia that participants moved to visit each other and carry their products. But we didn't see any problem in that. Everybody got to the CT through somebody, so everybody was trusted.' Moreover, exchanges across the three CTs were still embedded in a shared morality of solidarity, even if it was no longer strictly local. 'People were expected to behave responsibly when they joined, according to the solidarity we shared,' Covas adds.

With the subsequent addition of two more CTs, which made a total of five, the limits to personal exchange started to emerge. It became clear that some transparency was needed to guarantee the value of the *créditos* and price stability across the network. A rule of issuance was decided when the leaders of the five CTs agreed that the currency or scrip would be issued at a rate of twenty *créditos* per new participant. Each CT coordinator was in charge of managing the issuance of the scrip. The aim was to maintain trust in the vouchers as a means of payment. Besides keeping a stable relationship between products and money, it worked in practice as a form of microcredit for new entrants to start producing and trading. Members had to return the twenty *créditos* if they left the CT, so the means of payment would adjust again. For the network, these rules of issuance became the first institutions of impersonal exchange. They were a social innovation, created explicitly from the bottom up and by negotiation and agreement among the leaders.

The process of institution-building relied sometimes on the repetition of routines, rather than on negotiation and agreement. Around the end of 1996 the scheme appeared in a national TV show and from then onwards the initiators started to receive regular phone calls from people across the country asking how to start a CT. The know-how for this became increasingly standardised; it meant mobilising a minimum of twenty participants in a locality, printing vouchers (which had to be paid for in *pesos*), electing a coordinator and finding a venue for the market. Maintaining this model for all subsequent CTs was faster, cheaper and more practical than framing variants according to the locality. Scaling up took priority over local embeddedness and created further problems of impersonal exchange. The transfer of trust from old members to newcomers reached its limits because trust relationships with new coordinators had to be built from zero, without participants' referral. In order to accomplish this, the initiators designed training courses for prospective coordinators to introduce them to the system's principles of solidarity and its 'environmentalist-communitarian' ideology. Subsequent meetings were used for getting to know them and were dedicated to more practical matters such as choosing the vouchers and organising the CT. With this mechanism of standardisation and training, the total number of participants increased to 3,000 in seventeen CTs located in the main cities of Argentina.

By 1997, the network experienced its first case of forgery, making transparent management of *créditos* a pressing issue. In reality, not all participants and CTs accepted the vouchers of other CTs; this was broadly left to individual discretion. It then became clear that using non-state currency beyond the realm of personal exchange was going to need clearer rules and regulations. The initiators considered restricting the variety of currencies to reduce transaction costs, to make it more practical to move around and to increase the impact on household economies. To quote de Sanzo:

We promoted localisation as a principle, but it is a fact that people tend to travel to trade. We saw a significant dissatisfaction with new vouchers because people could not go everywhere with them. So new groups gradually preferred to use our *créditos* instead of ones printed locally.

However, this solution to reduce transaction costs created conflicts because other groups were not willing to accept the accumulation of power involved in a cross-regional currency. In general, scaling up from personal exchange also increased the chances of conflicting interests and tensions at the interpersonal level. Nevertheless, with an inter-regional currency, the diversity of supply and membership expanded further. Members became incredibly creative in widening the range of products offered: from fruits and vegetables to clothing and shoes, books and compact discs, home-made toiletries, furniture and electronics. Some services, such as haircuts, manicures, wedding parties and tarot fortune-telling, were also offered on the market premises. Others, such as legal counselling, car insurance, taxi and courier transport, holiday packages and education and training were advertised on bulletin boards. Even plots of land in the countryside and livestock were for sale.

In 1997, a meeting of CTs took place for the first time. It represented a new step towards building institutions of impersonal exchange. Although there were serious conflicts of leadership, the practice of regular meetings, however informal and unstructured, was inaugurated. More importantly, a monetary system of vouchers was organised to improve transparency. The metropolitan area of Buenos Aires was divided into four zones (North, South, West and Capital), each with its own vouchers controlled by a regional committee. Meetings subsequently became more regular and formal. Committees were established to discuss a broad range of issues – for example, the meaning of solidarity, the meaning of an alternative economic space, practical strategies (for example on access to basic inputs) and relations with other institutions and organisations. These meetings were a major step towards formalising a structure of impersonal exchange. Every CT was to have regular assemblies to elect a coordinator, among other purposes. Coordinators attended regional monthly gatherings that were held to control the issuance and distribution of vouchers in the region. Each area committee would send two representatives to a national committee, the highest body in the network. Its crucial function was to control the *créditos* issued and distributed in each region, so all vouchers would be acceptable across the country. This multi-level and multi-scalar organisation of the *Trueque* across the country worked for a while (Table 12.1). The CTs informed the regional committees of how many vouchers they had distributed that month (the agreed rule by then was fifty *créditos* per new entrant) and the meetings gave birth to a variety of ideas on empowerment and political emancipation.

TABLE 12.1 Organisation of the Argentine complementary currency networks

Types of agent	Organisations where they participate	Level of operation	Type of relation
Regional representatives	Inter-zone committees	National	Impersonal ties
Coordinators	Regional committees	Regional	Weak personal ties
Participants	*Club de Trueque*	Local	Strong personal ties

Far from being enthusiastic about the organisational design that came out of these meetings, the three initiators regarded the structure as a burden and the 'politicisation of the *Trueque*', as de Sanzo put it. For them, the committees were unnecessarily bureaucratic bodies that delayed the expansion of the *Trueque* and blocked the implementation of decisions. They viewed the alleged democratisation of the *Trueque* as a false pretence to pursue a project burdened by committees, detached from the 'real needs' of participants. The *Trueque* presented itself as a 'state within the state' in a political sense, and not just 'a market within the market', which was how they had conceived it. While the process fits the description of institutional innovation proposed by Moulaert and Nussbaumer (2005), the design of rules of action is nested in the critical power struggles outside the SSE initiatives. As noted by Bardhan (1989), the collective action needed for institutional innovation may be overwhelming and well beyond what innovation in the morality of solidarity and reciprocity can achieve.

The scheme took on a life of its own and transaction costs grew with scale, as predicted by Douglass North (1989; 1990). Most traders did not know each other and the currency system became vouchers that came from the organisers. That is to say, the currency was by then not only innominate but anonymous as well, like an institution of unknown origin. Trust was no longer transferred from old to new members and the training courses did not meet their intended goals. Newcomers were asked to sign a letter of agreement with the main principles of the *Trueque*, which was little more than an information sheet outlining the values of the organisation. They were also required to attend a couple of training sessions in which the system was explained to them, but in reality this happened only occasionally. It was in the course of trading that they became acquainted with the system and the other participants. The kind of trading they were used to practising was that of the regular market economy, which conformed to principles that were quite contrary to the solidarity principle that the *Trueque* stood for. Atomistic market exchange is disembedded from specific social relations and different from a system of reciprocity (Granovetter 1992). Institutional innovation, ascribed to SSE initiatives by Moulaert and Nussbaumer (2005), was gradually abandoned and replaced by institutional adoption, in this case of the rules of action that guided behaviour in the regular economy.

The initiators assumed that all newcomers shared the values of solidarity of the *Trueque* or would grow into them as they participated in the scheme. They thought that, while the bonds of personal exchange had long been overpowered, the new participants would be committed to the shared morality of the SSE. 'They signed the letter when they joined. This is a system of trust. Once in, we could assume they shared the values of solidarity,' said Covas. The expectation that there would be no shirking by participants was, to say the least, idealistic. Trust could not be transferred by interpersonal bonds (Uzzi 1996) because the number of participants was too large, making the mechanism no longer realistic or effective. Moreover, as more participants joined, the 'common principles' were increasingly perceived as those of the initiators. Ironically, those initiators, who had shown extraordinary creativity and ingenuity in launching the *Trueque*, organising it as a network and designing a device to replicate it as fast as demand required, eventually failed to keep pace with the changes. The CTs were out of control long before the leaders realised something had to be done. The question still remains as to whether remedial steps could have been taken.

There was a serious struggle for power between the supporters of the initiators and those who opposed them. Opponents thought that the three initiators were trying to control the *Trueque* and constrain democratic participation. They believed that the *Trueque* belonged to all participants and should be managed horizontally by all of them. The more agents interacted with each other, the more struggles and antipathies were aggravated. The antagonistic relationships between the various leaders eventually broke the multi-level and multi-scalar organisation of the *Trueque* and the control mechanisms were abandoned. The coexistence of very different organisational and managerial models led to a split in April 2001, and the *Trueque*, understood as one national network linking regional and interdependent CTs, ceased to exist (Hintze 2003). There were too many opinions or visions about what the *Trueque* should be: a complement, an alternative or an improved capitalist economy; a new kind of informal economy; a desperate survival strategy; an economy of reciprocity and solidarity; a means to learn participation and democracy; a market by and for the poor abandoned by the state to fend for themselves; an environmentally friendly local initiative; or an economy dominated by women.

Conclusion

The challenge for the scaling up of SSE initiatives often depends on whether scaling up fits with the views of the organisers. In the case of the *Trueque*, it was part of the discourse from the very beginning and created a structure for agents whose preferences favoured growth. This is a first critical condition for any discussion of scaling up, as noted by Peter North (2005).

The next challenge, as noted by Douglass North (1989; 1990), relates to the shift from personal to impersonal exchange and the need to design institutions to resolve the trade-off between growth and the uncertainties of including larger numbers of people. In theory, scaling up requires the collective creation of formal and informal institutions as part of a social innovation process. In its early days, the *Trueque* was regulated by personal exchange and comprised a handful of participants of more or less similar social background. Eventually the number of CTs grew to 5,000 and the number of participants to 2.5 million, according to some sources (Hintze 2003). Transaction costs soared, because exchange was between strangers and there was no state regulation. With the expansion of the *Trueque*, diversity grew and with it personal rivalries, power struggles, and divergent interests and intentions. In the longer run these could not be solved and the system collapsed.

The scaling-up sequence of the *Trueque* can be summarised as follows. In the first instance, the conditions of personal exchange prevailed and guided the actions of a small number of participants who trusted each other. The initiators considered that this small scale, typical of SSE initiatives, was a limitation to access resources and achieve a satisfactory economic impact at the level of the household. They decided to concentrate their time and efforts on scaling up the scheme and replicating it in other localities.

Second, replication in other localities was achieved through their personal network of contacts with whom there was a high level of reciprocal trust. New CTs would launch their own means of payment, automatically adhere to the principles of solidarity, and transfer bonds of reciprocity to their own networks of local participants. Crossing the boundaries of locality did not pose a problem as long as the interpersonal network expanded its trust to include newcomers and the shared morality was sustained. This first step of scaling up worked reasonably well and followed the mechanism of transfer of interpersonal trust, as identified by Uzzi (1996). It allowed participants to move freely from one CT to another, access more resources and generally enjoy greater economic impact. The transfer of interpersonal trust kept transaction costs under control and the level of adherence to the principles of solidarity was apparently acceptable.

This implicit adherence allowed the organisers to venture into a third phase, characterised by the creation of the first institutions of impersonal exchange by negotiation and agreement among leaders. The interpersonal transfer of trust had reached its limits but it was enough to keep actors working together towards institutional innovation. They could define rules for voucher issuance and incorporation of new members, and they standardised the regulation of CTs. Rules of action were enforced by reciprocal control among the participants. The initiators were no longer directly known to everyone, but their reputations were. A point to add to Uzzi's (ibid.) findings is the role of the initiators' reputation. In the weaving of an interpersonal network of networks there are referents on which more trust is placed than on others, and they act as the linchpins of the system. This explains why the original vouchers were preferred to the subsequent generations of local vouchers, even if they were equally without legal protection or financial reserve.

A fourth stage in the process of scaling up into institutions of impersonal exchange was the organisation of a multi-level and multi-scalar structure of governance across the country. This was meant to work as an apparatus of rules and institutions to regulate and coordinate economic action among extremely large numbers of participants. The institutions of impersonal exchange resulted from negotiations and agreements, which were binding but could not be controlled in any way. Enforcement relied on assumptions of voluntarism and individual adherence to the SSE morality of the scheme. This mechanism allowed participants to enjoy the benefits of a more diverse and richer local economy and a wider economic impact on their income. While it allowed the *Trueque* to scale up further, it proved not to be sustainable in the long run because of the lack of formal control mechanisms, like those of the state.

The experience of the *Trueque* in Argentina shows that there is potential for SSE initiatives to scale up from personal to impersonal exchange and benefit from a larger economy and yet not lose the morality of the SSE. However, in the absence of effective regulatory institutions, there are limits to how large SSE initiatives can become. The process of scaling up combines institutional innovation within the scheme (new rules of action) with the extension to newcomers of a shared morality concerned with the satisfaction of collective needs. This corresponds to the third stage in the evolution of the *Trueque* as described above. Three processes combined in that stage: 1) the extension of a morality of solidarity and reciprocity from old participants to newcomers was still possible; 2) the reputation of the leaders acted as the linchpin that sustained trust and glued the system together, even if trust among participants was not necessarily high; and 3) institutional innovation was an ongoing process of negotiation and agreement between the leaders and resulted in clear rules of action for the whole network. When any of these three necessary conditions is absent or becomes exhausted, the institutions created by the SSE can no longer guide the social action of participants. At that point, the initiative cannot expand further and may well contract.

13 | STATE AND SSE PARTNERSHIPS IN SOCIAL POLICY AND WELFARE REGIMES: THE CASE OF URUGUAY

Cecilia Rossel

Introduction

Globally, social and solidarity economy (SSE) participation in social policy implementation has grown in recent decades. In the United States (US) and Europe, and more recently in Latin America and Africa (see Chapter 14), many countries have been creating state–SSE partnerships for the provision of public social services, mainly oriented towards poor and/or marginalised populations. In some cases, stable models of collaboration between SSE and public administration have emerged.

Since the late 1990s, Uruguay has developed policies and programmes in which SSE actors – mostly non-governmental organisations (NGOs) – are playing an increasingly important role in the provision of public social services for the poor. This chapter analyses partnerships between SSE organisations and the government in social policy, and discusses the role of such partnerships in recent welfare reorientations to address new risks, their impacts on SSE, and their implications for the construction and sustainability of a new welfare mix. The underlying hypothesis is that SSE actors are becoming crucial for enabling welfare provisioning through different public programmes and policies. The chapter is mainly concerned with the question of whether adjustments in the welfare system are contributing to the growth of SSE while simultaneously threatening the sector's capacity to develop its full potential.

Recent research and evidence presented here show that SSE–state partnerships are facing numerous problems in relation to institutional structures and state–NGO relationships. This opens a diverse set of questions on the future sustainability of the collaboration model. By focusing on concrete state–SSE partnerships in the area of social policies targeting at-risk children and adolescents, this chapter aims to contribute to a deeper, evidence-based discussion about the conditions under which state–SSE mixes are emerging in social policy, their challenges and their political sustainability. Ultimately, this discussion intends to promote a better understanding of the role of social policy in enabling SSE and vice versa, paying particular attention to the risks involved in the process.

SSE as social service deliverer: rationale and limits

One of the most remarkable developments in the expansion of SSE in recent decades is the increasing engagement of NGOs, non-profit organisations and other SSE actors in the provision of public social services. In the 1980s, state–SSE collaborations in social policy gained the attention of researchers in developed countries. The following years showed a clear expansion and an increasing complexity of these collaborative settings. The possibility of SSE organisations delivering public social services also became a reality in less developed regions, including Latin America.

A growing body of literature explored the conditions under which these partnerships were taking place and their potential and limits. A catalogue of good qualities suggested the comparative advantage of the SSE over public administration in the implementation of social policies. Many authors advocated for the benefits of SSE involvement in social services, especially those directed towards the most excluded groups. Two types of arguments were emphasised in the early literature on partnerships in the 1980s and early 1990s. The first pointed out SSE's solidarity values as a key advantage for delivering social services that could effectively reach the poor (Kramer 1981), as well as the benefits of other SSE features, such as commitment to service quality, not having a profit maximisation logic (Weisbrod 1989), proximity to beneficiaries and receptivity to their needs (Uphoff 1995), and the flexibility and capacity for innovation (Knapp et al. 1990). The second argument claimed that the entry of SSE actors into the social policy arena as service providers gave citizens more options and was conducive to efficiency and efficacy in the use of resources (Kramer 1994; Smith and Lipsky 1989).

Within this discussion, there were many expectations about the benefits that engagement in the delivery of public services could bring to SSE actors themselves. Researchers started observing an increase in the number of organisations willing to become involved in welfare production and a significant growth in the SSE, observable in resources – both human and monetary – and also in diversity and 'market share' in the welfare arena (Corbin 1999; James 1987; Knapp et al. 1990; Salamon 1987; Smith and Lipsky 1989). At the same time, the 'field of action' of SSE widened and started to cross the borders of policy formulation processes (Robinson and White 1997; Taylor 2002), advancing quickly in terms of professionalism.

But it was not all good news. Strong theoretical and empirical concerns emerged about the tensions that might arise in a scenario where SSE organisations were agents of public service delivery. Several studies showed that competition for resources had a negative influence on the sector's fundamental values, because it undermined the collaborative and solidarity nature of SSE actors (Nowland-Foreman 1998). Also, the professionalisation and formalisation processes imposed by the control and accountability rules of the state opened the door for bureaucratisation. SSE organisations started to reproduce some of the traditional problems of public administration. At the same time, as administrative rules demanded results in the provision of services, SSE organisations tended to be more reluctant to focus on the poorest populations (Knapp et al. 1990; see also Froelich 1999).

In this context, perhaps the most important issue for researchers was the new economic dependency on state resources. This was due to shifts in the funding sources of organisations – especially NGOs – resulting in the overwhelming predominance of state resources, usually provided on a regular basis (Kramer 1981, 1994; Kramer and Grossman 1987; Salamon 1987; 1989). This could produce an asymmetrical relationship, technical dependence on the state (Smith and Lipsky 1989) and co-optation and quiescence in SSE organisations (Wolch 1990). Others predicted a potential threat to the sector's autonomy and ultimately its identity, which was strongly related to the idea of an innovative sector independent of the state and the market (Gronbjerg 1993). The advocacy and questioning role of some SSE actors could be undermined due to an overemphasis on service delivery in the context of contracting-out and other types of collaborative partnerships (Alexander et al. 1999).

Although much water has passed under the bridge since the period analysed in this literature, the main questions still seem to be relevant. Recent research indicates the existence of clear 'marketisation' trends within the non-profit sector relating to contract

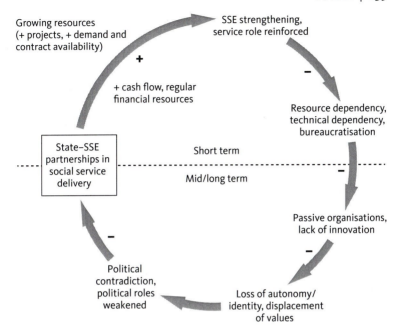

13.1 Main impacts on SSE when delivering services in partnership with the state

competition (Eikenberry and Drapal Kluver 2004) and the loss – or at least displacement – of SSE values in organisations (Abramovitz 2005). The debate around the challenge of strengthening non-profits, despite the deep transformation that the relationship between the sector and the government has gone through, is still at the core of research questions (Kearns 2003; Smith 2008). Figure 13.1 represents graphically the main elements of this debate.

Although it clarifies a number of aspects that relate to both short- and longer-term impacts, the perspective provided in Figure 13.1 does not tell us anything about the specific weights of and interactions between these positive and negative impacts. This remains one of the most important shortfalls in state–SSE partnership research, and is the question that ultimately guides this chapter.

Providing welfare services through NGOs and other SSE actors in Uruguay

Since its origins, the Uruguayan welfare state has been one of the most advanced systems in the Latin American region. The country has a long tradition of social protection based on universal access to education and health, labour market regulation and pensions designed to cover the majority of the working population (Filgueira and Filgueira 1994). However, with time, deep demographic, cultural and labour transformations resulted in 'stratified universalism' (Filgueira 2001), where coverage for certain benefits was available in principle for almost everyone, but in practice access was very stratified. This model combined a relatively strong state leading the development process in almost every dimension, with a relatively weak civil society. However, structural reforms carried out in the late 1990s and early 2000s tended to give other actors – SSE among them – a more important role in the public policy process. This implied a fundamental change in the social protection model that had prevailed since its creation in the first decade of the twentieth century (Midaglia 2000).

Liberal reforms carried out in the 1990s opened up opportunities for alternative forms of social policy implementation, privileging the use of contracts and the transfer of resources from the state to NGOs, associations and other SSE actors. Pressure was strong from international organisations (such as the World Bank and Inter-American Development Bank) to involve civil society in the new policy management model, and SSE actors entered the race to access new resources (as financial aid from international cooperation agencies gradually declined) (ibid.; Villarreal and Santandreu 1999).

Within this context, the first formal SSE–state collaboration experiences in public policy began in the mid-1990s, with a childcare programme (*Plan Caif*) that was designed to reach the poorest families in the country. The programme – conducted by the Uruguayan Child and Adolescence Institute (Instituto del Niño y Adolescente del Uruguay or INAU), the state institution responsible for policies addressing the situation of vulnerable children – assumed that the service would be delivered by civil society actors, namely NGOs and grass-roots organisations. The coverage of the initiative grew quickly: while in 1997 it covered around 7,500 children, this number had doubled within three years.

Immediately after the creation of the plan, INAU established a special office to regulate and manage agreements with the organisations that implemented the services. At the same time, other

INAU policies and new programmes emerged based on the logic of a stable collaboration with SSE organisations. The main features of this logic were: 1) a methodological specification of the service that was to be provided; 2) full financing of the service costs; 3) technical specifications for the personnel who should work in the service; 4) renewable contracts; 5) periodic administrative control of the organisations; and 6) competitive processes for assigning contracts (Midaglia 2000; Rossel 2008).

The 1990s were also characterised by another important change: the arrival, for the first time in the country's history, of the leftist party – Frente Amplio – in the local government of the capital, Montevideo. This transformed the relationship between SSE and public policy by providing the impulse behind the first formal SSE collaboration at a local level, namely a programme to provide child-care services to the most needy families in the city, framed within an ambitious decentralisation plan (Rossel 2008). At the same time, leftist representatives also directly opposed the alternative service delivery formats the national government was creating, arguing that they ignored the core values of SSE, including participation and representation (Midaglia et al. 2006; see also Rossel 2011).

Despite having a different ideological orientation, the national government also sought to partner with SSE actors for the delivery of public social services. Thus, these two programmes, along with other smaller-scale initiatives in other areas, became the pillar upon which the relationship between SSE and the state was built in the social service arena. The main argument at the time was that SSE was able 'to do things' that the government – because of financial or organisational rigidity – was unable to do (Rossel 2003).

With partnerships becoming more frequent, deep internal debates started emerging within the SSE sector; there were two clear positions with regard to being part of this new contracted-out approach. Those who were more convinced about the benefits of the change argued for the possibility for growth and the potential strength that – via new resources – SSE organisations could attain. In contrast, a more pessimistic point of view cautioned about the risks of becoming merely service providers or an embodiment of the liberal model, based on the retrenchment of the state and its substitution by SSE (Sanseviero 2006). There were also different opinions among public administration officers. Those who promoted the changes were convinced that contracting out services to NGOs and grass-roots organisations was the best – and only – way to expand coverage. But others believed that this decision could represent a loss of prominence for the role of the state, in a country where expectations of the presence of the state were still very strong (Rossel 2008).

By the beginning of the 2000s, SSE involvement in public service delivery had crystallised in the social policy agenda. The number of services developed by SSE actors kept growing, as did the number of beneficiaries. State and SSE partnerships in social policy received more and more resources every year. By 2004, approximately 80 per cent of INAU's beneficiaries accessed services that were delivered by SSE actors (Midaglia et al. 2006). The idea that the Uruguayan state had an 'executing agency'[1] in the SSE entered the debate.

Recent trends: from 'retrenchment allies' to 'welfare adjustment enablers'?

When the left-wing Frente Amplio party took over the reins of national government in 2005, there were many doubts about the direction that the party would give to SSE actors and their role in the implementation of social policy. The party traditionally had a strong discourse that was critical of retrenchment and structural reform. However, the impetus provided by the creation of the Ministry of Social Development combined with the effort made to combat the social emergency did not diminish SSE–state partnerships; on the contrary, more and more was demanded of them.

Since 2005, the Uruguayan state – with a very rigid structure and low capacity to recruit qualified professionals – has tended to rely almost entirely on partnerships with SSE actors every time there was a new policy or programme designed to protect excluded groups among the poor (usually those left out of the traditional welfare system). The Uruguayan welfare state has to deal with the generational imbalance of social protection and the exclusion of important social groups, including children, adolescents, youth and women (Filgueira et al. 2005). Even when the system still maintains some fundamental social services on a universal basis (education, for example), its capability to integrate the poorest has been weakening. This was particularly clear when a deep economic crisis affected the country in 2002.

With this context, the development of new policies and services

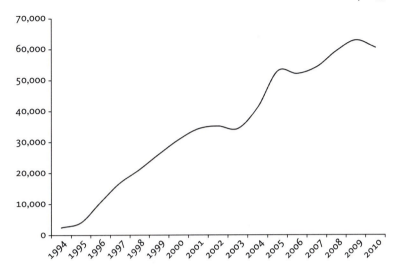

13.2 Number of beneficiaries of public social services delivered by SSE actors directly to children and adolescents, 1994–2010 (*source*: Based on Midaglia et al. 2009; Rossel 2011; Government of Uruguay 2005–10).

in recent years reveals the effort made to react to this situation. But the reality is that the main thrust of these new initiatives relies on the SSE to deliver, and sometimes even design, such services. This is the case of *Plan Caif* and the main programmes carried out by INAU, as well as many of the new initiatives that have been developed by the Ministry of Social Development since 2005 (Rossel 2011). In fact, a conservative estimate of the number of beneficiaries of child and adolescent public services delivered by SSE shows a significant increase: in 2000, the coverage of these services was twelve times that in 1994, and it had doubled by 2010 (see Figure 13.2).

This situation – although not significant when comparing, for example, resources to or beneficiaries of public education or health policies – contrasts with the traditional idea that the state is the only public social service provider. One study reveals that today around one out of every four programmes dedicated to children and adolescents are being implemented by SSE organisations contracted by the state. This proportion is higher when special protection programmes addressing vulnerability and poverty are included (Midaglia et al. 2009).

Evidence also shows that the involvement of SSE actors in delivering social services in Uruguay led them to play a crucial role in including groups that hitherto had been excluded or in tackling new problems and risks that previously had not been addressed. This trend has continued over two decades. However, because these partnerships are associated with welfare reform debates that are closely related to neoliberal reforms – such as the need for reducing state welfare costs and bureaucracy, improving the quality and efficiency of services and deepening the accountability of public administration – it is difficult to understand the significant growth that partnerships have had since 2005 under a government identified with the political left.

A possible hypothesis to guide future research on these questions could be that, when the peak of liberal reforms had passed, much of what had crystallised in that period persisted in the social protection architecture. This probably occurred (as it had in some developed countries), albeit in a more disorganised and fragmented way than is often depicted in the literature (Bode 2006). But there is a possibility that state–SSE partnerships in Uruguay are currently performing more than one role or are functioning in different ways compared with the early partnership era. In other words, even if one is critical of neoliberal reform, the retrenchment and decentralisation context that contributed to the emergence and expansion of state–SSE partnerships is not reason enough to dismiss their contribution to the construction of a new welfare mix.

Enabling or disabling SSE through policy partnerships?

When considering theoretical debates and the role of the Uruguayan SSE in the welfare adjustment process, questions arise about the impacts that these partnerships could be having on SSE organisations themselves. In the following pages I offer some preliminary evidence to advance a few answers. This is based on an analysis of policies for dealing with vulnerable children and adolescents that derives from previous research I have conducted, secondary information and interviews with SSE organisations related to those policies. These findings suggest a Uruguayan case that conforms very strongly to the image described in the literature (Kettl 2006; Kearns 2003; Salamon et al. 2000; Knapp et al. 1990; Smith and Lipsky 1989), although it is not identical (see Figure 13.3).

A number of SSE representatives perceived that partnerships

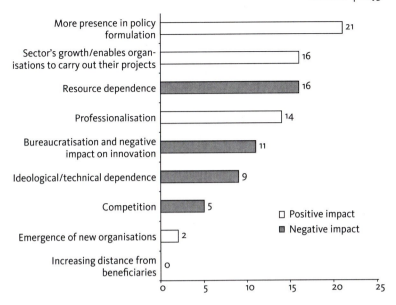

More presence in policy formulation — 21
Sector's growth/enables organisations to carry out their projects — 16
Resource dependence — 16
Professionalisation — 14
Bureaucratisation and negative impact on innovation — 11
Ideological/technical dependence — 9
Competition — 5
Emergence of new organisations — 2
Increasing distance from beneficiaries — 0

□ Positive impact
▨ Negative impact

13.3 Impacts of SSE actors' participation in partnership with the state in service delivery (*source*: Based on interviews with directors of SSE organisations that are delivering social services in partnership with the state, 2006–11).

allowed their organisations to have greater influence in policy formulation and service design: twenty-one out of twenty-nine actors identified this as a clear positive impact. This finding contrasts with that described in the literature, where 'policy influence' or a 'political goal' is frequently absent when considering service delivery partnerships exclusively (Rossel 2010). From the perspective of one SSE organisation involved in delivering child and youth services, the positive impact of partnerships on their organisation was observed in:

> the possibility to be permanently in dialogue with those who are responsible for policies … we became closer to public administrators, there are more and more spaces opened for interaction, and we are able to discuss policy designs. That's a great achievement.

Leaving this response aside for a moment, the second major finding related to the growth of the sector, in terms of financial and human resources. For some organisations, these benefits were closely linked to the possibility of increasing their cash flow. Partnerships implied a regular relationship and resource flow, which gave more certainty to organisations that were used to functioning in an uncertain environment.[2] At the same time, another representative from an SSE organisation indicated that partnerships with the state had allowed them to 'have a greater impact in the communities they work with, having more dynamism, efficiency and efficacy in the use of resources'.

Another positive effect of partnerships for SSE actors was professionalisation. Several researchers and most of the organisations interviewed recognised that stable collaboration with the state and its regular forms of control had allowed them to improve their management capacities, as well as their ability to formulate, monitor and evaluate projects (Rossel 2008). This was closely related to a transformation in the recruitment practices within SSE organisations, where a growing proportion of the personnel had professional qualifications and were remunerated.

However, the increasing amount of resources available for SSE has opened up competition, as noted in the literature. For example, a representative from an NGO that delivers services for several public institutions declared that 'nobody recognises there is competition among NGOs. There is, and it is very hard.' This competition has had a negative effect on coordination and networks within the SSE, creating an antagonism between organisations and obstructing the possibility of interaction and collaboration (Morás 2001; Rossel 2003; 2008).

The biggest negative impact seems to be the high level of dependency on state resources that occurs when SSE partnerships become more frequent (Gerstenfeld and Fuentes 2005; Midaglia 2000; Rossel 2011). Resource dependency is perceived as a threat for several reasons. First, it diminishes the technical independence of SSE actors, who start to feel as if they are part of the public administration, with less margin to pursue innovative ideas. As one youth service worker explained:

> The threat or weakness is in being part of the system. That happens to many small organisations, because they depend on the state. That leads them to not being able to think, to be so dependent that they can't help others, their peers, to get their head out of the water, because they can't confront the state. That's a big threat, because before, NGOs had much more independence.

The second reason concerns the possible loss of autonomy and capacity to confront the apparatus of public administration, specifically in the formulation of policy direction. This loss of autonomy could be direct or could result from self-censorship, as a way of avoiding tensions and conflicts with public administrators and being able to retain regular resources provided by them. This was explained by an organisation delivering child and youth services:

> The key is to diversify and not to stay only with the state's resources. That way, you can influence other actors, take a stand, and not transform yourself into an accomplice of a pseudo system.

At the same time, working in partnership with the state seems to generate a bureaucratisation process in SSE organisations, as has been noted in relation to other countries. This happens because of the growth in personnel, the increased reporting requirements, the accountability requirements from public administrators and the growing specialisation of organisational structures. This process has contributed to reducing the presence of voluntary members in the SSE. According to one SSE organisation, bureaucratisation had changed their 'mystique' and transformed them into a functional actor for the state, with a strong tendency towards 'routine activity and a utilitarian approach'. In the long term, SSE actors see these tendencies as real threats to the sector's autonomy and identity. This is observed in the awkwardness of being a 'partner' of the state, the difficulty of developing innovative ideas within the logic of collaboration with the state, and the replacement of SSE actors' traditional advocacy and political role with a service role. This perspective is clear in the following statements by two NGO directors:

> We are analysing the possibility to restructure and decide what kind of contracts we can have and which we consider we shouldn't carry on with, because there is a double difficulty: there has been a transfer of responsibilities from the state, and this has killed our organisation's initiative.

> Innovation declines and homogeneity starts being a value for the state ... which is thinking more in a service replica logic and not worrying if the service that is being delivered is the best answer to the social problem that it is trying to solve.

Among SSE organisations, there seems to be some fear of losing resource access if the relationship with public administration 'gets too political'. But the diminished importance of the political dimension can also be attributed to the routine and contract-seeking logic associated with these new set-ups. As one interviewee observed:

> Many organisations have transformed, absolutely, into performing merely an executive role, and have abandoned their questioning and political role ... I wonder where the political capacity of Uruguayan NGOs is? Where is it reflected? Nowhere.

Conclusion

While it is clear that SSE–state partnerships in Uruguay are enabling the expansion of welfare services for some groups in the population, it is far less clear whether this creates an enabling environment for the development and strengthening of the SSE. Moreover, the negative impacts that SSE actors themselves perceive caution against any assumptions regarding the political sustainability of partnerships. State–SSE partnerships for delivering social services have acquired an increasingly significant role in Uruguayan welfare provision, but this growth has generated significant tensions and contradictions that undermine the possibilities of realising the potential of the SSE to facilitate development and change.

It would be worrying, indeed, if resource dependency, competition and routine resulted in a loss of independence and autonomy, the loss of innovation capacity, a weakening of political roles, and a decline in values associated with solidarity and the primacy of social objectives over profit.

With this preliminary evidence, it is reasonable to hypothesise that these new state–SSE partnerships are not necessarily a solid base for a new form of politically sustainable 'welfare mix' in Uruguay. To be politically sustainable, such a mix would require the SSE to be, if not strong, then relatively cohesive. The brief examination of Uruguayan welfare partnerships explored in this chapter reveals that SSE–state partnerships seem more like a solution that enables organisations to survive and the state to bypass its rigid structure than a path for enabling SSE. Moreover, it seems that partnerships are affecting SSE development more negatively than positively, particularly if we assume development to mean the expansion of the sector's capabilities not only in service roles but also in relation to solidarity, advocacy and other features of political empowerment.

From a more general point of view, the model developed in Uruguay is closer to an outsourcing process that does not expect much more from the SSE than its implementing function. The fact that this situation has not really changed from the 1990s, when partnerships originated (under liberal reforming governments), until the present day (with the main party of the left ruling the country for the first time in history) could be a sign of the political relevance held by the SSE in the welfare equation, not only because of the scale of coverage provided by the SSE and the resources allocated by the state, but also because of the level of institutionalisation that the role of the SSE has gained in the process.

14 | EXTENDING SOCIAL PROTECTION IN HEALTH THROUGH SSE: POSSIBILITIES AND CHALLENGES IN WEST AFRICA

Bénédicte Fonteneau

Introduction

Social security systems originated in most African countries in the 1950s and 1960s. These systems were designed based on the assumption that developmental processes in Africa would follow the Western model. This explains why existing social security systems in Africa are often a replication of Western social security systems strongly linked to the labour market. But development processes in Africa have taken another turn. The majority of the population works in the informal or rural economies without any kind of formal social health protection. Existing state-run social security systems offer limited benefits to a small portion of the population, namely civil servants and workers employed by formal enterprises. In addition, administrations in charge of social security issues are, in many African countries, rather inefficient and sometimes ineffective in their duty (ISSA 2008).

Since the late 1980s, many community-based or non-governmental organisation (NGO) initiatives have offered health insurance packages to people not covered by their national state-run social security systems or unable to buy insurance packages from private (i.e. for-profit) companies. Many of these initiatives led to the creation of social and solidarity economy (SSE) organisations, particularly mutual health organisations (MHOs).

This had remained the situation for years, with African governments and the international community paying little attention to social security or social protection issues. More recently, however, social protection has been (re)appearing on public policy agendas thanks to the influence of major international organisations, in particular the International Labour Organization (ILO) and the World Bank (Barrientos and Hulme 2008; de Haan 2000).

In many developing countries, social protection systems are being substantially reformed. In the health sector, these processes are closely linked to the goal of universal coverage and new modalities of financing (WHO 2010). In several francophone African countries, social protection strategies being developed or under discussion classify the overall population according to their activity (formal/ public or private economy and rural/urban informal economy, including agriculture) and/or individual characteristics (vulnerable groups, specifically women, people with disabilities, children under five, and people with no revenue). For each group there are corresponding specific (private, public or community-based) mechanisms (insurance, assistance) and financing sources (government revenue, contribution of the population, international aid). SSE organisations are expected to play a major role in these new social protection models; MHOs should, according to the model elaborated in these countries, cover about 80 per cent of the population, namely all those working in the informal economy or in the rural sector (see, for example, Burkina Faso 2012; République du Sénégal 2012).

This chapter looks critically at social protection policies based on SSE initiatives. It starts with an empirical description of the development of MHOs in Africa and their relationship with the state. It then analyses the challenges associated with such policies from the perspective of both public policies and the SSE. This chapter focuses on the experiences in Mali, Senegal, Burkina Faso and Benin – all francophone countries in West Africa where the development of MHOs has been more significant than in other regions. Drawing on research conducted by this author, particular attention is paid to the cases of Senegal and Burkina Faso, where the development of MHOs and the proposed reforms relating to social health protection share some important characteristics.

The development of mutual health organisations in West Africa

MHOs as SSE organisations The emergence and expansion of MHOs in West Africa did not occur by chance. They first appeared in the late 1980s and early 1990s, coinciding with the beginnings of democratisation and the changing nature of civil society (Fonteneau and Galland 2006).[1] Many initiatives were undertaken by the population to respond to urgent needs and political issues. These initiatives were encouraged by development cooperation agencies that wanted to support the democratisation process. In this context, MHOs as non-profit, autonomous, mutual-interest groups were an appropriate form of organisation for such a collective initiative. Their role was further reinforced by the Bamako Initiative, launched in 1987 by the World Health Organization and the United Nations Children's Fund (UNICEF), and progressively implemented during the 1990s. Designed to secure access to quality primary healthcare in Africa, the Bamako Initiative rested on three principles. First, primary healthcare services must attain a sufficient level of self-financing, which requires patients to contribute through user fees. The second was the principle of better access to medicines, particularly generic pharmaceuticals. The third principle was community participation to enhance the quality of care. This principle depended on the idea that, if representatives from the local community sat on the boards of healthcare centres, this would make providers more transparent and responsive. More broadly, this last principle recognised that a range of actors should be involved in the healthcare system, including community-based organisations in charge of managing first-level healthcare centres.

Standard features of MHOs reflect the 'classical' criteria of SSE organisations (Defourny and Develtere 1999; Fonteneau and Galland 2006). They include:

- improve access to healthcare through risk-sharing and resource-pooling;
- not-for-profit;
- members are owners and beneficiaries at the same time;
- autonomy;
- participatory decision-making;
- voluntary membership.

Like other insurance systems, MHOs are based on a mechanism of risk-sharing and resource-pooling. But as SSE organisations, they are non-profit and do not select members based on their individual risk profiles. Access to healthcare through solidarity is thus the main objective of these organisations. The members of MHOs are also the owners, decision-makers and policy-holders. This feature requires strong participation and control mechanisms to make collective decision-making effective. Annual general meetings decide on issues such as budgets, accounts, what to do with surpluses and operational matters, as well as overall strategy. Membership is voluntary. This principle clearly distinguishes MHOs from compulsory insurance schemes such as most national and often state-run social security systems. As in any non-profit organisation, a person may choose to become a member but is never forced to join. From an insurance perspective, the voluntary character of MHOs can be challenging because an MHO has to find a way of ensuring that it can gather a sufficient number of members to share risks in an efficient and attractive way.

MHOs cannot be reduced to their insurance function, however. As participatory mutual interest organisations, MHOs fulfil functions beyond insurance, such as health education. They also act in a sector (healthcare) where the interests of users have been represented only recently. By organising potential users of health services, they become an interlocutor that represents members' interests vis-à-vis healthcare providers. In the same way, we observe MHOs (organised in networks, federations or platforms) representing their members in policy discussions and lobbying on different issues (such as health financing, quality of care, users' rights, and so on).

MHOs in West Africa: where do we stand? What, then, do we know about the development of MHOs in West Africa? As with many other SSE initiatives in Africa, there is a serious lack of comparative and reliable data on MHOs, although there have been some attempts to carry out multi-country inventories in West Africa (La Concertation 2004; 2007). The 2004 inventory of La Concertation identified 622 schemes in eleven countries; of these, 366 were functional. A subsequent inventory carried out by La Concertation in 2007 in fifteen countries (including some Central African countries) identified 188 functional MHOs. The difference between these findings suggests that some schemes may have stopped operating or might have remained too small to partake in further rounds of the inventory. But it also suggests an overall lack of monitoring at both the project level (when MHOs are supported by international or national development organisations) and the national level (by the state or other national programme), as the differences might also be explained by methodological factors (for example, geographical scope or types of MHOs taken into consideration in the surveys).

A better idea of current dynamics can be gauged from recent primary data extracted from surveys or monitoring reports of support organisations. With the exception of Burkina Faso, the initiatives described below do not reflect the entire scope of existing dynamics at the national level. These data (see Table 14.1) illustrate the relatively sober outcomes of MHOs in West Africa, despite the number of existing entities and the continuous creation of new MHOs by diverse local or international initiatives.

TABLE 14.1 Overview of data on MHOs in West Africa

	Network or support organisation	Number of MHOs	Number of beneficiaries (insured people)	References
Benin	Réseau Alliance Santé (Borgou district)	27	26,000	WSM 2009
	Réseau des mutuelles de Bembérèké (Borgou district)	8	6,880	WSM 2009
Senegal	Oyofal Paj (region of Kaolack)	11	22,000	Solidarité Socialiste 2012
Burkina Faso	National survey	165	100,479	Zett and Bationo 2011
Mali	Union Technique de la Mutualité (national)	81	n/a	UTM 2012

With a few exceptions, the size of MHOs remains relatively small, generally between 300 and 1,000 beneficiaries; a beneficiary is defined as a person covered by the insurance, namely a registered person who has paid a financial contribution. From an insurance point of view, this limited size restricts the pooling of resources and thus also the package of services that can be provided. The majority of MHOs cover only smaller risks (primary healthcare), while packages that include higher levels of risk, such as in-patient care, remain the exception.

In theory, MHOs are open to all types of members, whatever their socio-economic profile. In practice, and due to the community-based character of MHOs, members often share the same characteristics. They tend to be from households with limited and/or irregular revenue from their activity in agriculture or the informal economy.

MHOs are, for those populations, the only way to acquire health insurance. The membership of an MHO is often homogeneous (especially in the beginning), which can have negative effects in terms of risk diversification, since members coming from the same area or working in the same sector present similar risks.

Most MHOs are run by elected members, sometimes supported by 'managers' whose salaries are funded by temporary programmes of development agencies. Despite some tendency towards more professional management, this current management type has broadly demonstrated a number of weaknesses. For example, in terms of governance, a recent survey carried out in Burkina Faso (Zett and Bationo 2011) showed that while MHO general assemblies are mostly held according to MHO constitutions, board meetings are much more difficult to organise on a regular basis.

MHOs are also very dependent on the health sector, and in particular on the provision of care. However, the quality of care is generally low in health facilities in West Africa. In that sense, it may not be attractive to become a member of an MHO or to buy insurance products that facilitate access to health facilities providing poor-quality care. Especially in rural areas, MHOs often do not have options other than contracting with public health facilities. In urban areas, health facilities providing better quality of care exist but they are often not affordable for MHOs.

The low contributory capacity of the population is often used to explain the 'small, mutual and low contribution' collection argument. The amounts of contributions are relatively low (between 1,800 and 3,600 CFA francs per person per year, which is approximately equivalent to US\$3.72 to US\$7.43, or between 10,800 and 21,600 CFA francs per year for a household of six people, approximately equivalent to US\$22.3 to US\$44.5), and so it is difficult to argue that the ability (or inability) to pay is the cause of the weak development of MHOs across the region. This incapacity or unwillingness to pay should be considered together with the level of insurance package offered by most MHOs (i.e. mainly limited to small risks), the poor quality of care, and the prevalence of issues relating to management and trust.

The development of MHOs in West Africa has been initiated or supported by many stakeholders, including national support organisations, NGOs from the global North, and international development and aid agencies. Different support models – from minimal support to set-up phases to long-term and hands-on approaches – have been tested in various areas. Some such models have encountered more success than others, but all have faced the weaknesses of MHOs mentioned above. The associated education, information, training, operational support, monitoring and evaluation processes also require large amounts of human, technical and financial resources. The consequence of this diversity of support is that there is also a considerable dispersion and variety of MHOs, making it difficult to organise them into unions or federations at local and national levels.

The link between public authorities and MHOs

In most West African countries, authorities have promoted the development of MHOs. In 1998, the Malian Ministry of Health designed and supported the creation of an organism called Union Technique de la Mutualité (UTM) together with the French Agency for Development (Fischer et al. 2006). The UTM still fulfils its dual functions of being a technical office providing services to MHOs and a union representing the interests of MHOs. In other countries, such as Senegal and Benin, national authorities took other initiatives to create MHOs at the local or national levels; in general, very few of these attempts were successful. In many cases, an overly interventionist and top-down approach contradicted the member-based dynamics and autonomy principle that characterise MHOs and that are necessary to set up and sustain SSE organisations.

National authorities quickly recognised the potential role MHOs could play in the extension of social protection in health. From the mid-2000s onwards, several national health strategies mentioned MHOs as one of the policy options to improve access to healthcare, especially for the category of the population considered as poor. At the same time, tensions have arisen over which ministries should be in charge of these kinds of organisations. Different ministries often laid claim to the sector: the Ministry of Health, because MHOs are acting in their sector; the Ministry of Social Affairs, because MHOs deal with exclusion from healthcare and with poverty issues; the ministry in charge of social protection, due to MHOs' insurance function; or the Ministry of Domestic Affairs, because MHOs are considered to be civil society organisations. While efforts to gain influence and resources may have underpinned the competition, these disputes also reveal the multiple functions (political, economic and social) typically covered by SSE organisations.

MHOs encounter many obstacles, especially in their day-to-day relations with the public health sector and healthcare providers at the local level. Health providers seem to be reluctant to enter into contracts with this kind of insurance scheme. Contractual relations are complicated by the role played by MHOs in terms of patients' rights, and in particular by the voices they represent on issues relating to quality of care. Despite some changes, few classical health systems are open to recognising MHOs as a legitimate part of the health sector. These difficult relations between MHOs and health providers can certainly be explained by the closed nature of health systems (in Africa or elsewhere) and the providers' reluctance to include organisations that represent patients. At different levels, public health authorities could influence this relationship by, for example, informing and training healthcare providers in relation to the advantages and rules of contracting with MHOs. But, in practice, a limited number of steps in that direction have been taken by health authorities.

For a long time, MHOs have mainly functioned informally, without any legal status. Only Mali (in 1996) and Senegal (in 2003[2]) voted through laws regulating MHOs. In the mid-2000s, attempts stalled in Niger to legislate in order to control the development of MHOs, probably due to the weak and unpredictable development of MHOs (Fonteneau et al. 2005). In 2004, the West African Economic and Monetary Union (UEMOA) elaborated a specific regulation on what they have called '*mutuelles sociales*'.[3] This process has been supported by the French Agency for Development and implemented by the ILO through a participatory process involving ministries, MHOs, unions and support organisations. This regulation was adopted by all UEMOA members in 2009 and each country is currently in the process of translating this supra-national regulation into their own national legal frameworks.

Towards a new model to extend social protection in health

In parallel to this regulation process at the supra-national level, new social protection regimes are emerging in almost all West African countries. In French-speaking West Africa, these strategies, which aim to achieve universal health coverage, are still under discussion but look set to be adopted in several countries. In comparison with a few years ago, there is clearly a higher-level political commitment regarding social protection issues. In Burkina Faso, a permanent secretariat dedicated to the implementation of the Universal Health Coverage project was established in 2009. Several feasibility reports have been produced and were adopted by the Council of Ministers in 2013. After his election in 2012, the new Senegalese president, Macky Sall, set up a 'Cellule d'Appui à la Couverture Maladie Universelle' within the Ministry of Health and, more broadly, a 'Délégation Générale à la Protection Sociale et à la solidarité nationale' has been established under the office of the prime minister.

The social protection model being discussed is comprised of a mix of mechanisms targeted to different groups. The universal health coverage scheme currently being debated in Burkina Faso is characteristic of other national projects, such as those in Ghana and Rwanda.

Workers in the formal private and public sector would be still covered through compulsory contributory mechanisms managed by national social security institutions (the Caisse Nationale de Sécurité Sociale). The main innovation of these projects is to extend health coverage to the other 80 per cent of the population, namely those who are active in the agricultural sector or in the informal economy. Universal health coverage will be attained through primary local MHOs, while part of the financial contributions would flow to secondary MHOs that would manage the pooling of risk at the regional or departmental level. For people unable to contribute financially, assistance mechanisms would ensure free access to healthcare. In some countries (for example, Burkina Faso), these assistance mechanisms would be provided through MHOs. A technical platform (or third-party administrator) would assist in the management of risk-pooling and ensure links with the administration in charge of the insurance scheme (the Caisse Nationale d'Assurance Maladie).

SSE organisations as the main actors in the extension of social health protection in West Africa

According to the social protection model described above, MHOs could become one of the main actors in the extension of social health protection in West Africa. This constitutes a huge opportunity to improve access to healthcare for the majority of the population. In addition, the model is quite innovative in the sense that SSE organisations would become a central player in public–private partnerships and national health policy. However, while many community-based MHOs exist, most are still facing difficulties in terms of governance, management, scaling up membership and insurance, and managing institutional and operational relationships between health practitioners and authorities. This raises questions about the roles assigned to these MHOs as well as their objectives and functioning principles. Before analysing this model from an SSE perspective, some of the challenges from a public policy perspective are noted below.

Challenges for public policy As Hickey (2008) suggests, political institutions are a key dimension in social protection in Africa. They include institutions – both formal (elections and political party systems) and informal (patron–client relationships) – that define the 'rules of the game' within a given society (North 1990 cited in Hickey 2008). Social protection has a history of being fairly marginal in the agendas of West African political parties; however, since 2005, some social assistance programmes targeting pregnant women, the destitute or the elderly have been launched under presidential initiatives and funded by domestic resources. *Plan Sésame* in Senegal is one example; this was launched under the previous presidency (Abdoulaye Wade) to provide free health services for the elderly. But such programmes are often not elaborated in the long term; for instance, according to some authors (Ndiaye et al. 2013), the weak performance of the *Plan Sésame* in Senegal is due to poor design, which in turn requires a high level of improvisation by the administration supposed to implement it. Only very recently has social protection (in the broad sense) become a central topic during electoral campaigns, for example in Benin (2011) and Senegal (2012). While steps have been taken in both countries to address the issue of social protection, real political debates regarding the design and implementation of these policies are yet to be seen.

The new social protection model will require a high degree of design, regulation and monitoring capacity at the state level. But because the policy domain of social protection has lagged behind for so many years, the level of knowledge and expertise on these issues is often weak within government administrations (Fonteneau et al.

2005). Many social sector ministries have been marginalised and lack appropriate staff (Mathauer 2004 cited in Hickey 2008: 254), and administrations do not always have the capacity to critically inform and discuss different policy options proposed by donors. In addition, the regulation of such models presents many challenges due to the involvement of diverse (public and private) actors and ministries. Monitoring and evaluation of this social protection model will also require strong mechanisms to measure the achieved outcomes in terms of coverage of the population as well as client satisfaction and the effectiveness of the model to increase access to quality healthcare. These problems of a lack of human resources and administrative capacity within these bodies, as well as the lack of financial resources, seriously constrain their ability to function as they should.

At a more operational level, countries such as Senegal and Burkina Faso are exploring the idea of involving local authorities (districts, communes or *collectivités locales*) to fulfil some functions (for example, the collection of premiums). In theory, this involvement would make sense in the framework of the decentralisation process that confers some health-related responsibilities on local authorities (Boidin 2012). To be effective, their involvement would imply transferring financial and human resources from the central level, but, so far, these transfers remain slow or problematic (Touré 2011).

The lack of state capacity on social protection issues and the weakness or absence of political discussion on such scenarios do not foster a strong 'national ownership' discourse around social protection. Looking at this from a donor perspective, Niño-Zarazúa et al. (2012: 169) noted that:

> to date, donors have not engaged productively with the politics of social protection in sub-Saharan Africa where they have more often proposed new initiatives rather than built on existing ones, worked through NGOs and parallel project structures rather than the state, failed to develop good enough baselines on which arguments for scaling-up could be based, couched their ideas in terms of welfare rather than growth, and failed to identify powerful political actors to work with.

The planning related to social protection projects in West Africa is ambitious. Previous government plans in Senegal aimed to provide cover for 50 per cent of the population by 2015 (Boidin 2012). Burkina Faso aims for MHOs to cover 30 per cent of the population by 2015 (UNDP et al. 2011), but there is a discrepancy between the ambitions announced and the current level of development of MHOs. The number of existing MHOs is, of course, not sufficient to cover the 80 per cent of the population discussed earlier; new MHOs should be created at the local level. However, MHOs are not only risk-sharing mechanisms. After almost twenty-five years, many lessons have been learned about the complex social engineering process that is required in the creation of MHOs. This process reflects a mix of 'technical' factors (quality of healthcare, and so on), financial factors (willingness and capacity to pay premiums) and socio-political factors (social cohesion, trust, leadership, collective choice, etc.) that cannot be created mechanically from the top down. Even if MHOs are less community-based, the question remains as to under what conditions can public authorities initiate the creation of such SSE organisations.

A broad range of health financing options, including innovative financing mechanisms and development assistance, is currently under discussion at both domestic and international levels. Some ILO simulations (Berhendt 2008) suggest that, although well-designed programmes could be affordable in some African countries, current fiscal space and/or capacity for tax collection are too limited to support the financing of national social protection strategies or even of new social protection initiatives. Indeed, all African governments are concerned about the financial implications of introducing social protection programmes in a context of high poverty incidence and fiscal constraints (Niño-Zarazúa et al. 2012). The financing issue often remains vague in existing national social protection strategies. While they might foresee, theoretically, a financing mix made up of revenue from national governments, aid from international donors, private, community and NGO financing, household savings and out-of-pocket expenditure (Barrientos 2008), they often fail to consider the certainty, predictability and sustainability of these financial plans. In the short term, the implementation of specific social protection mechanisms still relies mainly on external temporary resources made available by donors, NGOs or the ad hoc revenues of national governments for presidential initiatives. With a few exceptions, donor interventions regarding social protection often remain donor driven in their approach and fragmented in their financing and implementation (Fonteneau 2013).

Challenges from an SSE perspective What are the theoretical challenges and opportunities presented by this model from an SSE perspective?

The role assigned to MHOs by this new social protection model has been very positively welcomed by MHOs and by their technical and financial partners. In some countries (Burkina Faso, for example), MHOs even lobbied to ensure that this role would be uniquely assigned to them and not open to any civil society organisation or other kind of intermediary body. For MHOs, this social protection model is an important recognition of the efforts and innovations that have been undertaken by the SSE. Potentially, it also allows for MHOs to be able to continue to provide services while being technically and financially supported in the context of a national strategy.

So far in West Africa, many individual MHOs have demonstrated the capacity to offer health insurance to specific groups, but no MHOs – not even those organised in networks – have succeeded in covering a significantly large group of the population with insurance packages covering larger risks. Recent experiences in Rwanda and Ghana have clearly demonstrated that better results can be achieved by MHOs when they are articulated with national social protection policies. MHOs could thus become more effective in increasing access to (quality) healthcare, although scaling up and increased professionalism will be essential. But the challenges relating to professionalisation processes and scaling up are complex to address for various reasons. As MHOs are still run by elected leaders or managers in a situation of precarious employment (short-term and low-paid contracts), professionalisation will not be that easy. Current managers may not have the necessary competencies and elected members could be reluctant to lose a 'space of power' at the community level. In terms of scaling up, the current embeddedness of MHOs in the community makes it difficult to link with other MHOs in order to merge the organisations themselves or their networks. In addition, MHOs should also be able to attract more members. However, this permanent objective remains challenging given, for example, the limited scope and quality of the services offered by MHOs (the fact that they cover only small risks and facilitate access to healthcare centres providing poor-quality services, for example).

MHOs present many advantages, particularly in terms of their proximity to members. Because of the weakness of public administration, this proximity could be used not only to collect insurance premiums but also as a way to enhance communication between the administration and members. Without such intermediary organisations, the implementation of a social protection mechanism for populations working in the informal economy or in the rural sector would be almost impossible. In Latin America, some governments have made an explicit choice to promote a plural economy by incorporating SSE in public policy design (Caruana and Srnec 2013; Chapter 7 in this volume). But in West Africa, despite the positive interest of the state with regard to MHOs, a limited number of effective policies (such as Mali's UTM) have been implemented so far to support their development and sustainability as SSE organisations. As such, the emerging models of social protection policy seem to be guided more by pragmatism than by an explicit political choice made by governments to support SSE.

SSE organisations are also autonomous organisations. As Defourny and Develtere (1999) put it, management autonomy distinguishes the social economy from the production of goods and services by governments. Such organisations enjoy the independence that informs the basic motivation behind every associative relationship (ibid.). This 'autonomy and independence' feature has also been recognised by the West African regional legal framework on '*mutuelles sociales*' (UEMOA 2009). Indeed, MHOs currently operate in a rather autonomous way from the state, deciding (in theory) on their own design, internal governance principles, financial contributions, insurance packages and relationships with healthcare centres. The new social protection model, however, will lead to a certain standardisation of MHOs in terms of functioning and structure, as well as the types of insurance packages offered to the population. This standardisation can have positive effects if it contributes to more equitable access to healthcare. But it could also hinder the autonomy of MHOs as SSE organisations, because of the limited functions MHOs would fulfil in the new social protection model (for example, collecting financial contributions).

Although MHOs are not a recent phenomenon in West Africa,

their articulation with formal public policies has tended to pre-cede their organisation and structuring at local, regional and national levels. So far, there is only one national union in West Africa, in Mali. In other countries, unions or federations exist but they mainly cover MHOs set up or supported by the intervention of a technical or financial partner or even a parent organisation. Yet such structures are of crucial interest not only in terms of MHOs' role in the new social protection model, but also in terms of recognising the nature of the SSE.

As SSE organisations, MHOs are based on participatory decision-making processes. In practice, the level of participation among exist-ing MHOs should not be romanticised. While members may formally have the right to decide in a general assembly, the influence of informed elites, leaders or external support organisations remains high. But participatory decision-making processes also allow mem-bers to be informed about their own rights as patients (in terms of quality of care, access to information, and so on) and to control the efficient functioning of their organisations. In the new social protec-tion model, both of these functions will have to be ensured vis-à-vis the state but also in relation to other actors managing the pooling of risk at all levels. The presence of member-based organisations in a social protection system potentially ensures representation of its members. By integrating MHOs within the welfare system, the state has recognised that governance should be based on a multi-stakeholder participatory process. This is an essential element if the transformative dimension of social protection is to be realised: namely, the capacity to address concerns relating to social justice and exclusion (Devereux and Sabates-Wheeler 2008). This transformative dimension also means that specific actors, in particular civil society, have a key political role to play beyond the provision of social protec-tion services or intermediation between the state and the population. As Michielsen et al. (2010: 655–6) put it regarding social protection in health, the transformative dimension is about 'transforming the social and institutional context of the health system to counteract exclusion and deprivation of the right to health and quality care'.

Conclusion

In this chapter, I have tried to describe the paradoxical situation that is taking place in West Africa with regard to the development of a new social protection model. The policies involved aim to extend social protection in health to the majority of the population through already existing – and yet to be created – SSE organisations, namely MHOs. This articulation between SSE organisations and public policy presents huge potential. But if one considers the design of this policy and the weaknesses that existing MHOs are still facing, many questions arise – not only about the realism and ownership of such policies but also about the challenges at stake for MHOs as SSE organisations.

A successful articulation between MHOs and national social protection policy is the joint responsibility of both the state and the MHOs and their partners. Beyond the technical, political and financial challenges relating to social protection strategies, national governments and administrations have somehow to 'invent' how to interact and establish structural dialogue with SSE organisations while respecting their autonomy. On their side, MHOs should reflect on the limits of the community-based model and on the way forward in terms of scaling up and professionalisation while defending what constitutes their added value: their proximity to the population, the participatory processes that enable voices to be heard, the representation of members' interests, and their capacity to play an effective role within a national social protection system. Finally, overcoming the fragmentation of the mutual 'movement' remains perhaps the greatest challenge for realising the potential of this model in West Africa. In this process, technical and financial partners bear a great responsibility. The way in which they design their intervention and support has a direct influence on how MHOs set up collective representative structures.

15 | ENABLING AGRICULTURAL COOPERATIVES IN UGANDA: THE ROLE OF PUBLIC POLICY AND THE STATE

Justine Nannyonjo

Introduction

It is widely accepted that cooperatives contribute to improving food security, job creation, income generation, resource mobilisation and broad-based economic empowerment, thereby enhancing sustainable human development. In both developed and developing countries, a sizeable population derives its livelihood directly or indirectly through cooperative-based activities. However, cooperatives too often remain limited in scale and scope, constrained by the lack of an enabling policy environment. Experience has shown that government policies can impede or enhance independent cooperative development (Hoyt 1989). For encouraging the development of cooperatives, public policy can have a significant effect in several ways. It can support the development of cooperatives through indirect policy measures, such as transparent laws and regulations that are based on consultation with the producers. More direct measures can also be taken, such as subsidies or grants to producer organisations. Governments can also facilitate collaboration with networks and intermediaries by encouraging their creation where they do not exist or by developing incentives for cooperatives to join existing networks. They can also support with the scaling up of successful and innovative cooperative models. However, the provision of public support can hinder the development of cooperatives' financial sustainability, self-reliance and autonomy.

There is increasing recognition of the challenges and limitations of existing policies to promote the development of cooperatives. In many countries, the current process of policy formation, measures and programmes undertaken are limited and ineffective, thus raising questions around how governments might enable cooperative development through public policy. This chapter analyses the role of the state and the effectiveness of the policy environment for cooperative development in Uganda, particularly in relation to agricultural cooperatives. The chapter begins by tracing the historical evolution of cooperatives within the public policy and political economy context. Since the 1990s, the Ugandan government has taken a number of significant measures aimed at strengthening the cooperative sector. By the end of 2013, the cooperative movement was composed of 13,202 cooperative societies (of which about 90 per cent were involved in agricultural marketing and production, and savings and credit); membership had grown from just over 1 million people in 1978 to about 4 million in 2012, representing about 12 per cent of the total population.[1] The process of policy formation and implementation, however, confronts numerous challenges and limitations. Furthermore, it is not clear how effective the approach has been. The cooperative sector has experienced frequent and dramatic shifts in circumstances related to both national and international policy, ranging from periods of rapid growth, loss of autonomy and economic collapse to what is currently a significant revival. The remainder of the chapter outlines the structure and activities of cooperatives before examining the role of, and challenges facing, government in enabling the development of cooperatives. A concluding section sums up the main findings and key challenges that remain.[2]

The development of agricultural cooperatives

The cooperative movement in Uganda was driven by the urge to resist private European and Asian interests that sought to monopolise domestic and export marketing, especially in the cotton and coffee industries. The first cooperative was formed in 1913 in the central region. Many other groups of farmers were later established across Uganda, including the Buganda Growers Association in 1923, whose goal was to control the domestic and export marketing of members' produce. A cooperative movement was therefore born to fight the exploitative forces of the colonial administrators and alien commercial interests. The colonial government at the time considered the emergence of such organisations premature and subversive and denied them legal backing that would have enabled them, among other things, to access credit from lending institutions. This forced cooperative groups to operate informally until 1946, when the Cooperative Societies Ordinance was enacted to legalise their operations.

A registrar for cooperatives was appointed and a Department for Cooperative Development created. However, many cooperatives refused to register under the ordinance as they perceived this as a means of increasing government interference in their activities.

Expansion in the 1950s and 1960s Renowned for his liberalism, Sir Andrew Cohen came to Uganda as governor in 1952 and appointed a commission of inquiry into the progress of the cooperative movement. The inquiry report of 1952 stipulated that:

- it was not the function of government to guide private enterprises, as doing so would arouse suspicion;
- the cooperative movement would be stronger if it were independent of government; and
- it was a legitimate and reasonable aspiration of cooperative societies to be free of government control.

In light of this, the government amended the Cooperative Societies Ordinance. This gave rise to the Cooperative Societies Act of 1952, which was more accommodating and provided a framework for rapid economic development. It provided enough autonomy to make registration acceptable to the cooperative groups. It also both provided for the elimination of discriminatory price policies and offered private Africans access to coffee processing. Thus, between 1952 and 1962, cooperative membership increased eight-fold and the tonnage of crops increased six-fold (Kabuga and Kitandwe 1995). The cooperative district unions acquired considerable importance, and by 1962 there were fourteen cotton ginneries and seven coffee curing works in the hands of cooperative unions. Many people were employed and cooperative unions became the most conspicuous institutions in the districts.

Following Uganda's political independence in 1962, the government favoured cooperatives as policy instruments for rural development. The 1952 ordinance was repealed by the Cooperative Societies Act 1963, which restored the office of the registrar, combining it with that of the Commissioner for Cooperative Development. Also restored were the powers of the departmental staff, who had complained that their advice was usually ignored as they did not have powers to enforce it.

A Cooperative College and a Cooperative Development Bank

were later established. Cooperatives were granted a 100 per cent monopoly to gin cotton, and, by 1965, cooperative unions handled 61 per cent of the volume of cotton. They also handled 40 per cent of the Robusta coffee and 90 per cent of the Arabica. Stimulated by heavy government support through direct assistance and subsidised services, the cooperative movement expanded immensely in many sectors including fishing, dairy, cattle marketing, hides and skins, savings and credit.

Loss of autonomy and declining performance in the 1970s and 1980s Gross mismanagement, corruption and embezzlement became common in the cooperatives during the late 1960s. This created discontent in rural areas and led to various commissions of inquiry, the repeal of the 1963 ordinance, and eventually its replacement by the Cooperative Societies Act 1970. The act gave the minister direct control over the affairs of registered cooperative societies, thus robbing the cooperative movement of its autonomy. Henceforth co-operative societies and unions were run like government parastatals. By the time Idi Amin came to power in 1971, there were over 2,500 primary cooperative societies with over 750,000 family members. There were thirty-six unions including four national unions and an apex organisation (Arain et al. 1967).

The Idi Amin regime (1971–79) saw a decline in the performance of cooperatives. Following his declaration of 'the economic war' that saw the expulsion of Asians from Uganda, the performance of the economy declined, with prices of controlled crops such as cotton and coffee (where cooperatives were dominant) dropping so low that farmers resorted to growing other crops. Nevertheless, cooperatives grew in number as civil servants and wage earners realised that they could overcome the credit squeeze only through the formation of cooperative savings and credit societies. By 1978 there were 3,054 primary cooperative societies, 41 unions and 1,100,000 cooperative members. Many consumer cooperative societies were also created to take advantage of scarce commodities distributed through government cooperatives.

During Obote's government (1980–85), cooperatives were encour-aged to form in order to benefit from the limited commodities and services provided by government. However, efforts to revive and use cooperatives for rural development were hampered by excessive government involvement that virtually turned cooperatives into government parastatals. Worse still, as the guerrilla war intensified, such efforts were destabilised as the war was largely fought in the cooperative movement's strongholds. Cooperatives incurred heavy losses in terms of both people and property. Obote's regime was toppled by that of Okello, which, in turn, was toppled by Yoweri Museveni's National Resistance Movement (NRM)[3] in 1986.

The NRM government adopted a structural adjustment programme in the late 1980s, which resulted in the liberalisation of agricultural markets, privatisation of public institutions, and cutting of funding for services in many sectors. This led to a further decline of cooperatives and the loss of their buying monopoly. The government marketing boards on which the cooperatives largely depended for crop and marketing finance were abolished, and, with that, the provision of crop finance by government stopped. In addition, cooperatives were heavily indebted, with severe weaknesses in entrepreneurship, management and commitment in leadership, which made it impossible to seize the opportunities that liberalisation policies offered. A new Cooperative Statute of 1991 was formulated to provide for a member-based, autonomous and member-controlled movement. Most government services were cut, including audit, training and loan funds. These measures, combined with the inability of cooperatives to adjust quickly to change, led to a sharp decline in the performance of cooperatives. Most unions collapsed due to the lack of crop finance. The Uganda Cooperative Alliance (UCA), as an apex body, was also affected, since it was supported by the cooperative unions.

Revival of cooperatives The malfunctioning and collapse of many cooperatives triggered a corrective response from both the state and the cooperative movement in the late 1990s. It was recognised that the potential of the cooperative enterprise in fostering development was yet to be harnessed due to internal problems relating to governance and leadership, poor capitalisation, inadequate knowledge, a lack of management information systems and expertise in managing cooperatives, and an inadequate legal and regulatory framework. The state therefore responded to the collapse of cooperatives by revising the cooperative legislation, streamlining the regulatory framework for the cooperative movement. The cooperatives themselves responded by reasserting their solidarity to find lasting solutions to the crisis. Many of them seized the opportunity offered by liberalisation to reinvent their business model. For the first time, cooperatives had the freedom to re-examine their organisational structure, with a view to meeting their own needs and interests (tackling poverty and social needs), rather than the interests of the state. The individualistic tendencies of neoliberalism and their adverse consequences, especially for the poor (unemployment, for example), also led people to regroup and regenerate solidarity to help each other survive the market forces. This new-found solidarity led to the replacement of the ineffective and inefficient cooperative unions or to the creation of new cooperative unions, resulting in the structural reorganisation of the cooperative movement (Wanyama 2012).

Contemporary cooperative structure, activities and challenges

The whole cooperative movement, including marketing cooperatives, has today been transformed through addressing many of the weaknesses described above: high degrees of dependency, lack of entrepreneurial culture, poor leadership and management, costly and unsustainable cooperative structures and lack of financial resources. A new approach has focused efforts at the grass-roots level, whereby grass-roots community-based organisations, parish farmers' associations and other smaller farmer groups have regenerated their solidarity and organised themselves into cooperative societies at the village or parish level under rural producer organisations (RPOs). RPOs were strengthened to act as cooperatives that market members' produce collectively.

At the sub-county level, area cooperative enterprises (ACEs), which are composed of between five and twenty RPOs, were created to act as smaller cooperative unions for the RPOs. ACEs market produce for their members and bargain for better prices, collect and disseminate market information, and process members' produce. They also link producers and input dealers, and support agricultural extension.

A further component of the restructured cooperative system is a link between RPOs, ACEs and savings and credit cooperatives (SACCOs), which has been termed a 'triangular model' (Figure 15.1). The RPOs supply produce to the ACEs, which look for markets for that produce. The SACCOs provide financial assistance to the

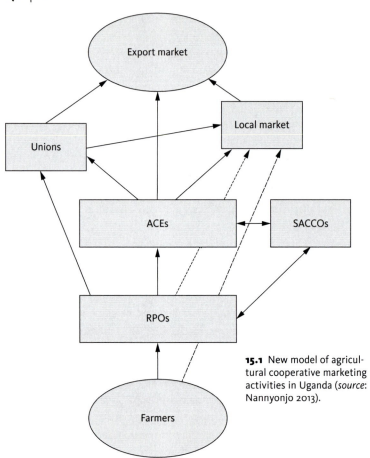

15.1 New model of agricultural cooperative marketing activities in Uganda (*source*: Nannyonjo 2013).

farmers, who are registered members of both the SACCOs and the ACEs. The produce supplied to ACEs can be used as security for obtaining loans from the SACCOs. An ACE may market produce to individual traders or to export traders. The RPOs and ACEs may also become members of unions and trade directly with them. This differs from the previous structure of cooperatives, which was vertical and hierarchical; produce would flow from farmers at the lowest level to export markets via primary societies, unions and marketing boards (Figure 15.2).

These reformed cooperatives are meant to be managed as profitable business units competing with other private traders in agricultural output markets. In the reformed system, cooperative

15.2 Old model of agricultural cooperative marketing activities in Uganda (*source*: Afranaa Kwapong and Lubega Korugyendo 2010).

marketing has been greatly expanded in scale and scope to include non-traditional crops[4] and other products such as honey and fish, in order to reduce the risks from crop failure and low prices during the peak production season.

Activities of cooperatives The current activities of cooperatives are organised in a four-tier, vertical structure of primary societies that consist of at least thirty people aged above twelve years. A minimum of two primary societies form a secondary society (union or ACE), while two or more secondary societies form a tertiary society. Secondary and tertiary societies form the apex association. There are 13,064 primary societies or RPOs, 129 secondary societies, of which 70 are ACEs, 8 tertiary societies and 1 apex association (the UCA). The UCA is responsible for lobbying, advocacy and resource mobilisation for capacity-building and advisory services to the co-operative movement, and promotion of relationships and alliances between stakeholders involved in the development of cooperatives.

The activities of agricultural cooperatives can be grouped under five categories. *Production and marketing cooperatives* are involved in the production and marketing of coffee, cotton, tobacco, maize and milk (among other products). There are also many cooperative societies involved in *agro-processing and value addition*, for example ginning cotton, processing coffee and honey, and making wines and medicinal syrups. There are twenty-four *dairy cooperatives* that supply breeding and veterinary inputs; provide cold storage and transportation of dairy products; and improve pricing and market access. *Consumer cooperatives* undertake wholesale trading and retailing of both farm inputs and cooperatives' products. They also promote fair trading practices, offer a ready market for producer' products and stabilise consumer prices.

There are also 5,166 SACCOs that offer several financial products, including credit extension, savings mobilisation, business advice and financial literacy. The promotion of SACCOs has contributed to improved outreach of financial services to rural communities, including to hitherto unserved populations (UCA 2012).[5] The integration of ACEs and SACCOs enables cooperative members to have access to services such as improved seeds and to acquire inputs at lower than open market prices, as well as providing them with extension services – all of this enables them to increase production and productivity (UCA 2013). For example, input sales through fifty-four selected ACEs that have links to SACCOs increased by 38 per cent to 195 metric tonnes during the year 2012–13 from 141 metric tonnes in 2011–12.[6]

Challenges of cooperatives Within the context of reforms, several challenges continued to hamper the development of cooperatives: internal problems relating to governance and leadership; poor capitalisation attributed to the limited sources of cooperative financing; inadequate knowledge about the formation of cooperatives, their leadership and governance, and markets; a dented image attributed to various disadvantages such as crop failure, market and price fluctuations, political instability, and loss of assets; weak management information systems characterised by paper-based files, a low level of use of information and communication technology (ICT) and poor data management practices; and poor infrastructure, especially in rural areas, including storage facilities, electricity and communication. Further, the legal and regulatory framework was inadequate and not implemented effectively to ensure that cooperatives function in the best interests of their members and the country. The absence of appropriate policies also undermined the existing cooperative law and efforts towards the further development of the movement. Thus there was a need for government to create an environment that was more conducive for cooperatives to expand and diversify their activities.

Enabling cooperatives: key issues and challenges for the state

A number of initiatives, described below, have emerged since the 1990s, specifying various support measures for cooperatives within the public sector to address the gaps and remaining challenges recognised above. These initiatives are in parallel to, and/or in collaboration with, similar initiatives undertaken by the private sector, civil society and the cooperative movement, affirming the principle that supporting cooperatives is a shared responsibility. The initiatives include: consultative formation of a cooperative development policy; amendment of cooperative laws and regulations; support for financial services and marketing institutions; strengthening of cooperative capacities; upgrading and modernisation of management information systems; promotional activities; and integration of gender and environmental concerns in cooperative development.

Clear policy guidelines for cooperatives The reformed cooperative system focuses on providing clear policy guidelines. At the national level, the *National Cooperative Policy* (MTIC 2011) outlines strategies to develop and strengthen the cooperative movement so that it might play a leading role in poverty eradication, employment creation and socio-economic transformation of the country. Key aspects relate to:

- instituting the necessary legal reforms to promote good governance that will facilitate the rebuilding and revitalisation of the cooperative movement;
- strengthening the Ministry of Trade, Industry and Cooperatives

(MTIC) and local government cooperative offices for effective service delivery;

- diversifying cooperative enterprises;
- enhancing productivity and competitiveness;
- providing cooperative training and education;
- promoting gender balance, fair representation of marginalised groups and good environmental practices within cooperatives;
- mitigating the spread and effects of HIV/AIDS and malaria using the cooperative network; and
- improving coordination within ministries, departments and agencies, linking cooperative development with national poverty eradication and development plans and programmes[7] and with private–public partnerships to facilitate implementation.

The policy resulted from a wide consultative process involving government officials, private sector executives, cooperative movement actors, academia, donors and mass media. Consultative workshops at regional and district levels have informed the policy, although attendance at workshops was restricted to senior representatives of institutions and thus excluded the participation of stakeholders at lower levels. Nevertheless, the process has helped to identify the priority areas for cooperative development, and to relate these to national development policies (ibid.). Strategic actions to achieve these priorities have also been arrived at through a consultative process. At the grass-roots level, members of cooperatives have been made more aware by their leaders and UCA staff of the principles of cooperatives, the governance structure, and their roles and responsibilities as cooperative members.

A national cooperative development plan has been set out to guide implementation of this policy. Monitoring and impact assessment of policy implementation are conducted by the policy analysis unit of the MTIC. The MTIC is also amending the Cooperative Societies Act and the Cooperative Societies Regulations 1992 to support the implementation of the *National Cooperative Policy* (ibid.).

Financial services support Policies to expand access to financial services have been a substantial component of rural development over the last two decades. The Poverty Alleviation Project (1994–98) was initiated with support from the African Development Bank

(AfDB); this was followed up with the Rural Microfinance Support Project I (2000–05), which was designed to increase the rural poor's access to microfinance services and to provide appropriate capacity-building and technical assistance.

However, lessons learned from these projects indicated that the country's capacity to ensure sustainable financial services at the local level continued to be eroded by: 1) the absence of strong retail capacity in microfinance institutions (MFIs); 2) the difficulties of extending financial services to rural areas, where most of the poor are concentrated, in a cost-effective manner; 3) weak institutional infrastructure, including a lack of service providers such as training institutes, accountancy services, credit reference bureaus and appropriate information technologies (AfDB Group 2009); and 4) many SACCO members being negatively influenced by politicians who presented the external funding as a government grant, increasing default rates (Fiorillo 2006).

A further lesson was that the success of wholesale lending is largely dependent on the quality of governance and management, and so efficient capacity-building is crucial. For example, SACCOs that sensitised their members about loan repayment were more successful in maintaining high repayment rates. It was found that external funds do not help a weak SACCO become strong, especially if the SACCO has weak management, ineffective governance or poorly performing portfolios. Furthermore, wholesale loans to weak SACCOs changed their orientation from being savings-led institutions to being simple mechanisms for the disbursement of external funds, resulting in a deterioration of loan portfolio quality and amounts of member savings. On the other hand, SACCOs that had qualified and dedicated management and governance teams, sensitised members, good policies and effective capacity-building showed sustained growth over time without any external funds (ibid.).

To accelerate access to financial services in rural areas, the government introduced a rural financial services strategy in 2006,[8] aimed at establishing SACCOs in every sub-county and emphasising savings mobilisation and providing loans for investment in rural enterprises. However, the supply-driven approach and provision of government-financed start-up capital created challenges in terms of repayment discipline and oversight, and resulted in a focus on loans rather than on savings, which continues to undermine the financial sustainability of SACCOs (IFAD 2013). Learning from this experience and recognising the importance of healthy institutions at the grass-roots level, the government is finalising a revised policy framework and new legislation for regulation of tier four MFIs, which include SACCOs and informal MFIs. Furthermore, the Bank of Uganda has developed a financial inclusion project (2012–15) to respond to emerging issues relating to financial innovations, financial literacy and education, consumer protection and broadening the provision of financial services that are geared towards the needs of different social sectors. A recent element in the rural economy, with important implications for rural finance, is the rapid spread of mobile phones and the appearance of new technology-driven financial services, including mobile banking, mobile cash, and agent and branchless banking (ibid.).

Access to, and utilisation of, financial and business development services is further facilitated by the Rural Income and Employment Enhancement Project (2010–14);[9] this is providing loans to cooperatives, small- and medium-sized enterprises and MFIs. It is contributing towards building rural financial infrastructure and enhancing links with mainstream financial institutions (such as commercial banks) through linkage banking and the sharing of client information. It is also promoting a savings and credit culture among the target rural population and enhancing their business management skills through training.[10]

Support to marketing institutions In partnership with cooperative unions and societies, a warehouse receipt system (WRS) and commodity financing have been established as marketing instruments to enable producers of commodities to increase access to commodity trade finance, improve stock quality, access better markets and maximise their returns. The system involves a farmers' group depositing produce into a certified warehouse where it is weighed and tested for quality. In return, the warehouse manager issues a receipt to the produce depositor that outlines the product details. This receipt can then be used by the farmer to look for a market instead of carrying the produce physically, and can be traded on the Uganda Commodity Exchange or used as collateral for obtaining bank loans.

The provision of finance receipts through such a system is expected to yield better returns. This instrument improves access to trade but can also provide input finance that is easily accessed using commodities as collateral. This minimises the need for crop finance and improves bargaining power, thereby leading to reduced exploitation of farmers by intermediaries. It also encourages links between SACCOs that provide funding for the producer and marketing cooperatives that deal in collective bulking. However, the level of participation by farmers in collective marketing and in the utilisation of the WRS to enhance their incomes is still low. This is due to limited awareness about the system, and partly due to farmers' concerns about delays in the processing system, including the slow response from banks in issuing discount receipts in order to provide loans to the farmers against the stocks in store.[11]

Strengthening cooperative capacities Capacity-building interventions are being carried out by the MTIC in collaboration with private partners, mainly on leadership and management. For example, in 2011–12, 234 cooperative leaders from seven districts were trained in financial management, governance, internal controls and risk management. Cooperative agricultural extension services are provided by district commercial officers, while training services are provided by the UCA and other stakeholders.[12] However, a large number of cooperatives interviewed (60 per cent) thought that more farmer training was needed given the rapid expansion of the cooperative movement.[13]

Existing cooperative management information systems are characterised by manual files, limited ICT equipment (such as internet access, computer hardware and software, and electrical power backup), low ICT literacy, and poor data and information management practices. This results in a lack of reliable and accurate data for cooperative planning, monitoring and decision-making at all levels, as well as low adaptability to technological changes among the cooperatives. However, some cooperatives are beginning to use computers, emails and other automated technologies. For example, the cooperative data analysis system (CODAS) is designed to support information links between the Department of Cooperatives in the MTIC and the cooperative movement, and it has been piloted in several districts. It is expected that CODAS will help with the analysis of data and dissemination of information on cooperative development indicators to aid planning.

Awareness-raising To revive cooperatives in the country, extensive community mobilisation, sensitisation and general education are also being carried out through meetings and workshops. The aim is to raise awareness within communities about cooperatives, gender issues, climatic change and health management, and to improve people's financial literacy and banking culture. More RPOs are joining cooperatives as a result of the 'cooperative sensitisation' process; for example, there was an increase of 21,049 members of RPOs in all ACEs in 2011–12 (representing a 39 per cent increase) as a result of 'sensitisation' of twenty-one RPOs.

Communities are also being encouraged to participate in various promotional activities. Among these is a Celebration of Cooperatives day, held on the first Saturday of July. During these celebrations, the members of cooperatives exhibit what they do and share knowledge on the development of the sector. A national cooperative development forum has also been established to facilitate interaction and information-sharing in the sector. These events aim to enhance links between cooperatives and to create awareness of and generate solutions to some of the challenges described above. However, despite increased community mobilisation and sensitisation, there is still a general lack of cooperative awareness and high levels of financial illiteracy among many communities. This calls for more awareness-raising efforts and 'cooperative sensitisation' (UCA 2012).

Cooperatives and gender The integration of gender in cooperative development is essential, and can be beneficial for expanding the membership in both number and quality. Deliberately gender-sensitive policies have been developed in all forms of cooperatives: namely, there has to be a woman and a youth on each committee. Gender training and sensitisation have helped ensure participation of both women and men in cooperative activities. This has led to an increase in the number of women participating in cooperative activities,[14] thus enabling women to access products and services and to improve their business skills and knowledge. Access to cooperative technologies (such as tractors and ox ploughs) has eased labour burdens for women, thus accelerating improvements in employment, education and health. Women now have more time to look after their families and also to venture into other economic and social activities. Some women involved in cooperatives have assumed management and leadership positions. This has also provided a platform for advocacy, leadership training and skills development. Through the UCA, youth clubs have also been formed in secondary schools and linked to SACCOs to increase youth awareness of and participation in cooperatives.

Concern for the environment In order to ensure that farmer livelihoods are also sustainable, environment and climate change issues are mainstreamed into cooperatives. This has been pursued through the training of UCA staff and cooperative leaders; for example, some cooperative members have been trained in tree nursery management and environmental mainstreaming, and tree planting was a key activity at the thirteenth Annual Saving and Credit Cooperative Association Congress held in Uganda in 2012. However, there is a need for further sensitisation, networking and training of communities to embrace renewable energy use.

Further challenges for government

In fulfilling its policy commitments to revive the cooperative movement, the government faces a number of institutional challenges:

- There are inadequate skilled *human resources* for supervision and technical services.[15] This is partly attributed to the restructuring of government departments following decentralisation, which left cooperatives with few staff, especially at the local government level. The remaining structures were not adequately facilitated or equipped to effectively service the entire cooperative movement. Currently, commercial officers handle all the commercial services at the district level (including trade, tourism, industry and cooperatives) yet cooperatives need close attention from a dedicated officer. Following decentralisation, the district commercial services department was merged with the production department (which is dominated by agricultural and veterinary officers) to supervise cooperatives. A ban on the recruitment of new staff for the MTIC in July 2011 has also denied the ministry the critical staff to perform its functions. There is thus a need for a scaling up of human resources to support cooperatives at local and central government levels.

- Insufficient *financial resources* seriously constrain the activities of the MTIC with regard to cooperatives, limiting extension services, awareness-raising and infrastructure development (MTIC 2012). Regulation and supervisory laws for cooperatives such as SACCOs are also not being effectively implemented due to the resource constraints faced by the cooperative registrar (UCA 2012). This allows errant leaders and management staff to flout their SACCO by-laws, policies and procedures as well as the cooperative law. There is a need for more financial resources to strengthen the Department of Cooperatives in order for it to perform its functions effectively.

- Various tensions characterise relations between cooperatives and the government. Three in particular stand out. First, externally dependent SACCOs have proliferated in rural areas as a result of some government officials mobilising people to start SACCOs in order to access funds under the government's Prosperity For All programme. This breeds confusion among the rural population, particularly when this approach is contrasted with the UCA's methodology of promoting self-sufficient SACCOs (ibid.). Second, SACCOs complain about political interference in their management and operations, particularly during the election of leaders and the recovery of overdue loans from defaulters. Third, as more resources are focused on the development of ACEs, there is a feeling among unions that the creation of ACEs has led to their marginalisation.[16] This suggests that the cooperative reform process may have been misperceived by, or not well justified to, the cooperative movement.

Conclusions and policy implications

This chapter has highlighted the important role that public policy has played in the development of cooperatives in Uganda since their formation in the early 1900s. Enactment of the cooperative laws during and after Uganda's independence in 1962, which granted a degree of autonomy to cooperatives, provided opportunities for the processing of produce, mobilisation, training and government support, and led to the expansion of cooperative operations and employment creation. However, government involvement in the activities of cooperatives and mismanagement, and later structural adjustment, subsequently led to a decline in cooperatives' performance. Since the 1990s, public initiatives have been undertaken to revive the cooperative sector. Besides incorporating cooperatives into relevant development plans, strategies and programmes, the government has established policies and has amended cooperative laws and regulations to create an enabling environment for cooperatives. Implementation of the cooperative development policy has led to an increase in the number of cooperatives and stronger links between them, the expansion of support services, and cooperatives' enhanced institutional capacities, while integrating gender and environmental concerns in cooperative development.

Various challenges and limitations of the existing policies to promote the development of cooperatives have been noted. The capacity to ensure sustainable financial services is still constrained by weak institutional capacity and political interference in the management and operations of financial cooperatives, which has led to a deterioration of loan portfolio quality and member savings, among other effects. Support infrastructure, particularly electricity and communication, is inadequate in rural areas where most of the cooperatives are located. Also, the process of developing cooperative policy and law does not appear to have been fully participatory, as consultation was restricted to the senior representatives of stakeholders, creating tensions between government and cooperatives. Development of the financial sustainability and self-reliance of cooperatives is still hindered by weaknesses in the regulation and supervision laws that apply to financial cooperatives. Moreover, government capacity to fulfil its policy commitments is limited by inadequate financial and human resources, and weak links with the cooperative movement. Further support is also needed for infrastructure development in rural areas. More efficient capacity-building for cooperatives is crucial, since the success of support programmes largely depends on the quality of governance and management. There is a need to increase and strengthen the capacity of government to fulfil its commitments and to build its credibility in order to pursue policies that will enhance the autonomy and independence of cooperatives.

16 | EMBEDDEDNESS AND THE DYNAMICS OF GROWTH: THE CASE OF THE AMUL COOPERATIVE, INDIA

Abhijit Ghosh[1]

Introduction

Cooperatives represent a unique business model. They have successfully organised individuals from diverse communities, playing a salient role in alleviating poverty (Mair and Marti 2009). Based on principles of self-help, democratic control, member participation and concern for community, cooperatives combine social goals such as empowerment with means to facilitate collective participation in economic activity. What distinguishes them from pure profit-making enterprises (Johnson and Whyte 1977) is their stated pursuit of hybrid goals and democratic means for achieving them. By placing the means of development in the hands of those who most need it, cooperatives follow a distinctive path to development.

However, the survival and growth of cooperatives cannot be presumed, as many fail or do not manage to make the transition from infancy to growth. To understand how they might grow successfully, it is important to recognise how they strategise within their context. In other words, we need to understand how cooperatives' growth strategies are embedded within the broader context. For this, it is vital to appreciate the patterns of reciprocal interaction (Ghosh and Westley 2005) between their scaling-up initiatives and the wider context that enables, constrains and constitutes these growth initiatives.

Recognising dichotomies in strategy research, scholars within the field of organisational and management studies have called for more dynamic and embedded views of strategy (Porter 1991). This dichotomy is evident in the neglect of strategic intent (agency) on the one hand and by the lack of attention paid to the extra-organisational context on the other. Specifically, Tsoukas (2009: 4) points out that strategy scholars have 'focused on strategy practitioners within the organization, refraining from systematically connecting organizational changes with extra-organizational contexts'. Drawing further attention to this dichotomy, Tsoukas (ibid.: 341) notes that in their attempt to:

> conceptualize strategy processes, some researchers have tended to build models that reduce the element of human agency to a minimum, relying on selection forces rather than on human intentionality to design viable organizations and strategies. Within this stream of research, the process rather than the content of strategy is emphasized and 'emergent' rather than 'planned' strategies are highlighted.

Similarly, Whittington (2007: 1581, emphasis added) criticises strategy process research (especially Mintzberg) for not paying sufficient attention to strategic intent:

> first by defining strategy as what the organization does, [Mintzberg] denies the sense of strategy as a kind of work that people do; second by stressing how organizational outcomes are *so frequently detached from strategic intent*, he reduces the strategy work to a vain, even *absurd endeavor to control the uncontrollable.*

Mintzberg's focus on 'emergent' strategies (Mintzberg and Waters 1985) at the expense of managerial intention and purpose risks trivialising managerial effort and agency in the formation of strategy (Whittington 2007). One is left with the notion of the organisation as a rudderless ship, as the phrase 'absurd endeavor to control the uncontrollable' suggests. To transcend this either/or dichotomous approach, I argue for an embedded view of strategy-making that rests on three pillars – strategic intent, strategic initiatives and the broader socio-political context – and that acknowledges the dynamic interaction between them. This view concurrently recognises the agency manifest in the initiatives of managers acting within a broad strategic intent as well as their reciprocal interaction with the broader socio-political context. Following Hamel and Prahalad (1989), strategic intent is defined as an organisation's obsession with and pursuit of an unreasonably ambitious goal disproportionate to the resources the organisation possesses. Strategic initiatives are defined as 'deliberate efforts by a firm at creating or appropriating economic value from the environment' (Lovas and Ghoshal 2000: 881). Furthermore, recent literature on strategy suggests that social enterprises may also be more pluralistic (Denis et al. 2007). Specifically, social enterprises are explicitly characterised by multiple social and economic objectives, as well as diffuse power distribution that allows a wide array of constituents and stakeholders to influence the nature of the goals pursued and the means adopted to achieve them. This is unlike what may be expected in traditional firms. Moreover, members of cooperatives share a multi-faceted relationship with their organisation, at once being members, owners, suppliers and customers in their day-to-day transactions with the firm (Schneiberg et al. 2008). In these enterprises, the needs of members and their voice and participation in decision-making are paramount. Given this embeddedness in their community and context, cooperatives represent an ideal form (Rothschild-Whitt 1979) for enunciating an 'embedded' view of strategy. Thus, in order to obtain a deeper understanding of the embeddedness of cooperatives' growth strategies, this chapter asks how those strategies are formed and embedded within the broader socio-economic and political context.

Background to the case study

This question is examined through a study of India's most famous cooperative, AMUL. Formed in December 1946 as a district milk producers' union of two village cooperative societies (VCSs), today AMUL is one of India's most reputable national brands and competes successfully with larger dairy multinationals. In 2012, AMUL served 630,000 member producers across 1,179 VCSs, procured 620 million litres of milk and registered sales of US$450 million.[2] Through the Gujarat Cooperative Milk Marketing Federation, it had a country-wide distribution network comprising forty-eight sales offices, 5,000 wholesale dealers, 1,000,000 retailers and about 10,000 AMUL preferred outlets, with a combined revenue of US$3.2 billion.

Drawing on ethnographic fieldwork conducted over a period of eight months in the Kheda district of Gujarat State – AMUL's area of operation – this chapter examines a phenomenal period during the history of AMUL (1946–62).[3] The analysis illustrates the reciprocal interaction between AMUL's strategic initiatives at the micro level and relevant events and processes unfolding at the macro level. Through this narrative, I delineate the broad contours of an 'embedded' view of strategy. In the final section, I discuss research findings and draw general conclusions from the case study.

The growth of AMUL

Early years (1946–55) AMUL was formed just before India's independence, to counter the monopoly power of a private company, Polson.[4] Polson, the main supplier of milk from Kheda district to the Bombay Milk Scheme (BMS), exploited the milk producers by paying them poorly. Given its colonial contacts, Polson managed to get an executive order for the exclusive supply of milk from the most important milk-producing villages in Kheda (Heredia 1997). This meant that producers could not sell their milk to any other private trader. Polson collected milk through intermediaries who would negotiate arbitrary prices with a few powerful men in the villages.[5] In the process of procurement and supply of milk to BMS, both Polson and the intermediaries made huge profits, while the producers received a pittance (Ghosh and Westley 2005). Faced with exploitation, the producers approached Kheda's leader, T. K. Patel (TKP), who, at the behest of Sardar Patel[6] and Morarji Desai,[7] called a meeting of milk producers. This resulted in the decision to create a milk union. Moreover, they petitioned the BMS commissioner, asking that the producers of Kheda be allowed to supply milk directly to BMS (bypassing Polson), threatening to go on strike and stop supplying milk to Bombay if this request was not met (Singh and Kelley 1981; Somjee 1982). The petition was ignored and consequently Bombay went without milk for fourteen days (Heredia 1997). The commissioner finally acceded to the producers' request to form their own cooperative. Thereafter, TKP and his fellow political organisers set about organising milk producers from village to village. Very soon, in November 1946, the first two VCSs commenced operations. By December 1946, they were registered as a milk union called the Kaira Union, popularly called AMUL (ibid.).

By 1947, India had become independent. AMUL was fortunate to be operating in a political context where the leaders of the Indian National Congress came to occupy significant political offices both at the level of Bombay State and nationally. AMUL, through TKP (an important congressman at the district level), had direct access to ministers in Bombay State and to Sardar Patel, India's first deputy prime minister. These political links were fundamental to assuring AMUL a relatively congenial environment for its growth. Likewise, another congress leader, Dinkar Desai, became the state civil supplies minister responsible for overseeing BMS. In the initial years, TKP managed to leverage his contacts to lease part of the government's research creamery and its vintage pasteuriser in Anand. Around 1949, Verghese Kurien, a mechanical engineer posted at the research creamery, befriended TKP and his member farmers. Along with H. Dalaya, a dairy technologist, they advised TKP to invest in proper equipment if AMUL wanted to stand any chance of competing with Polson. TKP, after much difficulty, was able to raise the money to buy the necessary equipment.

At this point, both Polson and AMUL supplied milk to BMS and competed in purchasing milk from producers. However, Dinkar Desai, who was sympathetic to the cooperative's effort, paid AMUL a slightly higher rate for processing and handling compared with what Polson received (Singh and Kelley 1981). This allowed the union to pay a higher price, organise more societies and attract more members into its VCSs. The result was immediate: in one year (1949–50) the number of VCSs increased from thirteen to twenty-seven, and membership doubled from 924 to 1,995. In 1950, Kurien and Dalaya officially joined AMUL.

Securing a monopoly in Bombay As a result of recognition for AMUL's contribution as a source of low-cost milk to the city of Bombay, the state's government announced an annual grant of 300,000 Rupees which allowed AMUL to extend a range of services to its members and to buy more equipment. AMUL received this yearly grant from 1950 to 1960, and it allowed AMUL to hire supervisors for organising more VCSs. By 1950, more than thirty VCSs had been organised with a total membership of about 4,000 milk producers. Between 1948 and 1952, AMUL's strategy was directed at maximising its sales to BMS – in this, it was largely successful (ibid.). By 1952, AMUL had doubled the number of VCSs to sixty-two and had almost tripled its membership to 11,300 compared with that in 1950. With the help of loans received from Bombay State in 1951, it was able to organise more VCSs and thus request monopoly rights from Bombay for supplying milk to BMS. Recognising AMUL's growing strength, BMS cancelled its contract with Polson from January 1952 and awarded AMUL the exclusive monopoly for milk supply (ibid.). This was a result of strong lobbying by AMUL's leadership and the policy of the civil supplies minister, who, when he took charge, let it be known that his government would increase the supply of milk from rural producers in Anand, assistance would be given to them, and 'cooperative effort would be encouraged in handling milk' (Heredia 1997: 99). This decision of the government made the union a leader, and Polson lost its dominant position in the industry (Singh and Kelley 1981). Thus, political lobbying by AMUL's leadership was significant not only in procuring the creamery but also in getting better prices for milk sold to BMS, in obtaining dairy development grants for AMUL, and in securing a monopoly for the supply of milk to BMS.

Barriers to continued growth By 1952–53, milk was flooding into AMUL and its existing facilities were being operated at full capacity. In an interview, Dr Kurien explained that 'our problem was how to handle all the milk that came in'. Even though Kurien realised the importance of BMS to AMUL's growth, he and Dalaya also understood that exclusive dependence on BMS could be its undoing. Kurien recognised the need to diversify.

In the meantime, BMS conceived a project to relocate the thousands of buffalo herded into Bombay, which were kept in unsanitary conditions and therefore posed a health and sanitation problem. This project, called the Aarey Milk Colony project, was inaugurated in 1949. Cattle keepers and their 15,000 buffalo were relocated to the outskirts of Bombay. Since so many producers also had to be relocated, their milk had to be accepted by BMS. Contracts for exclusive supply were drawn up with these producers (Brissenden 1952), assuring them a place to settle, fodder for their buffalo at a reasonable charge, and acceptance of all their milk. However, it was supposedly incumbent on the cattle keepers to sell all their milk to BMS. Aarey's pasteurising facility was established in 1951–52, once the buffalo had been moved to the colony. Things began to look grim for AMUL, as Aarey Milk Colony emerged as a captive milk source for BMS and a competitor to AMUL.

Additionally, buffalo are seasonal breeders whose capacity for milk production doubles during winter compared with summer production. Khurody, the milk commissioner of Bombay, wanted a steady and not an irregular flow of milk into the city. Kurien recollects his conversation with the milk commissioner:

it was clear to me and Dalaya that we cannot succeed without our own conversion facilities ... Dalaya first suggested that we need modern facilities for conversion to butter and milk powder ... So we had to set up a powder plant.

BMS was primarily concerned about having a cheap milk supply for the consumers of Bombay. To achieve this goal, Khurody preferred to import milk powder from New Zealand and reconstitute it into liquid milk to meet the city's demand. This policy of BMS, of first accepting Aarey Milk Colony's milk and then meeting the shortfall using cheap milk powder from New Zealand, led it to refuse almost 50 per cent of AMUL's winter surplus, especially from 1953 onwards.[8] Consequently, AMUL's relationship with BMS was marked by hostility, mostly due to the milk commissioner's policy of 'cheap supply'.[9] But AMUL would soon find an unlikely solution to its problems.

UNICEF's intervention and further growth Around this time, the milk conservation division of the United Nations Children's Fund (UNICEF) was looking for partners to help in the United Nations Food and Agriculture Organization's (FAO's) campaign for the eradication of hunger and malnutrition in children. On approaching the government, they learned that Bombay received most of its milk supplies from Kheda district. They proposed to donate milk-drying equipment worth 800,000 Rupees, in return for which the government would commit to distributing, through BMS and AMUL, 1,200,000 Rupees' worth of free milk to undernourished children in Kheda (Heredia 1997).

Meanwhile, AMUL, seeing its procurement to BMS reduced, was looking for a solution to its problem. Since cooperatives were preferred to other organisational forms and were promoted through government funding and subsidy, these were propitious times for AMUL. However, there was more drama in store. Kurien recollects what happened:

so he [Dalaya] said now we will have to set up a modern plant. Everyone consulted said powder cannot be made from buffalo milk. A Professor Ridette of New Zealand, a renowned authority, came here and told me that 'this is a fantastic project which is bound to fail'. They did not want India to manufacture milk powder. I said nothing doing. It will not fail. I was confident we could do it. BMS's milk commissioner [Khurody] did not want AMUL to develop its own capacity for conversion of milk into product … Khurody wanted us to be dependent only on BMS so that we could not bargain for a higher price. He did not want us to develop alternative means of disposal of milk since then we would not be under their control and could develop our own market. So the period before 1955 was one of dependence on BMS, while after 1955 we were independent.

Kurien and Dalaya, using Larsen and Toubro's laboratory powder plant, successfully demonstrated to the UNICEF officials that milk powder could indeed be made from buffalo milk, a necessary pre-requisite for the milk commissioner in Bombay to approve the project. A combination of technological confidence, commitment to the farmers' cause and political clout ensured that AMUL would be able to receive the equipment for manufacturing milk powder. The new dairy finally began in 1955 and was inaugurated by the first prime minister of India, Mr Nehru. Apart from the generous donation of equipment from UNICEF, the new dairy was also partially financed by the New Zealand government as well as by the government of Bombay. AMUL was now operating in an area of 600 square miles and embracing more than 20,000 farmer members. A strategy of forward vertical integration had evolved, partly through happenstance, and partly through deliberate managerial effort to partially solve the problem of seasonal milk surpluses. AMUL's diversification would be achieved in future through its foray into a range of products. This was a historic moment for AMUL, as it would be able to conserve 'flush season' milk by moving to product manufacturing from mere processing.

During the years immediately following the expansion, AMUL embarked on organising VCSs to bring in more producer members. AMUL's growth over the years has not resulted in any loss of representation or autonomy for its members. Two developments were particularly important in this regard. First, during my fieldwork at AMUL, I noticed that once a VCS (the basic constituent of AMUL) grew too big, it would often be split up into two VCSs, generally at the level of 'paras' or 'muvadas' (smaller village sub-units). This kept the membership of a VCS within a manageable size, thereby allowing better communication between members and their elected representatives at the VCS level. It also allowed for greater responsiveness to the needs of member-owners. This trend shows us that it is possible for a social enterprise to achieve scale economies without necessarily compromising autonomy, trust and responsiveness. Growth does not automatically trigger 'self-interest seeking with guile' (Williamson 1996: 49). Second, the social composition of the leadership changed over time, in ways that facilitated democratic governance. During the first decades of AMUL's existence, almost all the directors on the board came from the Patel community. With more land, money and education, they created the cooperative. After the 1980s, this trend was reversed as the Kshatriya community (by far the majority) started winning more seats on the board through the electoral process. Sheer numbers started to matter in the increasing democratisation, suggesting that the issue of elite capture of social and solidarity economy (SSE) organisations may in some contexts be a staged process that can be reversed with time (Ghosh 2011).

Import substitution: capturing the dynamics of embedded reciprocity In 1957, after AMUL was registered as a brand name and launched its own butter, it faced serious competition from New Zealand's Anchor butter and Polson butter. India's policies of supporting cooperative enterprises, as well as import substitution and some luck, helped AMUL to market its butter. This is explained by Dr Kurien:

> A person came to our dairy and after having met me said that if I needed any help from him, I can ask for it. That was T. T. Krishnamachari [TTK]. He was a businessman initially, before he went on to become a politician and a minister. So once we got his blessings, I wrote him a letter saying 'Would you cut the import of butter by 25 per cent?' He wrote back, 'As desired by you, I am ordering a cutback of 25 per cent.' No discussion, no meetings, no files, nothing. ...
>
> After six months, I wrote him another letter saying, 'I am making more butter, can you cut the import by 62.5 per cent?' He wrote back, 'As desired by you, I am ordering a cut of 62.5 per cent.' Then, after some time, he wrote informing me of the foreign

exchange crunch and said that he is ordering a 100 per cent cut in imports. 'Please make sure that the nation faces no shortage of butter; I leave that job to you.' That was the end of the matter.[10]

Nehru, soon after the first election of 1952, appointed TTK the minister for commerce. The second five-year plan (1956–61) envisaged a development strategy based on the promotion of 'heavy industry' by the public sector (Panagariya 2008). Nehru wanted India to be independent of foreign markets within a short period. This implied the development of the machinery sector so that future investments would not have to depend on external sources of supply (ibid.).

During the first two five-year plans, a relatively liberal trade regime was followed. This trend was accentuated when TTK, who wanted the economy to develop fast, decided to 'import here and now, anything and everything that was not being produced in India' (ibid.: 27). This policy of benign neglect of the trade policy by the finance ministry continued until 1957. In 1956, TTK was appointed the finance minister and, by 1957, India's rapid haemorrhage in its foreign exchange resources was alarming (ibid.).

Moreover, AMUL represented India's pride in indigenous ownership, which conformed with the government's policy of 'self-sufficiency' through import substitution. Kurien's requests for cuts in imports, although anti-competitive, were favourably received due to both the acute foreign exchange crisis and AMUL's ability to step up production to meet national demands. All these factors influenced the perception of AMUL as a national enterprise that not only was consuming less foreign exchange, but was also conserving foreign exchange. AMUL's actions seemed to be in concert with what the government wanted. Figure 16.1 captures the dynamics of micro–macro interaction based on a strategy of *reciprocal favours*.

India decided to severely restrict imports of non-essential items, including dairy products, partly to promote its policy of national development of dairy products but also to improve its balance of payments (Heredia 1997). This policy was further tightened after 1956, with the result that the manufacture of dairy products was now more profitable than milk processing. This was due to import restrictions and the 'increase in demand through increases in population and income and a change in tastes and preferences

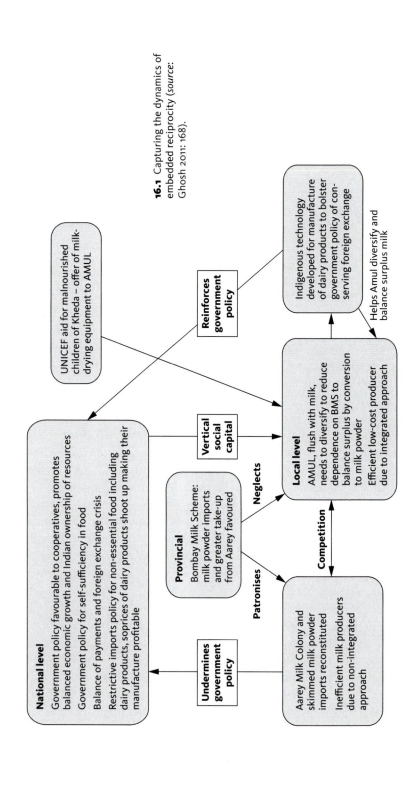

16.1 Capturing the dynamics of embedded reciprocity (*source:* Ghosh 2011: 168).

National level

Government policy favourable to cooperatives, promotes balanced economic growth and Indian ownership of resources

Government policy for self-sufficiency in food

Balance of payments and foreign exchange crisis

Restrictive imports policy for non-essential food including dairy products, soprices of dairy products shoot up making their manufacture profitable

UNICEF aid for malnourished children of Kheda – offer of milk-drying equipment to AMUL

Reinforces government policy

Vertical social capital

Neglects

Provincial

Bombay Milk Scheme: milk powder imports and greater take-up from Aarey favoured

Patronises

Competition

Undermines government policy

Local level

AMUL, flush with milk, needs to diversify to reduce dependence on BMS to balance surplus by conversion to milk powder

Efficient low-cost producer due to integrated approach

Indigenous technology developed for manufacture of dairy products to bolster government policy of conserving foreign exchange

Helps Amul diversify and balance surplus milk

Aarey Milk Colony and skimmed milk powder imports reconstituted

Inefficient milk producers due to non-integrated approach

of consumers' (Singh and Kelley 1981: 68). The relations between AMUL and the government were reciprocal; while AMUL helped India become self-sufficient in dairy products and to conserve valuable foreign exchange, the government in turn helped reduce competition, enabling the fledgling cooperative to survive.

AMUL's product diversification In 1956, Kurien 'visited Switzerland on the invitation of Nestlé but with a specific brief from the Ministry of Industries, Government of India' (Kurien 2005: 58). Although Nestlé had a licence to produce condensed milk from the government of India, the company was importing not just milk powder, but also sugar and tin plates. Dr Kurien requested that they try to manufacture condensed milk using buffalo milk. While Nestlé could bring in its experts to set up the plant, it was expected that the company would indigenise the labour force in the Indian plant in about five years. This was unacceptable to Nestlé, as it thought that the 'natives' would not be able to operate high-level technology (ibid.).

Kurien narrated this to the then commerce minister and impressed upon him the need for AMUL to manufacture condensed milk using buffalo milk and prove Nestlé wrong. AMUL's officials got to work. Some of the machinery required to produce condensed milk had already been installed when the 1955 dairy was commissioned. Soon after, in 1958, condensed milk was launched. This was the first time in the world that buffalo milk had been used to make condensed milk (Krishna et al. 1997). The total capital expenditure for sweetened condensed milk (approximately US$142,000) was met through grants provided by the government of Bombay (which amounted to US$80,000), by increasing the share capital, and partly from the union's retained earnings (Singh and Kelley 1981). Soon after its launch, Kurien wrote to the minister asking for a ban on the import of condensed milk; the government issued the ban (Kurien 2005). Thus, a similar story was being scripted now for another product, as a multinational company showed its hesitation in localising the manufacture of a product that had previously been imported.

AMUL's new dairy was expanded in 1959–60. This time, the expansion was for the purpose of producing cheese and baby food, given that India had a burgeoning infant population. By 1959–60, the prices of baby food and cheese had increased to a level whereby returns on these products were higher than returns on the sale of liquid milk or other dairy products (Singh and Kelley 1981). AMUL's decision to diversify into these products was also partly in response to Glaxo's refusal to manufacture baby food from locally available buffalo milk on the grounds of technical infeasibility. The government asked the Central Food Technological Research Institute (CFTRI) in Mysore to help in developing the process for manufacturing baby food from buffalo milk. In 1956, the CFTRI developed a formula for doing so and was looking for a producer, preferably Indian, to whom they could award the patent rights (ibid.). AMUL expressed its interest in the formula and improved upon it. This is recollected by a senior production manager at AMUL:

> In the 1960s the plant expanded; this time we purchased our own machinery, and we went for ultra-high temperature (UHT) processing of milk. Then we went into roller-dried infant food and cheese from buffalo milk. There were two things – converting buffalo milk to … match cow's milk and ultimately to substitute for mother's milk. The technology until [then] was all based on cow's milk … There was no work available as a reference on buffalo milk. So to formulate buffalo milk and manufacture an infant food was a challenge. That challenge was met and we came out with infant food fortified with vitamins and carbohydrates, which was marketed by Voltas.

The manager also explained that a similar story applied to cheese:

> We started on trial and error. The process took us almost three to four years … When we approached the Cow and Gate people and told them that we have an idea like this for formulating cheese from buffalo milk, we were told that 'you cannot make cheese … it tastes like soap and when you put it in the mouth, it gives you foam'. They never wanted us to be successful. But in 1965 we did it.

AMUL wanted to launch its baby food in competition with the giant corporation Glaxo, which was planning to set up capacity for manufacturing baby food in India. Glaxo had a manufacturing licence that specified that the state government would procure the milk required for baby food production. It also stated that, should the government not be able to procure the milk required to produce a total weight of 5 million pounds of baby food, then Glaxo could import cheap skimmed milk powder (SMP) for its manufacture. Therefore, Glaxo would probably use imported milk powder for many years, according to Kurien. Besides, Glaxo also had an import licence for baby food. With advantages like an established brand name, immense financial resources, and freedom to import cheap SMP and baby food, Glaxo would likely put AMUL at a serious competitive disadvantage.

AMUL therefore needed to be the first to the market to beat Glaxo. At the behest of AMUL, the government of India gradually reduced imports of baby food. When AMUL requested foreign exchange through the government of Bombay to import machinery for baby food, Khurody tried to block it, demanding that foreign exchange should go to Aarey instead in order to process the increasing quantities of milk (Heredia 1997). Kurien, however, argued that by undertaking manufacturing of cheese and baby food, AMUL would actually save the government 13.5 million Rupees in foreign exchange. Kurien's argument not only was cogent but showed AMUL in a light that was favourable to the government of India's long-term policy of becoming self-sufficient.

AMUL's expansion into cheese and baby food required a total investment of about US$400,000 (Singh and Kelley 1981). A large part of this expenditure was financed by a grant of US$336,000 from the government of India, with the union meeting the rest from its own sources (ibid.). This was the first time that baby food and cheese were made from buffalo milk. AMUL entered into an India-wide agreement for marketing baby food with Tata's Voltas company, which had a pan-India distribution network. This allowed AMUL to gain tremendous visibility and access. Between the late 1950s and the early 1960s, AMUL had established a toehold in the market for not only milk powder and butter but also condensed milk, cheese and baby food (Kurien 2005). The product diversification strategy was rolled out rapidly and AMUL – with its reasonable prices, good quality assurance and committed distributors, including Akbarelly's, Voltas and Spencers, along with advertising geniuses such as da Cunha's – was beginning to become a household name.

Conclusion

This study was motivated by the desire to understand the embeddedness of cooperatives' growth strategies within their unique socio-political context. It provides an in-depth understanding of how the dynamic reciprocal interplay between the strategic initiatives of actors at the micro level and the wider context – comprising competitors, governmental actors and multilateral agencies – is implicated in scaling up cooperatives.

Three key findings emerge. The first relates to AMUL's unique nature of political embeddedness, arising from the presence on its board of politicians affiliated to the congress party, and how this facilitated scaling up. The links of its elected leadership to the powers-that-be enabled access to the critical resources it needed for growth. AMUL's managers were able to leverage these political links to government bodies and agencies to obtain resources and favours for the cooperative's growth. This finding is very significant because, during their nascent stages, social enterprises need access to a variety of resources in order to grow. This is especially true in resource-constrained contexts of poor, developing countries (Mair and Marti 2009).

By studying strategy in its context, it is possible to identify and understand the nature of reciprocal interaction and embeddedness. I show that the context of the government and its agencies must be seen not so much as exogenous but as being involved and endogenous to the strategy formation process. This effect is particularly exaggerated in the case of cooperatives, given that members may constitute a significant voting bloc. Likewise, their representatives, who are often politicians, may provide direct or indirect access to levers that influence government policies. These links may allow cooperative leaders to use policy-making bodies to benefit their members rather than simply adopting strategies that are determined by exogenous policies.

Second, AMUL's scaling up through product diversification was embedded in the larger political economy of the nation. This context included national-level challenges of ensuring that adequate food was available for India's growing population, and the government's desire to promote indigenous efforts to realise its socialistic goals of self-sufficiency through import substitution. The context also involved a situation in which the nation faced an acute foreign exchange crisis, which made import substitution even more important. Given the burgeoning demand for milk products in the 1960s, and despite being faced with competition from much more powerful multinationals, AMUL used its resourcefulness to effect significant technological breakthroughs and to produce products from buffalo milk.

AMUL's growth was anchored by its visionary leadership through 'purposively embedding' its scaling-up strategy of product development within India's self-sufficiency regime. Such purposive embedding involved innovative product development strategies to make the most of local conditions and technologies. It also involved vigorous lobbying of the state and federal government by AMUL's leaders in a language couched in the logic of self-sufficiency but meant to nullify economic competition from multinationals through political means. This involved AMUL's leadership convincing the government to enact policies to substantially curb or ban cheaper imports from multinationals, thus enabling India to be self-sufficient through AMUL's 'import-substituting' product development strategy in light of the worsening foreign exchange crisis. I find that such purposive embedding of strategies involves an attuned leadership actively selecting part of the nation's political economy as the relevant context and aligning the organisation's scaling-up strategies to that context. Such purposive embedding implicates ideological rhetoric in securing a congenial institutional context for developing and launching innovative products into a market dominated by more resource-rich competitors.

Finally, I find that strategic intent was omnipresent. While strategies often appeared as a result of adaptation by AMUL's strategic actors to the circumstances faced by the organisation in relation to its wider environment, the broad strategic intent of 'serving Kheda's farmers' to help them achieve economic independence and to assure their well-being continued to guide the organisation throughout its history. Federated growth, built on the foundation of the basic grass-roots unit of the VCS, helped transcend the supposed 'big equals bad'/'small equals good' dichotomy. It allows for growth while keeping the basic units that constitute it small. How organisations are structured and the embeddedness of transactions in an ongoing history of social relations – as Granovetter (1985) pointed out – are important in keeping SSE enterprises from degenerating into an 'Oliver Williamson world' of under-socialised transaction cost strategising. Federated growth can enable an organisation to scale up while ensuring that the constituent village-level grass-roots units remain at a manageable size.

17 | TAKING SOLIDARITY SERIOUSLY: ANALYSING KERALA'S *KUDUMBASHREE* AS A WOMEN'S SSE EXPERIMENT

Ananya Mukherjee-Reed

This chapter analyses *Kudumbashree*, a unique social initiative comprising nearly 4 million women below the poverty line in the Indian state of Kerala, which is undertaking an important social and solidarity economy (SSE) experiment.[1] While Kerala has long been the highest ranked Indian state in terms of human development and has received international acclaim for its achievements, it still exhibits significant gender inequality and multiple forms of marginalisation (along the lines of caste, ethnicity, and so on) in the social, political and economic realms. *Kudumbashree* was initiated by the state government sixteen years ago as a poverty eradication programme. Since that time it has developed into a unique network in which marginalised women work collectively to plan and implement programmes and projects that address the structural causes of their poverty. While *Kudumbashree* groups participate in a wide range of social, educational and economic programmes, as well as actively engaging in the political realm, in this chapter we focus specifically on their SSE activities. More specifically, we highlight how the creation of strong bonds of solidarity, grounded in democratic decision-making and collective action, have enabled poor women to challenge existing power inequalities and establish innovative organisations.

Kudumbashree: a state-wide anti-poverty programme

In 1998, the Left Democratic Front (LDF) government of Kerala established a state-wide poverty eradication programme that it christened *Kudumbashree* (meaning prosperity of the family, rather than the individual). At this time, the LDF government was also rolling out a decentralised planning process, mobilised through the People's Plan Campaign. It sought to mobilise citizens and offer local communities greater opportunities to identify their own priorities and own solutions (Lakshmanan 2006; Issac and Heller 2003). The new anti-poverty programme was conceived from its inception as endemically linked to the decentralisation process.

The ambitious goal that was initially set for *Kudumbashree* was to eradicate absolute poverty in the state within ten years. To accomplish this goal, the government determined that the new initiative needed to undertake three broad tasks. First, it had to define poverty and identify the poor. It was recognised from the outset that multiple factors contribute to poverty, not income alone. Second, an organisational structure had to be established. This structure would need to be firmly rooted in the communities but at the same time be systematically connected to various state institutions. This preference for state–community linkage was a direct consequence of the People's Plan Campaign, a key contextual factor that shaped *Kudumbashree*. Third, the campaign's essential aim was to break the barriers between the state and its citizens, and to have plans actively shaped by communities from below. Accordingly, *Kudumbashree* had, from its very beginning, a community component and a bureaucratic component working in tandem. As the official poverty eradication programme of the state of Kerala, *Kudumbashree* is also a government agency that has a budget and paid staff and is part of the Ministry of Local Self-Government. As a government agency, its role is to provide support, training and coordination for the plans developed by community groups.

This community component has a three-tiered structure comprising the neighbourhood groups (NHGs) of about fifteen to forty families at the neighbourhood level; area development societies (ADSs) at the ward level; and community development societies (CDSs) at the village or municipal level. The NHGs provide a discursive forum for women as well as serving as the basic unit for planning[2] and functioning as thrift and credit societies (which fund women's enterprises). All of the groups are democratically run, with members from the lower-level groups electing representatives to the upper levels.

Through this three-tiered structure, *Kudumbashree* groups participate in the local planning process through which they develop and consolidate development plans, as discussed below (Rajan 2006; Kadiyala 2004). Micro plans formulated by the neighbourhood groups may be acted upon directly or they may be woven into mini plans in the ADSs, with these, in turn, compiled into larger village or municipality plans. One-third of the total development funds are set aside for these plans. With support from the government, these plans are operationalised by the *Kudumbashree* groups (Oommen 2008; Pillai 2007).

Agency and solidarity

One of the basic premises of *Kudumbashree* is that poverty can be addressed substantively only if the poor are active agents. While they differ in their terminology, numerous studies have documented *Kudumbashree*'s success in mobilising the agency of its members (Prakash and Chandarsekar 2012; Oommen 2008; Alkire and Chirkov 2007). For this chapter, the primary question is: how has the *Kudumbashree* movement succeeded in generating agency, especially collective agency, in such a comprehensive fashion, at such significant rates, across so many different areas (knowledge, leadership, etc.), across such a great expanse (state-wide) and among such large numbers (nearly 4 million poor women)?

With collective agency, which is our focus here, we are not concerned only with 'agents' being able to alter their individual situations (for example, attend school, develop a skill or earn an income). Rather, we are concerned about the processes through which individuals come together to form a collective that brings about a change in social relations, and particularly in relations of unequal power.

In this context, it might help to consider the notion of *social power* (Mukherjee-Reed 2008). Friedmann (1992), for example, has argued that people need access to three basic forms of resources to effectively exercise social power: 1) social resources such as defensible life space, surplus time, knowledge and skills, appropriate information, social organisation and social networks; 2) economic resources such as instruments of work and livelihood, financial resources, training and education; 3) political resources including access to formal democratic mechanisms, relations of solidarity, mechanisms of protest, media, and so on. The different resources complement each other and can be used to exercise agency across different realms in mutually supportive ways.

Arguably, the key to *Kudumbashree*'s success has been its ability to generate and access these types of resources in a *comprehensive* and *systematic* fashion through a dynamic relationship between its community and the state. With respect to social resources, the organisational and support structures have facilitated the creation of safe spaces, a regular supply of information and the formation of extensive social networks through the provision of training, organisational support and access to funds. Here, the role of the groups in enabling women to share their experiences has been crucial. In terms of political resources, the skills gained through involvement in the group structures enable women to take full advantage of the access (mediated by the state) to planning structures, as well as to engage in the formal electoral process, in public protests and lobbying efforts, among other things. In the economic realm, *Kudumbashree's* bureaucratic structure provides training and expert advice and facilitates access to capital from various public and private sources (Oommen 2008; Pillai 2007).

While the state in Kerala has indeed provided resources for the empowerment of women, this support only facilitates agency. The actual exercise of agency requires decisions and action by *Kudumbashree* women. They have taken the critical decision to come out of their homes, often in the face of major obstacles, and to encourage their neighbours to do so as well, in order to act upon their situation. By coming together in the neighbourhood, women have created safe spaces, have gained confidence and have learned to work together in organisations to effectively utilise resources, sometimes in the face of resistance by local government bodies (Rajan 2006).

Much more ethnographic research is necessary to determine whether participation in this movement has constituted a 'triple shift' for women and has added to their workload. However, oral interviews and testimonies of *Kudumbashree* leaders give us some indication of how to think about this question. Many of them endure very serious obstacles and social pressures, including emotional and physical abuse that could impede participation in *Kudumbashree*. So what motivates them? As one member, now an elected official in the local government and a veteran *Kudumbashree*, put it: '*Kudumbashree* has enabled me to transform my pain into power.'[3] She withstood years of emotional and physical abuse but continued in her role of leading and motivating women and bringing her community's issues to the public realm.

Moreover, by engaging in democratic decision-making to assess needs and develop plans aimed at promoting social justice (and not just their own group interests), and by acting collectively to implement these plans, Kerala's women have generated what is perhaps their greatest resource: strong and extensive bonds of solidarity. Grounded as they are in discursive democracy and collective action for social justice, these bonds go beyond kinship relationships and mutual self-interest. They are, arguably, what is most distinctive about *Kudumbashree* and the basis of their ability to engage in collective agency across the social, political and economic spheres. To understand *Kudumbashree*, it is necessary to take these bonds of solidarity seriously: that is, to problematise their formation and examine how they function.[4] In the next section, we examine specifically how these bonds of solidarity are formed and are drawn upon in the development of some key SSE initiatives.

Kudumbashree: an emerging social and solidarity economy?

Kudumbashree has developed a variety of income and employment schemes in the form of micro and group enterprises.[5] These range across the primary sectors (such as group agriculture), secondary sectors (garment manufacturing, food processing, etc.) and tertiary sectors (information technology, recycling, sustainable tourism, etc.). From the start these initiatives received financing through the thrift and credit associations, while recently the development of distribution channels (local markets and a home shopping network) has been actively promoted. Together, these initiatives form the basis of a complete SSE, in which the activities in different sectors are mutually reinforcing. Such an economy, however, is at best only in its initial phase. In the final section, we offer some reflections on the prospects and conditions for its development, especially in relation to the problem of extending bonds of solidarity. In this section, however, we focus on how solidarity has functioned in the successful development of two of *Kudumbashree*'s largest economic initiatives, one a government employment programme and the other involving group agriculture.

Kudumbashree and the Mahatma Gandhi Rural Employment Guarantee Programme In 2005, the Indian government passed the Mahatma Gandhi National Rural Employment Guarantee Scheme

(MGNREGS) Act, which put in place the largest public investment programme seen in the country in recent times. The programme provides a legal guarantee of 100 days of paid employment at minimum wage rates to adults in rural households who are willing to do unskilled manual work in public work programmes.

The MGNREGS envisages a central role for local decision-making bodies in determining the nature of the work to be undertaken and its allocation. In India, there is a three-tier structure of local self-governance (the *Panchayati Raj* system). At the base of this system are the *Gram Panchayat* (village council) and the *Grama Sabha* (village assembly). Each *Gram Panchayat* consists of one or more villages, while a *Gram Sabha* is a body covering the people on the electoral roll for a *Gram Panchayat*. It is the *Gram Panchayat* that convenes meetings of the *Gram Sabha* 'to disseminate information to the people as well as to ensure that development of the village is done through participation or consent of all households' (GOI 2012: 2–3). Above the village level, there are block *panchayats* and district *panchayats* in every state. With respect to the operationalisation of the programme, the MGNREGS Act states:

> Plans and decisions regarding the nature and choice of works to be undertaken in a Fiscal Year along with the order in which each work is to be taken up, site selection, etc. are all to be made in open assemblies of the *Gram Sabha* (GS) and ratified by the *Gram Panchayat* (GP). Works that are inserted at Block and District levels have to be approved and assigned a priority by the GS before administrative approval can be given. The GS may accept, amend or reject them (ibid.: 2).

In Kerala, there were two particular challenges with the programme. First, male workers showed relatively little interest in the scheme, as the MGNREGS wages were only about half of the standard rate for male workers in Kerala. Second, the deeply contradictory situation of women in Kerala threatened their potential participation in the scheme. Despite its exceptionally high human development indicators, Kerala's women remain largely excluded from public spaces by deeply engrained patriarchal norms. In the economic realm, this is reflected in the fact that women in Kerala rank towards the bottom of participation rates in the labour force in India (Table 17.1).

TABLE 17.1 Rural women's workforce participation rate (WPR) in India, 2009–10

State	Women's WPR (per thousand)
Andhra Pradesh	582
Himachal Pradesh	612
Rajasthan	425
Tamil Nadu	540
Kerala	341
All India	348

Source: GOI 2011: 33.

Kudumbashree members broke this tradition of non-participation in the public space. Because they had previously been organised in NHGs, ADSs and CDSs, *Kudumbashree* groups were capable not only of actively participating in the planning process, but also of mobilising their members to work in the MGNREGS programme. Through these efforts, 110,000 poor women are participating in the programme. For most, it is their first entry into the formal economy. Kerala ranks first in India in terms of women's participation in MGNREGS, with women's person days constituting 93 per cent of total person days for the year 2011–12.

The decision to participate in the programme was not an easy one for many of the women, as they frequently had to bear the wrath of their family members. There were two key factors, however, that were critical to their decision to get involved. As former *Kudumbashree* director, Muraleedharan (2012), explains:

> What prompted these women to come out and undertake work that they did not know, which involved a level of physical exertion that they were unfamiliar with and which ran the risk of disapprobation from their families? A commonly heard refrain was that this was work 'for the government', which gave it an aura of respectability that private manual work did not carry. Second was the power of the collective.

Another form of participation by *Kudumbashree* members provides further insight into the ability of the programme to engage women at such a high level. A central actor in the MGNREGS is the 'mate' (the work supervisor). Because of the confidence in *Kudumbashree*, the government made an executive decision to appoint all 'mates' for the programme from among the *Kudumbashree* ADSs, making Kerala the only state in the country where all mates are women. To ensure effective implementation, the Rural Development Department and the *Kudumbashree* Mission jointly trained 120,000 women mates, whose responsibilities entailed identifying work opportunities, mobilising groups for work, preparing estimates in consultation with the overseer or engineer, supervising work, providing amenities at the worksite, preparing and submitting muster rolls, and handling emergencies. Many women would cite the presence of a mate who was identified as 'one of us', as someone from their immediate neighbourhood, as a key factor in their involvement.

The central role that *Kudumbashree* members played in the MGNREGS has dramatically shaped the functioning of the programme in Kerala, embedding it in a broader discourse of awareness of the rights of women as women, workers and citizens. Moreover, women's participation in the planning of the MGNREGS has changed the make-up of electoral politics. In 2011, over 11,000 women from *Kudumbashree* contested the *panchayat* elections and of these 5,404 won. Overall in Kerala – where 50 per cent of seats are reserved for women – 60 per cent of all women elected as representatives in the *Gram Panchayats* were members of *Kudumbashree*.

It is necessary to highlight one additional impact of the involvement of *Kudumbashree* in the MGNREGS. Because of the skills that their members developed in the programme, particularly as supervisors and project managers, they received offers from private sector entities to manage and execute projects. This resulted in the development of another innovation – the women's labour collective. In various *panchayats* across the state, MGNREGS workers have come together in these collectives to take on agricultural work and to work on homesteads and plantations. Over a thousand of these collectives are in operation, and through these women are offered work at rates roughly double what MGNREGS offers (ibid.).

The *Sangha Krishi* (Group Agriculture) Initiative As in many other parts of the world, in Kerala vast quantities of agricultural land have been diverted towards residential and commercial development in recent years. At the same time, a fall in agricultural prices and rising wages have made farming a largely unprofitable activity, leading to a continuous fall in food production in the state. It is in this context that Kerala made the decision to develop a food security strategy. Unlike standard approaches to food security, though, Kerala went beyond the question of distribution to focus on increasing agricultural production in the state. Admittedly, it is the production of food and its deeply commodified nature that are responsible for food crisis and insecurity. One effect of this is the rise in food prices beyond what the poor can afford. How can this be addressed? Kerala's strategy was to encourage the poor to produce more food, so that the control on production costs and prices remains in their hands. Most interestingly, it established as one of its key goals of its food security strategy the incorporation of women into agricultural production. Just as members of *Kudumbashree* were able to organise to open up new economic spaces for women through the MGNREGS, so too were they able to respond in innovative ways to take advantage of the state's new food security initiative.

Kudumbashree women embraced the vision of the state and enthusiastically organised in an experiment termed *sangha krishi* (group farming). The radical idea behind the new programme was to increase agricultural production by bringing poor landless women into farming, not as agricultural workers but as farmers. This was to be accomplished by taking advantage of the significant amounts of land in the state that had being lying fallow for years due to low agricultural prices (and other employment opportunities for men). The initiative involved women organising themselves into collectives, leasing fallow land, rejuvenating it and farming it as independent producers.

The basis for this new initiative was in large part founded on the participation of *Kudumbashree* members in the MGNREGS programme. Not only did they participate in the planning and development of collective decision-making in the operationalisation of that programme, but some of the MGNREGS projects involved the reclamation of fallow land. From there, it was a small step to the promotion of group agriculture.

To date, the *Sangha Krishi* initiative has brought over a quarter of a million poor women into farming. Through more than 44,225 small collectives, *Kudumbashree* members are now cultivating some 10 million acres across the entire state of Kerala. On average, these women farmers earn 15,000 to 25,000 Rupees per year, with incomes varying depending on the crops grown and the number of yields annually.[6]

In addition to new and/or increased income, the solidaristic structure of *Sangha Krishi* has facilitated three important changes. First, it has brought about greater social inclusion and integration. On the one hand, not only has it allowed women to enter into the formal economy, but it has done so in ways that provide them with greater dignity and self-worth.[7] On the other hand, it has helped to incorporate particularly marginalised groups in the economy, such as members of the Scheduled Tribes and Scheduled Castes, and has also helped integrate them into diverse collectives.[8]

Second, it has radically transformed the structure of work for poor women as they have moved from being wage labourers to being independent producers. In the process they have gained control over their time and labour, over what they want to produce and how, and over their produce.[9] As farmers, they are now in a position to decide, depending on their needs, either to sell the produce or to use it for their own consumption.[10] Some groups have been so successful that they have even been able to purchase their own land.[11]

Third, there has been a significant change in the nature of agriculture in Kerala. The dramatic increase in the participation of poor women has not only increased food security but has gone a long way to promoting food sovereignty, as control over production is being broadened and democratised.

Conclusion: challenges and future directions

Kudumbashree has made remarkable progress in terms of developing SSE enterprise structures on the basis of strong bonds of solidarity among poor women. *Kudumbashree* has also taken some initial steps towards linking these economic initiatives together to form the basis for a local SSE (for example, by linking their own saving and lending practices to financing their own enterprises, through developing their own distribution channels, and by moving into new sectors).

Still, despite such important accomplishments, the SSE initiatives of *Kudumbashree* remain vulnerable and insufficient. They are insufficient in that they do not meet the needs and aspirations of their members for greater economic opportunities. There are still large numbers of women below the poverty line who remain excluded from the formal economy (Siwal 2009; Nidheesh 2008; Pillai 2007). The enterprises remain vulnerable for a variety of reasons. In micro-enterprises, *Kudumbashree* women work in very competitive, low-profit sectors and can easily be forced out of the market by exogenous shocks. In the group enterprises in manufacturing and service sectors, the work of *Kudumbashree* units is also precarious, as it depends on receiving orders from larger national and transnational firms that may transfer the work elsewhere depending on market and strategic considerations. While, in agriculture, *Kudumbashree* women have reduced their insecurity to some degree through collective action and democratic organisation, they are operating in a sector with relatively low profit margins. In addition, they remain dependent to a significant degree upon a government programme (MGNREGS) that may change, and/or on the willingness of landlords to rent them land.

So far, the ability of *Kudumbashree* members to progress has largely been predicated on structures of solidarity. There are a number of ways in which *Kudumbashree* can (and indeed is already attempting to) further leverage these bonds of solidarity among its members to extend its SSE initiatives. First, existing programmes that have been limited in their geographic scope can be extended. Second, increasing the capacity of group enterprises in some sectors (either by developing bigger units or clustering small units together) can have significant pay-offs: for example, by allowing for specialisation, increasing the ability to compete for large orders and extending potential markets (to the national and international realms). This is a strategy that is already being pursued to some extent by the textile production units. Third, *Kudumbashree* units can seek to move up supply chains to capture more of the value-added. Again, this already happens to some degree in agricultural and food processing. Fourth, *Kudumbashree* units can attempt to move into more profitable sectors. This is difficult, especially in the short term, as, among other factors, these sectors often involve higher skill and educational levels and are more capital intensive. One possible area that is being developed is sustainable tourism. Fifth, given the size of its membership base, *Kudumbashree* has tremendous potential to develop its own distribution channels and market to its members. Initial efforts have already been undertaken in this area in the form of home-shopping networks, local markets, and so on. These various directions for extending *Kudumbashree*'s SSE initiatives, which are already being explored, can be firmly grounded in the bonds of solidarity that already exist in the *Kudumbashree* network.

Kudumbashree has the potential to further develop these types of initiatives by working with external partners. The concern, of course, about such a strategy is the degree to which the units are able to retain, and even leverage, their character as SSE enterprises when working with external partners. Partnering with conventional firms is understandably challenging in this regard, as they operate based on completely different value presuppositions. This means that most such relations are purely commercial in nature.

The other alternative for *Kudumbashree*, of course, is to expand their circle of solidarity outward to work with other groups and networks that share their values. There are two major challenges involved here. The first is finding SSE actors that have complementary roles to play as partners (as buyers, suppliers, financiers or consultants, for example). The second set of challenges involves developing strong relationships of solidarity with such actors. One problem here is that, while some organisations formally subscribe to SSE values, they do not necessarily engage with partners on the basis of these values. Rather, they operate on the basis of commercial relations, even though these commercial relations may involve adherence to 'ethical standards' and involve sourcing 'sustainable' inputs and products. To the degree that they live up to such values, these are primarily internal to their enterprise. They do not engage in discourse with their partners about how to collaborate on the basis of solidarity.[12]

Even when partners are formally committed to developing relationships based on solidarity, problems can and do arise, especially when there are significant power differentials between partners (which are reflected in differential access to knowledge, levels of organisational capacity, etc.) and different cultural backgrounds (Akram-Lodhi 2013). Developing bonds of solidarity takes time and has significant costs. It is not just a matter of professing shared values; rather, it involves working together on the basis of those values through democratic discourse and shared risk. This requires that partners have strong internal bonds of solidarity within their organisation, for without these they cannot commit to or live up to the process of relationship-building with other organisations. On the basis of a strong internal culture, however, enterprises can develop overlapping relationships of solidarity, relationships that are essential for moving beyond SSE enterprises to a complete 'social and solidarity economy'.

There is a crucial question that the *Kudumbashree* experiment poses for the SSE. As we saw above, one of the key features of this experiment is the endemic link between communities and the state, inspired by the broad vision that the state's priorities and actions must be shaped by its citizens. Does this kind of state–community relationship engender a 'dependence' on the state? Indeed, *Kudumbashree* enterprises do receive support from the state and many observers view this support as 'undeserved subsidies to the poor'. Certainly, much more work is necessary to map the nature of the dependence and then to find solutions to the problem. However, the core issue in this exercise must concern how we view the state and its relationship to citizens, particularly those who are doubly or triply marginalised, as in the case of the majority of *Kudumbashree* women. Surely, while some perceptions of the state see state support as 'subsidy', others would see it as a step towards building a solidarity economy. The challenge is to guarantee that state support is linked to a broader vision of creating such a solidarity economy.

18 | DEMONSTRATING THE POWER OF NUMBERS: GENDER, SOLIDARITY AND GROUP DYNAMICS IN COMMUNITY FORESTRY INSTITUTIONS[1]

Bina Agarwal

Introduction

The concept of social and solidarity economy (SSE) is still evolving and contentious, and much is being claimed on its behalf. Nevertheless, there is a convergence in conceptualising it as being made up of various forms of citizens' associations – social movements, self-help groups (SHGs), and so on – which cooperate for production and exchange in inclusive ways, and interact with outside institutions, such as the state and markets, on behalf of citizens. Some scholars also present the SSE as an alternative to capitalist forms of development. However, these depictions of SSE are in terms of groups interacting with institutions and organisations outside those groups, rather than about intra-group dynamics. In fact, the latter can impinge on successful cooperation within the group, as well as on the group's effectiveness in dealing with extra-group institutions. Moreover, the social composition of groups, especially as predicated on gender and class, can make a key difference to intra-group dynamics. But are solidarity and a collective articulation of interests necessary conditions for the socially disadvantaged to have a voice within a group, or can their inclusion in sufficient numbers equally serve this purpose?

This chapter examines these neglected dimensions in the ongoing debate on SSE. In particular, it focuses on within-group dynamics based on gender and class, and demonstrates that, in given contexts, simply increasing the numbers of the disadvantaged in public institutions can go a long way towards improving outcomes for them, even without a collective articulation of their common interests. It draws on the author's detailed primary survey conducted in 2000–01 on community forestry groups in India and Nepal. Using the quantitative and qualitative data from the survey, the chapter explores the effect of a group's gender and class composition on the ability of women to participate effectively in local institutions of forest governance and the impact of their participation.

An analysis of these community forestry institutions (CFIs) demonstrates that increasing the proportion of women representatives in their executive committees can enhance both women's effective participation in the CFI's decision-making and institutional outcomes. The empirical results, for instance, show that women's substantial presence not only affects the rules of forest use but also leads to better forest conservation (improved efficiency) and reduced firewood shortages (which serve as a proxy for improved gender equity). The chapter then discusses how the groups can be scaled up (such as by forming federations) to strengthen their reach beyond the local as well as to enhance their bargaining power with the state. In this context, it also reflects on deliberative democracy as a means of promoting group cohesion and creating a sense of solidarity.

Some conceptual issues

It has long been accepted both in research and practice that the social composition of a governance group matters for enhancing equity and inclusion. But does it also matter for effective functioning? Can simply increasing the numbers of the disadvantaged to raise their proportions make a difference, as implied by the lobbying for quotas on gender or caste lines in institutions ranging from parliaments to village councils? Or is something more needed for effectiveness, such as shared values or ideologies? These questions have not been addressed to any great extent.

The question of the proportion of women in community decision-making groups raises at least three conceptual issues. The first relates to critical mass. We know from studies of women's participation in legislatures and corporations, especially in the context of Western countries, that women's numbers matter for enabling them to overcome conservative social norms and personal reticence (see, for example, Bratton 2005; Dahlerup 1988; Kanter 1977; Studlar and McAllister 2002). However, there is little statistical testing for a threshold effect. Such testing is essential to assess what percentage of women constitutes an effective presence.

Secondly, socio-economic heterogeneity among women could impact on the effectiveness of their presence. It could lead, for instance, to significant conflicts of interest between poor and well-off women, causing them to favour divergent decisions. It is equally possible, though, for such conflicts of interest to be weak where women face the same types of constraints, despite their socio-economic differences. For example, village women across classes face conservative social norms that restrict their mobility. They are also subject to a gender division of labour that holds them responsible, in greater or lesser degree, for tasks such as firewood collection and care work. And most women (including those from better-off households) own few productive assets (Agarwal 1994). Conceptually, therefore, there can be arguments both for and against women having common interests across economic and social difference (ibid.; Phillips 1995). In practice, these implicit commonalities and conflicts could play out in diverse ways, depending on context.

A third issue is whether women are likely to promote their interests through collective action. Implicitly sharing a common interest may not lead to an automatic recognition of that commonality, or an ability to forge alliances. To develop a sense of shared identity for promoting their common interests, women would need to move from being 'women in themselves' (a biological description) to 'women for themselves' (as a collective entity). Although this formulation evokes the Marxist distinction between 'class in itself' and 'class for itself', unlike that formulation it is not being suggested here that women suffer from false consciousness, which they would need to overcome to move from 'women in themselves' to 'women for themselves'. Rather, such a shift would depend on women overcoming the structural and ideological constraints they face. This would help them move towards identifying an agenda of shared concerns and building solidarity.

It is argued here that, in given contexts, simply the inclusion of larger numbers of women to raise their proportions within mixed-gender groups – 'women in themselves' – can go a long way to improving outcomes for women, even without a thrust to create a 'women for themselves' social consciousness, although a shift towards the latter could be additionally beneficial.

The impact of numbers: data and findings

What is the impact of increasing women's proportions in CFIs on institutional functioning and outcomes? CFIs are groups managing degraded forest land owned by the government but transferred to local communities or user groups to protect and manage, with a sharing of responsibilities and benefits. In India, most CFIs have emerged under the Joint Forest Management (JFM) programme launched in 1990. Nepal initiated a somewhat similar programme in 1993. The groups can make rules for the extraction of non-timber products and members have the right to share (with the forest department) the mature timber harvested. By the early 2000s, India had around 84,000 JFM groups involving 8.4 million households and 22.5 per cent of its forest land, while Nepal had around 10,000 groups involving about 1 million households and 11.4 per cent of its forest land.[2]

The data relate to 135 CFIs, sixty-five of which are located in three districts of Gujarat (Narmada/Bharuch, Panchmahals and Sabarkantha) in west India, and seventy are located in three districts (Baglung, Parbat and Gorkha) of Nepal's middle hills. In both countries, the CFIs have a two-tier organisational structure: a general body (GB) with members drawn from the whole village and an executive committee (EC) of nine to fifteen members. The EC is the core decision-making body. In interaction with the GB (and, to varying degrees, with the forest department), the EC defines the rules for forest use, product extraction and benefit-sharing, the penalties for breaking the rules, and the methods by which the forest should be protected. It also helps resolve conflicts among users within the village or across neighbouring villages. The members who constitute the EC thus play a crucial role in the functioning of the institution and in the distribution of benefits and losses from it. A focus on women's proportional strength in the EC and its impact can thus be revealing.

In selecting the sample for the study, the gender composition of the EC was therefore the main criterion used. The groups were divided into three mutually exclusive categories: ECs with up to two EC women, those with more than two women (but not all women), and ECs where all members were women. The two-woman marker was used since including at least two women in the EC is required in Gujarat (as in some other Indian states), even if this is not always followed in practice. Gujarat had very few all-women CFIs; its sample therefore included mainly two categories of CFIs. Nepal had enough all-women CFIs to provide comparable numbers in all three categories.

To protect a forest, communities restrict the entry of people and animals and monitor this by employing a guard, forming patrol groups, keeping an informal lookout for intruders, or using some combination of these methods. Some CFIs completely ban extraction of any kind while others allow regulated and limited extraction of specified products. Since rural women are the main collectors of non-timber items, especially firewood, they are particularly affected by forest protection rules and procedures. This can impinge on EC women's responses to forest management in terms of the rules framed and the efforts made towards forest protection and conservation.

Overall, as the following section establishes, women's greater presence in local environmental governance makes a significant difference on all these fronts (Agarwal 2010b). It enhances women's effective participation in decision-making; influences the nature of decisions made, especially the rules of forest use and their implementation; curbs rule violations; increases the likelihood of an improvement in forest condition; and reduces the likelihood of women facing firewood and fodder shortages. There is also a critical mass effect in relation to women's participation. The salient features of the main results are given below (for detailed statistical evidence see ibid.).

Participation in CFI decision-making It was found that, the higher the proportion of women in mixed-gender CFIs, the greater the likelihood of women attending EC meetings, speaking up at them, and holding office (i.e. becoming president, vice president, secretary or treasurer). To begin with, increasing women's numbers on the EC ensured at least some female presence in most meetings (Table 18.1). Overall, in 26 per cent of the EC meetings in Gujarat and 18 per cent in Nepal, no women attended. But in the case of ECs with more than two women in Gujarat, there was female presence in 87 per cent of the meetings held, compared with 59 per cent in the case of ECs with two women or fewer. Similarly in Nepal, in ECs with over two women, 94 per cent of the meetings had some female presence compared with 64 per cent of meetings in the case of ECs with two women or fewer. However, there were no meetings in either region where men were entirely absent.

A regression analysis (which controls for other variables that could also affect women's participation) further establishes the importance of women's numbers. In both Gujarat and Nepal, the likelihood of

TABLE 18.1 EC meetings with women attending in mixed-gender CFIs in Gujarat and Nepal

	Gujarat			Nepal		
	≤2 EC women	>2 EC women	All CFIs	≤2 EC women	>2 EC women	All CFIs
Number of meetings	136	167	303	139	196	335
Attendees who are women (%)						
0	41.2	13.2	25.7	36.0	6.1	18.5
>0	58.8	86.8	74.3	64.0	93.9	81.5
Detailed breakdown (%)						
>0 – <15	25.7	16.2	20.5	38.1	17.3	26.0
≥15 – <25	16.9	21.6	19.5	15.1	14.3	14.6
≥25 – <33	8.1	27.5	18.8	9.4	17.9	14.3
≥33	8.1	21.6	15.5	1.4	44.4	26.6

Source: Agarwal 2010b: 190.

meetings with no women present was significantly less if ECs had between 25 per cent and 33 per cent or more women than if they had less than 25 per cent. In both regions, there was a 36 point difference between ECs with 25 per cent to 33 per cent female members and those with a lower percentage in the percentage of meetings with zero women.

Women's attendance rate at EC meetings, which enables us to test for critical mass, also rose with an increase in the proportion of EC women. There was a verifiable critical mass effect for Nepal and an indicative effect for Gujarat. In both regions, the rate was significantly higher in groups with 25 per cent to 33 per cent EC women compared with groups with less than 25 per cent women.

EC women themselves recognised the importance of numbers in increasing their attendance, as they said during focus group discussions in several CFIs in Gujarat:

If more women attend ... then we can go to meetings regularly. More women in the Mandli [CFI] would be good. That would encourage women to attend meetings and speak up.

Similarly, the likelihood of at least some women speaking up is greater among ECs with a third or more women members. In Gujarat, for instance, the probability of at least one woman speaking up was 48 per cent greater in ECs that had a third or more women, compared with ECs that had less than a quarter women. For Nepal, the probability was 27 per cent higher, with a similar move from less than a quarter women to one-third or more women. Having more women ensured that at least some women voiced their views. Also, as the following quote from a village women's meeting in Gujarat indicates, many women themselves maintain that the presence of other women is helpful in enabling them to voice their views:

> It helps to have more women because then women will not be dominated or feel shy. After all, if there is only one woman and ten men, how will she speak? Women need each other to be able to speak up.

Interestingly, including landless women in the EC made an important difference. If present in sufficient numbers, landless women (compared with those from landed households) were found to be much more likely to attend EC meetings and voice their concerns, since they were less restricted by social norms and more compelled by their needs to speak up. For instance, most of them faced severe firewood shortages and had a stake in getting the committee to allow greater extraction of firewood. This led them to speak up more. These results highlight the importance of including in institutions of governance not simply any women but especially women who are economically and socially disadvantaged, so that their interests are better represented.

In addition, a larger proportion of women on the EC improves the chances of women becoming office holders, but the effect is complex. On the one hand, higher proportions alone are insufficient to ensure that a woman will hold office. In Gujarat, for instance, almost no CFIs had female officials, whatever the EC's gender composition. On the other hand, where the glass ceiling had been cracked, as in Nepal, the likelihood of EC women holding an official position increased significantly among ECs with more women. There was a threshold effect at around 25 per cent women (Figure 18.1). This is the minimum percentage needed to make a difference, but the likelihood increases further as we move towards 50 per cent women.

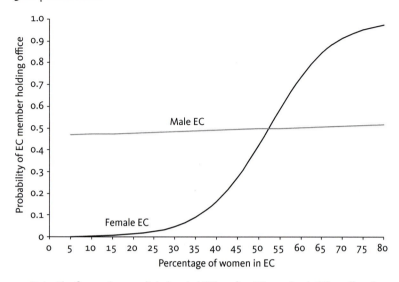

Note: The figure gives predicted probabilities of an EC member holding office, for specified values of the percentage of women in the EC, holding all other explanatory variables at their mean values.

18.1 Probability of an EC member holding office in mixed-gender CFIs in Nepal (*source*: Agarwal 2010b: 21).

Formulating forest use rules The power of numbers is also apparent in the rules that CFIs make for the use of forests. These rules determine whether anything can be extracted from the forest and, if so, what products can be collected, in what quantity, and how often during a year. The stricter the rules, the less is extracted. Strictness can vary widely across products and between CFIs for the same product. To test if the proportion of women on the EC affects strictness, I formulated a strictness index that aggregated the rules across products. The sampled CFIs showed considerable diversity in the extent of their strictness.

It was found that ECs with higher proportions of women differed notably from other ECs in the rules they framed for forest use, but the direction of the effect was unexpected. Given the pressures on women, especially for procuring firewood and fodder daily, we would have expected groups with more women to make relatively lenient rules, namely to allow greater extraction of these products. I found, however, that ECs with more than two women in Gujarat (compared with those with two women or fewer) and all-women

ECs in Nepal (compared with other ECs) tended to make stricter rules for forest use: that is, they extracted less from the forest. The only exception was Panchmahals district in Gujarat.

Several factors explain these unexpected results. In Nepal, all-women groups had less freedom to make lenient rules due to serious resource constraints – they controlled smaller and more degraded forests than male-dominated groups. They also faced greater difficulty in organising supervision for regulated extraction. Both factors restricted women's ability to extract more. Importantly, though, despite their needs and the pressure from the women of their constituency, the EC women resisted the temptation to make lenient rules for immediate gains at the cost of long-term forest regeneration. Moreover, almost all the EC members in Nepal's CFIs came from landowning families. This reduced the personal cost they incurred from framing strict rules. Landless women lack this choice.

Why was Gujarat's Panchmahals district an exception? Here, ECs with a greater female presence made less strict rules. An important reason lay in the fact that a substantial proportion of these women came from landless families, and they argued for greater extraction of forest products for daily use, especially firewood. Even these women, however, did not favour open access; rather, they preferred regulated procurement but for more days in the year. Hence, although women's class affected the strictness of rules framed, women of all classes gave primacy to community interest rather than being guided mainly by self-interest when placed in decision-making positions.

Rule violations were also affected by women's participation. In Nepal's CFIs, for example, ECs with more women had a lower incidence of rule-breaking. In Gujarat, violations by women and for firewood declined over time, while violations by men and for timber rose as the years of protection increased.

Impact on conservation Most importantly, conservation outcomes improved substantially with women's greater involvement in green governance. Forest condition was measured in the study through a range of indicators to capture the complexity of effects, but particularly changes in canopy cover and regeneration. Assessments by villagers, foresters and researchers were tested separately.

The majority of CFIs, irrespective of their gender composition, registered an improvement in forest condition by most indicators.

But women's presence brought additional benefits. In Gujarat, CFIs with more than two women in the EC (compared with those with two women or fewer) and in Nepal all-women CFIs (compared with other CFIs) were linked to significantly greater improvements in forest condition. In Nepal, I found a 51 per cent greater likelihood of an improvement in forest condition with all-women ECs compared with ECs with men.

Several factors underlie the better conservation outcomes of groups with more women on the EC. One is the ability of EC women to disseminate information about rules more widely within the community, since women can communicate with other women more easily than can men, given social norms. This increases awareness about forest closure rules and reduces inadvertent rule-breaking. Another factor is the enlargement of the pool of people protecting a forest – women can be especially effective in apprehending female intruders. In addition, the knowledge women have of plants and species and ecologically sound extraction practices is better used when they are on the EC. They can also convey village women's preferences for plants when plans for forest development are drawn up. Moreover, even if the eventual rules framed bring hardships for women, they are more likely to follow the rules and persuade other women to do so if they are part of the rule-making process than if they are excluded. Older women make an additional difference due to the experience and authority they bring.

Women's greater involvement in CFI decision-making can also help the CFIs fulfil many of the 'design principles' that Ostrom (1990) and other scholars have identified as conducive to building sustainable institutions for managing common pool resources. These principles place particular emphasis on the participation of users in the making and enforcement of rules and in resolving conflicts. The existing literature has largely failed to apply these principles to gender inclusiveness in CFIs.

Firewood shortages Firewood shortages are an important marker of gender inequality since firewood (gathered mainly by women and children) is the most important cooking fuel used in rural India and Nepal. A reduction in shortages can thus be seen as a proxy for a reduction in gender inequality of outcomes.

Women in ECs with more women are able to argue for an

increase in firewood extraction to an extent. Hence, in Gujarat, villages where CFIs had a larger percentage of female EC members were found less likely to report firewood shortages. Moreover, although not captured statistically, what matters to women is not only the fact that the forest is open for extraction but the period for which it is opened; a good deal of negotiation takes place between village women and the EC on these counts. In Nepal, however, even all-women groups reported persistent shortages since they could not extract much from the forests they received, which were considerably smaller and more degraded than the forests controlled by men. The persistence of cooking energy poverty also points to the limits of what can be achieved simply through participation in local bodies, and to the need to influence policy at higher levels (a point to which I will return).

Overall, the results from my analysis show that numbers, in themselves, have considerable power in enhancing women's ability to influence institutions of forest governance. This raises additional questions:

- How do we enhance women's presence in all CFIs?
- Can we move beyond numbers towards a more 'solidarity' type of cohesiveness? In particular, can women forge a collective voice as opposed to simply intervening individually? Can we establish institutional mechanisms whereby they can strategise and carve out collective goals?
- How can we move beyond the local to influence higher levels of decision-making?

These objectives, including that of increasing women's numbers, are interlinked, and the next section provides some reflections on the directions in which the answers may lie.

Enhancing women's presence, voice and influence

For increasing women's numbers and voice in CFIs, and especially poor women's numbers and voice, we need innovative institutional solutions. We also need institutional scaling up in order to raise the impact of women's presence beyond the local level. Building horizontal links between local institutions and establishing vertical links via federations could be potential ways of achieving both goals. In addition, forums of deliberative democracy could provide a means of reducing potential intra-group divergence and conflicts, and of promoting group cohesion and solidarity.

Promoting horizontal links Substantial potential lies in building strategic links between CFIs and other local women's collectives, such as village SHGs in India and similar types of groups (such as *amma samuhs*) in Nepal.

In fact, some non-governmental organisations (NGOs) in India are already experimenting with linking SHGs and CFIs to ensure a critical mass of female presence in mixed-gender CFIs. In rural Karnataka, for instance, the India Development Services (IDS) encouraged women's savings groups to join the CFIs in its sites. Some women went from door to door to persuade others to join. As a result, in several of the villages where IDS worked, 80 to 90 per cent of the women in the savings groups, and some outside these groups, joined the general bodies of CFIs and were quite vocal in mixed-gender meetings.[3] As women in one of the villages told me, 'without SHG membership we would have received no information about village forest committees. We are now united as women as well.'

The Mysore Resettlement and Development Agency (MYRADA), another NGO, went a step further. It specifically formed SHGs of poor women in forest communities in Karnataka's Uttara Kannada region in order to increase women's involvement in CFIs. In 2009, over 500 of these SHGs participated in forest protection and decision-making, thus energising the forest protection committees and enhancing their bargaining power with the forest department.[4]

Beyond numbers: towards group identity and solidarity Beyond numbers and personal interest, can women forge a group identity by overcoming divisions arising from social and economic differences? A number of feminist political theorists have argued that women can identify their common interests and sort out their differences arising from heterogeneity through democratic deliberation (Fraser 2005; Mansbridge 1990; Young 1997; 2000). But this will need forums for deliberation in which women can get to know each other, share information, discuss and resolve conflicts, identify priorities, strategise, and forge a sense of solidarity that can make them effective in promoting their collective interests.

Such a forum could take various forms. It could be a forum set up by SHGs linked to CFIs. Or it could be constituted of a sub-group of women EC members within mixed-gender CFIs who could strategise among themselves (just as women's caucuses do in parliament). They could also consult female non-members on what issues to take to the CFI. Both types of forum could be conducive to EC women sharing with other village women what transpires in the EC, and for village women to convey their problems to the EC women who are supposed to represent them.

Such sharing – or 'communication across difference', as Young (2000: 108) calls it – could also help EC women sort out differences among themselves and could lead to greater 'understanding across difference' (Young 1997: 52), especially where women across socio-economic classes have common interests in a natural resource. The observation of two CFI women who were also members of a women's SHG in Malwadi village, Karnataka, is illustrative:

> We discussed how benefits should be shared, whether we should differentiate between rich, poor, and middle-income households. We are poor. The poor often have no employment, so they need other sources of income, such as forest products for making leaf plates and pickle. They also extract gum. We have enough firewood and agriculture wage employment for now, but what about later? We have to discuss all this, and seek to resolve our differences.

In this way, a forum for deliberation could help women representatives take a collective view and arrive at group priorities about what forest products they want extracted, when and for how long the forest should be opened for extraction, which species to plant, and related matters. EC women would be more effective in mixed-gender CFIs if they spoke in a unified voice than as individuals speaking up without prior consultation.

Even if the outcome of deliberation favours some views over others, being able to express one's views could, in itself, make it easier for those who disagree to reconcile themselves to the decisions taken. Moreover, decisions arrived at through open discussion are likely to enjoy more legitimacy and lead to greater overall compliance and institutional sustainability. Over time, forums of deliberation could help the women build a sense of collective identity and solidarity that can equip them to deal better with government institutions as well.

Some authors, such as Fraser (1990), argue that equality is a necessary condition for deliberative (or communicative) democracy to work. My research indicates, however, that poor, low-caste rural women in South Asia are often less bound by tradition, and – especially if they are present in adequate numbers – they are more able to overcome the bounds of social norms that tend to restrict middle-class, upper-caste, rural women. Hence, while socio-economic equality would no doubt help, it is debatable whether it is a necessary condition for meaningful deliberation. Individual vulnerabilities can be overcome (even within hierarchical contexts) if poor women form a group and act collectively in their own interest.

Beyond the local So far, we have noted several encouraging examples of associative connections and strategic alliances between local groups that could enhance women's effective numbers, voice and influence in decision-making within CFIs and in the community. But, for many local problems, comprehensive solutions cannot be found locally.

For instance, although a critical mass of village women could have an impact on CFI decisions – such as by persuading CFIs to extract more firewood and other products – they cannot, on their own, change the popular perception that cooking energy is mainly the women's concern and not a community concern. Strategic alliances between women in CFIs and women in SHGs could well bring about some change, but do communities have the means to implement potential solutions? To establish firewood plantations, for example, communities will require control over the land used for this purpose. Similarly, the provision of clean fuel, such as biogas, at prices that the poor can afford requires technical and financial investment to design suitable models. Sophisticated technology, such as solar cookers, needs even greater investment in design, dissemination and maintenance. Therefore, although local government, such as village councils, could play an important role in the adaptation and dissemination of technology to users, research on design, testing and distribution on a wider scale usually require the involvement of higher levels of government. Energy- and environment-related policies that affect local communities are also usually formulated at the state and national levels.

Here, in addition to horizontal alliances between CFIs and

women's associations, women need bargaining power and vertical reach beyond the village. A federation constituted of a network of community-based organisations, as discussed below, could provide an answer.

Extending vertical reach through federations Broadly, a federation is an association of organisations. It can help realise economies of scale and provide bargaining power as an interest group, while retaining autonomy (Nair 2005). In South Asia, federations of SHGs and forestry groups have become an important way of building upward links, but these are usually single-focus federations: SHG federations connect SHGs, and forestry federations connect CFIs. What could prove innovative is the linking of these single-focus federations with each other.

In India, SHG federations are common: for example, by the mid-2000s, there were an estimated 69,000 such federations, 89 per cent of which were in southern India. Most of these were working at the village level, but some also worked at district level, and one at the state level (APMAS 2007). However, India has few federations of community forestry groups and most of these are far from gender equal.

In contrast, Federation of Community Forest Users of Nepal (FECOFUN), formed in 1995, is a national body with a demo-cratic structure that has elected representatives, and a constitution that mandates gender parity in committee membership and office-holding. In the mid-2000s, 10,000 of Nepal's 14,000 CFIs were members of FECOFUN (Ojha et al. 2007) and today most CFIs are part of the federation. Within each district, individual CFIs are connected to district-level committees, and elected representatives from each district form the national council and executive body. FECOFUN not only links forest user groups across the country, but it also takes up issues of forest policy with the government on their behalf (Britt 2007). On gender, however, its record is mixed. Notwithstanding FECOFUN's constitutional mandate of gender parity, some close observers note that the women who are included still remain largely a nominal rather than an effective presence (Britt 1997).

Indeed, in both India and Nepal, women's interests need to be better incorporated within forest federations. In India, this could

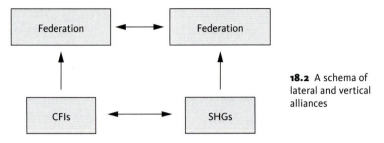

18.2 A schema of lateral and vertical alliances

be done by forging alliances between women's SHG federations and forest federations, to broaden the scope of both (see Figure 18.2). Forest federations would thus become more gender inclusive, expand their membership and reach, and enhance their lobbying power with the forest bureaucracy. In such alliances, SHG federations, which enjoy political clout in some regions, could bring the benefits of their influence to the CFIs. Examples of such collaboration between SHG and CFI federations suggest that this is possible. The NGO MYRADA, for instance, has built such links in a limited way, and the two types of federation have collaborated in tackling forest fires, river flooding and commercial logging. Similarly, in Uttara Kannada district (Karnataka), the federation of voluntary organisations for rural development – a network of twenty-one NGOs – works closely with SHG and forest federations in the district.

If federations with different strengths worked together, they could become more effective not only institutionally but also in lobbying with the upper echelons of the government to address issues such as domestic energy poverty, the marketing of non-wood forest products, and related concerns of village communities in general and of poor women in particular.

However, it should be emphasised that intra-group dynamics and inclusiveness must be built at all levels – from within a CFI at the village level to within federations of CFIs at higher levels, as well as within interlinked federations of CFIs and SHGs. This appears important both for gender equity (or other aspects of equity) and for the effectiveness of outcomes.

Conclusions

The empirical findings reported in this chapter demonstrate the power of numbers. Overall, the aims of both efficiency (more biomass regeneration and improved forest condition) and distributional equity (reduced firewood shortages, for example) are likely to be better realised with more women on the EC, and especially with more economically disadvantaged women. One-third appears to be a close approximation of the minimal presence women need to be effective, but achieving gender equality will require going beyond this proportion.

While this study did not measure solidarity directly, some observations can be made on this count. First, the power of numbers and common interests can produce beneficial results, even without an explicit forging of a common identity. The women who were included in the CFIs were fairly heterogeneous by class, age and (in Nepal) caste of household. What they shared were common interests in the resource, especially an interest in accessing firewood and fodder. Sometimes there were internal conflicts, which were observed especially in Nepal where class and caste differences were greater than in Gujarat. But, overall, shared interests vis-à-vis external factors (such as in keeping non-villagers out) were more important to the women than internal differences among themselves.

Second, to increase women's numbers and voice across CFIs at the local level, there is notable potential for forming federations of CFIs, as well as for forging strategic alliances between different segments of civil society groups, such as between CFIs and SHGs, and between federations of CFIs and SHGs. These alliances and associations, as conceptualised, could be based on shared interests, even if there is no forging of a common identity.

Third, links between civil society groups, even if initially based on strategic considerations, have the potential to evolve over time into networks guided by social solidarity considerations. This could add to the effectiveness of numbers. Some semblance of this can be seen in the workings of FECOFUN at the national level, where it intervened beyond forest issues to join national efforts to restore democracy in Nepal. But much more work is needed to establish common identity across difference. For this, as discussed in this chapter, a start can be made at the local level through processes of democratic deliberation. Meanwhile, numbers, even in themselves, continue to hold considerable power.

NOTES

Introduction

1 See also Piketty (2014), UNRISD (2010), World Bank (2005).

2 See also Utting et al. (2014), Fonteneau et al. (2011).

3 Derived from Gramsci (1971), 'Counter-hegemony' refers to the structuring by subaltern groups and 'organic intellectuals' of a discourse and politics that are inclusive of diverse struggles against oppression, domination and deprivation, capable of incorporating allies from other social groups, and able to counter – if not eventually dismantle – dominant 'hegemonic' power.

4 Data from the annual reports of Fairtrade International for 2004/05 and 2013.

5 See, for example, Amin (2009), Defourny et al. (2009), Jayasooria (2013), Coraggio (2007), OECD (2010), Fonteneau et al. (2011).

6 See, for example, Bernstein (2004).

7 The term 'polycentricity' refers to the notion that regulatory systems often involve different sets of rules associated with different (public, private and civil society) actors, operating at multiple (micro, meso and macro) scales.

8 For an analysis of how radical concepts are taken up by mainstream actors, see Cornwall and Brock (2005).

9 As regards spelling, 'fair trade' refers to the concept, movement or organisations promoting the concept, whereas 'Fairtrade' refers to the certified sub-system within the fair trade approach.

10 For an up-to-date mapping of public policy related to SSE, see http://reliess.org/?lang=en.

11 The concept of the double movement refers to a situation where the movement towards commodification and market liberalisation is countered by the spontaneous reaction of subjects to protect against heightened risk and vulnerability.

12 See Laclau and Mouffe (1985: 183).

2 McMurtry

1 See, for example, Kropotkin (1972) or Fontan and Shragge (2000) for this argument.

2 The definition of capitalism is often not explicitly articulated, which often leads to confusion. For this chapter, capitalism is defined as a social and economic system that is characterised by the tendency towards private and exclusionary ownership of the means of production for profit.

3 See Chapter 1 of McMurtry (2010) for a fuller explanation.

4 Marx, of course, was famously dismissive of the cooperative: 'Restricted, however, to the dwarfish forms into which individual wage slaves can elaborate it by their private efforts, the cooperative system will never transform capitalistic society' (cited in Thomas 1985: 275).

5 See Liebman (1985) for a detailed outline of the SSE in the NEP.

6 See McMurtry (2004) for some of these directions.

7 There is a good argument to be made that credit unions remain the most advanced form of microcredit yet developed.

8 See Loxley (2007) for a develop-

ment of the concepts of leakage and linkage.

9 It is important to note that this position is *not* advocating a 'retreat to the local' or 'particularism' above all else, but rather suggesting that a clearly articulated 'third' player (the SSE) should gain a meaningful seat at the political and economic table.

3 Bergeron and Healy

1 For a discussion of these concepts and how they are central to many of the competing meanings of SSE, see Amin (2009), particularly essays 1, 5 and 7.

2 J. K. Gibson-Graham is the pen name of Katherine Gibson and the late Julie Graham.

3 For more information, see www.communityeconomies.org.

4 The research of progressive feminist development scholars has also highlighted the diversity of household forms – often with consternation at the flawed assumption that guides much current policy that all households conform to the dominant patriarchal norm where women are the primary carers (Bedford 2009; Bergeron 2011; Chant 2006).

4 Millstone

1 See the Cooperative Development Foundation: www.cdf.coop/history-of-cooperatives (accessed 28 February 2013).

2 For a breakdown of the different types of utilities provision in the US, see also www.publicpower.org/files/PDFs/USElectricUtilityIndustryStatistics.pdf.

3 In contrast, many countries in mainland Europe have a more plural economy, with more small- and medium-sized businesses, family firms, employee-owned firms and cooperatives (Hutton 2012).

4 See Co-operatives UK: www.uk.coop (accessed 14 February 2013).

5 See the Democracy Collaborative:

democracycollaborative.org (accessed 26 February 2013); and Community Wealth.Org: http://community-wealth.org (accessed 27 February 2012).

6 See US Federation of Worker Cooperatives: www.usworker.coop/about workercoops (accessed 27 February 2013).

7 Governance and 'one member, one vote' are the key differences between workers' cooperatives and 100 per cent employee-owned companies.

8 See B-Corps: www.bcorporation.net (accessed 30 March 2013).

9 A mutual operates under the principle of mutuality, but, unlike cooperatives, members do not invest directly in the company. Instead, they have a customer relationship with the mutual, on the basis of which they are allowed to vote and participate in governance.

10 See Social Enterprise UK: www.socialenterprise.org.uk (accessed 30 March 2013).

11 Evergreen Cooperative: http://evergreencooperatives.com (accessed 28 February 2013).

5 Reed

1 In this chapter I focus on the Fairtrade International (FLO) network, which certifies (mostly) agricultural products as 'fair trade', without addressing the practices of the smaller World Fair Trade Organization (WFTO), which certifies producer organisations (many of which work in handicraft sectors).

2 See B-Corps: www.bcorporation.net.

3 The notion of scale in the neoclassical tradition most commonly refers to the benefits of economies of scale and typically focuses on the benefits that accrue to individual firms. In this discussion, the notion of scale is used in a more general fashion to refer to the potential benefits of growing SSE enterprises and the participation of SSE nterprises in the larger economy.

4 While manufacturing costs are the typical object of concern, this phenomenon may also relate to other costs, such as those for processing, transportation and marketing.

5 This need is expressed through concepts such as 'place-based' economies (Lionais and Johnstone 2009). FT exemplifies how international as well as local bonds of solidarity can promote dense SSE economies.

6 In the initial period, the focus on promoting SSE activity was seen as compatible with corporate participation, to the extent that regulatory efforts were also undertaken to make corporations more accountable. For a discussion of the notion of corporate accountability (and how it contrasts with corporate social responsibility), see Utting (2005), and see Reed and Mukherjee-Reed (2012) for the relationship to FT. For its part, FLO has largely dropped the ball on promoting stricter regulation over the years, focusing almost exclusively on its own certification programme that is predominantly based on consumer pressure.

7 This depends, of course, on the definition of SSE. There have been actors at different levels of the FLO system that did not seem to prioritise SSE production and exchange, such as Fair Trade USA (Jaffee 2010). The sharpest contrast here would be with the efforts of small producer organisations to set up their own labelling bodies, such as Comercio Justo México (Fair Trade Mexico) and the recent attempts by CLAC to develop a small producers' symbol (Coscione 2012; Smith and VanderHoff Boersma 2012).

8 This establishment of a parallel certification system in FLO came about as a result of two related dynamics. First, growth in sales led to an increased 'professionalisation' of the body, with more conventional business experts being hired and brought on to the board. Second, as institutions, the national labelling bodies had their own interests in growing sales (as this was their primary income source). The easiest way to do this was to make participation in FT more attractive to large corporations. These dynamics, in addition to helping to account for the parallel certification systems within FLO, also contributed to de-emphasising the earlier practice of promoting trade reform, which has largely fallen off the FLO agenda (Reed 2012).

7 Coraggio

1 This chapter draws on a paper prepared for the conference 'Estados Generales de la Economía Social y Solidaria', held in Paris on 17–19 June 2011. The paper was adapted for the United Nations Research Institute for Social Development conference 'Potential and Limits of Social and Solidarity Economy', Geneva, 6–8 May 2013. The original paper included case studies on Bolivia and Venezuela.

2 This refers to an anti-imperialist/anti-colonialist position in the global political system, as well as socially oriented by the interests of the majorities of the population.

3 While proximity services are activities typical of SSE policies in Europe and Canada, the central concern in Argentina is the need to increase jobs and income, regardless of the needs to be satisfied by the goods and services produced.

4 A description of advances in systematisation, not only for Argentina but also for the region, can be found in cases outlined on the Red de Investigadores Latinoamericanos de Economía Social y Solidaria website (www.riless.ungs.edu.ar).

5 Coverage of this case and of the Venezuelan case relies heavily on data organised by Susana Hintze (see Hintze 2011).

6 The above does not purport to be a comprehensive description of these economies, but merely an illustration of the ways in which they differ.

7 For the relevant constitutions, see: www.justicia.gob.bo/index.php/normas/doc_download/35-nueva-constitucion-politica-del-estado (Bolivia, 2008); www.asambleanacional.gov.ec/documentos/constitucion_de_bolsillo.pdf (Ecuador, 2008); and www.tsj.gov.ve/legislacion/constitucion1999.htm (Venezuela, 1999).

8 Bateman

1 See 'The great stabilisation', *The Economist*, 19 December 2009.

2 For example, a special branch of the Banca Nazionale del Lavoro was established in order to provide afford-able financial support packages for the wide variety of cooperatives (Bartlett and Pridham 1991).

3 See *The Economist*, 9 November 2013.

4 Prior to the 2012 study by Bate-man, all previous evaluations of the LEDA network in Latin America had been undertaken by the same small group of individuals who helped to design and establish the LEDAs and who for many years thereafter provided consulting services for the management and expansion of the LEDA programme – in other words, individuals hardly likely to want to be critical of their own programme design and management.

5 However, as several confidential informants close to the LEDA project openly admitted to the author after the report had been completed, the real rea-son why the UNDP solicited the Colom-bian government and other organisations to fund the LEDA network was precisely to avert its impending collapse.

6 Interview with Antonio Torres and Gustavo Flores, Economic Develop-ment Director and Lac Jubones Project Economist, Azuay Provincial Govern-ment Economic Department, Cuenca, 2 May 2012.

7 It was also decided that the top-down 'contract farming' model, the preferred agricultural supply chain model in the international development community, would not produce the desired economic *and* social results in the agricultural community.

8 Interview with Javier Andres Cuaical Alpala, General Manager, Alimentos Nariño, Tulcán, Colombia, 25 April 2012.

9 Mendell and Alain

1 In order to learn from experiences at the national, regional and local level in countries in the global North and South, FIESS was organised in Montreal, Quebec in 2011 to discuss collaborations between civil society and governments. It attracted 1,600 participants from sixty-two countries. These studies were coordinated by a scientific committee chaired by Marguerite Mendell.

2 All studies are available at http://reliess.org/centre-de-documentation/.

3 For more information on frame-work laws for the SSE, see http://reliess.org/framework-law/?lang=en.

4 The Małopolskie Social Economy Pact was officially signed by twenty-five entities in March 2008. However, only five NGOs had joined it by the time of the study. All OECD studies referred to in this chapter are available at OECD: www.oecd-ilibrary.org/industry-and-services/oecd-local-economic-and-employment-development-leed-working-papers_20794797.

5 Work integration enterprises aim to help marginalised people reintegrate into the traditional labour market through skills development activities in a commercial setting and personal counselling.

6 This pact has since been renewed and extended.

7 A new action plan for 2014–19 is currently being elaborated by SSE actors, representatives of various government ministries, networks of municipalities, local development agencies and researchers.

10 Grasseni et al.

1 These comprised a survey, participant observation and in-depth interviews.

2 The data presented here are part of a wider research project, 'Inside relational capital' (*Dentro il capitale delle relazioni*), carried out by CORES (Consumi, Reti e Pratiche di Economie Sostenibili or Consumption, Networks and Practices of Sustainable Economies) in 2011–13 under the scientific direction of Francesca Forno, Cristina Grasseni and Silvana Signori at Bergamo University (www.unibg.it/cores). By March 2013, 429 GAS were mapped in Lombardy, among which 204 group co-ordinators and 1,658 *gasistas* completed the CORES questionnaire online. The study was endorsed by the Italian Solidarity Economy Network (Tavolo RES: www.retecosol.org) and carried out in collaboration with Davide Biolghini and Giuseppe Vergani of Tavolo RES.

3 *Gasista* in the singular. We propose a gender-neutral plural, *gasistas*. The GAS charter is available on line (in Italian) at www.retecosol.org/docs/CartaReso703. pdf (accessed 9 September 2012).

4 A pilot study carried out in Bergamo established a protocol, which CORES replicated in Lombardy and is currently being extended to Sicily and Friuli, in collaboration with local facilitators with comparable knowledge of the local contexts.

5 'Serventi a Radio Onda d'Urto', broadcast November 2011, is available at http://navdanya.radiondadurto.org/ files/2011/11/Seventi-due.mp3 (accessed 8 April 2014).

6 See Federico De Musso's 2012 documentary 'L'altra faccia dell'Arancia' at http://vimeo.com/53209804.

7 The project 'Turning the Vicious Cycle Around: New Frontiers in the Fight Against the Mafia' was funded by the Swedish Research Council (2010–13) as a collaboration between Uppsala University and Bergamo University.

8 The notion of the solidarity economy 'district' follows the definition of Italy's 'industrial districts' (Becattini 2000; Trigilia 2005). This was considered the Italian 'third way' to globalisation, celebrated in the 1980s and 1990s as a way of avoiding consolidation, with a diffused network of small-scale, often family business-driven but highly specialised enterprises, thriving in the world market in terms of design, logistics and high-quality manufacture.

9 The full project is available online at http://resbergamasca.files.wordpress. com/2011/08/progetto-mercati-mc-6-3-2012.pdf (accessed 26 December 2010).

10 The self-evaluation protocol measures the following criteria: degree of environmental and health preservation, degree of engagement in social work, local provenance and food miles, degree of involvement in a relational economy, and participation in the activities to foster and diffuse the mission of a citizenship market. See http://resbergamasca.files.wordpress.com/2011/08/discplinare-mercato-mc-6-3-2012.pdf (accessed 26 December 2012).

11 The activities and projects of DES Brianza (DESBRI) are described at www. desbri.org.

12 Current qualitative research is being carried out on these phenomena by a number of scholars in the Community Economies Collective (see www.communityeconomies.org). Ethnographic observation of the Massachusetts solidarity economy initiatives was made possible by a Wenner-Gren Foundation

2013–14 grant, through the project 'Seeds of Trust' (www.wennergren.org/grantees/grasseni-cristina).

13 See the activities of the Worcester SAGE Alliance (Solidarity and Green Economy) at www.worcesterroots.org.

14 This has occurred, for example, through the Solidarity and Green Economy Coalition conferences that have taken place annually in Worcester, MA since 2011.

11 **Nelson**

1 See 'About BlueOrchard' on the BlueOrchard website: www.blueorchard.com/about-blueorchard.

2 Lending under Islamic finance law is an important exception, in which transactions must be structured so that lenders share the risk.

3 This section is based on only partial information about the behaviour of individual investors associated with the two organisations.

13 **Rossel**

1 See 'Hay 5.200 Ong que ejecutan las políticas sociales del Estado', *El País*, 8 October 2004: http://historico.elpais.com.uy/Suple/LaSemanaEn ElPais/04/10/08/lasem_naci_114809.asp.

2 Although there are no precise data available, actors involved in the government and in the SSE tend to agree that there is a growing number of new organisations being created as a result of this new situation (Rossel 2011).

14 **Fonteneau**

1 This overview draws largely on Fonteneau and Galland (2006).

2 The law was adopted by the assembly but the operational decrees have never been enacted.

3 This terminology has been chosen to cover mutual organisations providing health insurance without excluding the addition of other social risks.

15 **Nannyonjo**

1 Based on an estimated population of 34 million people in 2012.

2 This study consisted of: a desk review of existing documents; interviews with apex institutions, including the Uganda Cooperative Alliance (UCA) and Uganda Cooperative Savings and Credit Union Limited; interviews with government officials in relevant ministries; and field visits to fifteen randomly selected area cooperative enterprises (ACEs) and unions in four regions of Uganda, conducted during April and May 2013.

3 Previously called the National Resistance Army.

4 These include rice, maize, beans, bananas, fruits and vegetables.

5 Indeed, there was a significant increase in people using SACCOs, from 5 per cent in 2009 to 21 per cent in 2013. The estimated adult population using SACCOs increased five-fold from 128,000 in 2009 to 622,000 adults in 2013 (EPRC 2013: 16).

6 Based on data on fifty-four ACEs that are linked to SACCOs under the Maximising Cooperators' Benefits project.

7 These include the Poverty Eradication Action Plan, Prosperity For All programme and Plan for Modernisation of Agriculture.

8 Support to SACCOs includes equipment; subsidies for operational costs; and training in entrepreneurship skills, group formation and dynamics, ownership and governance issues.

9 Several other institutions, including the Support for Feasible Financial Institutions and Capacity Building Efforts (SUFFICE) programme, extend loans to SACCOs.

10 The Rural Income and Employment Enhancement Project (RIEEP) aims to contribute towards poverty eradication in rural Uganda by facilitating

access to and utilisation of affordable financial and business development services for about 1.4 million rural poor (AfDB Group 2009; MSC 2013).

11 Based on interviews with warehouse managers during August 2013.

12 Other stakeholders who support capacity-building for cooperatives are the Association of Microfinance Institutions of Uganda, SUFFICE, and the German Technical Cooperation (GTZ).

13 In a study by Afranaa Kwapong and Lubega Korugyendo (2010), farmer training was identified by ACEs as a desired area for government support.

14 For example, following training on gender for cooperatives in five regions in 2011–12, the number of women participating in cooperative activities increased by 18 per cent from 24,491 to 29,040 (UCA 2012: 22).

15 Based on several MTIC reports and interviews with officials in the MTIC in March and April 2013.

16 Based on interviews with five union leaders during April 2013.

16 Ghosh

1 The author would like to thank AMUL's MD Rahul Kumar, IRMA's former Director Dr Vivek Bhandari, National Dairy Development Board Chairman Dr Amrita Patel, the late Dr Verghese Kurien, and the entire AMUL and AMUL Research and Development Association family for contributing to this research output. I gratefully acknowledge the insightful comments and valuable suggestions received from Dr Paola Perez-Aleman, Dr Abhirup Chakrabarti and Dr Frances Westley on previous drafts of this chapter. I would also like to thank Dr Peter Utting of UNRISD for his incisive feedback and ILO's Partnership and Field Support Department for their generosity. I express my profound gratitude to International Development Research Center, Canada, Center for Strategy Studies in Organizations, McGill and Institute for the Study of International Development, McGill for sponsoring my fieldwork in India. I would also like to thank Dr Frances Westley, JW McConnell Chair in Social Innovation at SiG (Social Innovation Generation), University of Waterloo, for her invaluable guidance and inspiration.

2 Records of the Kaira Union. Details on AMUL's turnover as well as assets and liabilities are available from the author.

3 Data were obtained from both primary and secondary sources. Primary data were collected during my fieldwork in Kheda district through semi-structured, face-to-face interviews with 164 respondents, including member producers, senior executives, directors (current and retired) and AMUL veterans who had spent their entire careers with AMUL.

4 Polson received support for the continuation of its monopoly from the British colonial government.

5 Interviews conducted by the author.

6 Sardar Patel was a doyen of the nationalist movement and chief comrade of Gandhi. He would go on to become India's first home minister and deputy prime minister after India's independence. He was sympathetic to the grievances of Kheda's milk producers and to their movement for organising dairy cooperatives.

7 Morarji Desai was Sardar's right-hand man and would go on to become India's finance minister and then prime minister.

8 This situation continued from 1953 until 1956, when AMUL had to stop organising new VCSs, although membership in existing VCSs doubled. Between these years, procurement stagnated.

9 Khurody used imported milk powder to enhance the capacity utilisation of Aarey to artificially lower their fixed unit costs of operation.

10 Interview conducted by the author.

17 Mukherjee

1 I am extremely grateful to the women of *Kudumbashree* who have generously given me their time. I am particularly grateful to N. Jagajeevan, S. Muraleedharan and Anup Nayar for their continuous help and support. I also wish to thank Dhanya Chidambaram, Meena Nair and Hema Praveen for their assistance with research. The work was made possible with support from the Social Science and Humanities Research Council of Canada (SSHRC) and the Shastri Indo-Canadian Institute, Calgary, Canada.

2 Each NHG elects five volunteers to the following positions: president, secretary, infrastructure volunteer, community health volunteer and income activities generation volunteer (Siwal 2009).

3 As narrated by a *Kudumbashree* participant at a conference entitled 'Aspiring for women's full citizenship in Kerala: the *Kudumbashree* mission', 21 December 2011.

4 The notion of solidarity that we are employing here is grounded in Habermasian critical theory. Unlike the Durkheimian notions of mechanical and organic solidarity (which are based on shared life-world assumptions and promote shared interests in complex societies), this understanding presupposes a commitment to discursive decision-making. Moreover, it highlights the fact that building bonds of solidarity involves shared practice (in addition to discursive decision-making).

5 The majority of micro-enterprises have single proprietors, but some are owned by small groups. They have an investment of between 5,000 and 250,000 Rupees and are supposed to generate a minimum income of 1,500 Rupees per member. Formal group enterprises have a minimum of ten members and higher investment rates (Siwal 2009).

6 Based on interviews conducted between 2009 and 2011.

7 The case of a woman from Malappuram illustrates this point. Widowed and left with three young children, she found no means of survival other than cleaning dead bodies. Hardly adequate as a livelihood, it also brought her unbearable social ostracism. Now she is a proud member of a farming collective and wants to enter politics.

8 The author, in collaboration with local researchers, conducted a survey of 100 collectives across fourteen districts during 2011. The survey found that 15 per cent of the farmers were Dalits and Adivasis and 32 per cent came from minority communities.

9 One woman from Perambra – where *Kudumbashree* members have rejuvenated 140 acres that lay fallow for twenty-six years – summed up this transition by referencing the move from the MGNREGS programme to group farming: 'We have created life ... and food, which gives life, not just 100 days of manual labour.'

10 Since the farmers are primarily poor women, they often decide to use part of their produce to meet their own needs rather than selling it. Every group takes this decision democratically, depending on the levels of food insecurity of their members. In Idukki, where the terrain prevents easy market access and food insecurity is higher, farmers take more of their produce home – as opposed to Thiruvananthapuram, where market access is better and returns are higher.

11 A member of a joint liability group for farming in Mullasseri, Thrissur, relates that from their incomes of collective farming members were able

to buy land both individually and as a group. Each member now had assets worth 350,000 Rupees and sixteen more groups have been inspired by their example to come into collective farming.

12 Fair trade networks may provide the best example of this phenomenon (Hutchens 2009).

18 Agarwal

1 A longer version of this chapter was first published in the *Journal of Peasant Studies* in 2014 under the title 'The power of numbers in gender dynamics: illustrations from community forestry groups'.

2 For India see Bahuguna (2004). Nepal's figures are taken from its forest department.

3 Information gathered by the author during a field visit to IDS sites in 1998.

4 As narrated to the author by a project officer of the organisation.

CONTRIBUTORS

Bina Agarwal is professor of development economics and environment at the University of Manchester, United Kingdom.

Béatrice Alain is coordinator of RELIESS, an initiative of the Chantier de l'Economie Sociale, Canada.

Milford Bateman is a freelance consultant on local economic development policy and visiting professor of economics at Juraj Dobrila University of Pula, Croatia.

Suzanne Bergeron is director of women's and gender studies at the University of Michigan–Dearborn, United States.

José Luis Coraggio is director of the master's degree in social economy at the Universidad Nacional de General Sarmiento, Argentina, and co-director of the Latin American Network of Researchers on Social and Solidarity Economy (Red Latinoamericana de Investigadores en Economía Social y Solidaria, RILESS).

Bénédicte Fonteneau is a research expert at the Institute for Work and Society, University of Leuven, Belgium.

Francesca Forno is assistant professor of sociology and sociology of consumption at Bergamo University, Italy.

Abhijit Ghosh is assistant professor in strategic management at the Offutt School of Business, Concordia College, United States.

Georgina M. Gómez is senior lecturer in the Department of Human Resources and Local Development of the Institute of Social Studies (ISS) at Erasmus University Rotterdam, the Netherlands.

Cristina Grasseni is associate professor at the University of Utrecht, the Netherlands.

Stephen Healy is a senior research fellow at the Institute of Culture and Society at the University of Western Sydney, Australia.

Jean-Louis Laville is a professor at the Conservatoire National des Arts et Métiers (CNAM) in France and European coordinator of the Karl Polanyi Institute of Political Economy.

John-Justin McMurtry is currently graduate program director of the Social and Political Thought Program at York University, Canada.

Marguerite Mendell is a professor at the School of Community and Public Affairs and director of the Karl Polanyi Institute of Political Economy at Concordia University, Canada.

Carina Millstone is a research fellow at the New Economy Coalition in the United States.

Ananya Mukherjee-Reed is professor of political science at York University, Canada.

Roldan Muradian is visiting professor at the Postgraduate Social Science Programme on Development, Agriculture and Society (CPDA), Federal Rural University of Rio de Janeiro, and in the Department of Economics at the Federal Fluminense University, Brazil.

Justine Nannyonjo is head of the Modelling and Forecasting Division of the Research Department at the Bank of Uganda.

Paul Nelson is associate professor and director of the International Development Program at the Graduate School of Public and International Affairs, University of Pittsburgh, United States.

Darryl Reed is professor of business and society at York University, Canada.

Cecilia Rossel is associate professor in the Political and Social Sciences Department of the Universidad Católica del Uruguay.

Silvana Signori is an assistant professor in the Department of Management, Economics and Quantitative Methods at Bergamo University, Italy.

BIBLIOGRAPHY

Abebaw, D. and M. Haile (2013) 'The impact of cooperatives on agricultural technology adoption: empirical evidence from Ethiopia'. *Food Policy* 38: 82–91.

Abramovitz, M. (2005) 'The largely untold story of welfare reform and the human services'. *Social Work* 50(2): 175–86.

ADEL (2011) *Un camino al desarrollo humano local en Colombia*. Bogotá: Las Agencias de Desarrollo Económico Local (ADEL) and United Nations Development Programme (UNDP).

AfDB Group (2009) 'Rural Income and Employment Enhancement Project (RIEEP): project appraisal report'. Tunis-Belvédère: African Development Bank Group (AfDB Group). www.afdb.org/fileadmin/uploads/afdb/Documents/Project-and-Operations/Uganda-_Rural_Income_and_Employ ment_Enhance ment_Project_-_Appraisal_Report.pdf.

Afranaa Kwapong, N. and P. Lubega Korugyendo (2010) 'Revival of cooperatives in Uganda'. Policy Note 10. Washington DC: International Food Policy Research Institute (IFPRI).

Agarwal, B. (1994) *A Field of one's Own: Gender and land rights in South Asia*. Cambridge: Cambridge University Press.

— (2010a) 'Rethinking agricultural production collectives: the case for a group approach to energize agriculture and empower poor farmers'. IEG Working Paper 305. Delhi: Institute of Economic Growth (IEG).

— (2010b) *Gender and Green Governance: The political economy of women's presence within and beyond community forestry*. Oxford: Oxford University Press.

Agyeman, J. (2013) *Just Sustainabilities: Policy, planning and practice*. London: Zed Books.

Akram-Lodhi, H. (2013) *Hungry for Change: Farmers, food justice and the agrarian question*. Halifax: Fernwood Press.

Alexander, J., R. Nank and C. Stivers (1999) 'Implications of welfare reform: do nonprofit survival strategies threaten civil society?'. *Nonprofit and Voluntary Sector Quarterly* 28(4): 452–75.

Alkire, S. and V. Chirkov (2007) 'Measuring agency: testing a new indicator in Kerala'. In V. Pillai and S. Alkire (eds) *Measuring Individual Agency or Empowerment: A study in Kerala*. Thiruvananthapuram, Kerala: Centre for Development Studies.

Alonso, O. (2007) *Nuevas formas de propiedad y de gestión de las organizaciones en la transición hacia el socialismo del Siglo XXI*. Caracas: ILDIS.

Alperovitz, G. (2011) *America Beyond Capitalism: Reclaiming our wealth, our liberty and our democracy*. Takoma Park MD: Democracy Collaborative Press and Dollars and Sense.

—, T. Howard and T. Williamson (2010) 'The Cleveland model'. *The Nation*, 11 February.

Altenberg, L. (1990) 'An end to capitalism: Leland Stanford's forgotten vision'. *Stanford Historical Society* 14(1): 8–20.

Amin, A. (ed.) (2009) *The Social*

Economy: International perspectives on economic solidarity. London: Zed Books.

Amsden, A. (2001) The Rise of 'The Rest': Challenges to the West from late-industrializing economies. Oxford: Oxford University Press.

Andino, V. (2013) 'Políticas públicas para la economía social: caso de estudio Ecuador'. Montreal: RELIESS. www.reliess.org/centredoc/upload/VAndino-poltpubyecosol-Ecuador-RELIESS-final1367861067.pdf (accessed 13 February 2014).

Antsey, C. (2013) 'Viewpoint: the price of violence against women and girls'. BBC News, 8 March. www.bbc.co.uk/news/business-21696469 (accessed March 2013).

APMAS (2007) SHG Federations in India: A perspective. New Delhi: Access Development Services.

APPA (2013) 2013–14 Annual Directory and Statistical Report. Arlington VA: American Public Power Association (APPA). www.publicpower.org/files/PDFs/USElectricUtilityIndustry-Statistics.pdf (accessed 30 March 2013).

Arain, S. et al. (1967) Commission of Inquiry into the Affairs of all Cooperative Unions in Uganda. Kampala: Government of Uganda.

Arnsperger, C. (2013) 'Want to really help expand the social and solidarity economy? Then start rethinking money!'. United Nations Research Institute for Social Development (UNRISD) Think Piece. www.unrisd.org/thinkpiece-arnsperger (accessed 20 November 2013).

Arrow, K. (1969) The Organization of Economic Activity. The analysis and evaluation of public expenditure: the PPB system. Washington DC: Joint Economic Committee, 91st Congress, pp. 59–73.

Arruda, M. (2005) 'What is solidarity economy?' Transnational Institute website. www.tni.org/article/what-solidarity-economy.

Bacon, C. (2010) 'Who decides what is fair in fair trade? The agri-environmental governance of standards, access, and price'. Journal of Peasant Studies 37(1): 111–47.

Bahuguna, V. K. (2004) 'Root to canopy: an overview'. In V. K. Bahuguna, K. Mitra, D. Capistrano and S. Saigal (eds) Root to Canopy. New Delhi: Commonwealth Forestry Association and Winrock International, pp. 15–24.

Bajde, D. (2013) 'Marketized philanthropy: Kiva's utopian ideology of entrepreneurial philanthropy'. Marketing Theory 13(1): 3–18. http://mtq.sagepu b.com/content/13/1/3.

Bakker, I. (2007) 'Social reproduction and the constitution of a gendered political economy'. New Political Economy 12(4): 541–56.

— and S. Gill (eds) (2003) Power, Production and Social Reproduction. Toronto: York University Press.

Barco Serrano, S. (2011) 'Estudio de casos españoles: las políticas de economía social y el diálogo entre los poderes públicos y la sociedad civil'. Montreal: Chantier de l'Économie Sociale, FIESS 2011. www.reliess.org/centredoc/upload/FIESS_EC_Espana_Oct.-2011.pdf (accessed 13 February 2014).

Bardham, J. and C. Chetemi (2009) 'Collective action initiatives to improve marketing performance: lessons from farmer groups in Tanzania'. Food Policy 34(1): 53–9.

Bardhan, P. (1989) 'The new institutional economics and development theory: a brief critical assessment'. World Development 17(9): 1389–95.

— (1993) 'Analytics of the institutions of informal cooperation in rural development'. World Development 21(4): 633–9.

Barreiro, L. and L. V. Leite (2003) La

Confianza en la Economía Popular: El caso de la red de trueque Nodo Astral. Buenos Aires: Instituto de Investigación en Ciencias Sociales (IDICSO).

Barrientos, A. (2008) 'Financing social protection'. In A. Barrientos and D. Hulme (eds) *Social Protection for the Poor and the Poorest: Concepts, policies and politics.* London: Palgrave Macmillan.

— and D. Hulme (eds) (2008) *Social Protection for the Poor and the Poorest: Concepts, policies and politics.* London: Palgrave Macmillan.

Barry, J. J. (2012) 'Microfinance, the market and political development in the internet age'. *Third World Quarterly* 33(1): 125–41.

Bartlett, W. and G. Pridham (1991) 'Co-operative enterprises in Italy, Portugal and Spain: history and development'. *International Journal of Interdisciplinary Economics* 4: 33–59.

Bateman, M. (2000) 'Neo-liberalism, SME development and the role of business support centres in the transition economies of Central and Eastern Europe'. *Small Business Economics* 14(4): 275–98.

— (2005) 'SME development policy in the transition economies: progress with the wrong model'. In M. Harper and J. Tanburn (eds) *Mapping the Shift in Business Development Services: Making markets work for the poor.* London: Intermediate Technology Publications.

— (2007) 'Financial cooperatives for sustainable local economic and social development'. *Small Enterprise Development* 18(1): 37–49.

— (2010) *Why Doesn't Microfinance Work? The destructive rise of local neoliberalism.* London: Zed Books.

— (2012) *Local Economic Development in Latin America: A study of the role of the UNDP-supported LEDAs in promoting sustainable local economic and social development in Latin America.* Geneva: International Links and Services for Local Economic Development Agencies (ILS LEDA), United Nations Development Programme (UNDP).

— (2013) 'The age of microfinance: destroying Latin American economies from the bottom up'. *Ola Financiera* 15 (May–August).

— (2014) *The Zombie-like Persistence of Failed Local Neoliberalism: The case of UNDP's Local Economic Development Agency (LEDA) network in Latin America.* IDS Working Paper 14.3. Halifax, Canada: St Marys University.

— and H.-J. Chang (2012) 'Microfinance and the illusion of development: from hubris to nemesis in thirty years'. *World Economic Review* 1(1): 13–36.

—, B. Girard and R. McIntyre (2006) *Promising Practices: An integrated cooperative approach for sustainable local economic and social development in the Basque region of Spain.* New York NY: United Nations Development Programme.

—, J. P. Duran Ortíz and K. Maclean (2011) *A Post-Washington Consensus Approach to Local Economic Development in Latin America? An example from Medellin, Colombia.* Background note. London: Overseas Development Institute (ODI).

Baumol, W. (1990) 'Entrepreneurship: productive, unproductive, and destructive'. *Journal of Political Economy* 98(5): 893–921.

Becattini, G. (2000) *Il Distretto Industriale: Un nuovo modo di interpretare il cambiamento economico.* Turin: Rosenberg & Sellier.

Beckert, J. (2003) 'Economic sociology and embeddedness: how shall we conceptualize economic action?' *Journal of Economic Issues* 37(3): 769–87.

Bedford, K. (2009) *Developing Partnerships: Gender, sexuality and the reformed World Bank*. Minneapolis MN: University of Minnesota Press.

Bergeron, S. (2011) 'Economics, performativity and social reproduction in global development'. *Globalizations* 8(2): 151–61.

Berhendt, C. (2008) 'Can low income countries in sub-Saharan Africa afford basic social protection? First results of a modelling exercise'. In A. Barrientos and D. Hulme (eds) *Social Protection for the Poor and the Poorest: Concepts, policies and politics*. London: Palgrave Macmillan.

Bernard, T. and D. Spielman (2009) 'Reaching the rural poor through rural producer organizations? A study of agricultural marketing cooperatives in Ethiopia'. *Food Policy* 34(1): 60–9.

Bernard, T. and A. Taffesse (2012) 'Returns to scope? Smallholders' commercialization through multipurpose cooperatives in Ethiopia'. *Journal of African Economies* 21(3): 440–64.

Bernard, T., A. Taffesse and E. Gabre-Madhin (2008a) 'Impact of cooperatives on smallholders' commercialization behavior: evidence from Ethiopia'. *Agricultural Economics* 39(2): 147–61.

Bernard, T., M. E. Collion, A. Janvry, P. Rondot and E. Sadoulet (2008b) 'Do village organizations make a difference in African rural development? A study for Senegal and Burkina Faso'. *World Development* 36(11): 2188–204.

Bernstein, H. (2004) '"Changing before our very eyes": agrarian questions and the politics of land in capitalism today'. *Journal of Agrarian Change* 4(1&2): 190–225.

— (2008) 'Agrarian questions from transition to globalization'. In A. Haroon Akram-Lodhi and C. Kay (eds) *Peasants and Globalization: Political economy, rural transformation and the agrarian question*. London: Routledge, pp. 239–61.

Bijman, J., R. Muradian and A. Cechin (2011) 'Agricultural cooperatives and value chain coordination: towards an integrated theoretical framework'. In B. Helmsing and S. Vellema (eds) *Value Chains, Inclusion and Endogenous Development: Contrasting theories and realities*. London: Routledge.

Bijman, J., C. Iliopoulos, K. J. Poppe et al. (2012) *Support for Farmers' Cooperatives: Final report*. Brussels: European Commission.

Bingen, J., A. Serrano and J. Howard (2003) 'Linking farmers to markets: different approaches to human capital development'. *Food Policy* 28(4): 405–19.

Birchall, J. (1994) *Coop: The people's business*. Manchester: Manchester University Press.

— (2003) *Rediscovering the Cooperative Advantage: Poverty reduction through self-help*. Geneva: International Labour Organization (ILO).

Bode, I. (2006) 'Disorganized welfare mixes: voluntary agencies and new governance regimes in Western Europe'. *Journal of European Social Policy* 16(4): 346–59.

Boidin J. (2012) 'Extension de l'assurance maladie et rôle des mutuelles de santé en Afrique : les leçons de l'expérience sénégalaise'. *Economie Publique* 28–29(1–2): 47–70.

Borgen, S. (2004) 'Rethinking incentive problems in cooperative organizations'. *Journal of Socio-Economics* 33(4): 383–93.

Borras Jr., S. M., M. Edelman and C. Kay (eds) (2008) *Transnational Agrarian Movements: Confronting globalization*. Chichester: Wiley-Blackwell.

Borruso, M. T. (2012) *McKinsey on Cooperatives*. McKinsey & Company Industry Publications.

Borzaga, C. and J. Defourny (2001) *The Emergence of Social Enterprise.* London: Routledge.

Borzaga, C. and R. Bodini (2012) 'What to make of social innovation? Towards a framework for policy development'. Euricse Working Paper 036/12. Trento: European Research Institute on Cooperative and Social Enterprise (Euricse).

Bouchard, M. J. (ed.) (2013) *Innovation and the Social Economy: The Quebec experience.* Toronto: University of Toronto Press.

Boyer, R. (2007) 'Growth strategies and poverty reduction: the institutional complementarity hypothesis'. Working Paper 2007-43. Paris: Paris School of Economics.

— (2014) 'Welfare state and institutional complementarity: from North to South'. Paper presented at the UNRISD workshop on New Directions in Social Policy, Geneva, 7–8 April.

— and J. R. Hollingsworth (1997) 'From national embeddedness to spatial and institutional nestedness'. In J. R. Hollingsworth and R. Boyer (eds) *Contemporary Capitalism.* Cambridge: Cambridge University Press.

Bratton, K. A. (2005) 'Critical mass theory revisited: the behavior and success of token women in state legislatures'. *Politics and Gender* 1(1): 97–125.

Briceño, S. (2005) *Invest to Prevent Disaster.* Geneva: United Nations Inter-Agency Secretariat of the International Strategy for Disaster Reduction (UN/ISDR). www.unisdr.org/2005/campaign/docs/press-kit-english.pdf (accessed 13 April 2013).

Brissenden, C. H. (1952) 'The Bombay milk scheme'. *International Journal of Dairy Technology* 5(2): 108–14.

Britt, C. (1997) 'Federation building and networking: FECOFUN and experiences from user groups Nepal'. Discussion Paper. New Delhi: Ford Foundation.

— (2007) *FECOFUN'S Role in the Loktantra Andolan (2005–2006): Forest users support for community forestry and democracy in Nepal. Final report.* New Delhi: Ford Foundation.

Brodie, J. (2005) 'Globalization, governance, and gender relations: rethinking the agenda for the 21st century'. In L. Amoore (ed.) *The Global Resistance Reader.* London: Routledge.

Burkina Faso (2012) *Politique Nationale de Protection Sociale: Plan d'action 2012–2014.* Ouagadougou: Government of Burkina Faso.

Byrne, K. and S. Healy (2006) 'Cooperative subjects: towards a post-fantasmatic enjoyment of the economy'. *Rethinking Marxism* 18(2): 241–58.

Cameron, J. (2002) 'Domesticating class: femininity, heterosexuality and household politics'. In J. K. Gibson-Graham, S. Resnick and R. Wolff (eds) *Class and Its Others.* Minneapolis MN: University of Minnesota Press.

— (2009) 'Experimenting with economic possibilities: ethical economic decision-making in two Australian community enterprises'. In A. Amin (ed.) *The Social Economy: International perspectives on economic solidarity.* London: Zed Books.

— and J. K. Gibson-Graham (2003) 'Feminizing the economy: metaphors, strategies, politics'. *Gender, Place and Culture* 10(2): 145–57.

Canzanelli, G. (2010) *State of the Art Review on Local Economic Development Agencies.* ILS LEDA Paper 12 (October). Geneva: International Links and Services for Local Economic Development Agencies (ILS LEDA), United Nations Development Programme (UNDP).

— (2011) *Evaluation of Local and Territorial Development Agencies for Human*

Development: The ILS LEDA case. ILS LEDA Paper 15. Geneva: International Links and Services for Local Economic Development Agencies (ILS LEDA), United Nations Development Programme (UNDP).

Caruana, C. and C. Srnec (2013) 'Public policies addressed to the social and solidarity economy in South America: toward a new model?' *Voluntas* 24(3): 713–32.

CEC and K. Gibson (2009) 'Building community-based social enterprises'. In A. Amin (ed.) *The Social Economy: International perspectives on economic solidarity.* London: Zed Books.

Chagwiza, C., R. Muradian, R. Ruben and W. Tessema (2013) 'Collective entrepreneurship and rural development: comparing two types of producers' organizations in the Ethiopian honey sector'. In T. Ehrmann, J. Windsperger, G. Cliquet, T. Ehrmann and G. Hendrikse (eds) *Network Governance: Alliances, cooperatives and franchise chains.* Heidelberg: Springer.

Chakraborty, A. (2005) 'Kerala's changing development narratives'. *Economic and Political Weekly* 40(6): 541–7.

Chamberlain, P., M. Toye, G. Huot and E. Gruet (2011) 'Etude de cas Canada. Co-construction de politique publique pour l'économie sociale'. Montreal: Chantier de l'Économie Sociale, FIESS 2011. www.reliess. org/centredoc/upload/FIESS_EC_ Canada_Oct2011_FR.pdf (accessed 13 February 2014).

Chang, H.-J. (2007) *Bad Samaritans: Rich nations, poor policies and the threat to the developing world.* London: Random House.

— (2011) *23 Things They Don't Tell You About Capitalism.* London: Allen Lane.

Chant, S. (2006) 'Contributions of a gender perspective to the analysis of poverty'. In J. Jacquette and G. Summerfield (eds) *Women and Gender Equity in Development Theory and Practice.* Durham NC: Duke University Press.

Christiansen, J. and L. Bunt (2012) *Innovation in Policy: Allowing for creativity, social complexity and uncertainty in public governance.* London: Nesta. www.nesta.org.uk (accessed 13 February 2014).

Cittadini, R., L. Caballero, M. Moricz and F. Mainella (eds) (2010) *Economía Social y Agricultura Familiar: Hacia la construcción de nuevos paradigmas de intervención.* Buenos Aires: Ediciones INTA. www.inta.gov.ar/extension/ prohuerta/info/carpetas/economia_ social/economia_social_y_agricultura _familiar.pdf.

Cohen, G. A. (2001) *If You're an Egalitarian, How Come You're So Rich?* Cambridge MA: Harvard University Press.

Cohen, J.-L. and A. Arato (1994) *Civil Society and Political Theory*, Cambridge MA: MIT Press.

Cole, G. D. H. (1913) *The World of Labour.* London: Bell.

Conning, J. and J. Morduch (2011) 'Microfinance and social investment'. *Annual Review of Financial Economics* 3 (December): 407–34.

Contessi, S. (2014) 'Suolo'. *Antropologia Museale* 34 (December).

Contreras, C. A., C. Pernet and S. Rist (2013) 'Collective action, gender dynamics and the constraints for scaling up women initiatives in rural Mexico: the case of "El Color de la Tierra", an indigenous collective initiative in western Mexico'. Paper presented at the UNRISD conference on the Potential and Limits of Social and Solidarity Economy, Geneva, 6–8 May. www.unrisd.org/sse-draft-arias- et-al (accessed 20 November 2013).

Convergences (2011) 'Traditional and innovative sources of funding'. Study prepared for the 2015 Convergences World Forum. www. convergences2015.org/Content/ biblio/C2015% 20-%20Sources%20 of%20Funding_web.pdf (accessed 5 December 2013).

Cook, S., K. Smith and P. Utting (2012) 'Green economy or green society? Contestation and policies for a fair transition'. Occasional Paper 10. Geneva: United Nations Research Institute for Social Development (UNRISD).

Co-operatives UK (2012) *The UK Co-operative Economy 2012: Alternatives to austerity*. Manchester: Co-operatives UK. www.uk.coop/ sites/storage/public/downloads/ coop_economy_2012.pdf (accessed 12 February 2013).

Coraggio, J. L. (ed.) (2007) *La economía social desde la periferia: Contribuciones Latinoamericanas*. Buenos Aires: UNGS/Altamira.

— (2008) *Economía social, acción pública y política (hay vida después del neoliberalismo)*. 2nd edition. Buenos Aires: CICCUS.

— (2011) *Economía Social y Solidaria: El trabajo antes que el capital*. Debate Constituyente series. Quito: Abya-Yala.

— (2012) 'Las tres corrientes vigentes de pensamiento y acción dentro del campo de la Economía Social y Solidaria (ESS). Sus diferentes alcances'. Unpublished paper. base. socioeco.org/docs/a_las_tres_ corrientes_de_la_ess_27-2-13.pdf (accessed 23 October 2013).

Corbin, J. (1999) 'A study of factors influencing the growth of nonprofits in social services'. *Nonprofit and Voluntary Sector Quarterly* 28(3): 296–314.

Cornwall, A. and K. Brock (2005) '"Poverty reduction", "participation" and "empowerment" in development

policy'. Programme Paper 10. Geneva: United Nations Research Institute for Social Development (UNRISD).

Cornwell, J. (2011) 'Worker co-operatives and spaces of possibility: an investigation of subject space at collective copies'. *Antipode: A Radical Journal of Geography* 44(3): 726–44.

— and J. Graham (2009) 'Building community economies in Massachusetts: an emerging model of economic development?' In A. Amin (ed.) (2009) *The Social Economy: International perspectives on economic solidarity*. London: Zed Books.

Coscione, M. (2012) *La CLAC y la defensa del pequeño productor*. Santo Domingo: Editorial Funglode.

Crouch, C., W. Streeck, R. Boyer, B. Amable, P. A. Hall and G. Jackson (2005) 'Dialogue on dialogue on "institutional complementarity and political economy"'. *Socio-Economic Review* 3(2): 359–82.

Crowell, E. and D. Reed (2009) 'Fair Trade: A model for international co-operation among cooperatives?' In D. Reed and J. J. McMurtry (eds) *Cooperatives in a Global Economy: The challenges of co-operating across borders*. Cambridge: Cambridge Scholars Publishing.

Da Silva, J. G., M. E. Del Grossi and C. Galvão de França (2011) *The FOME ZERO (ZERO HUNGER) Program: The Brazilian experience*. Brasilia: Brazilian Ministry of Agrarian Development.

Dacheux, E. and D. Goujon (2011) 'The solidarity economy: an alternative development strategy?' *International Social Science Journal* 62(203–4): 205–15, March–June.

Dahlerup, D. (1988) 'From a small to a large majority: women in Scandinavian politics'. *Scandinavian Political Studies* 11(4): 275–98.

Dalla Chiesa, N. and M. Panzarasa (2012)

Buccinasco: La N'drangheta al Nord. Turin: Einaudi.

Daly, H. (1991) *Steady-state Economics: Second edition with new essays.* Washington DC: Island Press.

Danani, C. and S. Hintze (2011) *Protecciones y desprotecciones: La seguridad social en la Argentina 1990–2010.* Los Polvorines: Universidad Nacional de General Sarmiento.

Davis, K. E. and A. Gelpern (2010) 'Peer-to-peer financing for development: regulating the intermediaries'. *New York University Journal of International Law and Politics* 42(4): 1209–68.

de Haan, A. (2000) 'Introduction: the role of social protection in poverty reduction'. In T. Conway, A. de Haan and A. Norton (eds) *Social Protection: New directions of donor agencies.* London: Department for International Development.

Defourny, J. and P. Develtere (1999) 'The social economy: the worldwide making of a third sector'. In J. Defourny, P. Develtere and B. Fonteneau (eds) *Social Economy North and South.* Leuven/Liège: Katholieke Universiteit Leuven, Hoger Instituut voor de Arbeid, Université de Liège, and Centre d'Économie Sociale.

— (2009) 'The social economy: the worldwide making of a third sector'. In J. Defourny, P. Develtere, B. Fonteneau and M. Nyssens (eds) *The Worldwide Making of the Social Economy: Innovations and challenges.* Leuven: Acco.

Defourny, J. and M. Nyssens (2012) 'The EMES approach of social enterprise in a comparative perspective'. EMES Working Paper 12/03. Liege: European Research Network (EMES).

Defourny, J., P. Develtere and B. Fonteneau (1999) *L'Économie Social au Nord et au Sud.* Paris and Brussels: De Boeck.

Defourny, J., P. Develtere, B. Fonteneau

and M. Nyssens (eds) (2009) *The Worldwide Making of the Social Economy: Innovations and challenges.* Leuven: Acco.

della Porta, D. (2005) 'The social bases of the global justice movement: some theoretical reflections and empirical evidence from the first European social forum'. Civil Society and Social Movements Programme Paper 21. Geneva: United Nations Research Institute for Social Development (UNRISD).

Deller, S., A. Hoyt, H. Brent and R. Sundaram-Stukel (2009) *Research on the Economic Impact of Cooperatives.* Madison WI: University of Wisconsin Center for Cooperatives.

DeMartino, G. (2003) 'Realizing class justice'. *Rethinking Marxism* 15(1): 1–32.

Democrazia Km Zero (2012) 'La repubblica dei beni comuni'. www.democraziakmzero.org/files/2012/07/Democrazia-Km-Zero-La-Repubblica-dei-beni-comuni.pdf (accessed 6 September 2012).

Deng, H., J. Huang, Z. Xu and S. Rozelle (2010) 'Policy support and emerging farmer professional cooperatives in rural China'. *China Economic Review* 21(4): 495–507.

Denis, J. L., A. Langley and L. Rouleau (2007) 'Strategizing in pluralistic contexts: rethinking theoretical frames'. *Human Relations* 60(1): 179–215.

Devaux, A., D. Horton, C. Velasco, G. Thiele, G. López, T. Bernet, I. Reinoso and M. Ordinola (2009) 'Collective action for market chain innovation in the Andes'. *Food Policy* 34(1): 31–8.

Devereux, S. and R. Sabates-Wheeler (2008) 'Transformative social protection: the currency of social justice'. In A. Barrientos and D. Hulme (eds) *Social Protection for the Poor and the Poorest: Concepts, policies and politics.* London: Palgrave Macmillan.

Devika, J. and B. V. Thampi (2011)

'Mobility towards work and politics for women in Kerala State, India: a view from the histories of gender and space'. *Modern Asian Studies* 45(5): 1147–75.

Dewey, J. (1953) *Reconstruction in Philosophy*. Boston MA: Beacon Press.

Dieckmann, R. (2007) 'Microfinance: An emerging investment opportunity. Uniting social investment and financial returns'. Frankfurt: Deutsche Bank Research. www.dbresearch. com/PROD/DBR_INTERNET_EN-PROD/PROD0000000000219174.pdf (accessed 12 April 2013).

Dietz, R. and D. O'Neill (2013) *Enough is Enough*. San Francisco CA: Berrett-Koehler Publishers.

Dinerstein, A. C. (2013) 'The hidden side of SSE: social movements and the appropriation and "translation" of SSE into policy (Latin America)'. Paper presented at the UNRISD conference on the Potential and Limits of Social and Solidarity Economy, Geneva, 6–8 May. www.unrisd.org/sse-draft-dinerstein (accessed 20 November 2013).

Dreze, J. and A. Sen (1995) *India: Economic development and social opportunity*. Delhi: Oxford University Press.

Dubeux, A. M., A. M. Sarria Icaza, A. J. de Siqueira Medeiros, G. Cavalcanti Cunha and M. Paes de Souza (2011) 'Estudio de casos brasileños: la dinámica de relaciones entre los foros de economía solidaria y las políticas públicas para la economía solidaria en Brasil'. Montreal: Chantier de l'Économie Sociale, FIESS 2011. www.reliess.org/centredoc/upload/FIESS_EC_Brasil_Oct.-2011. pdf (accessed 13 February 2014).

EC (2010) 'Communication from the Commission: Europe 2020. A strategy for smart, sustainable and inclusive growth'. Brussels: European Commission (EC). http://eur-lex. europa.eu/LexUriServ/LexUriServ.do ?uri=COM:2010:2020:FIN:EN:PDF.

Eikenberry, A and J. Drapal Kluver (2004) 'The marketization of the nonprofit sector: civil society at risk?'. *Public Administration Review* 64(2): 132–40.

EPRC (2013) *Uganda 2013 Fin Scope III Survey Report Findings: Unlocking barriers to financial inclusion*. Kampala: Economic Policy Research Centre (EPRC).

Estrin, S. (1983) *Self-management: Economic theory and Yugoslav practice*. Cambridge: Cambridge University Press.

ETC Group (2011) *Who Will Control the Green Economy? Corporate concentration in the life industries*. ETC Group Communiqué 107. Ottawa: ETC Group. www.etcgroup.org/sites/ www.etcgroup.org/files/publication/pdf_file/ETC_wwctge_4web_Dec2011. pdf (accessed 12 February 2013).

Etzioni, A. (1988) *The Moral Dimension: Toward a new economics*. New York NY: The Free Press.

EuropeAid (2000) *An Evaluation of PHARE SME Programmes in the Transition Economies of Central and Eastern Europe*. Brussels: Evaluation Unit of the Common Service for External Relations (SCR), European Commission (DG1A). http://ec.europa.eu/europeaid/how/evaluation/evaluation_reports/reports/cards/951508final_en.pdf (accessed 12 December 2013).

Evers, A. and J.-L. Laville (eds) (2004) *The Third Sector in Europe*, Northampton MA and Cheltenham: Edward Elgar.

Farnsworth, K. (2012) *Social versus Corporate Welfare: Competing needs and interests within the welfare state*. London: Palgrave Macmillan.

Federation of Danish Cooperatives and Agricultural Council (1993) *Danish Farmers and Their Cooperatives*.

Copenhagen: Federation of Danish Cooperatives and the Agricultural Council.

Ferguson, J. (2009) 'The uses of neoliberalism'. *Antipode: A Radical Journal of Geography* 41(S1): 166–84.

Filgueira, C. and F. Filgueira (1994) *El largo adiós al país modelo: Políticas sociales y pobreza en Uruguay*. Montevideo: Arca.

Filgueira, F. (2001) 'Between a rock and a hard place: construyendo ciudadanía en América Latina'. In L. Gioscia (ed.) *Ciudadanía en tránsito*. Montevideo: Ediciones de la Banda Oriental and Instituto de Ciencia Política.

—, F. Rodríguez, C. Rafaniello, S. Lijtenstein and P. Alegre (2005) 'Estructura de riesgo y arquitectura de protección social en el Uruguay actual: crónica de un divorcio anunciado'. *Prisma* 21: 7–42.

Fiorillo, A. (2006) *The Effects of Wholesale Lending to SACCOs in Uganda: Final report*. Kampala: Financial Sector Deepening Project (FSDP). www.ruralfinance.org/fileadmin/templates/rflc/documents/ 118493 1557460_effect_wholesale_lending_SACCOs_uganda.pdf (accessed 26 March 2013).

Fischer, E. and M. Qaim (2012) 'Linking smallholders to markets: determinants and impacts of farmer collective action in Kenya'. *World Development* 40(6): 1255–68.

Fischer, K., I. Sissouma and I. Hathie (2006) *L'Union Technique de la Mutualité Malienne*. CGAP Working Group on Microinsurance: Good and Bad Practices, Case Study 23. Washington DC: Consultative Group to Assist the Poor (CGAP).

FLAI (2012) *Primo Rapporto su Agromafie e Caporalato*. Rome: Confederazione Generale Italiana del Lavoro (CGIL) and Federazione Lavoratori Agricoli Italiani (FLAI).

Flannery, M. and P. Shah (2014) 'Kiva responds'. Next Billion blog, 12 February. www.nextbillion.net/blogpost. aspx?blogid=3731.

Fontan, J.-M. and E. Shragge (2000) *Social Economy: International debates and perspectives*. Montreal: Black Rose.

Fonte, M., M. Eboli, O. W. Maietta, B. Pinto and C. Salvioni (2011) 'Il consumo sostenibile nella visione dei Gruppi di Acquisto Solidale di Roma'. *AgriRegioniEuropa* 7(27): 80.

Fonteneau, B. (2013) *Financing Social Protection in Health in Africa: Outline of a research project*. Leuven: HIVA/KU.

— and B. Galland (2006) 'Micro health insurance: the community-based model'. In C. Churchill (ed.) *Protecting the Poor: A microinsurance compendium*. Washington DC and Geneva: Consultative Group to Assist the Poor (CGAP) and International Labour Organization (ILO).

—, M. Kaïlou and A. Koto-Yérima (2005) *Diagnostic du potentiel de développement des systèmes de micro-assurance santé au Niger*. Brussels and Niamey: Coopération Technique Belge and Government of Nigeria.

—, C. Gueye, D. H. Ouattara and A. Koto-Yérima (2004) *Les défis des systèmes de micro-assurance en Afrique de l'Ouest: Cadre politique, environnement institutionnel, fonctionnement et viabilité*. Brussels: VLIR-DGIS.

—, N. Neamtan, F. Wanyama, L. Peirera Morais and M. De Poorter (2010) *Social and Solidarity Economy: Building a common understanding*. Turin: International Training Centre of the International Labour Organization (ILO).

—, N. Neamtan, F. Wanyama, L. Pereira Morais, M. de Poorter and C. Borzaga (2011) *Social and Solidarity Economy: Our Common Road Towards Decent*

Work. In support of the second edition of the Social and Solidarity Economy Academy, 24–28 October 2011, Montréal, Canada. Turin: International Training Centre of the International Labour Organization (ILO).

Forno, F. (2011) La Spesa a Pizzo Zero: Consumo critico e agricoltura libera, le nuove frontiere della lotta alla mafia. Milan: Altreconomia.

— (2013) 'Cooperative movement'. In D. A. Snow, D. Della Porta, B. Klandermans and D. McAdam (eds) Blackwell Encyclopedia of Social and Political Movements. Oxford: Blackwell.

— and C. Gunnarson (2010) 'Everyday shopping to fight the mafia in Italy'. In M. Micheletti and A. S. McFarland (eds) Creative Participation: Responsibility-taking in the political world. Boulder CO: Paradigm.

—, C. Grasseni and S. Signori (2014) 'Italy's solidarity purchase groups as "citizenship labs"'. In E. Huddart Kennedy, M. J. Cohen and N. Krogman (eds) Putting Sustainability into Practice: Advances and applications of social practice theories. Cheltenham: Edward Elgar.

Foucault, M. (1978) The History of Sexuality. Volume 1: An introduction. London: Allen Lane.

— (2008) The Birth of Biopolitics: Lectures at the Collège de France, 1978–1979. New York NY: Palgrave Macmillan.

Francesconi, G. N. and N. Heerink (2010) 'Ethiopian agricultural cooperatives in an era of global commodity exchange: does organizational form matter?' Journal of African Economies 20(1): 153–77.

Francesconi, G. N. and R. Ruben (2012) 'The hidden impact of cooperative membership on quality management: a case study from the dairy belt of Addis Ababa'. Journal of Entrepreneurial and Organizational Diversity 1(1): 85–103.

Fraser, F. (2005) 'Reframing justice in a globalizing world'. New Left Review 36: 69–88.

Fraser, N. (1990) 'Rethinking the public sphere: a contribution to the critique of actually existing democracy'. Social Text 25/26: 56–80.

— (2012) Can Society be Commodities All the Way Down? Polanyian reflections on capitalist crisis. Paris: Fondation Maison des Sciences de l'Homme.

Fridell, G. (2007) Fair Trade: The prospects and pitfalls of market-driven social justice. Toronto: University of Toronto Press.

Friedman, M. and R. Friedman (1980) Free to Choose. Orlando FL: Harcourt Inc.

Friedmann, J. (1992) Empowerment: The politics of alternative development. Cambridge MA: Blackwell.

Froelich, K. (1999) 'Diversification of revenue strategies: evolving resource dependence in nonprofit organizations'. Nonprofit and Voluntary Sector Quarterly 28(3): 246–68.

Fung, A. and E. O. Wright (2003) Deepening Democracy: Institutional innovations in empowered participatory governance. London: Verso.

Gaiger, L. I. (2007) 'A economia solidária no Brasil: refletindo sobre os dados do primeiro mapeamento nacional'. Presented at the second Seminario Nacional do Nucleo de Pesquisa sobre Movimentos Sociais, Universidad Federal de Santa Catarina, April.

Galak, J., D. Small and A. T. Stephen (2011) 'Microfinance decision making: a field study of prosocial lending'. American Marketing Association 48: 8130–7.

Galema, R. J. (2011) 'Microfinance as a socially responsible investment'. PhD thesis, University of Groningen, the Netherlands.

Genet, K. and T. Anullo (2010)

'Agricultural cooperatives and rural livelihoods: evidence from Ethiopia'. *Annals of Public and Cooperative Economics* 83(2): 181–98.

Gerstenfeld, P. and A. Fuentes (2005) *Caracterización del Tercer Sector en las políticas de formación de capital humano en Uruguay.* Estudios y Perspectivas. Montevideo: Economic Commission for Latin America and the Caribbean.

Ghosh, A. (2011) 'Embeddedness and the dynamics of strategy processes: the case of AMUL cooperative, India'. PhD thesis, McGill University.

— and F. Westley (2005) *Amul: India's cooperative success story.* Hawaii: Academy of Management.

Giagnocavo, C., L. Fernandez-Revuelta Perez and D. U. Aguilera (2012) 'The case for proactive cooperative banks and local development: innovation, growth, and community building in Almería, Spain'. In S. Goglio and Y. Alexopoulos (eds) *Financial Cooperatives and Local Development.* London: Routledge.

Gibson-Graham, J. K. (2003) 'Enabling ethical economies: co-operativism and class'. *Critical Sociology* 29(2): 1–3.9.

— (2006) *A Postcapitalist Politics.* Minneapolis MN: University of Minnesota Press.

— (2008) 'Diverse economies: performative practices for "other worlds"'. *Progress in Human Geography* 32(5): 613–32.

— and G. Roelvink (2011) 'The nitty gritty of creating alternative economies'. *Social Alternatives* 30(1): 29–33.

—, J. Cameron and S. Healy (2013) *Take Back the Economy: An ethical guide to transforming our communities.* Minneapolis MN: University of Minnesota Press.

Gilbert, A. (2006) 'Good urban governance: evidence from a model city?'

Bulletin of Latin American Research 25(3): 392–419.

Gitter, S., J. Weber, B. Barham, M. Callenes and J. L. Valentine (2012) 'Fair Trade-organic coffee cooperatives, migration, and secondary schooling in southern Mexico'. *Journal of Development Studies* 48(3): 445–63.

GOI (2011) *Employment and Unemployment Situation in India 2009–10: National sample survey 66th round.* NSS Report 537(66/10/1). New Delhi: Government of India (GOI), Ministry of Statistics and Programme Implementation.

— (2012) *MGNREGA Sameeksha: An anthology of research studies.* New Delhi: Government of India (GOI), Ministry of Rural Development. www.indiawaterportal.org/sites/indiawaterportal.org/files/mgnrega_sameeksha.pdf.

Goïta, M. and M. Koumare (2011) 'Etude de cas maliens: emploi et travail, sécurité et souveraineté alimentaire et économie sociale et solidaire'. Montreal: Chantier de l'Économie Sociale, FIESS 2011. www.reliess.org/centredoc/upload/FIESS_EC_Mali_Oct.-2011.pdf (accessed 13 February 2014).

Gómez, G. M. (2009) *Argentina's Parallel Currency: The economy of the poor.* London: Pickering & Chatto.

— (2010) 'What was the deal for the participants of the Argentine local currency systems, the Redes de Trueque?' *Environment and Planning A* 42(7): 1669–85.

Goodman, D., M. DuPuis and M. Goodman (2012) *Alternative Food Networks: Knowledge, practice, and politics.* New York NY: Routledge.

Government of Canada (2009) *Collaboration on Policy: A manual developed by the Community-Government Collaboration on Policy.* Ottawa: Social Development Partnerships Program,

Government of Canada and Caledon Institute of Public Policy.

Government of the Italian Republic (2007) 'Disposizioni per la formazione del bilancio annuale e pluriennale dello Stato'. Law no. 244 of 24 December 2007, article 1, paragraphs 266–8. *Gazzetta Ufficiale* 300, 28 December 2007, Suppl. Ordinario no. 285. www.normattiva.it/uri-res/N2Ls?urn:nir:stato:legge:2007-12-24;244!vig.

Government of Uruguay (2005–10) *Annual Reports*. Montevideo: Ministerio de Desarrollo Social (MIDES) and Instituto del Niño y Adolescente del Uruguay (INAU). www.mides.gub.uy/innovaportal/v/4312/3/innova.front/memorias_anuales (accessed 6 June 2014).

Graham, J. and J. Amariglio (2006) 'Subjects of economy: introduction'. *Rethinking Marxism: A Journal of Economics, Culture and Society* 18(2): 199–204.

Grameen Foundation (2010) 'Financing microfinance'. Microfinance Africa website, 13 July. http://microfinanceafrica.net/news/financing-microfinance/ (accessed 16 December 2014).

Gramsci, A. (1971) *Selections from the Prison Notebooks*. London: Lawrence and Wishart.

Granovetter, M. (1985) 'Economic action and social structure: the problem of embeddedness'. *American Journal of Sociology* 91(3): 481–510.

— (1992) 'Economic institutions as social constructions: a framework for analysis'. *Acta Sociologica* 35: 3–11.

Grasseni, C. (2013) *Beyond Alternative Food Networks: Italy's solidarity purchase groups*. London: Bloomsbury.

— (2014) 'Seeds of trust: alternative food networks in Italy'. *Journal of Political Ecology* 21: 178–92. http://jpe.library.arizona.edu/volume_21/Grasseni.pdf.

Green, D. (1997) *Silent Revolution: The rise of market economics in Latin America*. New York NY: Monthly Review Press.

— (2012) *From Poverty to Power: How active citizens and effective states can change the world*, 2nd edition. Oxford and Rugby: Oxfam International and Practical Action Publishing.

Gronbjerg, K. A. (1993) *Understanding Nonprofit Funding*. San Francisco CA: Jossey-Bass.

Gudeman, S. (2012) *Economy's Tension: The dialectics of community and market*. Oxford: Berghahn Books.

Gutberlet, J. (2009) 'Solidarity economy and recycling co-ops in São Paulo: micro-credit to alleviate poverty'. *Development in Practice* 19(6): 737–51.

Habermas, J. (1984) *The Theory of Communicative Action. Volume I: Reason and the rationalization of society*. Boston MA: Beacon Press.

— (1987) *The Theory of Communicative Action. Volume II: Lifeworld and system: a critique of functionalist reason*. Boston MA: Beacon Press.

Hamel, G. and C. K. Prahalad (1989) 'Strategic intent'. *Harvard Business Review* 67(3): 63–76.

Harrison, B. (2011) 'Kiva: an analysis of microfinance, NGOs and development discourse'. Master's thesis, Carleton University, Ottawa.

Hart, K., J.-L. Laville and A. D. Cattani (2010) *The Human Economy*. Cambridge: Polity Press.

Hartley, S. E. (2010) 'Crowd-sourced microfinance and cooperation in group lending'. Kiva Working Paper, March. Kiva.org. http://dash.harvard.edu/bitstream/handle/1/3757699/Hartley_Kiva_DASH.pdf?sequence=2 (accessed 16 December 2014).

Harvey, D. (2010) *The Enigma of Capital and the Crises of Capitalism*. London: Profile Books.

Hazell, P., C. Poulton, S. Wiggins and

A. Dorward (2010) 'The future of small farms: trajectories and policy priorities'. *World Development* 38(10): 1349–61.

Healy, S. (2008) 'Caring for ethics and the politics of health care reform'. *Gender, Place and Culture* 15(3): 267–84.

Healy, S. and B. Shear (2011) 'Occupy Wall Street: a gift for the economy'. *Truthout*, 27 October.

Helper, S. (1990) 'Comparative supplier relations in the US and Japanese auto industries: an exit-voice approach'. *Business Economic History* 19: 153–62.

Heredia, R. (1997) *The Amul India Story*. New Delhi: Tata McGraw Hill.

Hernandez-Espallardo, M., N. Arcas-Lario and G. Marcos-Matas (2013) 'Farmers' satisfaction and intention to continue membership in agricultural marketing cooperatives: neoclassical versus transaction cost considerations'. *European Review of Agricultural Economics* 40(2): 239–60.

Heyer, J., F. Stewart and R. Thorp (2002) *Group Behaviour and Development: Is the market destroying cooperation?* UNU-WIDER Studies in Development Economics. Oxford: Oxford University Press.

Hickey, S. (2008) 'Conceptualising the politics of social protection in Africa'. In A. Barrientos and D. Hulme (eds) *Social Protection for the Poor and the Poorest: Concepts, policies and politics*. London: Palgrave Macmillan.

Hillenkamp, I. and J.-L. Laville (eds) (2013) *Socioéconomie et Démocratie: L'actualité de Karl Polanyi*. Toulouse: Erès.

Hillenkamp, I., F. Lapeyre and A. Lemaître (2013) *Securing Livelihoods: Informal economy practices and institutions*. Oxford: Oxford University Press.

Hillenkamp, I., I. Guérin and C. Ver-schuur (2014) 'Economie solidaire et théories féministes: pistes pour une convergence nécessaire'. *Review of Solidarity Economy/Revue d'économie solidaire* 7.

Hinkelammert, F. J. and H. Mora Jiménez (2009) 'Por una economía orientada hacia la reproducción de la vida'. *Iconos: Revista de Ciencias Sociales* 33(January): 39–49.

Hinrichs, C. and T. Lyson (2009) *Remaking the North American Food System: Strategies for sustainability*. Lincoln NE: University of Nebraska Press.

Hintze, S. (2001) 'Las políticas para la economía social y solidaria en América Latina: sostenibilidad y protección del trabajo asociativo y autogestionario'. PhD thesis, Universidad Autónoma de Barcelona.

— (2003) *Trueque y Economía Solidaria*. Los Polvorines, Argentina: Instituto del Conurbano (ICO), Universidad Nacional de General Sarmiento.

— (2011) *La política es un arma cargada de future: La economía social y solidaria en Brasil y Venezuela*. Buenos Aires: CLACSO/CICCUS.

Hobsbawm, E. J. (1962) *The Age of Revolution*. London: Weidenfeld and Nicolson.

Hochschild, A. R. and B. Ehrenreich (eds) (2003) *Global Woman*. New York NY: Henry Holt.

Hodgson, G. (2006) 'What are institutions?' *Journal of Economic Issues* 40(1): 1–25.

Hollingsworth, J. R. and R. Robert (eds) (1997) *Contemporary Capitalism*. Cambridge: Cambridge University Press.

Holloway, G., N. Nicholson, C. Delgado, S. Staal and S. Ehui (2000) 'Agroindustrialization through institutional innovation: transaction costs, cooperatives and milk-market development in the east-African highlands'. *Agricultural Economics* 23(3): 279–88.

Hope, A. and J. Agyeman (2011) *Cultivating Food Justice: Race, class, and sustainability*. Cambridge MA: MIT Press.

Horvat, B. (1982) *The Political Economy of Socialism*. New York NY: M.E. Sharpe.

Hoyt, A. (1989) 'Cooperatives in other countries'. In D. Cobia (ed.) *Cooperatives in Agriculture*. Englewood Cliffs NJ: Prentice-Hall.

Hutchens, A. (2009) *Changing Big Business: The globalization of the fair trade movement*. Cheltenham: Edward Elgar.

Hutton, W. (chair) (2012) *Plurality, Stewardship and Engagement: The report of the Ownership Commission, March 2012*. Borehamwood: Mutuo.

IFAD (2013) *Republic of Uganda: Project for financial inclusion in rural areas*. Rome: International Fund for Agricultural Development (IFAD). www.ifad.org/operations/projects/design/109/uganda.pdf (accessed 30 October 2013).

ILO (2010) *Women in Labour Markets*. Geneva: International Labour Organization (ILO).

— (2011) *Towards a Greener Economy: The social dimensions*. Geneva: International Labour Organization (ILO).

— (2013a) *The Informal Economy and Decent Work: A policy resource guide, supporting transitions to formality*. Geneva: International Labour Organization (ILO).

— (2013b) *Global Employment Trends 2013: Recovering from a second jobs dip*. Geneva: International Labour Organization (ILO).

— and ICA (2014) *Cooperatives and the Sustainable Development Goals: A contribution to the post-2015 development debate brief*. Geneva and Brussels: International Labour Organization (ILO) and International Co-operative Alliance (ICA). www.ilo.org/wcmsp5/groups/public/---ed_emp/documents/publication/wcms_240640.pdf (accessed 2 May 2014).

IPCC (2013) *Climate Change 2013: The physical science basis. Working Group I contribution to the Fifth Assessment Report of the Intergovernmental Panel on Climate Change*. New York NY: Cambridge University Press.

Isaac, T. M. and P. Heller (2003) 'Democracy and development: decentralized planning in Kerala'. In A. Fung and E. O. Wright (eds) *Deepening Democracy: Institutional innovations in empowered participatory governance*. London: Verso, pp. 77–110.

Isaac, T. M. T., R. W. Franke and P. Raghavan (1998) *Democracy at Work in an Indian Industrial Cooperative*. Ithaca NY: Cornell University Press.

ISSA (2008) *Dynamic Social Security for Africa: An agenda for development*. Geneva: International Social Security Association (ISSA).

Jackson, T. (2009) *Prosperity without Growth: Economics for a finite planet*. London and New York NY: Earthscan and Routledge.

Jaffee, D. (2010) 'Fair Trade standards, corporate participation, and social movement responses in the United States'. *Journal of Business Ethics* 92(2): 267–85.

Jameel, J. (2000) 'Microfinance and the mechanics of solidarity lending: improving access to credit through innovations in contract structure'. *Journal of Transnational Law & Policy* 9(1): 183–208.

James, E. (1987) 'The nonprofit sector in comparative perspective'. In W. Powell (ed.) *The Nonprofit Sector: A research handbook*. New Haven CT: Yale University Press.

Jayasooria, D. (ed.) (2013) *Developments in Solidarity Economy in Asia*. Selangor, Malaysia: JJ Resources for Centre for Social Entrepreneurship, Binary University.

Jeantet, T. and J.-P. Poulnot (eds) *L'économie sociale, une alternative planétaire: Mondialiser au profit de tous*. Paris: Charles Léopold Mayer.

Jeffrey, R. (1987) 'Culture and governments: how women made Kerala literate'. *Pacific Affairs* 60(4): 447–72.

— (2004–05) 'Legacies of matriliny: the place of women and the "Kerala model"'. *Pacific Affairs* 77(4): 647–64.

Johnson, A. G. and W. F. Whyte (1977) 'The Mondragon system of worker production cooperatives'. *Industrial and Labor Relations Review* 31(1): 18–30.

Kabuga, C. and J. W. Kitandwe (1995) 'Historical background of the cooperative movement'. In C. Kabuga and P. Batarinyebwa (eds) *Cooperatives: Past, present and future*. Kampala: Uganda Cooperative Alliance.

Kadiyala, S. (2004) 'Scaling up *Kudumbashree*: collective action for poverty alleviation and women's empowerment'. Food Consumption and Nutrition Division (FCND) Discussion Paper 180. Washington DC: International Food Policy Research Institute.

Kanter, R. M. (1977) 'Numbers: minorities and majorities'. In R. M. Kanter (ed.) *Men and Women of the Corporation*. New York NY: Basic Books, pp. 206–44.

Karim, L. (2011) *Microfinance and Its Discontents: Women in debt in Bangladesh*. Minneapolis MN: University of Minnesota Press.

Kawano, E. (2013) 'Social solidarity economy: toward convergence across continental divides'. United Nations Research Institute for Social Development (UNRISD) Think Piece. www.unrisd.org/thinkpiece-kawano (accessed 20 November 2013).

Kearns, K. (2003) 'The effects of government funding on management practices in faith-based organ-izations: propositions for future research'. *Public Administration and Management: An Interactive Journal* 8(3): 116–34.

Kelly, M. (2012) *Owning Our Future: The emerging ownership revolution. Journeys to a generative economy*. San Francisco CA: Koehler Publishers.

Kersting, S. and M. Wollni (2012) 'New institutional arrangements and standard adoption: evidence from small-scale fruit and vegetable farmers in Thailand'. *Food Policy* 37(4): 452–62.

Kettl, D. (2006) 'Managing boundaries in American administration: the collaborative imperative'. *Public Administration Review* 66: 10–19. Special issue on Collaborative Public Management.

King, R., M. Adler and M. Grieves (2013) 'Cooperatives as sustainable livelihood strategies in rural Mexico'. *Bulletin of Latin American Research* 32(2): 163–77.

Kiva.org. (2013) 'About us'. Kiva website. www.kiva.org/about (accessed 17 December 2013).

— (n.d.) 'Lending teams: connect with Kiva's lender community'. Kiva website. www.kiva.org/teams?category=Other (accessed 5 December 2013).

Knapp, M., E. Robertson and C. Thomason (1990) 'Public money, voluntary action'. In H. K. Anheier and W. Seibel (eds) *The Third Sector: Comparative studies of nonprofit organizations*. Berlin: De Gruyter.

Kramer, R. (1981) *Voluntary Agencies in the Welfare State*. Berkeley CA: University of California Press.

— (1994) 'Voluntary agencies and the contract culture: dream or nightmare?' *Social Service Review* 68(1): 33–60.

— and B. Grossman (1987) 'Contracting for social services: process management and resource dependencies'. *Social Service Review* 61(1): 32–55.

Krishna, A., N. Uphoff and M. Esman (1997) *Reasons for Hope: Instructive experiences in rural development.* West Hartford CT: Kumarian Press.

Kropotkin, P. (1972) *Mutual Aid: A factor in evolution.* New York NY: New York University Press.

Kunwar, R. M., R. P. Acharya, G. Khadka, B. H. Poudyal, S. Shahi, S. Dhakal, S. Pariyar and B. Bhattarai (2013) 'Public policy for social and solidarity economy: a case study from Nepal'. Kathmandu: Practical Solution Consultancy Nepal. www.reliess.org/centredoc/upload/SSEreport-Final.pdf (accessed 13 February 2014).

Kurien, V. (2005) *I Too Had a Dream.* New Delhi: Roli Books.

Kydd, J. and A. Dorward (2004) 'Implications of markets and coordination failures for rural development in least developed countries'. *Journal of International Development* 16(7): 951–70.

La Concertation (2004) *Inventaires des Mutuelles de Santé en Afrique de l'Ouest.* Dakar: La Concertation.

— (2007) *Inventaires des Mutuelles de Santé dans 11 Pays d'Afrique de l'Ouest et Centrale.* Dakar: La Concertation.

Laclau, E. and C. Mouffe (1985) *Hegemony and Socialist Strategy: Towards a radical democratic politics*, 2nd edition. London: Verso.

Lahaye, E., R. Rizvanolli and E. Dashi (2012) 'Current trends in cross-border funding for microfinance'. CGAP Brief. Washington DC: Consultative Group to Assist the Poor (CGAP). www.cgap.org/sites/default/files/Brief-Current-Trends-in-Cross-Border-Funding-for-Microfinance-Nov-2012.pdf (accessed 25 March 2013).

Lakshmanan, P. (2006) 'Participatory planning process in Kerala'. In

P. P. Balan and M. Retna Raj (eds) *Decentralised Governance and Poverty Reduction: Lessons from Kerala.* Thrissur, Kerala: Kerala Institute of Local Administration, pp. 120–9.

Lalvani, M. (2008) 'Sugar cooperatives in Maharashtra: a political economy perspective'. *Journal of Development Studies* 44(10): 1474–505.

Lampe, J. (1979) 'Modernization and social structure: the case of the pre-1914 Balkan capitals'. *Southeastern Europe/L'Europe du Sud-Est* 5(2): 11–32.

Lander, E. (2007) 'El estado y las tensiones de la participación popular en Venezuela'. *Consejo Latinoamericano de Ciencias Sociales/OSAL (Observatorio Social de América Latina)* VII(22): 65–86.

Larson, A. (1992) 'Network dyads in entrepreneurial settings: a study of governance of exchange processes'. *Administrative Science Quarterly* 37: 76–104.

Laville, J.-L. and M. Nyssens (2000) 'Solidarity-based third sector organizations in the "proximity services" field: a European Francophone perspective'. *Voluntas: International Journal of Voluntary and Nonprofit Organizations* 11(1): 67–84.

Laville, J.-L. and R. Sainsaulieu (2013) *L'Association: Sociologie et économie.* Paris: Fayard-Pluriel.

Laville, J.-L., B. Levesque and M. Mendell (2007) 'The social economy: diverse approaches and practices in Europe and Canada'. In A. Noya (ed.) *Social Economy: Building inclusive economies.* Paris: Organisation for Economic Co-operation and Development (OECD), pp. 155–89.

Lee, E.-A. and Y.-S. Kim (2013) 'Social economy and public policy development: a South Korean case'. Montreal: RELIESS. www.reliess.org/centredoc/upload/Social

Economy_KoreanCaseStudy_Final Revision_201309_.pdf (accessed 13 February 2014).

Lemus, B. and D. Barkin (2013) 'Rethinking the social and solidarity economy in light of community practice'. Paper presented at the UNRISD conference on the Potential and Limits of Social and Solidarity Economy, Geneva, 6–8 May. www.unrisd.org/sse-draft-lemus-barkin (accessed 20 November 2013).

Levi, Y. and P. Davis (2008) 'Cooperatives as the "enfants terribles" of economics: some implications for the social economy'. *Journal of Socio-Economics* 37(6): 2178–88.

Lévi-Strauss, C. (1966) *The Savage Mind*. Chicago IL: University of Chicago Press.

Levin, H. M. (2006) 'Worker democracy and worker productivity'. *Social Justice Research* 19(1): 109–21.

Lewis, M. and P. Conaty (2012) *The Resilience Imperative: Cooperative transitions to a steady-state economy*. Gabriola Island, Canada: New Society Publishers.

Liebman, M. (1985) *Leninism under Lenin*. London: Merlin Press.

Lionais, D. and H. Johnstone (2009) 'Building the social economy using the innovative potential of place'. In J. J. McMurtry (ed.) *Living Economics: Canadian perspectives on the social economy, cooperatives and community economic development*. Toronto: Emond Montgomery.

Lipietz, A. (2001) *Pour le tiers secteur*. Paris: La Découverte-La Documentation Française.

Logue, J. (2005) *Economics, Cooperation, and Employee Ownership: The Emilia-Romagna model – in more detail*. Cleveland OH: Ohio Employee Ownership Centre.

Lorek, S. and J. Backhaus (eds) (2012) *Sustainable Consumption During Times of Crisis. SCORAI Europe workshop proceedings: First trans-Atlantic SCORAI workshop, May 1*. Sustainable Consumption Transition Series, Issue 1. Bregenz, Austria: Sustainable Consumption Research and Action Initiative (SCORAI).

Lovas, B. and S. Ghoshal (2000) 'Strategy as guided evolution'. *Strategic Management Journal* 21(9): 875–96.

Loxley, J. (2007) *Transforming or Reforming Capitalism: Towards a theory of CED*. Toronto: Fernwood Press.

Luhman, N. (1996) *Confianza*. Barcelona and México: Anthropos and Universidad Iberoamericana.

MAAIF (2010) *Agricultural Sector Development Strategy and Investment Plan: 2010/11–2014/15*. Kampala: Ministry of Agriculture, Animal Industry and Fisheries (MAAIF).

Mair, J. and I. Marti (2009) 'Entrepreneurship in and around institutional voids: a case study from Bangladesh'. *Journal of Business Venturing* 24(5): 419–35.

Makelova, H., R. Meinzen-Dick, J. Hellin and S. Dohrn (2009) 'Collective action for smallholder market access'. *Food Policy* 34(1): 1–7.

Malkin, E. (2008) 'Microfinance's success sets off a debate in Mexico'. *New York Times*, 5 April. www.nytimes.com/2008/04/05/business/worldbusiness/05micro.html?pagewanted=all&_r=0.

Mansbridge, J. (1990) 'Feminism and democracy'. *American Prospect* 1 (Spring).

Maroni, L. and D. Ponzini (2013) 'Il patto degli 11 grani: una filiera del grano nel Parco Agricolo Sud Milano'. In Tavolo per la Rete Italiana di Economia Solidale (ed.) *Un'Economia Nuova: Dai GAS alla zeta*. Milan: Altreconomia, pp. 67–70.

Mathauer, I. (2004) 'Institutional analysis toolkit for safety net interventions'. World Bank Social Protection Discussion Paper 0418. Washington DC: World Bank.

Mathew, G. (1995) 'The paradox of Kerala women's social development and social leadership'. *India International Centre Quarterly* 22(2/3): 203–14.

Mauss, M. (1954) *The Gift*. London: Cohen and West.

May, C. (2008) *PGS Guidelines: How participatory guarantee systems can develop and function*. Bonn: International Federation of Organic Agriculture Movements (IFOAM). www.ifoam.org/sites/default/files/page/files/pgs_guidelines_en_web.pdf.

Mazzucato, M. (2013) *The Entrepreneurial State: De-bunking public vs. private sector myths*. London: Anthem Press.

McGranahan, D. (1975) 'Preface'. In UNRISD, *Rural Co-operatives as Agents of Change: A research report and a debate*. Geneva: United Nations Research Institute for Social Development (UNRISD).

McMurtry, J. J. (2004) 'Social economy as political practice'. *International Journal of Social Economics* 31(9): 868–78.

— (2009) 'Ethical value added: fair trade and the case of Café Femenino'. *Journal of Business Ethics* 86(1): 27–49.

— (2010) *Living Economics: Canadian perspectives on the social economy, cooperatives and community economic development*. Toronto: Emond Montgomery Publishers.

Meadows, D., J. Randers and D. Meadows (2004) *The Limits to Growth: The 30-year update*. White River Junction VT: Chelsea Green Publishing.

Meehan, J. (2004) *Tapping the Financial Markets for Microfinance: Grameen Foundation USA's promotion of this emerging trend*. Washington DC: Grameen Foundation USA.

Menard, C. K. (2007) 'Cooperatives: hierarchies or hybrids?' In K. Karan-tininis and J. Nilsson (eds) *Vertical Markets and Cooperative Hierarchies*. Dordrecht: Springer.

Mendell, M. and N. Neamtan (2010) 'The social economy in Quebec: towards a new political economy'. In L. Mook, J. Quarter and S. Ryan (eds) *Why the Social Economy Matters*. Toronto: University of Toronto Press.

Mendell, M., B. Enjolras and A. Noya (2010) *L'Économie Sociale au Service de l'Inclusion au Niveau Local: Rapport sur deux régions de France: Alsace et Provence-Alpes-Côte d'Azur*. OECD Local Economic and Employment Development (LEED) Working Papers 2010/14. Paris: Organisation for Economic Co-operation and Development (OECD). http://dx.doi.org/10.1787/5kgonvhxwgbp-en (accessed 13 February 2014).

Mendell, M., R. Spear, A. Noya and E. Clarence (2010) *Improving Social Inclusion at the Local Level Through the Social Economy: Report for Korea*. OECD Local Economic and Employment Development (LEED) Working Papers 2010/15. Paris: Organisation for Economic Co-operation and Development (OECD). http://dx.doi.org/10.1787/5kgonvg4bl38-en (accessed 13 February 2014).

Mendell, M., V. Pestoff, A. Noya and E. Clarence (2009) *Improving Social Inclusion at the Local Level Through the Social Economy: Report for Poland*. OECD Local Economic and Employment Development (LEED) Working Papers 2009/01. Paris: Organisation for Economic Co-operation and Development (OECD). http://dx.doi.org/10.1787/5kgonvgopnnt-en (accessed 13 February 2014).

Micheletti, M. and D. Stolle (2012) 'Sustainable citizenship and the new politics of consumption'. *Annals of the American Academy of Political and Social Science* 644(1): 88–120.

Michielsen, J., H. Meulemans, W. Soors, P. Ndiaye, N. Devadasan, T. De Herdt, G. Verbist and B. Criel (2010) 'Social protection in health: the need for a transformative dimension'. *Tropical Medicine and International Health* 15(6): 654–8.

MicroRate (2009) *State of Microfinance Investment: The 2009 survey*. Arlington VA: MicroRate. www.microrate.com/media/downloads/2012/04/The-State-of-Microfinance-Investment-09-Summary-Paper.pdf (accessed 5 December 2013).

— (2012) *The State of Microfinance Investment 2012: MicroRate's 7th annual survey and analysis of MIVs*. Arlington VA: MicroRate and Luminus. http://microrate.com/media/2012/10/MicroRate-The-State-of-Microfinance-Investment-2012.pdf (accessed 5 December 2013).

Midaglia, C. (2000) *Alternativas de protección a la infancia carenciada: La peculiar convivencia de lo público y privado en el Uruguay*. Buenos Aires: Consejo Latinoamericano de Ciencias Sociales (CLACSO).

—, F. Antía and C. Castillo (2009) *Repertorio de Programas Sociales: La protección social a la infancia y la adolescencia*. Montevideo: MIDES-Observatorio Social.

—, M. Castillo and F. Antía (2006) 'Las tercerizaciones de las prestaciones sociales: un debate político inconcluso'. Unpublished report.

Ming-yee, H. (2007) 'The International Funding of Microfinance Institutions: An overview'. Paper commissioned by LuxFlag. www.microfinancegateway.org/sites/default/files/mfg-en-paper-the-international-funding-of-microfinance-institutions-an-overview-nov-2007_0.pdf (accessed 16 December 2014).

Mintzberg, H. and J. A. Waters (1985) 'Of strategies, deliberate and emergent'. *Strategic Management Journal* 6(3): 257–72.

Molyneux, M. (2006) 'Mothers in the service of the new poverty agenda: progresa/opportunidades'. *Social Policy Administration* 40(4): 49–70.

Mook, L., J. Quarter and S. Ryan (eds) (2010) *Researching the Social Economy*. Toronto: University of Toronto Press.

Morais, L. P. (2014) 'Estrategias de supervivencia y elaboración de políticas públicas: El papel de la economía social y solidaria en Latinoamérica y la contribución de Brasil hacia la construcción de políticas emancipadoras'. Occasional Paper 4. Geneva: United Nations Research Institute for Social Development (UNRISD).

Morás, L. E. (2001) 'Desafíos de la articulación público-privado en la gestión de programas sociales: síntesis sobre aspectos controversiales en la relación público-privado'. Technical report for the Fifth Forum on State–NGO Collaboration for the Design and Implementation of Social Policies, 'Mañanas complejas' Cycle.

Morrow, O. and K. Dombroski (forthcoming) 'Enacting a post-capitalist politics through the sites and practices of life's work'. In K. Strauss and K. Meehan (eds) *Precarious Worlds: New geographies of social reproduction*. Athens GA: University of Georgia Press.

Mouffe, C. (2005) *On the Political*. Abingdon and New York NY: Routledge.

Moulaert, F. and J. Nussbaumer (2005) 'Defining the social economy and its governance at the neighbourhood level: a methodological reflection'. *Urban Studies* 42(11): 2071–88.

Moulaert, F. and O. Ailenei (2005) 'Social economy, third sector and solidarity relations: a conceptual synthesis from history to present'. *Urban Studies* 42(11): 2037–53.

MSC (2013) *The Rural Income and Employment Enhancement Project (RIEEP)*. Kampala: Microfinance Support Centre (MSC). www.msc.co.ug/index.php/projects/rieep (accessed 30 October 2013).

Msemakweli, L. (2009) 'Co-operative marketing reforms in Uganda'. Kampala: Uganda Cooperative Alliance (UCA). www.uca.co.ug/publications/marketingreforms.pdf (accessed 26 March 2013).

MTIC (2011) *National Cooperative Policy*. Kampala: Ministry of Trade, Industry and Cooperatives (MTIC).

— (2012) 'Ministerial policy statement: MTIC. Presented to the Parliament of the Republic of Uganda for the debate on the budget estimates for the financial year 2012/13'. Kampala: Ministry of Trade, Industry and Cooperatives (MTIC).

MTTI (2011) 'Ministerial policy statement: MTTI. Presented to the Parliament of the Republic of Uganda for the debate on the budget estimates for the financial year 2010/11'. Kampala: Ministry of Tourism, Trade and Industry (MTTI).

Mujawamariya, G., M. D'Haese and S. Speelman (2013) 'Exploring double side-selling in cooperatives: case study of four coffee cooperatives in Rwanda'. *Food Policy* 39: 72–83.

Mukherjee-Reed, A. (2008) *Human Development and Social Power*. London and New York NY: Routledge.

Muraleedharan, S. (2012) 'Women, work and a winning combination'. *The Hindu*, 14 November. www.thehindu.com/todays-paper/tp-opinion/women-work-and-a-winning-combination/article4094352.ece.

Murray, R., J. Caulier-Grice and G. Mulgan (2010) *The Open Book of Social Innovation*. London: The Young Foundation. www.nesta.org.uk/sites/default/files/the_open_book_of_social_innovation.pdf (accessed 16 May 2014).

Nair, A. (2005) 'Sustainability of microfinance self-help groups in India: would federating help?' World Bank Policy Research Working Paper 3516. Washington DC: World Bank.

Nannyonjo, J. (2013) 'Enabling agricultural cooperatives through public policy and the state: the case of Uganda'. Draft paper prepared for the UNRISD Conference 'Potential and Limits of Social and Solidarity Economy', 6–8 May, Geneva. www.unrisd.org/80256B42004CCC77/%28httpInfoFiles%29/FA3911B9091BF39BC1257B7200356723/$file/Justine%20Nannyonjo.pdf.

Ndiaye, A., M. Ba, R. Ndao and N. Dangoura (2013) *L'exclusion sociale et les initiatives de gratuité des soins de santé au Sénégal: exemple de la prise en charge des personnes âgées par le Plan Sésame*. Dakar: Centre de Recherche sur les Politiques Sociales (CREPOS) and Health Inc.

Neamtan, N. (2009) 'Social economy: concepts and challenges'. *Universitas Forum* 1(3).

Nidheesh, K. B. (2008) 'Rural women's empowerment is the best strategy for poverty eradication in rural areas'. *International Journal of Rural Studies* 15: 1–3.

Nike Inc. (2009) *Corporate Responsibility Report 2007–2009*. www.nikebiz.com/crreport/content/pdf/documents/en-US/full-report.pdf (accessed February 2014).

Nilsson, J. and G. Hendrikse (2010) 'Gemeinschaft and Gesellschaft in cooperatives'. In J. Windsperger, M. Tuunanen, G. Cliquet and G. Hendrikse (eds) *New Developments in the Theory of Networks: Franchising, cooperatives and alliances*. Vienna: Springer.

Nilsson, J., G. Svendsen and G. T.

Svendsen (2012) 'Are large and complex agricultural cooperatives losing their social capital?' *Agribusiness* 28(2): 187–204.

Niño-Zarazúa, M., A. Barrientos, S. Hickey and D. Hulme (2012) 'Social protection in sub-Saharan Africa: getting the politics right'. *World Development* 40(1): 163–76.

North, D. C. (1989) 'Institutions and economic growth: an historical introduction'. *World Development* 17: 1319–32.

— (1990) *Institutions, Institutional Change and Economic Performance*. Cambridge and New York NY: Cambridge University Press.

North, P. (2005) 'Scaling alternative economic practices? Some lessons from alternative currencies'. *Transactions of the Institute of British Geographers* 30: 221–33.

— (2007) *Money and Liberation: The micropolitics of alternative currency movements*. Minneapolis MN: University of Minnesota Press.

Nowland-Foreman, G. (1998) 'Purchase-of-service contracting, voluntary organizations, and civil society'. *American Behavioral Scientist* 42(1): 108–23.

Obern, C. and S. Jones (1981) 'Critical factors affecting agricultural production cooperatives'. *Annals of Public and Cooperative Economics* 52(3): 317–49.

Ocampo, J. A. (2006) 'Foreword: Some reflections on the links between social knowledge and policy'. In P. Utting (ed.) *Reclaiming Development Agendas: Knowledge, power and international policy making*. Basingstoke: Palgrave Macmillan and UNRISD.

OECD (2010) *SMEs, Entrepreneurship and Innovation: OECD studies on SMEs and entrepreneurship*. Paris: Organisation for Economic Co-operation and Development (OECD) Publishing.

Oikocredit (2012) *Annual Report 2011*. Amersfoort, The Netherlands: Oikocredit. www.oikocredit.coop/k/n171/news/view/8995/8951/annual-report-2011-online.html (accessed December 5, 2013).

— (2013) *Global Movement of Investors*. Amersfoort, The Netherlands: Oikocredit. http://oikocreditusa.org/global-movement-of-investors3 (accessed 14 April 2013).

Ojha, J., H. Sharma, D. R. Khanal, H. Dhungana, B. Pathak, G. Pandey, B. Bhattarai, N. Sharma and B. Pokharel (2007) 'Citizen federation in democratizing forest governance: lessons from Community Forestry Users' Federation of Nepal'. Paper presented at the International Conference on Poverty Reduction and Forests, Regional Community Forestry Training Center and Rights and Resources Initiative, Bangkok, 3–7 September.

Oommen, M. A. (2008) 'Micro finance and poverty alleviation: the case of Kerala's *Kudumbashree*'. Working Paper 17 (April). Kochi, Kerala: Centre for Socio-economic and Environmental Studies (CSES).

Oommen, T. K. (2009) 'Development policy and the nature of society: understanding the Kerala model'. *Economic and Political Weekly* 44(13), 'Global Economic and Financial Crisis', 28 March–3 April, pp. 25, 27–31.

Ortiz-Miranda, D., O. Moreno-Perez and A. Moragues-Faus (2010) 'Innovative strategies of agricultural cooperatives in the framework of the new rural development paradigms: the case of the region of Valencia (Spain)'. *Environment and Planning A* 42(3): 661–77.

Ostrom, E. (1990) *Governing the Commons: The evolution of institutions for collective action. Cambridge: Cambridge University Press.

— (2009) 'Beyond markets and states: polycentric governance of complex economic systems'. Prize lecture, Nobel Prize Foundation. www.nobel prize.org/nobel_prizes/economic-sciences/laureates/2009/ostrom-lecture.html (accessed 13 May 2014).

Pacione, M. (1999) 'The other side of the coin: local currency as a response to the globalization of capital'. *Regional Studies* 33(1): 63–72.

Palacios, M. (1980) *Coffee in Colombia, 1850–1970: An economic and political history*. Cambridge: Cambridge University Press.

PAMAS (2010) *Etat des lieux des mutuelles de santé des régions de Diourbel, Fatick, Kaffrine et Kaolack*. Dakar: Republic of Senegal and Belgian Development Agency.

Panagariya, A. (2008) *India: An emerging giant*. New York NY: Oxford University Press.

Parrenas, R. S. (2008) *The Force of Domesticity: Filipina migrants and globalization*. New York NY: New York University Press.

Pascucci, S., C. Gardebroek and L. Dries (2012) 'Some like to join, others to deliver: an econometric analysis of farmers' relationships with agricultural co-operatives'. *European Review of Agricultural Economics* 39(1): 51–74.

Pavlovskaya, M. (2004) 'Other transitions: multiple economies of Moscow households in the 1990s'. *Annals of the Association of American Geographers* 94(2): 329–51.

Pencavel, J., L. Pistaferri and F. Schivardi (2006) 'Wages, employment, and capital in capitalist and worker-owned firms'. *Industrial and Labor Relations Review* 60(1): 23–44.

Pérez-Ramírez, M., G. Ponce-Díaz and S. Lluch-Cota (2012) 'The role of MSC certification in the empowerment of fishing cooperatives in Mexico: the case of Red Rock Lobster co-managed fishery'. *Ocean and Coastal Management* 63: 24–9.

Pesquera, A. (2011) 'How cities came to link rural producers with urban food markets in Colombia'. Leading by Example, Programme Insights. Oxford: Oxfam.

Phillips, A. (1995) *The Politics of Presence: The political representation of gender, ethnicity and race*. Oxford: Oxford University Press.

Piketty, T. (2014) *Capital in the 21st Century*. Boston MA: Harvard University Press.

Pillai, V. (2007) 'A note on *Kudumbashree*'. In V. Pillai and S. Alkire, *Measuring Individual Agency or Empowerment: A study in Kerala*. Thiruvananthapuram, Kerala: Centre for Development Studies.

Place, F., G. Kariuki, J. Wangila, P. Kristjanson, A. Makauki and J. Ndubi (2004) 'Assessing the factors underlying differences in achievements of farmer groups: methodological issues and empirical findings from the highlands of Central Kenya'. *Agricultural Systems* 82(3): 257–72.

Polanyi, K. (1944) *The Great Transformation: The political and economic origins of our time*. Boston MA: Beacon Press.

— (1968) *Primitive, Archaic, and Modern Economies*. New York NY: Anchor Books.

Poole, N. and A. de Frece (2010) *A Review of Existing Organizational Forms of Smallholder Farmers' Associations and Their Contractual Relationships with Other Market Participants in the East and Southern African ACP Region*. AAACP Paper Series 11. Rome: Food and Agriculture Organization of the United Nations (FAO).

Portanova, M., G. Rossi and F. Stefanoni (2011) *Mafia a Milano: Sessant'anni di affari e delitti*. Milan: Melampo.

Porter, M. E. (1991) 'Towards a dynamic theory of strategy'. *Strategic Management Journal* 12(S2): 95–118.

Poulton, C., A. Dorward and J. Kydd (2010) 'The future of small farms: new directions for services, institutions, and intermediation'. *World Development* 38(10): 1413–28.

Prahalad, C. K. (2004) *The Fortune at the Bottom of the Pyramid: Eradicating poverty through profits*. Upper Saddle River NJ: Wharton School Publishing.

Prakash, C. S. and K. S. Chandarsekar (2012) 'SHGs and socio-economic empowerment: a descriptive analysis based on *Kudumbashree* project in Kerala'. *International Journal of Business and Management Tomorrow* 2(2): 1–10.

Rajan, J. B. (2006) '*Kudumbashree*: a forum for gender mainstreaming'. In P. P. Balan and M. Retna Raj (eds) *Decentralised Governance and Poverty Reduction: Lessons from Kerala*. Thrissur, Kerala: Kerala Institute of Local Administration, pp. 151–62.

Rankin, K. N. (2001) 'Governing development: neoliberalism, microcredit, and rational economic woman'. *Economy and Society Volume* 30(1): 18–37.

Rawls, J. (1999 [1971]) *A Theory of Justice*. Cambridge MA: Harvard University Press.

Razavi, S. (2012) 'World Development Report 2012: A commentary'. *Development and Change* 43(1): 423–37.

Razeto Migliaro, L. (2013) '¿Que es la economía solidaria?' www.luisrazeto.net/content/%C2%BFqu%C3%A9-es-la-econom%C3%AD-solidaria (accessed 4 November 2013).

Reardon, T., C. Barrett, J. Berdegue and J. Swinnen (2009) 'Agrifood industry transformation and small farmers in developing countries'. *World Development* 37(11): 1717–27.

Reddy, C. S. and S. Manak (2005) 'Self-help groups: a keystone of microfinance in India – women's empowerment and social security'. Mimeo, Mahilka Abhivruddhi Society, Andhra Pradesh (APMAS), Hyderabad.

Reed, D. (2009) 'What do corporations have to do with Fair Trade: positive and normative analysis from a value chain perspective'. *Journal of Business Ethics* 86(1): 3–26.

— (2012) 'Fairtrade International (FLO)'. In D. Reed, P. Utting and A. Mukherjee-Reed (eds) *Business Regulation and Non-state Actors: Whose standards? Whose development?* Abingdon and New York NY: Routledge.

— and A. Mukherjee-Reed (2012) 'From non-state regulation to governance? Shifting the site of contestation'. In D. Reed, P. Utting and A. Mukherjee-Reed (eds) *Business Regulation and Non-state Actors: Whose standards? Whose development?* Abingdon and New York NY: Routledge.

—, B. Thomson, I. Hussey and J. F. Lemay (2010) 'Developing a normatively grounded research agenda for Fair Trade: examining the case of Canada'. *Journal of Business Ethics* 2 (Supplement 2): 151–79.

Reich, R. B. (2008) *Supercapitalism: The battle for democracy in an age of big business*. Cambridge: Icon Books.

Renard, M.-C. (2010) 'In the name of conservation: CAFE practices and fair trade in Mexico'. *Journal of Business Ethics* 92(2): 287–99.

République du Sénégal (2012) *Stratégie Nationale de Développement Economique et Social*. Dakar: Republic of Senegal.

Rizzo, M. (2011) *Supermarket Mafia: A tavola con Cosa Nostra*. Rome: Castelvecchi.

Roberts, A. (2008) 'Privatizing social reproduction'. *Antipode: A Radical Journal of Geography* 40(4): 535–60.

Robinson, M. and G. White (1997) *The Role of Civic Organizations in the Provision of Social Services: Towards synergy*. Helsinki: World Institute for Development Economics Research.

Rogers, P. (1994) 'Agricultural cooperatives and market performance in food manufacturing'. *Journal of Agricultural Cooperation* 9: 1–12.

Roodman, D. (2009) 'Kiva is not quite what it seems'. Center for Global Development website. www.cgdev. org/blog/kiva-not-quite-what-it-seems (accessed 15 April 2013).

Rosenberg, R. (2007) 'CGAP reflections on the Compartamos initial public offering'. Focus Note 42. Washington DC: Consultative Group to Assist the Poor (CGAP). www.cgap.org/ sites/default/files/CGAP-Focus-Note-CGAP-Reflections-on-the-Compartamos-Initial-Public-Offering-A-Case-Study-on-Microfinance-Interest-Rates-and-Profits-Jun-2007. pdf (accessed 5 December 2013).

Rossel, C. (2003) 'Un modelo para armar: el intercambio institucional Estado-sociedad civil en tres políticas sociales innovadoras'. *Cuadernos del CLAEH* 86–7: 5–44.

— (2008) *Tercer sector y co-gestión de políticas públicas en España y Uruguay: Un matrimonio por conveniencia?* Madrid: Instituto Nacional de Administración Pública (INAP).

— (2010) 'Third sector and social service delivery: the "black box" of citizen's participation in public management and its impact on corporative welfare regimes'. *Revista Reforma y Democracia* 47 (June): 1–27.

— (2011) 'Te amo, te odio, dame más: ONGs, participación y representación en el primer gobierno de izquierda en Uruguay'. Buenos Aires:

Consejo Latinoamericano de Ciencias Sociales (CLACSO) (unpublished).

Rothschild-Whitt, J. (1979) 'The collectivist organization: an alternative to rational-bureaucratic models'. *American Sociological Review* 44: 509–27.

Roy, A. (2010) *Poverty Capital: Microfinance and the making of development*. London: Routledge.

Roy, D. and A. Thorat (2008) 'Success in high value horticultural export markets for the small farmers: the case of Mahagrapes in India'. *World Development* 36(10): 1874–90.

Ruben, R. and J. Heras (2012) 'Social capital, governance and performance of Ethiopian coffee cooperatives'. *Annals of Public and Cooperative Economics* 83(4): 463–84.

Rubino, M. (2012) 'Spesa di gruppo, è boom: 7 milioni di Italiani nei "Gas"'. *La Repubblica*, 29 October. www. repubblica.it/economia/2012/10/29/ news/spesa_di_gruppo_boom_7_ milioni_di_italiani-45427020 (accessed 31 October 2012).

Ruggie, J. G. (1982) 'International regimes, transactions, and change: embedded liberalism in the postwar economic system'. *International Organization* 36(2): 379–415.

— (2002) 'Taking embedded liberalism global: the corporate connection'. In D. Held and M. Koenig-Archibugi (eds) *Taming Globalization: Frontiers of governance*. Cambridge: Polity Press.

Sachs, J. D. (2005) *The End of Poverty: Economic possibilities for our time*. Toronto: Penguin.

Safri, M. and J. Graham (2010) 'The global household: toward a feminist postcapitalist international political economy'. *Signs* 36(1): 99–126.

Salamon, L. (1987) 'Partners in public service: the scope and theory of government–nonprofit relations'. In W. Powell (ed.) *The Nonprofit Sector:*

A research handbook. New Haven CT: Yale University Press.

— (1989) 'The changing partnership between the voluntary sector and the welfare state'. In V. Hodgkinson and R. Lyman (eds) *The Future of the Nonprofit Sector: Challenges, changes and policy considerations*. San Francisco CA: Jossey-Bass.

— and H. K. Anheier (1997) *Defining the Nonprofit Sector: Across national analysis*. Manchester: Manchester University Press.

—, L. Hems and K. Chinnock (2000) 'The non-profit sector: for what and for whom?' Working Papers Series 37. Baltimore MD: Center for Civil Society Studies, Johns Hopkins University.

Sanseviero, R. (2006) *El Estado y las organizaciones sociales: De la 'sociedad de la desconfianza' al reconocimiento la promoción y la auto regulación*. Análisis y Propuestas. Montevideo: Friedrich Ebert Stiftung.

Santos, B. de Sousa (ed.) (2007a) *Democratizing Democracy*. London: Verso.

— (ed.) (2007b) *Another Production is Possible: Beyond the capitalist canon*. London: Verso.

— and C. Rodríguez-Garavito (2013) 'Alternatives économiques: les nouveaux chemins de la contestation'. In I. Hillenkamp and J.-L. Laville (eds) *Socioéconomie et Démocratie: L'actualité de Karl Polanyi*. Toulouse: Erès, pp. 127–47.

Schmidt, R. H. (2013) 'Core values of microfinance under scrutiny: back to basics?' In D. Köhn (ed.) *Microfinance 3.0.: Reconciling sustainability with social outreach and responsible delivery*. Berlin: Springer, pp. 41–67.

Schneiberg, M., M. King and T. Smith (2008) 'Social movements and organizational form: cooperative alternatives to corporations in the American insurance, dairy and grain

industries'. *American Sociological Review* 73(4): 635–67.

Scott, J. C. (1976) *The Moral Economy of the Peasant*. New Haven CT and London: Yale University Press.

Sen, A. (2009) *The Idea of Justice*. Cambridge MA: Harvard University Press.

Seroka, J. and R. Smiljković (1986) *Political Organizations in Socialist Yugoslavia*. Durham NC: Duke University Press.

Serrano, A. (2008) *Bolivia en Proceso*. La Paz: Universidad Mayor de San Andrés.

Servet, J.-M. (2010) 'Microcredit'. In J.-L. Laville, A. D. Cattani and K. Hart (eds) *The Human Economy*. London: Polity.

Seyfang, G. (2001) 'Community currencies: a small change for a green economy. An evaluation of local exchange trading schemes (LETS) as a tool for sustainable local development'. *Environment and Planning A* 33(6): 975–96.

— (2002) 'Tackling social exclusion with community currencies: learning from LETS to time banks'. *International Journal of Community Currency Research* 6. https://ijccr.files.wordpress. com/2012/05/ijccr-vol-6-2002-3- seyfang.pdf.

Signori, S. (2006) *Gli Investitori Etici: Implicazioni aziendali. Problemi e prospettive*. Milan: Giuffrè Editore.

Sinclair, H. (2014) 'The Kiva fairytale: it's a microlending superstar – but who is it really serving?', NexThought Monday, 10 February. www.nextbillion.net/blogpost.aspx?blogid=3726.

Singer, P. (1996) *Introdução a Economia Solidária*. Sao Paulo: Editoria Fundação Perseu Abramo.

— (2007) 'Economía solidaria: un modo de producción y distribución'. In J. L. Coraggio (ed.) *La economía social desde la periferia: Contribuciones Latinoamericanas*. Buenos Aires: UNGS/ALTAMIRA.

Singh, S. P. and P. L. Kelley (1981) *Amul:*

An experiment in rural economic development. Delhi: Macmillan India.

Siwal, B. R. (2009) *Gender Framework Analysis of Empowerment of Women: A case study of* Kudumbashree *programme*. New Delhi: National Institute of Public Cooperation and Child Development.

Smart Campaign (2013) 'New client protection certification program sets the bar for microfinance'. PRWeb website, 24 January. www.prweb. com/releases/2013/1/prweb10358 249.htm (accessed 19 April 2013).

Smith, A. (1776) *The Wealth of Nations*. London: Everyman's Library.

Smith, A. M. and F. VanderHoff Boersma (2012) 'Comercio Justo México: potential lessons for Fairtrade?' In D. Reed, P. Utting and A. Mukherjee-Reed (eds) *Business Regulation and Non-state Actors: Whose standards? Whose development?* Abingdon and New York NY: Routledge.

Smith, S. (2008) 'The challenge of strengthening nonprofits and civil society'. *Public Administration Review* 68: 132–45.

— and M. Lipsky (1989) 'Nonprofit organizations, government and the welfare state'. *Political Science Quarterly* 104(4): 625–48.

Solidarité Socialiste (2012) *Rapport de Suivi du Programme Sénégal*. Brussels: Solidarité Socialiste.

Somjee, A. H. (1982) 'The techno-managerial and politico-managerial classes in a milk cooperative'. *Journal of Asian and African Studies* 17(1/2): 122–35.

Soper, K. (2007) 'Re-thinking the "good life": the citizenship dimension of consumer disaffection with consumerism'. *Journal of Consumer Culture* 7(2): 205–29.

Spear, R. (2000) 'The cooperative advantage'. *Annals of Public and Cooperative Economics* 71(4): 507–23.

—, G. Galera, A. Noya and E. Clarence (2010) *Improving Social Inclusion at the Local Level Through the Social Economy: Report for Slovenia*. OECD Local Economic and Employment Development (LEED) Working Papers 2010/16. Paris: Organisation for Economic Co-operation and Development (OECD). http:// dx.doi.org/10.1787/5kgonvfx2g26-en (accessed 13 February 2014).

Staal, S., C. Delgado and C. Nicholson (1997) 'Smallholder dairying under transaction costs in East Africa'. *World Development* 25(5): 779–94.

Standing, G. (2011) *The Precariat: The new dangerous class*. London and New York NY: Bloomsbury Academic.

Steinman, S. (2011) 'National case study: Republic of South Africa. The need for a state–civil society dialogue to develop public policies for the social and solidarity economy'. Montreal: Chantier de l'Économie Sociale, FIESS 2011. www.reliess.org/ centredoc/upload/FIESS_CS_South-Africa_Oct.-2011.pdf (accessed 13 February 2014).

Stiglitz, J. (2012) *The Price of Inequality: How today's divided society damages our future*. New York NY: W. W. Norton & Company.

Strøm, Ø. and R. Mersland (2010) 'Microfinance mission drift?' *World Development* 38(1): 28–36.

Studlar, D. and J. McAllister (2002) 'Does a critical mass exist? A comparative analysis of women's legislative representation since 1950'. *European Journal of Political Research* 41(2): 233–53.

Sullivan, H. and C. Skelcher (2002) *Working Across Boundaries: Collaboration in public services*. Basingstoke: Palgrave Macmillan.

Sum, N.-L. and B. Jessop (2013) *Towards a Cultural Political Economy*. Cheltenham: Edward Elgar.

Swedberg, R. (1990) *Economics and Sociology: Redefining their boundaries. Conversations with economists and sociologists.* Princeton NJ: Princeton University Press, pp. 116–29.

Tavolo per la Rete Italiana di Economia Solidale (2010) *Il Capitale delle Relazioni.* Milan: Altreconomia.

— (2013) *Un'Economia Nuova: Dai GAS alla zeta.* Milan: Altreconomia.

Taylor, M. (2002) 'Government, the third sector and the contract culture'. In U. Ascioli and C. Ranci (eds) *Dilemmas of the Welfare Mix: The new structure of welfare in an era of privatization.* New York NY: Kluwer and Plenum.

Tharakan, P. M. (2008) 'When the Kerala model of development is historicised: a chronological perspective'. Working Paper 19 (July). Kochi, Kerala: Centre for Socio-economic and Environmental Studies (CSES).

Thomas, P. (1985) *Karl Marx and the Anarchists.* London: Routledge and Kegan Paul.

Thompson, E. P. (1963) *The Making of the English Working Class.* London: Victor Gollancz.

Timmer, P. (2010) 'Reflections on food crises past'. *Food Policy* 35(1): 1–11.

Touré, C. (2011) *Recherche Transnationale sur la Décentralisation en Afrique de l'Ouest et du Centre: Apprendre des expériences locales et intersectorielles. Cas du Sénégal.* Dakar: International Development Research Centre (IDRC) and Réseau Ouest et Centre Africain de Recherche en Education.

Trentmann, F. (2007) 'Citizenship and consumption'. *Journal of Consumer Culture* 7(2): 147–58.

Trigilia, C. (2005) *Sviluppo Locale: Un progetto per l'Italia.* Bari: Laterza.

Tsoukas, H. (2009) 'Practice, strategy making and intentionality: a Heideggerian onto-epistemology for strategy-as-practice'. In D. Golsorkhi, L. Rouleau, D. Seidl and E. Vaara (eds) *The Cambridge Handbook of Strategy as Practice.* Cambridge: Cambridge University Press.

UCA (2008) *Development of the Cooperative Movement in Uganda.* Kampala: Uganda Cooperative Alliance (UCA). www.uca.co.ug/publications/coophist.pdf (accessed 26 March 2013).

— (2012) *Annual Report for the Year 2010/2011.* Kampala: Uganda Cooperative Alliance (UCA).

— (2013) *Annual Report for the Year 2012/2013.* Kampala: Uganda Cooperative Alliance (UCA).

UEMOA (2009) 'Règlementation de la mutualité sociale'. Conseil des Ministres de l'UEMOA, Ouagadougou, 26 June.

UNDESA (2005) *The Inequality Predicament: Report on the world social situation.* New York NY: United Nations Department of Economic and Social Affairs (UNDESA).

UNDP, ILO and Global South–South Development Academy (2011) *Sharing Innovative Experiences: Successful social protection floor experiences.* New York NY: United Nations Development Programme (UNDP).

Unger, R. (2006) *What the Left Should Propose.* London: Verso.

United Nations (2009) *Human Development Report 2009.* New York NY: Oxford University Press.

United Nations System Task Team (2013) *Realizing the Future We Want for All: Report to the Secretary-General, June 2012.* New York NY: United Nations System Task Team.

UNRISD (2004) *Research for Social Change.* Geneva: United Nations Research Institute for Social Development (UNRISD).

— (2005) *Gender Equality: Striving for justice in an unequal world.* Geneva: United Nations Research Institute for Social Development (UNRISD).

— (2010) *Combating Poverty and Inequality: Structural change, social policy and politics*. Geneva: United Nations Research Institute for Social Development (UNRISD).

— (2013a) 'Opening session'. Conference on the Potential and Limits of Social and Solidarity Economy, Geneva, 6–8 May. http://youtu.be/Hcjq9e9vPGo.

— (2013b) 'Potential and limits of social and solidarity economy. An UNRISD conference co-hosted with the ILO'. Event Brief 1. Geneva: United Nations Research Institute for Social Development (UNRISD). www.unrisd.org/eb1 (accessed 19 April 2013).

UNTFSSE (2014) *Social and Solidarity Economy and the Challenge of Sustainable Development*. Geneva: United Nations Inter-Agency Task Force on Social and Solidarity Economy (UNTFSSE). www.unrisd.org/sse.

Uphoff, N. (1995) 'Why NGOs are not a third sector: a sectoral analysis with some thoughts on accountability, sustainability and evaluation'. In M. Edwards and D. Hulme (eds) *NGOs – Performance and Accountability: Beyond the magic bullet*. London: Earthscan-Kumarian.

UTM (2012) *Rapport d'activité*. Bamako: Union Technique de la Mutualité (UTM).

Utting, P. (2005) 'Rethinking business regulation: from self-regulation to social control'. Programme Paper on Technology, Business and Society 15. Geneva: United Nations Research Institute for Social Development (UNRISD).

— (2012) 'The challenge of political empowerment'. Capacity.org, 24 March. www.capacity.org/capacity/opencms/es/topics/value-chains/the-challenge-of-political-empowerment.html.

— (2013a) 'Social and solidarity economy: a pathway to socially sustainable development?' United Nations Research Institute for Social Development (UNRISD) Think Piece. www.unrisd.org/thinkpiece-utting (accessed 20 November 2013).

— (2013b) 'What is social and solidarity economy and why does it matter?' United Nations Research Institute for Social Development (UNRISD) Think Piece. www.unrisd.org/sse-utting (accessed 20 November 2013).

— (2013c) 'Pathways to sustainability in a crisis-ridden world'. In R. Genevey, R. Pachaur and L. Tubiana (eds) *Reducing Inequalities. A sustainable development challenge. A Planet for Life 2013*. New Delhi: TERI Press.

—, N. van Dijk and M. A. Matheï (2014) *Social and Solidarity Economy: Is there a new economy in the making?* Geneva: United Nations Research Institute for Social Development (UNRISD).

—, S. Razavi and R. Varghese Buchholz (2010) *The Global Crisis and Transformative Social Change*. London: Palgrave Macmillan.

Uzzi, B. (1996) 'The sources and consequences of embeddedness for the economic performance of organizations: the network effect'. *American Sociological Review* 61: 674–98.

Vail, J. (2010) 'Decommodification and egalitarian political economy'. *Politics and Society* 38: 310–46.

Valentinov, V. (2004) 'Toward a social capital theory of cooperative organization'. *Journal of Cooperative Studies* 37(3): 5–20.

— (2007) 'Why are cooperatives important in agriculture? An organizational economics perspective'. *Journal of Institutional Economics* 3(1): 55–69.

van Zeeland, A. (2013) 'Challenges for sustainability of SSE: the interaction between popular economy, social movements and public policies – case study of the Global Alliance of Waste

Pickers'. Paper presented at the UNRISD conference on the Potential and Limits of Social and Solidarity Economy, Geneva, 6–8 May. www.unrisd.org/sse-draft-vanzeeland (accessed 20 November 2013).

VanderHoff Boersma, F. (2009) 'The urgency and the necessity of a different type of market: the perspective of producers organized within the Fair Trade market'. *Journal of Business Ethics* 86(1): 51–61.

Varese, F. (2011) *Mafias on the Move: How organized crime conquers new territories.* Princeton NJ: Princeton University Press.

Velasco Olivarez, M. (2011) 'Estudio de casos bolivianos: las Políticas Públicas de Economía Social y el diálogo entre los poderes públicos y la sociedad civil'. Montreal: Chantier de l'Économie Sociale, FIESS 2011. www.reliess.org/centredoc/upload/FIESS_EC_Bolivia_Oct.-2011.pdf (accessed 13 February 2014).

Vergani, G. (2013) 'I sistemi partecipativi di garanzia: l'esperienza di "Per una pedagogia della terra" nei territori dei Des di Como, Monza e Varese'. In Tavolo per la Rete Italiana di Economia Solidale (ed.) *Un'Economia Nuova: Dai GAS alla zeta.* Milan: Altreconomia, pp. 177–82.

Vienney, C. (1980–82) *Socio économie des organisations coopératives,* 2 volumes. Paris: Coopérative d'Information et d'Édition Mutualiste.

— (1994) *L'Économie Sociale.* Paris: La Découverte.

Villarreal, N. and A. Santandreu (1999) 'Ciudadanía y estado: las ONGs y las políticas públicas'. *Cuadernos de Marcha* 157: 49–57.

Vitali, S., J. B. Glattfelder and S. Battiston (2011) 'The network of global corporate control'. *PLoS ONE* 6(10): e25995. http://arxiv.org/abs/1107.5728 (accessed 20 February 2013).

Wade, R. (1990) *Governing the Market.* Princeton NJ: Princeton University Press.

Wanyama, F. O. (2012) *Cooperatives for African Development: Lessons from experience.* New York NY: United Nations Department of Economic and Social Affairs. http://social.un.org/coopsyear/documents/WanyamaCOOPERATIVESFORAFRICANDEVELOPMENT.pdf (accessed May 2013).

— (forthcoming) 'The contribution of cooperatives to sustainable development'. Background paper. Geneva: International Labour Organization (ILO).

—, P. Develtere and I. Pollet (2009) 'Reinventing the wheel? African cooperatives in a liberalized economic environment'. *Annals of Public and Cooperative Economics* 80(3): 361–92.

Warren, D. and S. Dubbs (2010) *Growing a Green Economy for All: From green jobs to green ownership.* College Park MD: The Democracy Collaborative, University of Maryland.

Weatherspoon, D. and T. Reardon (2003) 'The rise of supermarkets in Africa: implications for agrifood systems and the rural poor'. *Development Policy Review* 21(3): 333–55.

Weisbrod, B. (1989) 'Rewarding performance that is hard to measure: the private nonprofit sector'. *Science* 244: 541–6.

Weiss, L. (1998) *The Myth of the Powerless State: Governing the economy in the global era.* Cambridge: Polity Press.

White, T. (2013) 'Seeds of a new economy: how community-supported agriculture promotes diverse economic activity'. PhD thesis, University of Massachusetts, Amherst.

Whittington, R. (2007) 'Strategy practice and strategy process: family differences under the sociological eye'. *Organization Studies* 28(10): 1575–86.

WHO (2010) *The World Health Report. Health Systems Financing: The path to universal coverage.* Geneva: World Health Organization (WHO).

Wiggins, S., J. Kirsten and L. Llambi (2010) 'The future of small farms'. *World Development* 38(10): 1341–8.

Williamson, O. (1981) 'The economics of organization: the transaction cost approach'. *American Journal of Sociology* 87: 548–77.

— (1985) *The Economic Institutions of Capitalism: Firms, markets and relational contracting.* New York NY and London: The Free Press and Macmillan.

— (1996) 'Economic organization: the case for candor'. *Academy of Management Review* 21(1): 48–57.

Wolch, J. (1990) *The Shadow State: Government and voluntary in transition.* New York NY: Foundation Center.

Wollni, M. and M. Zeller (2007) 'Do farmers benefit from participating in specialty markets and cooperatives? The case of coffee marketing in Costa Rica'. *Agricultural Economics* 37(2–3): 243–8.

World Bank (2001) *Engendering Development.* Washington DC: World Bank Group.

— (2005) *A Better Investment Climate for Everyone: World development report 2005.* Washington DC: World Bank.

— (2006) *Gender Equality as Smart Economics.* Washington DC: World Bank Group.

— (2012) *World Development Report 2012: Gender equality and development.* Washington DC: World Bank Group.

Wright, E. O. (2010) *Envisioning Real Utopias.* London: Verso.

WSM (2009) *Renforcer la Protection Sociale par l'institutionnalisation des Mutuelles de Santé au Bénin.* Brussels and Cotonou: Wereldsolidariteit (WSM).

Yang, D. and Z. Liu (2012) 'Does farmer economic organization and agricultural specialization improve rural income? Evidence from China'. *Economic Modelling* 29(3): 990–3.

Young, I. M. (1997) *Intersecting Voices: Dilemmas of gender, political philosophy, and policy.* Princeton NJ: Princeton University Press.

— (2000) *Inclusion and Democracy.* New York NY: Oxford University Press.

Yunus, M. (2007) *Creating a World without Poverty: Social business and the future of capitalism.* New York NY: PublicAffairs.

Zelizer, V. (1989) 'The social meaning of money: "special monies"'. *American Journal of Sociology* 95: 342–77.

Zett, J.-B. (2013) 'Politiques publiques pour le développement de l'économie sociale et solidaire: étude de cas. Burkina Faso'. Montreal: RELIESS and Uniterra. www.reliess.org/centredoc/upload/Economie Sociale_BF_2014.pdf (accessed 13 February 2014).

— and F. Bationo (2011) *Inventaires des mutuelles de santé dans la perspective de l'assurance maladie universelle au Burkina Faso.* Ouagadougou and Brussels: Recherche Commanditée par Solidarité Socialiste.

INDEX

Aarey Milk Colony (India), 289, 297
Abbruzzi (Italy), earthquake in, 201
Accion International, 208
accountability, 181
Act on Public Benefit and Voluntary Work (2003) (Poland), 172
actor's 'voice' of social and solidarity economy players, 34–5
adolescents, programmes for, 236, 244
advance payments to farmers, 186–7
advocacy for social and solidarity economy, 106–7
African Development Bank (AfD), 276–7
agency, 302–4; of poor people, 302
agri-food systems, development of, 116–17
agriculture, organic, investment in, 206 see also community-supported agriculture
Agro Azuay cooperative (Ecuador), 160
Alimentos Nariño (Colombia), 162–4
alliances, formation of, 37
Almeria miracle, 153
alter-globalisation, 2, 12, 35, 46
alternative economies, 78
AMUL cooperative (India), 3, 4, 25–7, 35, 284–99; growth of, 287–97; political embeddedness of, 298–9; product diversification of, 295–7
Anchor butter, 292
Andalusian Pacts (Spain), 172, 179
Andhra Pradesh, microfinance institutions in, 220
Annual Saving and Credit Cooperative Association Congress (Uganda), 281
Another economy, idea of, 139, 149
'another world is possible', 12
Arcipelago Siqiliyah, 192–3, 198
area development societies (ADSs) (Kerala), 301
Argentina, 17, 131, 142, 143, 145, 146, 147; community currency system in, 221–35; scaling up of social and solidarity economy in, 22–3; social economy policy in, 132–6
Argentina Trabaja programme, 135
association, 202, 204
asymmetry of information, 181
Australian Agency for International Development, 82
authoritarian models, dangers of, 51–3
autonomous spaces, need for, 16
autonomy, 26, 266, 327; loss of, 247, 267 (of cooperatives, 269–70); of cooperatives, 282, 291, 292; trade-off with dependency, 23
Azuay province (Ecuador), 160, 161

B-corporations, 89; to be included in social and solidarity economy, 101
baby food: production of, 295–6; reducing imports of, 297
Bamako Initiative, 252
Bamboo Workers' Union (Nepal), 174
bananas, as Fairtrade products, 111
Bank of Uganda, 278
banking, ethical, 197
Bankruptcy Act (Argentina), 135
basic income programmes, in South Africa, 77
Basque region, social and solidarity economy in, 4
beneficiaries of mutual health organisations, definition of, 254
Benin, 259; mutual health organisations in, 256
Bergamo: alternative food network in, 185; GAS network in, 193
Big Society, 58
Blue Orchard Microfinance Investment Managers, 205, 210–11
Bogotá, proto-cooperatives in, 161–2
Bolivia, 131, 132, 142, 144, 145, 146, 177; constitution of, 147

Bombay, monopoly milk marketing in, 288–9

Bombay Milk Scheme (BMS), 287–90

'bottom of the pyramid' model, 54

Brazil, 17, 107, 131, 132, 142, 143, 145, 147, 178, 181; co-construction of policy in, 136–9; solidarity economy conferences in, 170; social and solidarity economy in, 179 (regulation of, 177)

Brazilian Forum for Economic Solidarity (FBES), 137–8

bread, local marketing of, 198

bricolage, 31

BRICS countries, 70

Buen Vivir programme (Ecuador), 139–41

Buenos Aires, *trueque* system in, 230

buffalos: herds of, in Bombay, 289; milk of (powdering of, 290–1; production of, 289–90; used in baby foods, 296; used to make condensed milk, 295)

Buganda Growers Association, 267

build-operate-transfer (BOT) investment model, 19, 159

bureaucratisation, 17, 23, 138, 238, 247

Burkina Faso, 30, 251, 254, 255, 260; agricultural cooperatives in, 126; consultation processes in, 177; microfinance in, 170; social and solidarity economy in, 174–5; Universal Health Coverage project, 258

burn-out of activists, 198

butter, marketing of, in India, 292–3

Buzzcar company, 96

Caisse Nationale de Sécurité Sociale (Senegal), 258

Caja Laboral Popular (CLP) (Spain), 153

Cajamar cooperative bank, 153

Calvert Funds, 205

Cameron, David, 58

Canada, social and solidarity economy in, 25, 178

capacities, discourse of, 29–30, 58, 111

capitalism, 53, 69–70; alternatives to, 51–2; as determining force, 77; definition of, 80; emergence of, 59; investor-driven, 151; replacement of relations of, 4

car-pooling cooperatives, 96

care, 74, 78, 81–2, 83, 85; as resource, 72; attributed to migrant women, 76; divorced from gender dimensions, 85; unpaid, 33; work, invisibility of, 74

care economy, 32

caste differences, 329

Celebration of Cooperatives day (Uganda), 280

Cellule d'Appui à la Couverture Maladie Universelle (Senegal), 258

Central de Trabajadores de Argentina (CTA), 136

Central Única dos Trabajadores (CUT) (Argentina), 137

Chambre Régionale de l'Économie Sociale et Solidaire (CRESS, France), 173

Chantier de l'Économie Sociale (Quebec), 171, 176

charity, 42

childcare programmes, 236, 240, 241, 243, 244, 245

children, eradicating malnutrition among, 290

China: agricultural cooperatives in, 125; farmers' organisations in, 119

Citizen Participation Law (Ecuador), 175

citizenship, 96; active, 34; exclusion from, 42

civil society, 44–7, 182, 256, 264; democratisation of, 55; in South Africa, 176; relationship with government, 167; role of, 54

class, within capitalism, 80

class differentiation, 325, 329

Cleveland model, 92

climate change, 1, 5

Club de Trueque (CT), 226; failure of, 232

co-construction of social and solidarity economy policy, 19–20, 28, 33, 133, 166–82; as means of realising potential, 168–9; ensures effectiveness, 171; in Brazil, 136–7; reasons for, 168–72; reduces information asymmetry, 169; reduces transaction costs, 169; requirements for, 172–81

Co-operative Group (UK), failure to buy Lloyds Bank, 71

'co-opitalism', 28

co-optation, 4, 17, 37
coalitions, of social and solidarity economy actors, 20
coffee: as Fairtrade product, 107, 110, 111; production of, 119, 121, 274 (in Rwanda, 126; in Uganda, 268–9)
Cohen, Andrew, 268
Cohen, G. A., 64–5
Coldiretti farmers' union (Italy), 186
collective action, 20–7; costs of, 16, 123; of women, 315
collective bargaining, 133
collective brand law (2009) (Argentina), 135
collectivités locales, 260
Colombia, 19, 30, 150; local economic development policy in, 157–8, 161–4
Comissão Nacional de Avalição da Educação Superior (CONAES) (Brazil), 138
Comité Sectoriel de Main-d'oeuvre-Économie Sociale Action Communautaire (CSMO-ÉSAC) (Quebec), 173
commercialisation, 28
commodification, 7
common pool resources, 66–7; management of, 121, 322
common sense understandings of terms, 36
commons, 66
communication across difference, 325
communicative action, 64
communism, 59, 60, 151
community, as site of social and solidarity economy decision-making, 70
community currency system, in Argentina, 221–35
community development institutions, 88; financial, 88–9
community development societies (CDSs) (Kerala), 301
community economics approach, 72–85
Community Economics Collective (CEC), 73, 80–1, 82; project of, 79
community economies, formation of, 14
community forestry institutions: in Nepal, 313–29; mixed-gender, 325; women's participation in, 315–17

community land trusts, 89
community production system, 145
community value achieved by projects, 71
community-supported agriculture (CSA), 186
Compartamos microfinance institution (Mexico), 218
compensatory social programmes in situations of crisis, 130
competition for resources between social and solidarity economy actors, 238, 246, 248; for state resources, 23
condensed milk, production of, 295
conditionality, 20, 181
Confederación Empresarial Española de la Economía, 173
Conselho Nacional de Economia Solidária (CNES) (Brazil), 138
conservative social norms, affecting women, 315
Consultative Group to Assist the Poor (CGAP), 205
consumption: changing practices of, 97; seen as opposite of citizenship, 96
contestation, within social and solidarity economy structures, 34
cooking energy, concern of women, 326
cooperation, 74, 78, 140, 202, 204, 211; advantages of, 16; as resource, 72; divorced from gender dimensions, 85
Cooperative College (Uganda), 268
cooperative data analysis system (CODAS), 279–80
Cooperative Development Bank (Uganda), 268
Cooperative Group (UK), 95
Cooperative Societies Act (1952) (Uganda), 268
Cooperative Societies Act (1963) (Uganda), 268
Cooperative Societies Act (1970) (Uganda), 269, 276
Cooperative Societies Ordinance (Uganda) (1946), 267–8
Cooperative Societies Regulations (1992) (Uganda), 276
Cooperative Statute (1991) (Uganda), 270
cooperatives, 1, 3, 18, 47, 67–8, 83, 87, 89, 90, 102, 104, 141, 159, 210; agricultural,

117, 118–22, 151, 153, 160, 161, 266–83 (in Africa, 16; in Uganda, development of, 267–71; new generation of, 24; structural tensions in, 122–6); articulation with local government, 19–20; as aspect of local economic development policy, 155; as core of social and solidarity economy model, 151–5; as percentage of world GDP, 88; benefits of, 266; capacities, of, strengthening, 279–8; dairy-related, 274; development policies for, 266; enabling measures for, 275; farmer-owned, 160, 163–4; financial, 141, 151, 203, 271–2; for livelihood production, 119; for marketing, 119; for recycling, 204; gender issues in, 280–1; governance structures of, 125; hybrid goals of, 284; in agro-processing, 274; in production and marketing, 274; in Uganda (activities of, 273–4; challenges of, 274–5); independence from government, 268; labour cooperatives, 135; legislation in Argentina, 135; longevity of, 93; malfunction and collapse of, 270; milk-producing, in India, 284–99; model of, 49; of consumers, 274; on mafia-confiscated land, 193; operating principles of, 67; outperform general economy, 91; policy guidelines for, 275–6; proto-cooperatives in Bogotá, 161–2; raising awareness of, 280; registration of, 88; role of, in Latin America, 150–65; serve needs of communities, 92; set-up costs of, 125; strengthening of, in Argentina, 134; worker-owned, 89 *see also* electricity consumer cooperatives; Mill, John Stewart, view of cooperatives; *and* savings and credit cooperatives
Coordination Nationale des Organisations Paysannes (Mali), 174
coping with crisis, 9; forms of, 5
CORES survey of alternative food networks, 190–1, 200, 201
corporate social responsibility, 37, 51, 114
Correa, Rafael, 139, 159
Costa Rica, coffee production in, 119–20

cotton, production of, 274; in cooperatives, 268–9
counter-hegemonic movement, 10, 37; formation of, 35
Covas, Horacio, 227, 228, 232
Cow and Gate company, 296
credit, 75; access to, 19, 28; revolving, scheme for, 83
credit unions, 68, 210, 304 *see also* social credit movement
créditos, forgery of, 229
crisis, 7, 44–7; economic decisions made during
critical mass: in community action groups, 314; of women in movements, 326
crowdfunding, 1, 80
crowdsourcing, 95
cultural identity, respect for, 140
currency, local printing of, 227–8

Dalaya, H., 288, 289
day care, provision of, 180
debt, 21, 83; among poor farmers, 218; sovereign, 148
decentralisation, 30, 33; in Uganda, 281; of responsibility for social and solidarity economy, 177–8
decision-making, 91, 105, 118, 305, 323; centralisation of, 148; hierarchical, 126; in cooperatives, complexity of, 126; structures of, 90; women's participation in, 304, 317–19 *see also* participation
delegation, 21
democracy, 7, 42, 89, 151, 233, 284, 311, 323, 326; associative, 47; at community level, 70; GAS as 'schools' of, 188; use of term, 36 *see also* cooperatives, governance structures of *and* solidarity, democratic
democratisation, 55
denunciation, politics of, 77–8
dependency, 36
deregulation, 6
Desai, Dinkar, 287–8
Desai, Morarji, 287
Desjardins cooperative (Canada), 3
Deutsche Bank, 208, 220; study report, 206

development: different forms of, 2; re-imagining of, x, 9, 77–8; use of term, 36
developmental state, model of, 155–6
DhanaX lending organisation, 205
difference, economic *see* economic difference
digital enterprise, 15
disabled people, provision for, 180
distance to the road, factor of, 120–1
distretti di economia solidale (DES) (Italy), 185, 196
distributivist movement, 61
division of labour, 21, 225, 226; gendered, 315; in households, 81
double movement, 21

Economia Solidária (ECOSOL) (Brazil), 137–8
economic difference, 72, 73, 80–2, 84
economics, as playground of liberalism, 65–7
économie social, emergence of term, 58
economies of scale, in farmers' marketing groups, 124
economy: divorced from capitalism, 85; imagining of, 77–8, 80–2; redefinition of, 144
Ecuador, 18, 19, 30, 107, 131, 132, 142, 144, 146, 150, 179, 181; constitution of, 141, 147; new economic and social model in, 159–61; participation of civil society in, 175; participatory budgeting in, 177; social and solidarity economy in, 139–41
efficiency–equity pendulum, 28
electricity consumer cooperatives, 87, 93–4
elite capture, 16, 28, 30, 37; in NGOs, 46
Elsa, an entrepreneur, 83
emancipation, 33
embeddedness, of cooperatives, in India, 284–99
Emilia-Romagna, cooperatives in, 152
employee stock ownership plans (ESOP), 89
employment: generation of, 9, 180 *see also* full employment
empowerment, 33–4; of women, 26, 27, 303; use of term, 10

energy: alternative sources of, 68–9; renewable, 94
entrepreneurial charity, 209
environment, concern for, 281
environmental efficiency, need for, 98
environmental impacts of production, 97
environmental standards, 95
equality, 2, 64–5; necessary for democracy, 326 *see also* gender equality
equity capital: access to, 90–1; provided by microfinance sector, 212
estate production of Fairtrade goods, 111–12, 113
ethical banking *see* banking, ethical
ethical frameworks, 14, 58
ethical learning by doing, 21, 31
ethical value-added framework, 69–71; concept of, 71
ethicality, active, 31
ethics, 79, 82–4, 101; of economic development, 82; social and solidarity economy as site of, 66–7
Ethiopia, 120; cooperatives in, 119, 126
European Union (EU), 157–8; call for coordinated European response, 174; recognition of hybrid enterprises, 170
exclusion: from healthcare, 256; of women, from formal economy, 309
external support, of farmers' marketing groups, 124–5
externalisation of social and environmental impacts, 95, 98
extractive industries, 32, 148; moving beyond, 146

Facebook, 191
FAGOR company (Spain), 153
fair price principle, 162
Fairtrade, 3, 15, 21, 100–15, 138, 149, 170, 180, 213; as social and solidarity economy advocacy, 106–7; as social and solidarity economy exchange, 105–6; as social and solidarity economy production, 104–5, 109; as social and solidarity economy regulation, 108–9; certification, benefits of, 108; contribution to scaling of social and solidarity economy, 104; corporate participation

in, 114; heterogeneous advocacy in, 112; heterogeneous exchanges in, 110–12; heterogeneous production in, 110; heterogeneous regulation in, 112–13; heterogeneous social movements in, 113–14; labelling bodies for, 108, 110; limits of, for scaling social and solidarity economy, 109–10

Fairtrade Africa, 107, 112

Fairtrade International, 108

Fairtrade Labelling Organizations International (FLO), 107, 108, 112–13

Fairtrade Towns, concept of, 107

Fairtrade Universities, concept of, 107

family-driven collectives, in food networks, 188–9

farmers: collective agreements with, 186; participation in social programmes, 123; women as, 308–9

farmers' groups: collective action among, 117; coordination costs of, 124; economies of scale in, 124

farmers' markets, 19, 116–29, 162, 279; solidarity-driven, 196–7

farmers' organisation, coping with tensions in, 12, 127

Federation of Community Forest Users of Nepal (FECOFUN), 174, 327, 329

feminism, 45, 78; encounter with development, 73

finance *see* solidarity finance

financial markets, instabilities of, 28

financialisation, 28

firewood: collection of, 314 (by women, 315, 317, 320, 321, 325); shortages of, 319 (dealing with, 322–3)

Flannery, Jessica, 208

Flannery, Matt, 208

Fome Zero programme (Brazil), 162, 177

food: alternative networks of, 21, 30; cheap imports of, 32; fairness in production and distribution of, 21; prices of commodities, 116; rising prices of, 308 *see also* baby food *and* organic food

Food and Agriculture Organization (FAO), 290

food justice, 201

food networks, alternative, 185–201

food security, 25, 102

food sovereignty, use of term, 10

for-profit sector, 86, 89, 156, 205, 219

Fordism, 53

forestry groups, community-based, 25–7, 30, 35 *see also* community forestry institutions

forests: conservation of, 314, 321–2; formulating user rules for, 320–1; women as protectors of, 322

Foro Brasileiro de Economia Solidaria (FBES), 173–4

fossil fuel companies, avoidance of investment in, 206

Foucault, Michel, 7, 84

France, 181

Frankfurt School, 63

free rider problem, 4

Free Trade Area of the Americas (FTAA), opposition to, 131

French Agency for Development, 256, 257

Frente Amplio (Uruguay), 241, 242

full employment, 8

gender, 72–85, 102, 111; composition of committees, 194, 316–19; composition of groups, 27; essentialised notions of, 85; in composition of farmers' marketing groups, 123; quotas, 314; traditional relations of, 33

gender equality, 314, 327; business case for, 75–6; instrumentalisation of, 79; promotion of, 140

gender inequality, 300; marked by firewood shortages, 322

gender issues: in community forestry, 313–29; in cooperatives, 280–1

gender sensitisation, 280

Ghana, 258; mutual health organisations in, 262

Gibson, Katherine, 82–4

Gibson-Graham, J. K., 73, 80, 199, 225

ginger tea, production of, 83

Glaxo: plans baby food manufacturing in India, 296; unwillingess to use local milks, 296

Global Alliance of Waste Pickers, 35

global warming, 8

glocal movements, 35

GLS Bank, 220
governance, 24; collaborative, new forms
    of, 7, 167; good, 34
governing in complexity, 166
government, 182; as strategic enabler, 168;
    commitment to social and solidarity
    economy, 177–8; public, new paradigm
    of, 168; role of, 166; support for social
    and solidarity economy, 180
Gram Panchayat system (India), 305
Gram Sabha system (India), 305
Grameen Foundation, 216, 219
Gramsci, Antonio, 7
grassroots organisations, relations with
    political, 132
green economy, 15, 36, 93–4
greening of economy, 98
group identity, of women, 324–6
group size, optimal, 124
growth: jobless, 8; models of, 8
gruppi di acquisto solidale (GAS),
    185–201; emergence of, 186–8; formal
    incorporation of, 195; motivations for
    joining, 188
Gujarat, community forestry in, 316
Gujarat Cooperative Milk Marketing
    Federation, 286

Habermas, Jürgen, 63–4; *The Theory of
    Communicative Action*, 63
Haiti, earthquake in, 213–14
health insurance, 250, 255; offered by
    mutual health organisations, 262;
    unwillingness or inability to pay, 255
health organisation, mutual *see* mutual
    health organisations
healthcare, 15, 23, 97; education in,
    253; financing of, 251; in social and
    solidarity economy sector, 250–65;
    primary, 252; universal, 258
healthy living, 15, 21
hegemony, 36
HIV/AIDS, monitoring of, 276
Homenet, 35
horizontal links, promotion of, 324
household labour, 72; rendered more
    visible, 81; unpaid, 73
households: function internationally, 81;
    more egalitarian, 75

hydrocarbons, nationalising profits of, 146

identity politics, 6; post-industrial, 20
Idi Amin, 269
import substitution, 298; in Indian dairy
    industry, 292, 292
inclusion, 2, 6, 133, 172, 309, 314
India: community forestry groups in, 27,
    313–29; cooperatives in, 284–99
India Development Services (IDS), 324
Indian National Congress party, 287
indigenous communities, 142
indigenous ownership, 293
individual: self-maximising autonomous,
    68; thinking beyond, 67–9
industrialisation, models of, 8
inequality, 5–6, 8; inefficiency of, 78–9 *see
    also* equality
informal economy, 174; formalisation of,
    134; unionisation of, 102
information asymmetry, 169–71
innovation: capacity for, 237;
    discouragement of, 247; multi-
    dimensional, 54
institution-building, 22; process of, 229;
    role of microfinance in, 216–17
institutional complementarities, 31–4
institutional innovation, 30, 223–4, 232
institutionalisation of social and solidarity
    economy, 17; in Latin America, 130–49
Instituto Nacional de Asociativismo y
    Economía Social (INAES) (Argentina),
    134
Instituto Nacional de Economía Popular y
    Solidaria (IEPS) (Ecuador), 139
instrumentalisation, 17, 28, 36
intention, of investors, 214–15
Inter-American Development Bank, 134,
    240
Inter-Ministerial Team for Systematic
    Solutions for the SSE (Brazil), 179
Intercontinental Network for the
    Promotion of Social and Solidarity
    Economy (RIPESS), 109
interdependence: as resource, 72;
    relations of, 14
intergovernmental collaboration, 178–80
intermediaries, 216; cutting-out of, 106,
    162; openness of, 175; profits of, 287

International Co-operative Alliance, 35
International Forum on the Social and
Solidarity Economy (FIESS), 167
International Labour Organization (ILO),
xi, 8, 69, 250, 257
International Monetary Fund (IMF), 154
International Network for the Promotion
of Social and Solidarity Economy, 35
investment: ethical alternatives, 209;
pro-social, 206–9, 216; social and
solidarity-based, 202–20; with
awareness, 214
irrigation, community-based, 121
isomorphism, institutional, 4, 13, 28, 37, 51
Italy: alternative food networks in,
185–201; cooperative sector in, 151–2

Jiron farming cooperative (Ecuador), 160
John Lewis Partnership, 94
Joint Forest Management (JFM)
programme (India), 316
justice, 64, 66, 72, 83; social, 74–6, 101
(and environmental, use of term, 10);
social, 74–6

Kaira Union *see* AMUL
Kant, Immanuel, 62
Kerala: social and solidarity economy in,
4, 25–6; women's projects in, 300–12
Keynesianism, 44
Kiva lending scheme, 21, 202–3,
208–9, 212–19; Atheists, Agnostics,
Freethinkers and Skeptics group, 217;
Christians group, 217
knowledge: of investors, 214–15; technical,
sharing of, 105, 106
Korea, South, social and solidarity
economy in, 171–2, 179
Krishnamachari, T. T. (TTK), 292–3
Kudumbashree programme (Kerala),
25–7, 300–12; as social and solidarity
economy, 304–9
Kurien, Verghese, 288, 289–90, 295, 297

La Concertacion survey of healthcare in
Africa, 253
Lac Jubones dairy processing plant
(Ecuador), 160, 163
land: as part of social and solidarity

economy, 106; confiscated from mafia,
193
land erosion, 142
land reform, 32
land-grabbing, 200
landless women, 321; needs of, 319
Landless Workers' Movement (Brazil) *see*
Movimento dos Trabalhadores Rurais
Sem Terra (MST)
landlessness, in Brazil, 139
Latin American and Caribbean Producer
Association (CLAC), 107, 112
learning by doing, 167
learning from history and ideas, 11–14
Left Democratic Front (LDF) (Kerala), 300
legislation for social and solidarity
economy, 170–1; in Quebec, 174; in
Spain, 174
lemon cultivation, mafia infiltration in,
192
Lenin, V. I., 60
Leo XIII, *Rerum Novarum*, 61
Leroux, Monique, 93
liberalisation, 7
liberalism, 65–7, 69, 70; and social and
solidarity economy, 61–5; effects of,
on social and solidarity economy, 13;
embedded, 2, 7, 35; theory of, 60
local, moving beyond, 326–7
local currency, loans provided in, 213
local developmental states (LDS): in
Colombia, 161–4; in Latin America,
150–65; model of, 164–5 (and
cooperatives, in Latin America,
158–64)
local economic development agencies
(LEDAs), 157–8
local exchange trading systems (LETS), 221
local governments: key role of, 30;
transfer of authority to, 30
local heroes, required by social and
solidarity economy organisations, 92
local production and consumption cycle,
162
Lombardy, GAS networks in, 191

mafia: associated with agricultural
monocultures, 192; cleansed from
local economies, 192

magnetic debit cards, use of, 135

Mahatma Gandhi Rural Employment Guarantee Programme (MGNREGS) (India), 304–7, 310

mailing lists, 191

male breadwinner, assumption of, 8

Mali: healthcare legislation in, 257; mutual health organisations in, 264; social and solidarity economy in, 174

Małopolskie Social Economy Pact (Poland), 169–70

Manos a la Obra programme (Argentina), 133–4

marginalisation, 300

market: cyclicity of, 103; embedding of, 52; principle of, 50, 149; relation to state, 44; relations with, 11; self-regulating, basis for authoritarianism, 52 *see also* quasi-markets

Market and Citizenship association, 196

market economy: cause of divisions, 43; integration into, 49

market failures, investment related to, 213–14

market forces, excesses of, protection against, 31

marketing institutions, support for, 278–9

marketisation, 37, 69; in non-profit sector, 238; of life, 63

Marks, Peter, 95

Marxism, 64, 80

Massachusetts (USA): solidarity economy initiative in, 185; food network in, 199–200

'mate' (work supervisor) system, 306–7

Mauss, Marcel, 53

Max Havelaar, Fairtrade labelling body, 108

May 1968 protests (France), 45

McKinsey and Company study, 90

medicines, access to, 252

membership: of agricultural cooperatives, homogeneity of, 123–4; control by, in cooperatives, 68; of cooperatives, 120 (size of, 291); of farmers' marketing groups, 124; of mutual health organisations, diversity of, 254–5; participation by, 90, 95; voluntary, 252

micro-level strategising, 25

microcredit, 53, 68, 76; biases within, 28

microenterprises, 102, 310; informal, 156

microfinance, 18, 21, 278; and institution-building, 216–17; and pro-social investment, 203–6; as economic trap, 220; commercial investment in, 210–11; commercialisation of, 31, 202, 204, 205, 217–18; high repayments in, 212; in Burkina Faso, 170; over-lending in, 203, 218, 219; repayment rates in, 205; scandals in world of, 22; social and solidarity investment in, 202–20

microfinance investment vehicles (MIV), 205

middle-class effect, 120

milk: production and marketing of, in India, 284–99 *see also* condensed milk

Mill, John Stewart, view of cooperatives, 60

Millennium Development Goals (MDG), 6; agenda to succeed, 9

Ministerio de Inclusión Económica y Social (MIES) (Ecuador), 139

mixed economy, 144; three-sector, 141–2

modernity, characteristics of, 42

Mondragon Cooperative Corporation (MCC), 3, 4, 152–3; internationalising of, 71

monocultures, 32

Monza-Brianza *distretto di economia solidale*, 198, 200

moralisation of the poor, 43

Movimento dos Trabalhadores Rurais Sem Terra (MST) (Brazil), 35, 139, 147

multi-functionality, of agricultural cooperatives, 126

multi-scalar activism, challenges of, 29

Muraleedharan, S., 306

mutual assistance, practices of, 14

mutual associations, 3, 43, 47; use of term, 89

mutual health organisations (MHOs), 23–4, 250; advantages of, 263; development of, in West Africa, 251–6; fragmentation of movement, 265; relations with public authorities, 256–7; structural features of, 252; weaknesses of, 255

mutuelles sociales, 257, 263

MYCR lending organisation (Denmark), 205

Mysore Resettlement and Development Agency (MYRADA), 324, 328

National Commission for Microfinance (CONAMI) (Argentina), 135

National Plan for Wellbeing (Ecuador), 139–41, 169

National Registry of 'Agents' of Local Development and Social Economy (Argentina), 134–5

National Resistance Movement (Uganda), 270

National Secretariat of Solidarity Economy (SENAES) (Brazil), 137

National Solidarity Economy Council (Brazil), 179

natural disasters, investment related to, 213–14

natural resources, rules for exploitation of, 141

nature, rights of, 141

Nehru, Jawaharlal, 291, 293

neighbourhood groups (NHGs) (Kerala), 301

neighbourhood revitalisation, programmes for, 172

'neither state nor private', 59, 70

neo-developmentalism, 18

neo-populist tendencies in social and solidarity economy, 4

neoliberalism, 9, 29, 77–8, 150–65, 244; and social and solidarity economy-market relations, 14–20; as field of specific techniques, 84; effects of, 271; gender issues in, 76; self-defence against, 144

Nepal: community forestry groups in, 27, 313–29; informal unions in, 174; social and solidarity economy in, 179

Network of Asian Producers, 107

networks, 35, 198; creation of, 24

New Economic Policy (NEP) (USSR), 60

new goods, services and processes, production of, 30

new social movements, 6

New Zealand: import of milk powder from, 290; part funding of dairy in India, 291

Niger, healthcare legislation in, 257

non-governmental organisations (NGOs), 1, 45, 124, 163, 195, 236, 324; competition among, 246; dependent on state resources, 238; generation of income streams, 6; in provision of public services, 237; involved in health insurance, 250; issue of elite capture, 46; provision of welfare services through, 239–42

non-market production, 72, 77

non-profit sector, 12, 45, 46, 47, 101, 170–1, 217–19, 239, 252

normative theory, 58

North, Douglass, 222, 225–6, 231, 233

Obote, Milton, 269–70

Observatorio Español de la Economía Social (Spain), 173

Occupy movement, 6, 8

Ocean Spray company, 94

Oikocredit Academy, 215

Oikocredit social investment network, 21, 202–3, 208, 209–10, 212–19

oranges: ethical and organic, 198; Sicilian (itinerant sale of, 192; marketing of, 197); trade fairs of, 193

organic food, market for, 95

Organic Law of the Popular and Solidarity Economy (Ecuador), 169

Organisation for Economic Cooperation and Development (OECD), 167

Ostrom, Elinor, 66–7

Overseas Private Investment Corporation, 211

Ownership Commission (UK), 97

ownership of policy, 181

Oxfam, 162

Panchayati Raj system (India), 305

Panchmahals district of Gujarat (India), 321

Paraguay, 131

Parmesan cheese, production of, 201

participation, 21, 34–7, 241; in community healthcare, 252; in mutual health organisations, 264; of memberships, by digital means, 95–6; of women, 26–7, 306 (in local elections, 307; in planning processes, 301); popular, definition of, 34; sustained, 22 *see also* decision-making

participatory budgeting, in Ecuador, 177

participatory guarantee systems, 200

Partido dos Trabalhadores (PT) (Brazil), 137–9

Patel, Sardar, 287

Patel, T. K. (TKP), 287

paternalism, 42

patients, rights of, 257

patriarchy, 33, 81, 305

People's Plan Campaign (Kerala), 300–1

personal and impersonal exchange, 222, 233

philanthropy, 51; venture philanthropy, 53, 54 *see also* solidarity, philanthropic

Philippines: research project in, 82–4; women targeted as ideal migrant workers, 74

Pioneer Valley, Massachusetts, cooperative project, 199

Plan Caif (Uruguay), 240, 243

Plan Sésame (Senegal), 259

plural economy: in framework of democracy, 52–3; perspective, 50; promotion of, 263

Poland, 179; local development strategies in, 177; social and solidarity economy in, 169–70

Polanyi, K., 7, 12, 21, 53

Policy Alleviation Project (Uganda), 276

policy partnerships, 244–8

political connections, required to leverage resources, 25

pollution, generation of, 8

Polson company, 287–9, 292

polycentricity, 32

poor people: as active agents, 302; food problems of, 308; integration of, 242; perceived as 'subsidised', 312

Popular and Solidarity Economy Act (2011) (Ecuador, 139)

poverty, 9, 114, 130, 159, 243, 256, 261, 300; definition of, 301; in Colombia, 161; of cooking energy, 323; reduction of, 9, 12, 24, 26, 37, 43, 74, 101, 102, 108, 113, 142, 208–9, 271, 275, 300–2 (associated with Fairtrade system, 112;

in intergovernmental collaboration, 178–80)

power relations, reconfiguration of, 34

price, competition on, 94–5

priority of people over capital, 68

privatisation, of water (banned, 141; resistance to, 195)

Pro-Huerta programme (Argentina), 135

productivity, increasing of, 102–3, 145

professionalisation, of social and solidarity economy, 238, 246, 262

profit, 68: above-normal, 97; aversion to, 61; distribution of, proportional, 49; maximisation of, 237; non-distribution of, 47–8 *see also* for-profit sector *and* non-profit sector

Programa Nacional de Alimentação Escolar (Brazil), 177

progress, ideology of, 43 (questioned, 45)

Progress out of Poverty Index, 219

Prometheanism of social and solidarity economy, 63, 69, 71

Provence-Alpes-Côte d'Azur (PACA) region (France), 176

proximity services, 6, 46; provision of, 30

public company, history of, 87–8

public investment, 44

public policy, on healthcare, changes in, 259–62

public services, delivery of, 181

public spaces, recognition of, 42

public works programmes, 305

public–private partnerships, 23

publicly traded companies: possibility of replacing, 86; structural growth of, 98–9

quality of life, claims for, 45

Quality of Life surveys, 152

quality standards: application of, 120; in agri-food industry, 125–6

quasi-markets, 181

Quebec, 30, 32–3, 181; co-construction of policy in, 178; day-care centres in, 172; social and solidarity economy in, 4, 25, 171, 179

rationality of human decision-making, 46

Rawls, John, 62–3; *A Theory of Justice*, 62

re-embedding economy into society, 191–4
re-institutionalisation, 148
reciprocity, 28, 50, 52, 140, 149, 235
redistribution, 28, 44, 148, 149; principle of, 50
redundancies, 92
reflexivity, enhancement of, 5
registration of micro-enterprises, 135
regulation, 22, 31
remittances, 76; from women domestic workers, 74, 82–3
renewable energy, investment in, 206, 213
representation, 21, 241
Réseau de Veille sur la Commercialisation des Céréales (Burkina Faso), 174
resources, social, mobilisation of, 302–3
responsiveness, 212–14
Retegas.org, 187
Rio+20 conference, x; *The Future We Want* report, xi
risk-sharing, 22, 212–14
Rochdale Society of Equitable Pioneers, 87
rotating savings and credit associations (ROSCA), 203–4
Rousseau, Jean-Jacques, 62
Rousseff, Dilma, 138
routine activity, tendency towards, 247–8
rules, of cooperatives, internally crafted, 125
Rural Electrification Administration (USA), 87
Rural Income and Employment Enhancement Project (Uganda), 278
Rural Microfinance Support Project (Uganda), 277
rural producer organisations (RPOs) (Uganda), 271
Rwanda, 258; coffee cooperatives in, 126; coffee production in, 120; mutual health organisations in, 262

Sachs, Jeffrey, 67
safety nets, social, 51
Sall, Macky, 258
Sampayo, Fernando, 222
Sangha Krishi Initiative (India), 307–9
Sanzo, Carlos de, 227, 229–30, 231

São Paulo, recycling cooperatives in, 204
savings and credit cooperatives (SACCOs), 271–2, 277–8, 281
savings groups, 324
sbarchinpiazza initiative (Italy), 192
scaling up: limits, risks, tensions and dilemmas of, 27; of cooperatives, 266; of small networks, 226; of social and solidarity economy, xi, 1–37, 100–15, 221, 224–6, 233, 234, 299, 310, 323 (global movement forming, 10; horizontal, 4, 101–2; in Argentina, 22–3; in provision of welfare, 236; integrative, 3–5, 29; raising public awareness of, 145; transversal, 4, 103; vertical, 4, 102–3); of *trueque*, 226–33
Scheduled Tribes and Castes (India), 309
self-censorship by organisations, 247
self-help groups (SHGs), 324, 325; federations of, 327–8; of women, 27
self-sufficiency, 298
Sen, Amartya, 65–6
Senegal, 30, 251, 259, 260; agricultural cooperatives in, 126; healthcare legislation in, 257; mutual health organisations in, 256
Seoul Social Economy Centre, 171
Serventi, Mauro, 192
sharing economy, emergence of, 96–7
Sicily: anti-mafia solidarity activity in, 185; GAS networks in, 191–3
Singer, Paul, 10, 29
Sistema Nacional de Comércio Justo e Solidário (Brazil), 138, 180
Slovenia, 179; social and solidarity economy in, 177
small scale initiatives, 234
Smart Campaign, 219
Smith, Adam, *The Wealth of Nations*, 225
social and solidarity economy (SSE), x–xi, 159; actors in, protagonists in healthcare, provision, 258–9; and publicly traded companies, 87–90; and twenty-first-century development challenge, 7–10; appraisal of, 57–71; as alternative to capitalist development, 313; as institutional innovation, 223–4; as new synergy, 47–51; as poverty reduction strategy, 74; as site of moral

development, 61; as social services deliverer, 237–9; as socio-pedagogic laboratory, 21; characteristics of organisations in, foster growth, 90; classical criteria of, 252; competing with publicly traded companies, 14–15; complementary roles of actors in, 311; conceptualisation of, 224, 313; contested term, 57; contribution of microfinance to, 211–19; definition of, 58–9, 101; definitional ambiguity of, 57; development of, stages of, 12; diversity of enterprises in, 86; driving forces of, 5–7; empowerment of, 18; encompasses diversity of organisations, 41; expansion of, 3; formal business types contained in, 101; fragmentation within field of, 36; growth possibilities of, 91–4; history, theory and strategy of, 11–14, 41–56, 58; institutional base of, 52; institutionalising of, in Latin America, 130–49; legal and administrative forms of, 130; legislation on, 169; linking of local initiatives, 309; long-term support for, 180–1; organisations of (not structured for rapid growth, 94; poorly understood by local authorities, 92; risks of growth, 94–7); rebuilding of, after neoliberalism, 150–65; regarded as fringe economy, 3; relations with market, 14–20; relations with state, 17–20; role of cooperatives in, 150; sound environmental practices in, 93; structural constraints on, 5; theorisation of, 59–61; thickening presence of, 25; 'turn' in public policy, 24 (in Latin America, 17); use of term, 1–2, 36; weak original conditions of organisations, 27; widening field of action of, 238 *see also* co-construction of social and solidarity economy policy *and* scaling up of social and solidarity economy
social capital, 127, 130, 152; use of term, 118
social contract, redefinition of, 46
social credit movement, 61
social economy, 1, 2; definition of, 70; in Argentina, 133; in Brazil, 136–9; legal forms of, 48–9; regional poles of, 33; use of term, 47–9 *see also économie sociale*
Social Economy and Fair Trade meeting (Bolivia), 170
Social Economy Development Academy (Poland), 173
Social Enterprise Promotion Act (Korea), 178
social entrepreneurship, 53, 54
Social Farm programme (Argentina), 135
social impact bonds, 54
social impacts, measurement of, 71
social innovation, 44–7
social movements, new varieties of, 20
Social Policy Observatory of Małopolskie (Poland), 173
social power: concept of, 302; reassertion of, 2
social production enterprises (Venezuela), 143–4
social protection, 6, 8, 33, 44, 240, 242; in healthcare, 250–65
social security systems, in Africa, 250
social services, provision of, 6, 236
social value achieved by projects, 71
solidarity, 20–2, 83, 85, 101, 105, 140, 149, 194, 202, 203, 204, 211, 219, 223, 228, 229, 232, 235, 237, 252, 300–12, 324; concept of, invention of, 41–3; costs of, 311; democratic, 12–13, 28, 31, 43, 55–6 (challenges of, 51–4; evolution of, 41); in community currency system, 221–35; in community forestry, 313–29; in nineteenth century, 47; in practice, 20–7; measurement of, 329; new mechanisms of, 33; of women, 324–6; philanthropic, 12–13, 37, 42–3 (return of, 53–4); value chains in, formation of, 26
solidarity economy, 2, 47, 50–1, 131, 137, 151, 159, 170; aspects of, 50; conditions for, 18; districts and networks of, 192; reproduced in diagram, 142–3; research into, 199 *see also économie sociale*
solidarity finance, 21–2; new mechanisms of, 33
solidarity purchase groups, laboratories for sustainable citizenship, 194

solidarity purchasing, 188–91; solidarity prices in, 201

South Africa, social and solidarity economy in, 176

South Asia, social and solidarity economy in, 25–7

South Asia Microfinance Network, 216

Spain: cooperatives in, 152–3; social and solidarity economy in, 172

Special Credit Institutes (Italy), 152

state: as regulatory authority, 62; central distributive, 68; complementarity with market, 44; dependence on, 312; institutions of, diminished, 29; intervention by, discredited, 156; limited political will of, 28; lobbying of, 299; local developmental, 31–2; necessity of, 131; new forms of intervention by, 144; partnerships in social and solidarity economy, 236–49; relations with, 11; relations with social and solidarity economy, 17–20; resources of, dependency on, 246, 248; retrenchment of, 6; return of, 142; role of, 70, 143, 146 (downplayed, 32; in development and change, 28; in healthcare, 259); social, 55; twentieth-century, 43–4; withdraws from social service provision, 57 see also government

Stiglitz, Joseph, *The Price of Inequality*, 78

strategic pillars of transformative change, 27–8

strategic planning in communities, 71

strategy, 299; definition of, 285; human agency in, 285

Streetnet, 35

structural adjustment, 9, 54, 116

subjects-in-becoming, 82–4

subsidiarity, 20, 181

subsidies, 32

subsistence production, 74

Sun-Maid company, 94

Sunkist company, 94

supply chains, short, 198, 200

sustainability, 6; financial, of co-operatives, 266, 283; use of term, 36

Sustainable Development Goals (SDG), xi, 6

sustainable livelihoods, 102

sustained participation, of investors, 215–16

Tanzania, 120; agricultural cooperatives in, 126

Tavolo RES solidarity network (Italy), 196, 200

taxation, progressive, 32

tea, Fairtrade labelling of, 110, 111

third sector organisations, 12

time banks, 221

tobacco companies, avoidance of investment in, 206

top-down approaches, 28, 36, 51, 167, 256

tourism, sustainable, 310

trade unions, 136

transaction costs, 116–17, 121, 128, 231, 233, 299; definition of, 225–6; intermediate, 17, 121; of high value goods, 122; of perishable goods, 122; reduction of, 169–71, 229–30

Transfair USA organisation, 15

transformative change: strategic pillars of, 27–8; use of term, 10

trueque scheme (Argentina), 22, 221–35; failure of, 233; politicisation of, 231 see also scaling up, of *trueque*

trust, 228; definition of, 223–4; transfer of, 229, 232, 234

Uganda: agricultural cooperatives in, 266–83; National Cooperative Policy, 275–6; social and solidarity economy in, 123–4

Uganda Cooperative Alliance (UCA), 270

unemployed workers, re-employment of, 135

Unidades Económicas Populares (UEPs) (Ecuador), 140–1

Unifresh company, 164

Union of Soviet Socialist Republics (USSR), collapse of, 59, 81

Union Technique de la Mutualité (UTM) (Mali), 256

United Kingdom (UK), social and solidarity economy organisations in, 86–99

United Nations (UN), 6

UN Children's Fund (UNICEF), 252; in milk production, 290
UN Development Programme (UNDP), study of LEDAS, 157
UN Inter-Agency Task Force on Social and Solidarity Economy, xi
UN Non-Governmental Liaison Service (UN-NGLS)
UN Research Institute for Social Development (UNRISD), xi, xii–xiii
United States of America (USA): community economies in, 185–201; social and solidarity economy organisations in, 86–99, 152
Unitrabalho network (Brazil), 137–9
Unlad Kabayan savings group, 83
Uruguay, 131; scaling up of social and solidarity economy in, 22–3; welfare regimes in, 236–49
Uruguayan Child and Adolescence Institute (INAU), 240–1, 243

value-added, low, in commodity and service sectors, 27
Venezuela, 18, 131, 132, 142, 143, 144, 145, 146, 147
vertical reach, extension of, 327–8
Via Campesina organisation, 16, 35, 114, 147
violence, gender-based, 75
voice of women, 323–4
Voltas company, 296, 297
voluntarism, 235
voluntary action, 74; relations of, 49
volunteering, 49
vulnerability, 5
vulnerable employment, 8

Wade, Abdoulaye, 259
warehouse receipt system (WRS) (Uganda), 278
weapons companies, avoidance of investment in, 206
weatherisation projects, 199
welfare: exclusion from, 23; rethinking

of regimes of, 23; role of social and solidarity economy organisations in, 23
welfare policies, restoration of, 144
welfare regimes, in Uruguay, 236–49
welfare state, 41, 44; decline of, 59; in Uruguay, 242; model of, 8
West Africa: healthcare in, 250–65; social and solidarity economy in, 123–4
West African Economic and Monetary Union (UEMOA), 257
women: as managers of microfinance groups, 204; collective voice of, 323; entering formal economy, 309; excluded from public spaces, 305; 'for themselves', 315; freeing up time of, 33; greater cooperative outlook of, 74; in households, essentialised, 81; in social and solidarity economy, 300–12; in waged workforce, 8; inclusion of, 27; knowledge of plants, 322; participants in cooperatives, 280; positioned as global saviours, 85; presence of, beneficial, 322; subordination of, 29; targeted for development projects, 74; voice of, 323–4; workloads of, 26, 303
see also farmers, women as
Worcester Roots organisation (USA), 200
work integration enterprises, in Quebec, 171–2
worker management, 140, 143
workers' councils, 154
workers' self-management, 45; in former Yugoslavia, 153–5
World Bank, 72, 79, 134, 240, 250
World Council of Churches (WCC), 209
World Health Organization (WHO), 252
World Social Forum (WSF), 2, 12, 46, 131

Yugoslavia, former, 151; workers' self-management in, 153–4

Zamagni, Stefano, 152
Zero Hunger programme (Brazil) *see* Fome Zero
Zipcar company, 96